Becoming Af
in Ameri

Becoming African in America

Race and Nation in the Early Black Atlantic

JAMES SIDBURY

OXFORD
UNIVERSITY PRESS
2007

OXFORD
UNIVERSITY PRESS

Oxford University Press, Inc., publishes works that further
Oxford University's objective of excellence
in research, scholarship, and education.

Oxford   New York
Auckland   Cape Town   Dar es Salaam   Hong Kong   Karachi
Kuala Lumpur   Madrid   Melbourne   Mexico City   Nairobi
New Delhi   Shanghai   Taipei   Toronto

With offices in
Argentina   Austria   Brazil   Chile   Czech Republic   France   Greece
Guatemala   Hungary   Italy   Japan   Poland   Portugal   Singapore
South Korea   Switzerland   Thailand   Turkey   Ukraine   Vietnam

Published by Oxford University Press, Inc.
198 Madison Avenue, New York, New York 10016

www.oup.com

Library of Congress Cataloging-in-Publication Data
Sidbury, James.
Becoming African in America : race and nation in the early Black Atlantic / by James Sidbury.
p. cm.
Includes bibliographical references and index.
ISBN 978-0-19-532010-7
1. African Americans—History—To 1863.   2. African Americans—Race identity. 3. Black
nationalism—History.   4. American literature—African American authors—History and criticism. 5. English
literature—Black authors—History and criticism.   6. Antislavery movements—History—18th century.
7. African Americans—Migrations—History.   8. United States—Emigration and immigration—History.
9. Africa—Emigration and immigration—History.   10. United States—Race relations.   I. Title.
E185.18.S53 2007
973'.0496073—dc22   2007004017

9 8 7 6 5 4 3 2 1

Printed in the United States of America
on acid-free paper

For Robert Sidbury and Astrid Oesmann

Acknowledgments

I have worked on this book for a decade, building up debts to institutions, colleagues, and friends and family. It is impossible to single out everyone who has helped along the way, but there are many to whom I am especially indebted.

I have been teaching at the Department of History at the University of Texas since before I began this project, and the department and university have provided crucial support, including a Dean's Fellowship, a Faculty Research Assignment, and support as a fellow of the Mastin Gentry White Professorship in Southern History. The university also provided supplemental support that allowed me to accept fellowships funded by the Mellon Foundation at the American Antiquarian Society in Worcester, Mass., and at the John Carter Brown Library in Providence, R.I. This book began to take its final shape during the time that I spent at the AAS and JCBL, and I am deeply grateful for that time, and for those who have made those libraries such wonderful places to work on early American history, especially John Hench, Joanne Chaison, and Caroline Sloat at the Antiquarian Society, and Norman Fiering at the JCBL. I also want to acknowledge the help and support that I received from the community of scholars working at the AAS while I was there. Finally, the College of Liberal Arts at Texas granted me course release to participate in an interdisciplinary seminar run by the university's Humanities Institute.

I am also grateful to a number of people with whom I have worked over the years I have been writing this book. At the University of Texas, I have been lucky to work under three supportive departments chairs—Brian Levack, Carolyn Boyd, and Alan Tully. Even more important, almost all of the members of the department that they have chaired maintain a serious commitment to scholarship without taking themselves too seriously, making the department a wonderful place to work. I especially want to thank Erika Bsumek, Judith Coffin, Carolyn Eastman, William Forbath, George Forgie, Joan Neuberger, Denise Spellberg, our much missed former colleague Mauricio Tenorio, and Charters Wynn for their friendship and for more conversations about the meanings of Africa in early America than they can possibly have enjoyed. Other colleagues, some at the University of Texas and some not, took time from their own research to read parts of this book while it was being written: Randall Burkett, Jorge Cañizares-Eguerra, Christine Daniels, Laurent DuBois, Toyin Falola, Elijah Gould, Jack P. Greene, Cathy Jurca, Neil Kamil, Kevin Kenny, Julie Hardwick, Michael Johnson, Mieko Nishida, Peter Onuf, Robert Olwell, Stephan Palmié, Eliza Richards, and Julius Scott. A smaller group read the entire work in manuscript, or read multiple drafts of different parts—some did both—and the final product is immeasurably better than it would have been without their help: W. Jeffrey Bolster, Vincent Carretta, Ellen Goellner, Antony G. Hopkins, Susan Juster, Catherine Molineux, and David Oshinsky. An anonymous reader for Oxford University Press helped me sharpen the argument and, hopefully, avoid being misunderstood. Susan Ferber has been a wonderful editor, mixing enthusiasm for the project and a helpful eye for clumsy prose and garbled logic with friendship that didn't waiver when I missed deadlines.

I presented parts of this book at various conferences and colloquia over the past several years. I'm grateful to seminar participants and audience members at the American Antiquarian Society, Boston College, Brown University, the California Institute of Technology, Hartwick College, Johns Hopkins University, the University of Michigan, Michigan State University, and Rice University, and to participants in the Works in Progress series at Princeton University's Center for African American Studies. Claude Clegg III, Douglas Egerton, and Howard Jones provided particularly helpful suggestions when serving as commentators on panels at professional meetings.

I have been lucky while at the University of Texas to work with graduate students who are gifted scholars and wonderful people. Watching them develop into excellent historians has been one of the unalloyed pleasures of my professional life. Sara Fanning, Kenny Aslakson, Lissa Bollettino, and Paul Conrad have done research or clerical work on this project. Much more importantly, they and their colleagues—Kristen Tegtmeier-Ortel, Theresa Case, Kevin Roberts, Tim Buckner, and Patrick Luck—have raised issues and forced me to engage with new fields through their scholarship. That has made me a better historian, and working with them has made me a happier person.

Of course most "professional" debts are far more than professional. In thanking those who have read or talked about my work over the years, I am thanking them for the friendship and support that did so much to make the work interesting. Others have not read manuscripts, talked about interpretive problems, or shared archival horror stories, but they have lived with this project, at least indirectly and certainly involuntarily, for many years. Thanks, especially, to Anne Sidbury, Scott Mennella, Mercy Sidbury, Patty Haley, Bill Haley, and Timothy Powell.

This book is dedicated with thanks to two people whose support has never wavered in all the years that I have known them.

Contents

Becoming African
in America

Introduction

In 1849, Ira Aldridge, the black actor known throughout much of Europe as the "African Roscius," sought to capitalize on his growing fame by publishing a memoir. After a short discussion of the racial characteristics of the "regular coast of Guinea nigger," the memoir turns to Aldridge's royal African origins. Aldridge's grandfather, an unusually "enlightened" prince "of the Fullah tribe," had reportedly asked an American missionary to educate his son Daniel—the actor's father—so that Daniel could contribute to the work of "civilizing his countrymen," and the grandfather sought to contribute to the same project by ending Fullah involvement in the Atlantic slave trade. The missionary took Daniel Aldridge to New York to "receive the advantages of a Christian education," a fortuitous decision, because the grandfather's crusade against the slave trade angered the "principal chiefs" of the Fullah. A civil war ensued in which "the reforming Prince . . . together with his whole family, and personal attendants and connexions" were "savagely butchered." Daniel Aldridge had sailed to America "just in time to avoid a similar fate."

After his narrow escape from the slave-trading rebels, Daniel continued to pursue his father's dream. He took advantage of the opportunity that he had been granted by attending Schenectady College and becoming a minister who was admired by all who knew him. He then bided his time. Upon learning of the death of the "rebellious chief who had headed the conspiracy" against his father, Daniel Aldridge married a "young wife . . . of his own colour," and together they sailed to Africa to redeem his native land and reclaim his rightful place as the reforming leader of his people. Within a month of their arrival in Africa, Ira Aldridge was born, but the young family was not destined for happiness in the land of the Fullah. Daniel's efforts to spread "Gospel seeds" and to put an end to the barbarism of the slave trade stimulated another civil war in which "the enlightened African was defeated, barely escaping . . . with his life." He and his young family sought shelter with friends and allies in surrounding villages, remaining in hiding for nine years until they were finally able to arrange their escape to America.[1]

If this account of Ira Aldridge's origins seems fantastical, that is because it is. The great actor was almost certainly born in New York, where he grew up, attended the city's famous African Free School during the 1820s, and got his start as an actor in the nearby "African Theatre" during the early years of that decade. Soon after opening, the African Theatre became popular enough to threaten the profits of nearby white-owned theatres, as a result of which it was attacked and forcibly closed.[2] Ira Aldridge then left New York to pursue a career in England. By 1825 he had made his London stage debut, and over the following forty-two years he built a reputation as a Shakespearian actor that stretched from England to France and across the continent to Serbia and Russia. He died in 1867 while on tour in Poland, having become the first person of African descent to achieve success as an actor on the modern European stage, and his legacy remained powerful enough for Paul Robeson to have consulted with Aldridge's daughter on the eve of his own London debut as Othello.[3]

Contemporaries described Aldridge as a powerful stage presence—one reviewer said that he played Othello "wisely and restrainedly in a majestically classical style"—but as his appropriation of the title "the African Roscius" suggests, his race and background formed an unavoidable context within which theatergoers received his performances, and he wisely sought to spin his background for maximum advantage.[4] The tale that he told of his African origins was implicitly cast in just such terms when the importance of his escape to America was summarized: "Thus was he saved in his infancy to vindicate in his manhood the cause of his whole race."[5] His theatrical triumphs were victories for all "Africans," and a part of the rise of "civilized" African people in the West.

In the allegorical tale that he told of his origins, his royal ancestors had rejected both the supposed heathenism of Africa and their people's involvement in the slave trade. They had fought valiantly if unsuccessfully to bring "civilization" to their "savage land," and they had paid a heavy price for their failure to do so. Aldridge's father was a Fullah leader by birth if not by education, but his mother was a black American, and Ira himself must have been conceived in the United States though he was born and lived the first nine years of his life in West Africa. His authenticity as an "African" might seem odd at first glance—an identity at least as deeply rooted in the dias-

Figure I.1. Ira Aldridge as Aaron in Shakespeare's *Titus Andronicus*, 1852 [Engraving (Prints and Photographs Division, Library of Congress [227A])].

pora as on the continent. This understanding of African identity had little to do with the celebrations of indigenous cultural traditions that would become signs of authenticity in the twentieth century.

It is not particularly surprising that a professional actor fashioned a dramatic allegorical story of his past, but it is revealing. Ira Aldridge presented his African roots in diasporic and civilizing terms that had dominated discussions of African identity in the United States when Aldridge was growing up. His alma mater, the famous African Free School of New York City, had been a center of such thought. Those discussions of African identity grew out of and fueled efforts by Anglophone black people to Christianize and "civilize" the indigenous peoples of Africa, efforts that have been largely forgotten in modern celebrations of cultural diversity and tolerance, but efforts that acquired great currency during the decades surrounding 1800. The sense of African identity that arose in that period is the subject of *Becoming African in America*.

The terms "Africa" and "African" and the perception that the continent of Africa (or the sub-Saharan portion of it) comprises a unified cultural and/or "racial" unit are European in origin. Between 1650 and 1750 plantation slavery emerged and then flourished in many of Britain's American colonies, and Britons in England and America used "Africans" interchangeably with "Negroes" and "blacks" to refer to the people they purchased and imported into the Americas, as well as to the American-born (or creole) descendants of those victims of the slave trade. Little surprise, then, that "African" became a degrading term. Over the course of the eighteenth century several factors, including the intensification of the Atlantic slave trade, the increasing economic and cultural integration of plantation America into European society, and the growing currency of Enlightenment notions of human progress, helped produce a conventional image of Africa in the Western imagination as a primitive and pagan place. "Africans," according to this view, were a savage people who existed outside of the narrative of Western progress.[6]

During the second half of the eighteenth century a group of African-descended authors and activists living in England and America began to present themselves as "Africans" despite the negative connotations that term carried in many whites' minds. People like Ignatius Sancho, James Albert Ukawsaw Gronniosaw, Quobna Ottobah Cugoano, and Olaudah Equiano or Gustavus Vassa in England, as well as Phillis Wheatley, Venture Smith, and John Jea in North America published texts, usually autobiographical, in which they discussed or alluded to their pasts in Africa or their heritages as children of the slave trade.[7] One effect of their collective effort was the elaboration of an alternative understanding of "Africanness" that could provide a source of pride and unity for the diverse victims of the Atlantic slave trade. These authors did not, however, entirely escape the racist origins of the terms they sought to reinterpret, in part because they worked within Western literary and cultural traditions. Thus, the African identity that they claimed was not an ethnic identity—like Temne, Igbo, Kongo, or Yoruban—that might either have had or have been gaining intelligibility among residents of Africa fortunate enough to have escaped the slave trade. It was instead a new diasporic identity that was founded on emerging European perceptions that residents of Africa shared a "racial" essence.[8] Transforming a term so laden with connotations of primitivism and savagery into a source of pride required these authors to counter conventional Enlightenment portrayals of Africans' place—or absence of a place—in the progressive universal history of humanity forged by Enlightenment thinkers. In short, the authors had to re-place Africa within the Enlightenment's grand narrative of human history.[9] Concern about these questions was not limited to published authors. Black artisans and other working people living in American seaboard cities founded a wide range of churches, schools, and fraternal organizations during the decades surrounding 1800, and many included the term "African" within their titles. Tracing the black discourse on African identity from the realm of published texts into the realm of the actions and less formal and sometimes anonymous writing by members of local institutions—from intellectual history to sociocultural history—constitutes one of the central goals of this book.

The first two chapters of *Becoming African in America* trace these themes through the works of early black authors, focusing special attention on the ways these authors addressed one of the central challenges inherent in asserting an African identity—the problem of ethnic diversity within Africa. The first chapter shows how Wheatley and Sancho, having been labeled "African" writers, accepted that label and subtly altered what it meant to be "African" within what they wrote. Neither Africa nor African identity plays a central role in their texts, but the identity is present and acknowledged. Both were aware of the ethnic diversity on the continent and understood that it undercut any notion of an indigenous "African" identity. Both responded by creating a narrative of African identity that took its meaning from the diaspora rather than from conditions on the continent, a narrative that began with enslavement and the experience of the Middle Passage. Peoples of various ethnic backgrounds became "African" together by virtue of sharing the oppression of Atlantic slavery. The resulting sense of African identity was forged through the common experience of slavery and did not rest on a notion of an essential difference between "Africans" and other peoples, whether Europeans, Asians, or Native Americans.

Chapter 2 traces the black discourse on African identity that Wheatley and Sancho unknowingly initiated into the first generation of slave autobiographers. Most of the men who wrote these narratives—and all were men—had lived in African villages or in slave communities in the plantation regions of America, experiences foreign to both Wheatley and Sancho. Perhaps as a result, when they asserted African identities in their narratives, they confronted ethnic division more directly. Equiano, the most celebrated among them, used that confrontation to develop a mythic vision of an

African unity that predated the ethnic division that haunted Africa in the age of the slave trade. He and Cugoano, his collaborator, sought a way to recreate the unity among sub-Saharan Africans that they perceived to have been broken in postbiblical times. The tension between this mythic and nearly essentialist sense of African identity and the more contingent, experiential, and temporally recent sense of identity offered by Sancho and Wheatley became a central and persistent aspect of the black discourse on African identity.

The first generation of narrators contributed more than a descent-based sense of unity to black discussions of African identity.[10] Unlike Wheatley and Sancho, these authors wrote as political activists working within the emerging antislavery movement in England and North America during the 1780s and 1790s. Not surprisingly, they were more attuned than their predecessors to questions surrounding the social betterment of those they claimed as African brethren. Anxiety for the lives of their fellow "Africans" was perhaps inherent in antislavery activism, but the first generation of narrators did not rest satisfied with arguments for ending the slave trade and emancipating the enslaved. They pushed for a broader social transformation through which they introduced to the black discourse on African identity a commitment to what would later be called "racial uplift." This concern fueled many of the most dynamic and progressive forces in early black activism.

The turn to racial uplift within black antislavery thought was rooted in the critique of the Atlantic slave trade as, to borrow the title of Philip Gould's recent analysis, a "barbaric traffic."[11] Ending the illegitimate trade in human beings would open the door to the fundamental social transformations that came in the wake of "humane" commerce, transformations that these authors believed had put Europe on the path of human progress and would do the same for Africa. They understood this projected social conversion in religious terms, and they expected twinned revolutionary changes on the coast of Africa through which "pagan" Igbos, Kongos, and Temne would be converted to Christianity while also learning to produce nonhuman commodities for exchange in the Atlantic market. In this way the residents of Africa would overcome ethnic division, become Christian, and emerge as an "African" people who could assume their rightful position in the world of nation-states. It was, then, in the program for social and religious "reform" that the black discourse on African identity became an explicitly transformative discourse that aimed not at returning to Africa or recapturing an African past—though it often did entail black American missionary outreach to the residents of Africa—but rather at converting the supposedly pagan and backward residents of the continent into progressive Christians who would assume their place within God's narrative of human progress. Such a transformation would end the slave trade in the Atlantic, end slavery in the Americas, and end the degradation of Africa. It would benefit Britons and Americans as well as the newly emerging Africans, constituting a crucial and divinely ordained step toward the millennium.

Equiano went beyond a theoretical discussion of these changes. He agreed to serve as commissary—the chief provisioning officer—of the first British expedition to settle what became the colony of Sierra Leone. This initial mission was organized by the prominent London abolitionist, Granville Sharp, and was designed to send the city's "Black Poor" to found a colony on the coast of Africa that would serve as a beachhead for the projection of "civilization" and legitimate commerce into the continent.[12] Sharp's "Province of Freedom" got off to a disastrous start, in no small part due to corruption that Equiano was fired for trying to prevent, but a group of philanthropic bankers allied with Sharp formed the British Sierra Leone Company, won a charter from Parliament, and stepped in to organize a new colony.

The first settlers who founded Freetown, Sierra Leone, were former North American slaves who had fled from their masters to win freedom fighting with the British during the American Revolutionary War. Roughly 3,000 of these "black loyalists" sailed from New York City to Nova Scotia after the Treaty of Paris was signed in 1783, but many became frustrated by the discrimination they encountered in Nova Scotia and sought a fresh start and a more hospitable new home. Slightly more than 1,000 of these self-styled "Nova Scotians" accepted the British government's offer of free transportation to Sierra Leone and created a settlement at Freetown that became central to many blacks' visions of an "African" people and nation.

Chapters 3 and 4 traverse the Atlantic to juxtapose the efforts of one group of black Americans to build lives in Africa and those of several other groups to assert "African" identitites and to develop interpretations of their pasts, their presents, and their futures—in other words, to develop a coherent vision of their collective history—as Africans. Chapter 3 begins by tracing the rise of the African Baptist Church of Savannah, Georgia, one of the early churches to describe itself as "African," and the progenitor of black Baptist churches in Canada, Sierra Leone, and much of the British Caribbean. The chapter then turns to two institutions founded by black New Englanders at roughly the same time—African Freemasonry and the African Union Societies of Newport and Providence, Rhode Island—to trace their distinct but parallel efforts to build "African" institutions and identities. Leaders of these institutions sought to reconcile their deep faith in a Christian God with the prevalence of "paganism" in Africa, reaching toward a belief that American slavery represented God's plan for bringing the light of true religion to the Dark Continent. This conviction gave all three groups a shared stake in the efforts of those Black Loyalists who would move to Sierra Leone in 1792.

These men and women had been evacuated from the United States following the Revolutionary War and had been settled in Nova Scotia. They might seem at first glance to have been an obscure and peripheral group, but nothing could be further from the truth.[13] The Black Loyalists came from slave and free black communities throughout the United States, and they retained ties to their home communities while creating new ties through their engagement with Africa. They had strong links to the African Baptists of Savannah (David George from that church was one of their leaders); to the African Masons of Boston (John Marrant's preaching played a prominent role for both groups); and to the African Union Societies, who sought to join the loyalists in Sierra Leone. Chapter 3 closes with a discussion of the Black Loyalist experience in Nova Scotia, the way that experience fueled the movement to Sierra Leone, and the influences of the Loyalists' decision to emigrate on self-styled "Africans" in the United States.

Chapter 4 picks up this story by following the Loyalists—they came to call themselves "Nova Scotians"—in their exodus to an African promised land. It traces their efforts to put into practice the transformative project that Gustavus Vassa had outlined at the conclusion of his *Interesting Narrative*. In these settlers' struggles with the Sierra Leone Company, which governed the colony, and their efforts to forge relationships with the Koya Temne people who surrounded the colony, the Nova Scotians confronted some of the complexities inherent in the emerging diasporic vision of African identity. In the process they, and some black New Englanders who hoped to follow them, began to privilege an alternate way to think of the links connecting "Africans" to one another. As the Nova Scotians' frequent invocations of Exodus suggest, they increasingly saw themselves as God's newly chosen people. Such a claim to chosen-ness was not new to black Christianity, but when used to define an "African" people, it offered a link between affiliative secular narratives of identity that rested on shared oppression, and mythic filiative narratives that asserted literal blood kinship. The Nova Scotians' attempt to build an "African" community of chosen people reached a climax in 1800, when many of them insisted that their colony was distinct from the Sierra Leone Company's trading venture and sought to expel white Company officials from Freetown, Sierra Leone.

Chapters 5 and 6 turn toward what would be the most successful efforts to bring these distinct problems together, the emergence of the African church movement in various cities along the eastern seaboard—especially Baltimore and Philadelphia—and the efforts of the sea captain, Paul Cuffe, to initiate a black-controlled emigration movement that he hoped would forge persistent ties between Sierra Leone and blacks in North America, helping to create an "African" people and a diasporic "African" nation. During the 1790s, charismatic religious leaders in Baltimore and Philadelphia became increasingly convinced that they and their fellow black parishioners would never be allowed to worship freely within white churches. Daniel Coker, Absalom Jones, Richard Allen, and a host of less prominent blacks responded by leading their followers out of their integrated churches to found separate "African" congregations. Similar movements arose in other northern cities as well as in Charleston, South Carolina. These new churches became organizational hubs for the free black communities that emerged in the wake of the American Revolution, hosting numerous celebrations of various political triumphs of the antislavery movement. In the sermons and other texts produced by "African ministers," as well as in the speeches commemorating the end of the Atlantic slave trade or different state emancipatory acts, black leaders asserted claims about the relationships among those enslaved in America, the creole men and women who had escaped slavery in America, and the residents of Africa.

These early nineteenth-century preachers and orators followed an interpretive arc that paralleled that of the Nova Scotians and their North American contemporaries. Their portrayals of "African" identity continued to reflect the tensions between filiative and affiliative stories of kinship, but they increasingly appealed to the language of a chosen people. The status of "Africans" as a chosen people rested upon black people's shared history of oppression. It was, after all, the slavery that blacks suffered in the Atlantic world and the parallels between that slavery and the sufferings of the biblical Israelites that marked Africans as chosen. Appeals to chosen-ness claimed more, however, than simple affiliative kinship, for they pushed the bonds joining "Africans" to one another into mythic time, and into a category that was at least as "deep" and "real" in its own way as "blood" kinship.

As black religious leaders and political activists articulated these claims in various public forums, Cuffe, the Quaker son of an African-born man and a Native American woman, began pursuing a program of racial uplift that won the support of many African church leaders. Cuffe, a Massachusetts ship captain, may have been the wealthiest black man in the United States during the first two decades of the nineteenth century; beginning around 1808 he decided to devote himself to the advancement of his race. His program probably grew out of his knowledge of discussions of African emigration among various "African" benevolent societies in New England during the 1790s. Cuffe built on those earlier discussions by contacting Britons involved with Sierra Leone and seeking first to clear the way for renewed black American emigration to that colony, and then to recruit emigrants and transport them. He succeeded in taking one group before he was forced to suspend his efforts during the War of 1812.

War with Britain kept Cuffe in the United States, but it could not prevent him from pursuing his goals. In fact, by forcing him to remain on land, it pushed him to elaborate a clearer vision of racial uplift and also permitted him to intensify his organizational efforts among black Americans. Chapter 6 explores the way that Cuffe reached out to the leaders of the African Church movement in Baltimore, Philadelphia, New York, and Boston, and the way that he expanded beyond that movement by contacting black leaders in Richmond, Virginia, and Charleston, South Carolina. It traces the parallel and related efforts of black religious leaders to institutionalize their independence from white denominational structures and to provide a religious foundation for "Africans" as a distinct American people—most famously in the establishment of the African Methodist Episcopal Church (AME Church) as an independent denomination—and of Paul Cuffe to create an ongoing commercial and political connection among blacks of the diaspora and those settled in Freetown.

Cuffe won the active support of Daniel Coker and Richard Allen, the two most important founders of the AME, of Peter Williams Jr., an "African minister" of New York, and of many other black leaders from Richmond north along the Atlantic seaboard. Cuffe envisioned a pattern of commerce in which black commercial elites in North American cities would pioneer and profit from the legitimate African commerce that would replace the slave trade, fostering conditions in which a diasporic African people would rise into being and establish a "Historians' nation." He organized "African Societies" in seaboard American cities and initiated what he hoped would become an ongoing correspondence between them and the Friendly Society that he had helped form during his earlier visit to Freetown. Each of these black "African" societies was also put in touch with the white philanthropic African Institution of London. When peace arrived in 1815, Cuffe had cemented an alliance with black elites in American port cities, he had met with and won the approval of white American political leaders (including President James Madison and Secretary of the Treasury Albert Gallatin), and he had maintained his good relations with Britons influential in Sierra Leone. He returned from a second voyage to Freetown in 1816 as an almost-universally respected figure working to implement an innovative vision of a diasporic African commercial nation that would include Sierra Leone while encompassing "Africans" everywhere. This new nation would create a powerful "African" mercantile class within American cities while helping to bury the slave trade and bring slavery to an end.

The year 1816 stands as a high water mark for the early black discourse on African identity, encompassing both the establishment of the AME and Cuffe's triumphant return from Freetown. In December a group of white political leaders gathered in Washington to found an organization—the

American Colonization Society (ACS)—that hoped to build on Cuffe's efforts, but that paradoxically worked to drive black American assertions of African identity underground. The ACS sought to convince free black Americans that they had little future in the United States and thus that they would be better off "returning" to the land of their forebears and settling in an American colony in West Africa. Cuffe was favorably disposed toward the ACS's embryonic program and its request for his support, but he died shortly after it was formed. His allies in various American cities—Richard Allen and James Forten in Philadelphia, Daniel Coker in Baltimore, Peter Williams Jr. in New York—were also inclined to view the Colonization Society as a potentially useful ally, but immediate, overwhelming, and unyielding opposition from the black public quickly convinced Cuffe's allies to abandon their public support.

They did not, however, give up all hope that they could cooperate with—perhaps even co-opt—the powerful whites funding the Colonization Society. Chapter 6 concludes with the story of the first expedition sent to Africa by the ACS, and of the efforts of two of Paul Cuffe's close friends and supporters—John Kizell, a Nova Scotian leader of the Friendly Society that Cuffe had helped to found in Freetown, and Daniel Coker, one of the founders of the AME, and Cuffe's point man in Baltimore—to take control of the fledgling colony away from the white officials sent out by the Colonization Society. Kizell, who served as the local host of the venture, and Coker, who was the leader of the settlers, sought to found a black "African" colony on Sherbro Island (off the coast of southern Sierra Leone) that might develop into a commercial center of the sort that Cuffe envisioned. The settlement at Sherbro disintegrated in a welter of recriminations, as Coker and Kizell sought to blame each other for its failures and to retain favor with leaders of the Colonization Society in the United States. Coker largely won the battle of reputations, but both moved back to Sierra Leone, and neither played any further role in the ACS's efforts in Africa. As they withdrew, the vision of an African nation that had grown out of early black authors' assertions of African identities and that had flowered in Paul Cuffe's nationalist project began to lose its grip on black activists within the United States and on black emigrants moving to the American colony that was soon founded in Liberia.

Chapter 7 then traces the demise of the black discourse on African identity through the 1820s. Some of this story is straightforward and familiar. As black American antislavery activists became increasingly convinced that the ACS served slaveholders' interests and that asserting an "African" identity played into the Society's efforts to portray Africa as the natural home for black Americans, fewer and fewer blacks referred to themselves as Africans. "Colored" institutions began to supplant "African" ones. Orators insisted that free blacks living in the United States were "Americans" rather than "Africans," and that their futures lay in the New World rather than the Old. While acknowledging the broad contours of this familiar story, chapter 7 begins from the premise that the substantial support that Cuffe and his followers had rallied behind the cause of emigrationism could not have disappeared overnight, and it traces the ways that black activists sought to keep alive some engagement with Africa. At the same time the black settlers who moved to Liberia saw themselves less as "Africans" than as pioneers building an "American" society in Africa—as "Americo-Liberians." Chapter 7 traces both of these developments, while arguing that the turn away from Cuffe's expansive view of African identity and peoplehood weakened arguments for racial uplift. The language of "colored Americanism" offered ample tools to claim equality under the law, and it contributed significantly to the struggle to abolish slavery. In comparison to the language of "African" identity, however, it offered fewer tools that could be used to argue for the socioeconomic betterment of blacks as a distinct group.

The epilogue looks ahead to the reemergence of black discussions of African identity and of black emigrationism during the 1850s. It examines the efforts of Martin R. Delany, sometimes called the "father of African nationalism," to encourage black emigration from the United States during the 1850s, and to the sense of African identity that he articulated while advocating emigration. The epilogue suggests both the persistence of many ideas initially offered by the first generations of self-styled "Africans," and some of the costs of the demise of the remarkable vision that activists like Equiano, Allen, Coker, and Cuffe had developed.

Becoming African in America tells the story of the rise and unfortunate demise of an unusually open and progressive nationalist discourse, one attuned to both the struggle for formal legal freedom and equality—for abolition—and to the need to develop autonomous sources of economic sufficiency and power. It is not, and should not be understood to be, an intervention in the rich scholarly literature on the transmission of indigenous African cultures (e.g., Yoruban or Igbo) to the Americas. Beginning in the early twentieth century with the classic debate between Melville Herskovits and E. Franklin Frazier, historians, anthropologists, sociologists, and art historians have argued over how to understand the profound and complex influences of African cultures on African-born and creole slaves and their descendants in the New World.[14] There has been a natural but mistaken tendency by many (but not all) to view black Americans' assertions of "African" identity as a reflection of the power and persistence of this kind of cultural transmission.[15] *Becoming African in America* argues that the first recorded discussions of "African" identity in England and North America arose in tension with, and in partial opposition to, memories and experiences of the indigenous cultures of Africa, rather than directly out of them.

In telling this story, *Becoming African in America* seeks to collapse some of the conventional historiographical distinctions between sociocultural and intellectual history by recovering the sophisticated ways that "rank-and-file" self-styled "Africans" understood their relationships to the God in which they believed, the two lands to which they felt allegiance, and to the peoples of Africa and the diaspora whom they considered brethren. The discourse on African identity was the most important language in early black American religious and political activism, and properly understanding it fundamentally revises our picture of the rich and complicated roots of later African nationalist thought in the United States and the black Atlantic.

As is so often true of histories of the black experience in the United States, *Becoming African in America* is at once a profoundly—almost conventionally—"American" story, and a unique example of the distinct history of a group that was excluded from much that the United States offered to those of European descent. The processes through which black writers, preachers, activists, and orators made sense of their collective past in ways that promised a more hopeful future shared something with the strong sense of "English-ness" that had paradoxically fueled white colonists' movement for independence during the 1760s, and they anticipated the struggles that Irish, Italian, and other European immigrants would experience as they developed "American" identities from the 1840s into the twentieth century. Being black—or African—in America has never been the same, however, as being white (or Italian, Greek, Polish, English) and these first efforts of "African" activists to create an ongoing vibrant exchange that would link the freedom struggle of black Americans to the economic development and growth of "civilization" in Africa failed. That vision has, however, returned to inspire advocates of racial justice from Martin Delany, to Marcus Garvey, to W. E. B. DuBois, to Randall Robinson. It certainly included aspects that strike modern observers as imperialistic and condescending toward the peoples of Africa, but it also included a vision of progress that rested on a more humane foundation than the belief that winners should take all. Assertions of African identity allowed blacks to fight to spread the material blessings of the growing Atlantic economy to those who were otherwise excluded.

1

The First "Africans"

Africa and Africans in the Poetry of Phillis Wheatley and the Letters of Ignatius Sancho

Before the 1760s, there were many black people in English letters, but there were no prominent black producers of English letters. Shakespeare's Othello had been succeeded by heroic, comic, and tragic figures on the stage; Aphra Behn's Oroonoko opened the door to numerous enslaved black characters in fiction; less elite literary genres were peopled by countless black men, women, and children playing a variety of roles in English life. Both elite and popular graphic art brought even more black bodies into English society and Anglophone culture.[1] Blacks could be found as princes, jesters, victims, heroes, criminals, slaves and loyal retainers in English culture. Nonetheless, the complex of oppressive forces arrayed against the millions of black people who actually lived in the British Empire blocked their access to literacy and to the kinds of learning that would have been necessary to produce an accomplished writer.

By the second half of the eighteenth century some things had begun to change. Increasing numbers of creoles among those enslaved by Britons, including many native English-speakers, lowered the linguistic hurdle that had to be cleared by aspiring writers. More important, doubts about the morality of slavery intensified among white Britons, leading some to attempt to ameliorate slavery while others offered encouragement and material support to individual slaves they perceived to have special talents. A vogue for black servants within British aristocratic households further increased the small but significant number of blacks with access to some education. Even when taken together, these changes never began to provide reliable opportunity to talented blacks caught up in the machinery of British slavery. The vast majority of the victims of Atlantic slavery were sold into miserable lives on

17

Caribbean sugar islands where their masters worked them to death. The changes did, however, produce conditions in which a small and extraordinary group of people who combined relative good fortune with unusual ability managed to overcome the persistent structures of oppression that they faced, and author texts that found their way into print in Anglo-America and England.[2] Two of these writers—Phillis Wheatley and Ignatius Sancho—achieved significant fame prior to the American Revolution.

Perhaps inevitably, they came to be read not simply as writers, but as black writers, so their texts carried the burden of "proving" that blacks shared the same natural intellectual capacities as whites. Given their unsought roles as racial emblems, it was significant that both appeared on the cultural stage at least in part as "African" writers, something that helped initiate a tradition through which black writers and activists would, over the course of several decades, elaborate a language of African identity. That language would form one foundation of black nationalist and pan-African thought.

I

The differences between these two iconic figures are immediately apparent. Sancho became famous for writing letters that were published in the *Letters of the Late Ignatius Sancho, an African*; Wheatley, a poet, published *Poems on Various Subjects, Religious and Moral.*[3] Wheatley lived on the periphery of British culture, literally slaving her youth away as a domestic servant in a Boston, Massachusetts, home. She only traveled to England once in her life. Sancho, by contrast, was at home in the metropole, presiding over a grocery store in Westminster. He lived at the political and cultural center of London, and thus of the empire. Given these backgrounds, it may not be a surprise that Sancho's letters reveal a devotee of irony and sarcasm, while Wheatley's writing is more inclined toward piety and sincerity. There were, however, similarities in the path that each of them took to reach literary celebrity, and their biographies can be seen to have created an initial template for the emergence of "Africans" as a people within English Atlantic culture.

In this sense the trajectories they traced and the personas they projected, from representations of their earliest memories to stories of their emergence as well-known "Africans," influenced early black discussions of African identity. Those trajectories took off when Wheatley and Sancho entered the homes of benevolent owners, and they culminated in the creation of one African, Sancho, who was a citizen of the republic of letters, and another, Wheatley, who was a member in good standing of an international evangelical sorority. Africa, then, did not stand as a true origin or even an important beginning for either of them as an author.[4] Though Wheatley included an imagined portrayal of being seized by slavers in one poem, and Sancho once said inaccurately that he was "not sorry" to have been "born in Afric"—inaccurately, in the sense that his biographer reported that he was born on a slave ship rather than in Africa—their lives as African authors began elsewhere.

This is less clear in Wheatley's case, because she does not present it plainly in her own words. Instead, we must rely (or choose not to) on the testimonial that her master, John Wheatley, penned for the beginning of her book, portraying Phillis Wheatley's life as an author as having begun when she entered his household. She then formally endorsed the accuracy of John Wheatley's letter in her own preface to the poems.[5] Wheatley traced her genealogy as an author to the moments when she was saved from the normal fate of enslaved people rather than to something in her childhood on the coast or hinterland of Africa. Wheatley's genealogy as an African, on the other hand, necessarily reached slightly farther back in time and space than Sancho's, stretching to the moment of her enslavement, but not to her birth in Africa.

Sancho portrayed his early life more explicitly in his *Letters* than did Wheatley in her poems, though his story, too, involves complications. They begin with the fact that he did not publish his collected letters during his lifetime. Instead, a friend and correspondent—Frances Crewe—compiled them for publication after Sancho's death.[6] The first volume of his letters opened with a biographical sketch whose beginning has generally been treated as a factual account, despite its almost mythological quality. Joseph Jekyll, the author, reported that Sancho had been born on a slave ship en route to the Caribbean, sold in Cartegena, and then brought to London sometime around 1731 at the age of two. Sancho himself makes little direct reference to this part of his past in the letters, but it seems certain this was one of the tales with which he earned his reputation as a master storyteller.[7]

Sancho's own source for this story, however, cannot be traced. Tristram Shandy notwithstanding, he obviously could not have remembered his own birth, and because he was reportedly orphaned by the age of two, his parents could not have told him. Nor does his description of his early life in England—he noted in a letter having been "unlucky" enough as a youth to have been "placed in a family who judged ignorance the best and only security for obedience"—conjure visions of a kindly owner recounting for her young slave his difficult early years.[8] The accuracy of the tale cannot be verified, but the story of a fundamentally homeless and abandoned orphan being saved through the liberality of a philanthropic aristocratic household profoundly shapes the narrative of his life. It makes Sancho's embrace by the Duke and Duchess of Montagu the event that saved him from a life of unremarkable drudgery and, in the process, propelled him along a path that led to literary success. The path was not smooth. Upon receiving his freedom and a small financial bequest, he left the security of the Montagu household and, according to his account, fell prey to his passions, squandering his money on pleasurable vices. He did not, apparently, lose the battle with his appetites, for he came through this wild period to settle into the life of a "civilized" person. Setting aside his temporary fall from the path of virtue, his story resembles Wheatley's. Like her, he had begun anew in the life for which he much later gained fame when he became a slave in an elite and "philanthropic" household (for Wheatley, a "Christian" household).

Neither Wheatley nor Sancho credited their patrons for all of their success; neither gave the impression that white liberality had worked some sort of alchemical magic on passive and inert black objects in order to create African authors. Sancho stressed his own determination, having begun to acquire literacy through "unwearied application" while still living with his first decidedly unphilanthropic English owners; and Wheatley, in a proposal seeking subscribers for a never-published second volume of poetry, referred to the "sacred fire which [was] self-enkindled in the breast of this young African." John Wheatley's letter preceding Phillis Wheatley's poems also portrayed her as someone with a natural gift for learning, and Sancho, after reading her poems, referred to hers as a "mind animated by Heaven." Both Sancho and Wheatley acknowledged with gratitude the help of white patrons, but neither sought to understate the hurdles they cleared in acquiring the knowledge necessary to become African authors.[9]

Both knew, however, that knowledge and talent alone were not enough. The books of Sancho and Wheatley would not have been published had they not gained reputations by getting early work into print. Both Sancho's and Wheatley's books contained their most famous earlier publications. Sancho's *Letters* included a letter to the novelist Laurence Sterne, as well as two others that had been printed in newspapers during his lifetime. Wheatley's book included a poetic memorial to the famous evangelist George Whitefield, which had been published in several broadside versions as well as having been sent to Whitefield's British patron, the Countess of Huntingdon. Early local prominence rested in part on attracting influential patrons, and that interconnected accomplishment—attracting patrons and gaining local acclaim—served as an important stepping-stone toward the novel status of "African" author.

The problems becoming an African author were manifold. Wheatley's short introductory note in the preliminary material of her book pointed out the "disadvantages" she had "laboured under, with regard to learning," and the first poem in her book introduces the classical poet Terence—a North African—to ask the muses why he "alone of Afric's sable race" had been graced with their inspiration.[10] Challenges like these notwithstanding, she and Sancho both managed to acquire the abilities and to cultivate the patrons necessary to become "African" authors, but little about each author's persona as an "African" author accords with modern assumptions about African identity. Both took forthright stands as defenders of other black people and asserted allegiance to them, but neither presented race or racial identity as the major determinant of their senses of self. They were instead at home in their respective societies—Wheatley as a resident of Massachusetts and Sancho as perhaps the only eighteenth-century black Briton who enjoyed and exercised his right to vote in Parliamentary elections—frequently using the first-person plural ("we") to describe themselves as New or Old Englanders, respectively.[11] From those positions they advocated stances on a broad array of public issues and sought to hold their home societies—Massachusetts and England—to their "true" liberty-loving standards.

Public advocacy was not, however, the primary role claimed by either author. Wheatley and Sancho were, above all else, cultural citizens, and it was as cultural citizens that they spoke (or wrote) most forcefully. For Wheatley this involved a dual claim to a poetic and a Christian persona. She was a poet—an "African" poet—writing for the glory of a Christian God from within a tight evangelical sisterhood that supported her both practically and emotionally.[12] It is hardly surprising that assertions of racial identity that find their way into her poetry are occasionally expressed in the biblical idiom of Ethiopianism.[13] Both she, as an "African," and fellow blacks whose suffering she protested could, she suggested, find their highest calling in serving Christ. By reminding white Christians that all men were God's children—that Christ was an "Impartial Saviour" and that "Negros, black as Cain,/May be refin'd, and join th' angelic train"—she hoped to inspire them to welcome all black people into Christian brother- and sisterhood while simultaneously calling all black people to salvation.[14]

Sancho considered himself a Christian as well, though his beliefs were far more ecumenical than Wheatley's. He forcefully insisted that Christ promised salvation to all—"Jew, Turk, Infidel, and Heretic"—and carefully cultivated a tolerant and accepting public stance.[15] He projected the persona not of an evangelical man of faith, but of a man of feeling and sentiment. He was moved by art and by suffering, and he felt a sentimental kinship with anyone in the world whose suffering was brought to his attention. This position offered him a valuable stance from which to condemn the treatment of enslaved blacks and to appeal to "feeling" whites to join the battle.[16] But his stance as a cultured man of feelings within his letters extended far beyond his advocacy of antislavery. It found expression in his admiration for literature and the arts—especially for the evocation of emotion in them. He also exhibited what can seem to those schooled in eighteenth-century (or later) American norms, a surprising air of gallantry and sometimes condescending playfulness in his correspondence with elite women, but this, too, was a well-established convention in Sancho's London.[17] He was an "African," but an African who found his "chief pleasure . . . [in] books," English books, and whose closest companions were other cultured Britons. He embraced all of suffering humanity, and especially enslaved black people, because they suffered most horrifically and unjustly and did so at the hands of cultured Britons, the very Christians they should have been able to look to for compassion and help. His vision of heaven was one in which all distinctions disappeared. It was a place "big enough for all the race of man"—not the *races* of man—and a place where he hoped to "see and mix amongst the whole family of Adam."[18] Just as he frequently described himself as a "Blackamoor," a term of racial identity rooted in *Othello* and other British literature rather than black experiences in the African diaspora, he stood, as a man of feeling, on a foundation built by seventeenth- and eighteenth-century British writers.[19]

The life stories of Ignatius Sancho and Phillis Wheatley as told by their contemporaries and as encoded in their literary works became important models of "African" life and racial potential in the anglophone world. The biographies they offered were shaped, as had long since become the custom for biographical representation in the West, into coherent narratives that told the story of the "making" of the subject, and each offered a narrative that lent itself to a universalist conception of what it meant to be "African." Each became an "African" author by traversing a trajectory that started after leaving Africa. Their beginnings lay instead in Wheatley's and Sancho's self-perceived good fortune in landing—as a result of some effort in Sancho's case—in households that recoiled from the brutality visited upon most enslaved black people and instead fostered the talents of these future authors. From these beginnings Sancho and Wheatley developed public voices that were deeply entrenched in Anglo-American culture and were understood by Sancho and Wheatley to be just that. It bears repeating that Wheatley and Sancho, unlike many later participants in this black discourse on African identity, did not write autobiographical narratives, so the images of Africa and Africans that they offered were not conveyed primarily through their life stories, but their life stories could not help affecting those images. Fleshing out those images requires returning to the poems and letters, and to the way they found their way into print.

II

On October 25, 1770, an enslaved young woman from Massachusetts wrote to Selina Hastings, the Countess of Huntingdon, expressing sympathy over the death of George Whitefield, the celebrated evangelist. Whitefield had been the countess's personal chaplain, and Phillis Wheatley, the letter writer, enclosed a poetic eulogy. The "Tongues of the Learned," she insisted, were insufficient to honor the noble Whitefield and how "much less the pen of an untutor'd African." Others, including the countess, found her talents quite sufficient, and this short letter, along with the poem that it enclosed, initiated a process that transformed this relatively unknown and "untutor'd" author into the famous "African" poetess. Huntingdon ultimately shepherded a book of Wheatley's poetry into print in 1772 and ensured its wide circulation.[20]

Five years later the *Letters of the Late Rev. Mr. Laurence Sterne* were published. Among these celebrated exchanges was one with the black grocer named Ignatius Sancho. Sancho had initiated their epistolary relationship by writing to thank Sterne for a sympathetic portrayal of the enslaved in a scene in *Tristram Shandy*. Sancho had already composed and published music as well as a work of music criticism that has been lost, but it was his letter to Sterne (and Sterne's responses) that propelled him to renown. A decade later when he died, friends collected and published two volumes of his letters, including the one he had written to the famous novelist.[21]

Like Wheatley, Sancho ascended to the ranks of literary fame. Both quickly came to be used by pro- and antislavery polemicists arguing alternatively for the inferiority or equality of the peoples of Africa and their descendants, for "mastery of the arts and letters was," as the literary critic Henry Louis Gates Jr. points out, "Enlightenment Europe's sign of that solid line of division between human being and thing."[22]

While critics have generally continued to focus on the political meanings of the works of Wheatley and Sancho, the stakes of these political readings changed during the second half of the twentieth century. By then, overt defenses of racism began to recede into a few particularly odious cultural redoubts, and critical discussion shifted away from using Wheatley and Sancho as evidence for or against racial equality and toward judging the degree to which their works had bolstered or subverted either slavery as an institution or late eighteenth-century white cultural authority. Critics from the left sometimes revived charges that Wheatley's poems and Sancho's letters slavishly followed white models, but they did so to very different effect, suggesting that these early black writers had failed to develop the cultural autonomy necessary to undermine slavery and racism. Others agreed that the fundamental question to ask about Wheatley and Sancho was whether or not they should be understood to have fought the good fight, but these critics rejected interpretations that saw Wheatley and Sancho accommodating to Western racism. These critics found subversive subtexts within the poems and letters, subtexts that undercut racism and argued for emancipation in the only terms open to black writers at that time. No longer did these

Figure 1.1. Engraving of Ignatius Sancho from the Frontispiece of *Letters of the Late Ignatius Sancho, An African* [Harry Ransom Humanities Research Center, University of Texas (Austin) Libraries].

two authors' works carry the burden of the biological essence of a "race," but Wheatley and Sancho continued to be seen as "representative" figures who were to be judged by their success as advocates for their "race."[23]

It is hardly surprising that much has changed in critical discussions of these authors between the era of the slave trade and the present. What has stayed the same from the eighteenth century to the present, however, is that they have been seen as the first important black authors to write in English, and thus as crucial initiators and shapers of a black literary tradition. As such, the labels under which they wrote were important. Wheatley introduced herself to the Countess of Huntingdon as an "untutor'd African." Sancho, who also invoked an African identity at various times in his letters, was labeled "an African" in his book's title. If neither author presented an "African" identity as the key to her or his literary persona, each did assert such an identity in various texts.

These assertions have not garnered much scholarly analysis, in part because they are often peripheral to the main concerns of the poems and letters, but they take on much greater importance when seen within the context of the time. Wheatley and Sancho wrote on the eve of an era during which free people of color in England and throughout North America began to form churches and social organizations that formally asserted the "African" identity of their members. From the late 1780s through the early 1820s, black authors and activists most frequently chose to identify themselves and their organizations as "African."[24] This can sound natural and easy to modern ears, but making such claims required Wheatley, Sancho, and others to counter several traditions and realities. They wrote in the face of long-standing Western beliefs about the continent of Africa and its residents, more immediate and demeaning ideas about racial difference that developed alongside the Atlantic slave trade, the shared experiences of brutal oppression that black people in America and Britain faced largely as a result of plantation slavery, and the welter of village, dynastic, and ethnic identities then salient in the West and Central African societies from which most eighteenth-century English-speaking blacks traced their origins. Becoming "African" in English was complicated.[25]

Wheatley and Sancho had no control over their white contemporaries' perception of them as Africans, but they could and did try to reshape what those perceptions meant. Sancho first caught the public eye through Sterne, but he held it by offering valued literary and artistic opinions to white Londoners, opinions that were, of course, even more valued because they came from an unexpected and exotic source.[26] Wheatley was also savvy about the novelty of being an "African" writer. She probably played to the Countess of Huntingdon's well-known racial sympathy when she identified herself as an "untutor'd African" in her initial letter, and she surely came to realize the significance of race for the reception of her writing when the countess asked her to sit for an engraving that appeared shortly afterward as the frontispiece of the book.[27] As England and its North American colonies stumbled toward war, Sancho and Wheatley wrote themselves into the public eye as "African" authors.

Figure 1.2. Engraving of Phillis Wheatley from the Frontispiece of *Poems on Various Subjects, Religious and Moral* [Harry Ransom Humanities Research Center, University of Texas (Austin) Libraries].

Aside from Sancho's single brief admiring notice of Wheatley's poetry,[28] these authors did not refer to each other's work, but their approaches to African identity can be read as a conversation, because the texts that both produced spoke to later black authors and readers. The implicit narratives of African identity that emerge from the conversation between Wheatley and Sancho reflect their life experiences. Their understandings of themselves as "African" authors—as "African" people—did not grow out of an authentic firsthand appreciation of the cultural richness and variety of West and Central Africa, nor did they reach back to the fields, big houses, or slave communities of Britain's plantation societies. Both authors were distant observers of those experiences, and though they were certainly victims of the slave trade, they showed far more awareness of their good fortune in escaping the horrors that the trade visited on most who were caught in its web than of their status as victims. As a result, they struggled toward a sense of kinship with other "Africans" through Christian love and universal brotherhood (in Wheatley's case) or through the conventions of the sympathetic man of feeling (in Sancho's). As "Africans" who knew far more about British letters than about West African societies, their Africas were more deeply rooted in the books they read than in spiritual, political, or other cultural practices of any African "homeland." They were "Africans" because others called them Africans, but they left no evidence of wanting to escape that designation. Instead they embraced it gently, asserting that as "Africans" they and their "brethren" should be recognized as free and equal people in London, Boston, and throughout the Atlantic.

Their ties to their "brethren" were not exclusive, and the "African" identities that Wheatley and Sancho put forth were not rooted in very profound notions of racial difference. Neither portrayed "Africans" as alike in ways that made them fundamentally different from other peoples. Both claimed strong senses of affiliation with other black people in England, the Americas, and Africa. They shared a fate with others whom whites labeled "African," and they expressed allegiance to "African" people because of the oppression they all shared. Later writers working within the tradition that Wheatley and Sancho did so much to found would forge historically deeper notions of identity based on claims to "real" kinship or filiation, notions that would rest on narratives that stretched farther into the past than did those of Wheatley and Sancho.[29] Neither of these approaches to African identity was (or is) inherently more important, more progressive, or more admirable than the other. The tension between what I am calling filiative and affiliative approaches to African identity—between claims to a kind of "blood" kinship and claims to a sense of allegiance that rested on oppression originating in slavery and the modern diaspora—became an animating force in the early black discourse on African identity.

Sancho and Wheatley became emblematic figures from the moments they achieved public attention, though it is of course true that arguments over their meanings as emblems could be sharp. Not surprisingly, then, they both made the path that led from humble slave to celebrated author a subject of their writing, though when viewed from the perspective created by later slave narratives, it was a surprisingly minor subject. Neither opted for autobiography, the genre that would become the privileged choice of nineteenth-century black authors, but each embedded a life story in her or his non-autobiographical work, and in each case biographical details contributed to an antislavery argument.[30] As published authors, they underscored the injustice of enslaving individuals who could write so eloquently, and, by extension, the bondage of countless others who would have written just as eloquently had slavery and enforced ignorance not prevented them from doing so.

As a result, neither portrayed the continent of Africa or the peoples who lived there in much depth. Sancho could not have given a firsthand account if he was, in fact, born on a slaver, and Wheatley, according to an oral tradition passed down in the white Wheatley family, lacked "any remembrance of the place of her nativity, or of her parents, excepting the simple circumstance that her mother *poured out water before the sun at his rising*."[31] Still, each did write a single extended portrayal of the continent, and each rooted that portrayal at least in part in Western literary conventions of a garden of tropical plenty that reached back to the Garden of Eden: Sancho referred to a land "blessed with the most fertile and luxuriant soil," while Wheatley used even more explicit biblical imagery when she described "pleasing Gambia" whose "soils spontaneous" produced such "exhaustless stores" as to convince observers that "Eden blooms again." The poem contrasts this natural abundance, however, with the cultured and elevated British virtues that had bred a scientist like Newton and a poet like Pope. Most important for this argument, her unlettered Africa, in both its natural riches and cultural poverty, was as rooted in Western letters (as opposed to indigenous African societies) as was her civilized England.[32]

These idealized portrayals of the continent were also edenic in the sense that they presented Africa as a fallen paradise. Sancho's description of the continent's natural bounty immediately gave way to the report of a diabolical alliance between "the Christians' abominable traffic for slaves" and "the horrid cruelty and treachery of the petty kings" of Africa, a conspiracy that explained how God's intended blessing had transformed this garden of earthly delight into the home of "poor wretched natives." And, in what was Wheatley's most widely read reference to Africa, her poem "On being Brought from AFRICA to AMERICA," she claimed that "'twas mercy brought" her to Christian America from the "*Pagan* land" of her birth.[33] Wheatley and Sancho, like Britons more generally, understood Africa to be a place of natural bounty, but also a place whose divine and natural gifts had been so overshadowed by the sins of men as to have been transformed into false gifts. Both the visions of bounty and the condemnations of sinful behavior were conventional aspects of the image of Africa then current among whites in England and North America. These "African" authors did emphasize, however, Christian Britons' participation in the sins that had caused man's fall from the original Garden.

These passages describing Africa play minor roles in either author's body of work. They served, however, to open one path through which an image of Africa rooted in biblical and Western literary traditions entered black discourses on the "African," and they acted as conduits through which early Western notions of exotic Africa entered this nascent black anglophone tradition. These passages also help make sense of aspects of the later discourse on African identity that were absent from the work and legacies of Sancho and Wheatley. One of the most important of these involved the two authors' portrayals of "Africans" as people, or, to be more accurate, of themselves as "African" persons. *Africans* must be placed in quotation marks precisely because Wheatley and Sancho very rarely referred to residents of Africa—the people who might first come to modern minds thinking of Africans. In addition to the brief references mentioned above, Wheatley included an often-quoted explicitly imagined allusion to her African father in one poem, and Sancho's letters include a couple of references to individuals born in Africa. But in their published work neither displayed much interest in or knowledge of the residents of Africa.[34]

Instead, when Sancho or Wheatley claimed to be "African" in a letter or poem, they were usually asserting outsider status. Sancho sometimes made such claims as part of an ironic effort to underscore his disinterestedness when attempting to exercise the political prerogatives of an insider: twice when writing to newspapers about public policy he signed his letters "AFRICANUS." He used similar rhetorical strategies in more private letters, spicing his complaints about governmental actions with comments about what "a poor starving Negroe" had to do with "politics?—aye, or poets and painters?" while elsewhere insisting that even "a poor, thick-lipped son of Afric" had the right and ability to pass judgment on events.[35] Similarly, Wheatley attempted to shame deists for the lack of faith represented by their belief in a rational universe when she asked whether "Ethiopians must be employ'd" to show them the error of their ways; needless to say, she then did just that. In another poem she took on the rhetorical stance of "the Afric muse" to offer an escape from grief by reminding Massachusetts Lieutenant Governor Andrew Oliver that, however sad the loss of his wife, she had found a better home in heaven, something that should be cause for joy. And then, in a more complicated invocation of the outsider's voice that allowed Wheatley to advocate antislavery in the guise of a less controversial plea, she argued for American liberty in the face of British oppression by insisting that the power of "Liberty" could make "strong the weak/And (wond'rous instinct) Ethiopians speak."[36]

The rhetorical stance of the "African" was that of an outsider with judgment unsullied by self-interest or prejudice. These claims to disinterestedness often gained strength by ironically acknowledging prejudice against black people (e.g., Wheatley's poem to the deists and Sancho's "poor starving Negroe"), for neither Sancho nor Wheatley left evidence of taking seriously any claim that they lacked moral or intellectual authority to speak to public or private issues.[37] Much that they contributed to the emerging black discourse on African identity rests, in fact, on their insistence that they could speak to those issues as *Africans*, and that being African afforded them a valuably different perspective.

If, however, it was most often in the guise of a rhetorical presentation of the self that Wheatley and Sancho explicitly invoked the "African" (or "Ethiopian"), each did write on rare occasions about black people in the Atlantic and about black people's plight in a world in which American slavery profoundly constrained them. On these occasions, Sancho and Wheatley portrayed blacks as members of a wounded race worthy either of the sentimental engagement of all people of feeling (Sancho) or of the active religious and social advocacy of all Christians (Wheatley). Thus Sancho's famous letter to Sterne was written in thanks for the novelist's sympathetic portrayal of Sancho's "miserable black brethren," a portrayal powerful enough to have "drawn a tear" from Sancho and, presumably, from any other feeling man. Elsewhere Sancho decried the "unchristian and most diabolical usage of my brother Negroes." And he invoked the tribal prejudices of biblical times by comparing the illustrious Bostonians who marveled that poetry as eloquent as Wheatley's could come from the pen of a slave to the "Priests and Levites" in Christ's parable of the Good Samaritan, for these American worthies left the gifted Wheatley just as they had found her—enslaved. Wheatley's poetry included fewer of these references—and Sancho's letters were hardly brimming with them—but she did point out the presumption of American patriots who expected divine favor in their struggle with Britain even as they held "in bondage Afric's blameless race."[38]

Wheatley warned that God would hold the slavery of this blameless race against the supposedly liberty-loving New Englanders. Similarly, Sancho's invocations of black innocence portrayed his "brethren" as worthy of human sympathy. In both cases, however, the vast majority of black people was given little role beyond that of object of others' evil (or, potentially, of their benevolence). The "black race" was worthy of the sympathy of those able to confer it and of the Christian outreach of those who had received an evangelical call, but neither Sancho's letters nor Wheatley's poems provided much scope for black people as a group to engage in collective action to improve their situation in Africa or plantation America. Whites should extend a helping hand to those they had victimized, but neither author offered a vision of what would much later come to be called racial uplift.

Wheatley left evidence in her private correspondence of a more complicated and variegated sense of black people and their possibilities. She supported the efforts of several African-born residents of Newport, Rhode Island, in league with Samuel Hopkins, a local white minister as well as a friend and follower of Jonathan Edwards, to spread Christianity in Africa. Residents of the continent suffered from a "spiritual Famine," but because their minds were "unprejudiced against the truth," she hoped that devoted missionaries might be able to fulfill the psalmist's prediction and lead

"Ethiopians" to "stretch forth" their "hands to God." Wheatley left clear evidence that she understood the residents of Africa to be far more than passive vessels waiting to be filled by missionaries from the New World when she responded to the suggestion of John Thornton, a British philanthropist, that she enter a marriage of religious convenience and take up the missionary banner by traveling to Africa herself. Thornton's presumptuous attempt to direct Wheatley's religious commitments and her romantic life from across the Atlantic must surely have rankled, and she rejected the proposal out of hand. In doing so, she pointed to the absurdity of the assumption that her black skin would ensure acceptance among the indigenous peoples of Africa by joking that she would appear to be "like a Barbarian . . . to the Natives," because she was "an utter stranger to the Language of the Anamboe."[39] Wheatley, unlike at least one of her white patrons, knew perfectly well that her standing as an "African poet" in the United States would have no bearing on her acceptance among native residents of Africa. She understood that black people in Africa were as likely as white people in Europe to take language and shared customs into account when deciding who belonged in their communities and who should be trusted as a friend, much less as a prophet. Phillis Wheatley had, after all, been enslaved in Africa.

However narrow the portrayals of blacks in Sancho's *Letters*, he also certainly appreciated the range of black experience in the Atlantic. His wife was West Indian, and he included a number of goods produced in plantation America on the trade card advertising his grocery store. He lived in London and followed current events closely. He no doubt knew many black people who had the immediate experience of plantation slavery that he was fortunate enough to lack, and he would have known of numerous revolts on slavers and on Britain's Caribbean islands.[40] Nonetheless in the texts of Sancho and Wheatley, members of the "African race" were passive victims and worthy objects of sympathy rather than active shapers of their own destinies. The degree to which this image of Africans as helpless victims reflected the true beliefs of the two authors as opposed to tactical judgments about how to win white support for the amelioration and ultimate abolition of slavery is both impossible to know and largely irrelevant. The focus on blacks as victims worthy of sympathy would continue to inform affiliative narratives of African identity that began, like Wheatley's and Sancho's, with enslavement and the Middle Passage.

Phillis Wheatley's picture of an African identity based on consensual affiliation is, in many ways, less complicated than Sancho's. Wheatley was, above all else, an evangelical Christian, and her ties to other blacks—to those she called her "nation" in a letter to her black friend Obour Tanner[41]—were always mediated through her understanding of all humans as potential children of Christ. In one broadside version of her ode to Whitefield she came

Figures 1.3a, b. Trade card advertising Sancho's grocery. Sancho's card advertised tobacco and included an image of an enslaved African gathering cut sugar cane [V & A Images/Victoria and Albert Museum, London]. Many thanks to Catherine Molineux for telling me about this image.

closer to proclaiming a special destiny for Africans than anywhere else in her poetry. There she called for "ye Africans" to accept Christ not only because he was an impartial Savior, but because he would make them "free, and Kings, and Priests to God." But even this invocation is far from the portrayals of blacks—sometimes "Africans"—as a chosen people that later black writers and religious leaders would offer, for even here Wheatley explains Whitefield's promise about Christ's offer to Africans as part of a list of similar promises regarding Christ's vision for the "wretched," the "hungry Souls," the "thirsty," and the "preachers," as well as for all *Americans*."[42] This is not to downplay the claim that Christ could be understood to be offering freedom and political power to Africans (though of course the poem can also be read in a less radical vein without secular implications), nor that the poem treated Africans as a distinct group in God's eyes. It is, however, to point out that even the strongest reading of the liberatory promise of the poem cannot remove it from the religious framework in which Africans share brotherhood with Americans, hungry souls, and others through Christ's promise of salvation to all believers.

Emotional bonds of affiliation tied Wheatley's Africans, "the members of her" nation, to one another, but those black believers like Wheatley were tied by other, perhaps equally strong bonds to Christians of every hue and ethnic background. And though she did not include much along these lines in her poetry, there is a strong sense in two letters—one to the American Indian missionary Samson Occom and one to the British merchant John Thornton—that she saw the conversion of Africans as part of a more general missionary effort to all unbelievers.[43] Wheatley was, then, an African, but in her eyes Africans were a distinct part of a broader human family shaped by Christian universalist doctrine, and her strong feelings for members of her "African" nation existed within the context of her belief in the kinship of all believers through Christ.

The secular world was more important for Sancho's letters than for Wheatley's poetry, in large part because he based his universalism less on an evangelical Christian desire to bring pagans to Christ, than on a pedagogical project to teach savages to be civilized. As a result, Sancho's allegiance to Africa and Africans can be sketched out in greater detail. It begins with the two related but different ways in which he portrayed himself as a black person in his letters. The first, as noted earlier, involved calling himself a "moor" or a "blackamoor," references that clearly cast Sancho's blackness into a world of allusions rooted in British literature rather than Atlantic or American slavery.[44] Sancho made these literary roots explicit when he referred to the "Blackamoors . . . from Othello to Sancho the big" to fashion himself a black literary presence within English culture and English life. But in this same letter—a playful one to his good friend John Meheux—he invoked the other traditional trope that he used to describe himself as an African, that of racially demeaning stereotype, by testifying that there could have been no "Blackamoors in the Ark" because, as the patriarch of a household that included "Mrs. Sancho and the children five-deep," he knew that Noah could never have kept them all fed. "We eat like hogs."[45] Sancho's willingness to play with this demeaning image underscores his assurance of his standing as a civilized Briton, the successful African product of pedagogical self-fashioning.

Sancho's derogatory reference to his family is not a lone example. Like other similar passages, it invokes long-standing Western traditions of animalistic blacks in an ironic voice that acknowledges the literary convention while assuming that readers would not think that Sancho belonged in such a category. In the specific case of Meheux, Sancho played the role of an older, wiser, and more aesthetically astute advisor throughout their correspondence, so he could safely use self-deprecation and the deprecation of his family—immediate and "racial"—without fearing that Meheux would miss the false modesty. Similarly, when he called himself a "poor thick-lipped son of Afric," or signed a letter claiming to be "as much as a poor African can be, sincerely, Yours to command," he invoked the complexities of his position. These involved *both* the complexion that he shared with those whom Britons—even many antislavery Britons—continued to think animalistic and available to be commanded, *and* the fact that no one in Sancho's social circle mistook him for such a person.[46] Recognizing in these references the intended jokes without losing track of the critique of those who accepted the truth of the conventions that animated the jokes provides one key to understanding the kinship with other black people expressed in Sancho's letters.

An "African" in his letters, he shared both faults and grievances with his "brethren." These come through most clearly when his letters to Jack Wingrave, who had left the household of his parents, with whom Sancho was friendly, to enter the colonial service in India, are read in juxtaposition to his letters to Julius Soubise, a black friend in whom Sancho saw both the potential of his own youth and the tendency to excess that had once threatened that potential. The first letter in the first volume of Sancho's *Letters* was, in fact, written to Jack Wingrave in India in 1768, warning of the imminent arrival of Soubise, who had recently been hustled onto a ship bound for India, probably in part to escape a charge of raping a serving girl of the Duchess of Queensberry.[47] In it Sancho described the "little Blacky" as someone whose gifts include "every thing but—principle," a warning rooted in Soubise's record as a borrower, but not a repayer of money.

Four years after this letter to Wingrave, Sancho wrote to Soubise. He commended his sometime protégé for reforming his ways and encouraged him to continue to fight his tendency toward irresponsibility by praying for the "strength to imitate" the virtues of the Duke and Duchess of Queensberry, Soubise's original aristocratic patrons.[48] Only then would Soubise be able to surmount the "miserable fate of almost all of our unfortunate colour," which included "ignorance, . . . slavery, and the contempt of those very wretches who roll in affluence from our labours."[49] The horrible fate of other black people should serve as incentive to encourage Soubise to acquire the virtues of good Christian English aristocrats. Soubise's very kinship with other blacks, kinship in the eyes of the British at any rate, should stimulate him to become as British as he could make himself. This is what Sancho himself had done following a period of dissipation when he first found himself independent of white oversight.

Sancho's presentation of his initial bout with liberty can seem to skirt uncomfortably close to modern racist stereotype. Judgmental readings of that sort are not only anachronistic, however, they might block further inquiry into the affiliative connections Sancho was asserting with this uneasy portrayal of his black "brethren." These connections were only alluded to in his paternalistic advice to Soubise, but they became explicit in the pointed criticism that he leveled at Jack Wingrave in 1778 and then again in 1780.[50] In the earlier of these letters Sancho responded to Wingrave's complaints that the inhabitants of Bombay, who were "chiefly Blacks," were "a set of canting, deceitful people." Sancho pointedly reminded Wingrave that the first Western visitors to India had found the "Natives" to be "a simple, harmless people," but that interaction with the British had taught them "knavish—and diabolical arts" and turned them "upon their teachers." Nor did Sancho limit his comments to India. He noted with "reluctance" that "your country's conduct"—Sancho no longer claimed Britain here—had been "uniformly wicked in the East—West Indies—and even on the coast of Guinea." Yes, "even" on the coast of Africa, British explorers had corrupted what should have been, in Sancho's eyes, the universally beneficent forces of commerce and Christianity while wreaking havoc on each of the places they settled.[51] But if Wingrave would only resist these evil forces by gently attending to the natives' feelings and humanity, then "even Savages" might come to respect him.

Unfortunately, Jack Wingrave was not a particularly astute student: two years later he expressed sentiments that again threatened the respect of his once-savage correspondent. At that point Wingrave apologized to Sancho for having to bow to local custom by refusing to associate in public with two people of color whom Sancho had called to his attention. He received unfettered sarcasm in response: "I praise thee *sincerely*, for the *whole* and every *part* of thy *conduct*, in regard to my two sable brethren. I was an ass, or else I might have judged from the national antipathy and prejudice through custom even of the Gentoos [a derogatory Portuguese slang term for Hindus] toward their woolly-headed brethren, and the well-known dignity of my Lords the Whites, of the impropriety of my request.—I therefore not only acquit thee honourably—but condemn myself for giving thee the trouble to explain a right conduct."

Sancho held the mirror of "obviously" irrational Hindu prejudice before Wingrave's eyes, reminded the middle-class bookseller's son of the arrogance of English aristocratic prejudice, and then moved on to model a

gentler alternative. He was writing, he noted, with "a pen of thy father's"—
a reminder that some Wingraves were willing to associate with dark
friends—and then he drove his point home by praising Jack Wingrave's
"honest brother" and predicting that he would become "as much a
W[ingrav]e as his Indian brother." Having left his correspondent sharing
Hindu color prejudice rather than following his father's example of British
liberality, Sancho turned Jack into an Indian, rather than an English,
Wingrave. Young Wingrave's refusal to reject racism constituted a descent
from English civility. In a sense much more fundamental than skin color,
Wingrave had gone native in India.

This set of exchanges with Soubise and Wingrave sheds important light
on Sancho's sense of kinship with other black people. He accepted British
conventions in which people from the Indian subcontinent, like those
from Africa, were "blacks," and if he himself was both black and "African,"
he took almost as great umbrage when Wingrave slandered Indians as
when he shunned Africans; no doubt Sancho recognized the roots these
two prejudices shared. Indians, like Africans, were savages.[52] But while
both may have remained uncivilized so long as they continued in their
native ways and remained separate from Europeans, it was through their
interactions with British traders and settlers that they had become
immoral and untrustworthy. And Sancho's kinship with all of these
groups—East Indians, West Indians, and those living on the coast of
Guinea—grew out of his personal experience of corruption through contact with Englishmen. Like Soubise, he had fallen into dissipation when
allowed to indulge the passions that living with the British had unleashed.
Unlike Soubise, Sancho had pulled out of his descent and gained the self-
control necessary to live well as a Briton in England.[53] He had become a
good, humble, honest grocer. The experience left him with what often
comes across in his letters as an annoying air of self-satisfaction, and a
powerful sense of his superiority to other "Africans." It also left him as he
approached death with a strong sense of the position of Africans in the
British world as a people defined by others' oppression. He had escaped
from the fate of his brethren by accepting that definition and evading
much of the oppression by learning how to become "British." If he had
stumbled early on in this process, if, to invoke one of the oldest of clichés
related to British colonization, he had learned to curse, the lessons that he
sought to impart to Wingrave suggest that this self-styled "African" had
come to think himself superior as a Briton to most of the "British." Unlike
the Caliban of cliché, Sancho had learned to speak without cursing and to
write like those who authored Prospero's books. He encouraged Soubise to
follow his example, and his *Letters* stood as encouragement for other
Africans in the empire to do the same.[54]

III

The senses of allegiance to Africa and Africanness that Sancho and Wheatley expressed reached back only to the moment of enslavement, but that does not mean that they were simple. While neither author was conscious of beginning a discursive tradition—a black Atlantic discourse on African identity—each did seek, at least implicitly, to situate an African identity within the immediate settings in which they lived, and within the broader anglophone Atlantic culture of which they were a part. That identity was rooted in history and in literature, but the historical roots were much shallower than the literary ones. When Sancho spoke of blackamoors and Othello or when Wheatley wrote of Ethiopians and Terence, each consciously tapped into long-standing Western traditions that looked to Africa as the home of an exotic difference that helped make England "English," Europe "European," and Western Christendom "civilized."[55] Neither Wheatley nor Sancho accepted these literary/cultural traditions uncritically; like most creative writers they revised and played off of them, sometimes to great effect. But always when they rooted an "African" (or Ethiopian) identity in literary tradition, they manipulated images that they consciously pulled from descriptions of Africa and Africans that had been imposed from without. They were Africans because Europeans called them African, and to be an African was to be an exotic other whose cultural definition had been fashioned by Europeans over the course of millennia, and refashioned in Britain throughout the era of the slave trade.

That was not, however, all that being "African" meant in their texts. For if each referred most consistently to literature (or cultural history), each left ample evidence of an allied sense of allegiance to Africa and "Africans" that found its roots in what can anachronistically be labeled social history. When Wheatley or Sancho referred to their black "brethren," or to a black "nation," or when they decried the evils that their "fellow blacks" suffered, or when they sought the alleviation of that suffering, they implicitly claimed to share as "Africans" in the oppression faced by those suffering on slavers or under plantation slavery. Each had ample basis for staking that claim—after all, Wheatley had been kidnapped and sold into Atlantic slavery and Sancho had been born on a slaver. These historical roots—that is, roots in the historical experiences of black people rather than in the history of European or British culture—were important but they were shallow. They did not extend farther back in time than the moment of enslavement in Africa, and the sense of identity that those roots nourished could sometimes extend to encompass non-Africans who suffered similar fates. Wheatley's public support of Samson Occom's mission to American Indians, like Sancho's rebuke of Jack Wingrave for showing a lack of respect for the natives of India, underscores the degree to which affiliation based on shared oppression broadened to create alliances that reached beyond the peoples of Africa's diaspora, even as it fueled the historical component of the two authors' senses of African identity. Other than Wheatley's brief allusion to Terence, neither offered anything in their texts that pushed a sense of kinship uniting peoples of Africa and its diaspora back onto the continent of Africa or to the history of its peoples there. That was, after all, where enslavement had occurred.

Theirs was a peculiar form of collective identity and one that may best be explained using present-day terminology. Being "African" for Wheatley and Sancho was analogous to having an ethnic identity in twentieth-century America. It was not freely chosen, for they were born into the ascribed category of Africans. That category of people—Africans—was distinct; they were a people apart, but what set them apart, aside from whites' belief that they were different, was a shared history of oppression in England and her colonies. If that history set blacks apart and made them distinct—as Cuban Americans or Italian Americans retained distinctiveness during the twentieth century— it did not make Africans essentially different from other people.

One of the legacies, then, that these first two celebrated "African" authors left for black anglophone writers who came after them, was this historical and affiliative conception of being African. From the perspective of the early twenty-first century such a vision of African identity can look "assimilationist" or integrationist, but regardless of one's position on modern identity politics, it is deeply misleading to try to yoke these eighteenth-century authors to either side of a debate of which they could not have been aware. But if the affiliative identity in the work of Sancho and Wheatley lacks *direct* relevance to modern debates over racial identity, that identity is of profound historical importance to those debates. By unintentionally initiating a black discourse on Africanness, and by initiating it on a footing that embedded a racial or proto-national identity within a claim of universal human kinship—whether Christian or based on Enlightenment universalism—their work established one of the two poles between which the black discourse on Africanness has moved. The wave of black anglophone writers who immediately followed, including John Marrant, Quobna Cugoano, and Olaudah Equiano, would develop a filiative narrative of African identity, perhaps in partial reaction to the senses of Africanness offered in the texts of Wheatley and Sancho.

2

Toward a Transformed Africa

"African" Writers and the Autobiographical Turn

The African authors who published in the immediate wake of Sancho and Wheatley introduced new forms and new arguments to the emerging tradition of black Atlantic literature. These black writers, anticipated by James Albert Ukawsaw Gronniosaw and including John Marrant, Quobna Ottobah Cugoano, and Olaudah Equiano (or Gustavus Vassa), helped introduce autobiography into black writing. The success of *The Interesting Narrative of the Life of Olaudah Equiano, or Gustavus Vassa, the African, Written by Himself* helped make autobiography the privileged form among black writers, a position it retained for more than a century. The autobiographical turn taken by these writers brought in its wake a more consistent concern with concrete experiences of the slave trade and with plantation slavery in the Americas. In short, as many have noticed, these writers effectively founded the slave narrative as a genre.[1]

This new emphasis influenced the black discourse on African identity. Gronniosaw, Cugoano, and Equiano all reported having been born in Africa, and Marrant spent part of his early life in the plantation South, so it stands to reason that all produced texts that raised the kinds of questions about racial and African identity that Wheatley and Sancho had approached through indirection.[2] These writers were not a unified group advocating a single vision, but their works, when read together, posed fundamental questions about the nature of kinship among those born in or descended from sub-Saharan Africa. Equiano's *Interesting Narrative* provided an answer by implicitly positing a mythic story of filiative unity among African peoples that reached back into biblical times. African unity had, according to Equiano, been splintered in modern times, and that splintering had produced the ethnic checkerboard of eighteenth-century Africa while stimulating disruption and inhumanity through the "Barbaric Traffic" that had carried so many into American slavery.[3] The shared oppression that Sancho and Wheatley presented as the foundation of African identity remained crucial for these writers, but the role of affiliative ties shifted, for it was the common experience of oppression and slavery that created an opportunity for Africans to recapture a preexisting but broken unity from their mythical past. Within texts authored by Equiano and his friend Cugoano, a story of literal kinship among "Africans" took its place beside the affiliative picture of African unity found in the works of Sancho and Wheatley.

Gronniosaw, Equiano, and Cugoano, like others who will receive less attention here—Venture Smith, John Jea, and George White—all either wrote consciously and directly about Africa or wrote as "Africans." Equiano and Cugoano, whose books bring together major themes that run through the whole body of work by this group, introduced another new element to the discourse founded by Wheatley and Sancho by offering concrete steps through which African unity could be (re)created. The plan that Equiano and Cugoano proposed was, they believed, God's rather than their own, and Cugoano warned of His vengeance against any who failed to contribute to the divinely mandated changes that would transform the pagan residents of Africa into civilized Christian Africans. Those changes would extend beyond the conversion of "pagans" to Christianity. They would reconstitute "Africans" as a Christian people who would cease selling one another and begin producing nonhuman commodities to trade with Europe and America. The rising African people would then find their proper place within the narrative of human progress. Equiano and Cugoano sought to create a new Africa, not to return to or defend an old one. Ending slavery and the slave trade was a part of their plan, but only a part of a more fundamentally transformative vision that would restore God's chosen people to their rightful place. In putting forth this vision, Equiano and Cugoano introduced general themes that became crucial to future black discussions of African identity, including a commitment to the mythic unity of African peoples, a concern with the practical realities of reforming the societies of the Atlantic rim, and a conviction that blacks were special favorites of God.

I

The African American literary tradition is not synonymous with a black discourse on African identity. Although Wheatley and Sancho were the first widely read black authors to write in English, they had predecessors.[4] It was, however, the first autobiographical writers, most of whom published a few years later, who built on Wheatley's and Sancho's limited engagement with Africa and African identity and pushed it in new directions. That process began during the 1780s, while Sancho and Wheatley were still very much in the public eye and reached an important climax during the 1790s when Gustavus Vassa publicly claimed the name Olaudah Equiano and became the most prominent of a group of London-based black activists fighting to end the slave trade and slavery in the British Atlantic world. All eighteenth-century black authors were unavoidably caught up in the cultural politics of the time because of contemporary debates centering on the natural capacities of black people, debates in which the ability to write—not just to master the technical skills of literacy but to produce "literature"— emerged as the crucial sign of the difference between humans and animals.[5]

In this context, the autobiographical turn took on important meaning. The ability to render life as a written book gave a black person's life, and by extension the lives of all black people, a different meaning.[6] Two early autobiographical texts—the narratives of John Marrant and James Albert Ukawsaw Gronniosaw—make little or no explicit claim to African identity, but their stories raise implicit questions about what black people shared with one another. Equiano and Cugoano would offer answers to those questions.

In *A Narrative of the Lord's Wonderful Dealings with John Marrant, a black* (1785), the author told of his youth as a free person in Florida, Georgia, and South Carolina, his spiritual awakening, his experiences as a captive among the Cherokee, and ultimately of his decision to leave the South for London and the life of a mariner. He closed the narrative announcing his intention to cross the Atlantic once again in order to minister to the black community of Nova Scotia.[7] He fulfilled that intention, and when returning from the Maritime Provinces, he also visited Boston, where he preached to the Prince Hall African Masonic Lodge of that city—the first African Masonic Lodge in America and perhaps the first New World institution to lay claim to "Africa" within its title. Marrant's life, like his narrative, highlights questions central to the black Atlantic.

Perhaps because Marrant was born in New York and then moved to South Carolina, he did not mention Africa. Indeed his narrative often skirted questions of identity rather than addressing them directly. In one of the anecdotes that has captured the attention of many readers, Marrant described his conversion to "true" Christianity. While enjoying the life of a popular musician in Charleston, he accepted a friend's dare to interrupt a sermon by the celebrated George Whitefield by standing up and playing a tune on his French horn. Upon entering the hall, however, Marrant was convinced that Whitefield was speaking directly to him, and when the preacher declared "PREPARE TO MEET THY GOD, O ISRAEL," Marrant "was struck to the ground, and lay both speechless and senseless near half an hour." Later Whitefield declared to his new convert: "JESUS CHRIST HAS GOT THEE AT LAST," leading Marrant to give up his sinful ways for a new life as a Christian.[8] Marrant went on from this incident to proselytize among his family, then among Native Americans, and finally among different groups of black people in South Carolina, England, Nova Scotia, and Boston.

Race plays little overt role in this narrative, but when Marrant claimed that Whitefield, or perhaps more accurately the Holy Spirit speaking through Whitefield, had called him as "Israel" to God, he introduced a theme to which other black narrators would return when trying to establish a shared history for black people. Jacob originally received the name Israel from God at Bethel just before entering Egyptian bondage; perhaps predictably, both Jacob as an Old Testament figure and Bethel as a spiritual site would become central to many African Americans' conceptions of themselves as a chosen people. Marrant himself later raised the notion of blacks' history as a chosen people in a sermon, arguing that "Africans" descended from ancient Egyptians, that they were "sons of Cain," and that they had been among the masons who participated in building the great Temple of Solomon.[9] By representing blacks as God's chosen, and by linking their shared history both to Israel and to Egypt's glory, Marrant introduced biblical tropes of a shared African past that would reappear in blacks' struggle against slavery and racism.

Gronniosaw's narrative of his life experiences raised questions that pertained more directly than did Marrant's to the relationship between Africa and the histories of black people in Britain and America.[10] Having experienced enslavement in Africa, slavery in America, and Christian conversion, Gronniosaw used *A Narrative of the Most Remarkable Particulars in the Life of James Albert Ukawsaw Gronniosaw, An African Prince* to raise questions about Christianity, slavery, and identity. He reported having been born to a royal family "in the city of Bournou" in Africa and told the story of his journey from his inland home to a slave-trading city on the Gold Coast, and from there to Barbados where he was sold to a Dutch-speaking New York master. In New York, he converted to Christianity and received freedom. He remained close to his former owners, but when the last of them died, he took to sea, eventually reaching Europe. Gronniosaw described how he first settled in England, then traveled to Holland in search of former religious associates of his American master, and finally returned to England to start a family and continue his pursuit of salvation. At the end of his account, Gronniosaw described himself and his wife as "pilgrims ... travelling through many difficulties towards our HEAVENLY HOME, and ... waiting patiently" to be delivered "out of the evils of this present world."[11]

The adult Gronniosaw founded his story of enslavement on his intuition, while still a young boy, of the inadequacy of animist religion and of the existence of a single god. Gronniosaw presented himself as having been alienated from his parents and from the culture of Bournou since early childhood. He had been disliked by his siblings for the "grave and reserved . . . disposition" produced by his religious dissatisfaction, and for having been a relentless seeker after first truths—"I was frequently lost in wonder at the works of the Creation." His father also found him exasperating, once rebuking him for asking silly questions like "who made the *First Man*?" The young Gronniosaw insisted that there must be "some GREAT MAN of power which resided above the sun, moon, and stars" that his people worshipped. Due to the melancholy rooted in this spiritual dissatisfaction, he convinced his parents to allow a visiting merchant to take him to the Gold Coast where he could see "houses with wings . . . walk upon the water, and . . . also see the white folks." The merchant, of course, sold the boy to those white folks.

Africa, in Gronniosaw's stories, was a place to escape: even as a child he began to perceive religious Truth, and God favored him by guiding him into Christian lands. He represented Bournou as a place so spiritually deluded that he could have found neither salvation nor happiness had he remained there. When, in the text, he was saved from execution by being sold into Atlantic slavery, he explicitly celebrated the "miracles" that the "ALMIGHTY was pleased to work" for him, and he again praised God for the fact that the captain of a slaver chose to buy him.[12] In neither case did he portray the entire story of his enslavement as evidence of God's favor, but, like Wheatley, the kinship he could feel toward any group besides Christians had to involve shared faith in "True" religion.

Though Hannah More, his famous amanuensis, referred to Gronniosaw as "an African Prince" in the title of the narrative, never in the body of the text does she report him calling himself an "African," and it is not just the term *African* that is missing from Gronniosaw's narrative.[13] The logic of his tale moves away from the assertion of an African identity. He portrayed his life as a spiritual journey that began early and lasted through adulthood. Ill at ease in a Bournou blighted by spiritual ignorance, he found and accepted God's guidance in the search for "Truth," but he never found an earthly home. Gronniosaw did not present "race" (or an African heritage) as an essential or defining aspect of his personality, although he told several stories in which race mattered to others, as when he was exploited by English or American whites or helped by Quakers. The home that he anticipated at the end of the narrative was not to be found in England, Africa, or anywhere else on earth, and he and his English wife anticipated taking that trip together. The pilgrimage that was his life would not culminate when a chosen people found a promised land in the secular world, but when a sanctified couple received their heavenly reward. Within his narrative, the kinship that he felt toward Christian believers had trumped that which he felt toward his literal family, even when he was living in Bournou and had never been exposed to Christianity. He had no choice but to live in a secular world in which being an "African" mattered, but he cared much more about a spiritual world in which it did not.

When read together, the narratives of Marrant and Gronniosaw can be seen to have asked how to understand black people's place within a world that oppressed them because of their color, and also within a sacred universe that promised equality among all people and that could only be understood through the Bible. These authors helped to initiate a tradition of black autobiographical writing that later writers transformed into the genre of the slave narrative. Gronniosaw portrayed his life as an individual pilgrimage from the paganism of Bournou to slavery to the Christian hope for salvation. The simultaneous movement from slavery and sacred darkness to freedom and salvation reappeared in Equiano's later narrative and ultimately became a staple of former slaves' autobiographies. In his captivity narrative, Marrant's experience of racial oppression left him with "sorrow in" his "heart for my brethren, for my kinsmen, according to the flesh"; and that sorrow convinced him to sail from the relative comfort of London to evangelize among former slaves who had escaped to freedom in Nova Scotia.[14] He explained his mission to America in part as the result of his desire to minister to his brother, who, he reported, was among the Black Loyalists who had escaped to Nova Scotia from South Carolina after the American Revolution. His evangelical goals extended beyond his literal kin, however, as he showed by invoking the apostle Paul's lamentation that Israelites would not accept Christ.[15] Through this allusion he closed his narrative with the intention, finally, to take up Whitefield's charge and go, as Israel, to create his people. He hinted at the conviction that blacks were God's new chosen people, a conviction that he later stated more forthrightly while preaching in America.[16] Neither Marrant nor Gronniosaw sought to unify secular and sacred visions of either a single "African" past or a projected common future, but the issues they raised became important when Equiano and Cugoano, who read their respective works, took up that challenge.[17]

II

As the 1780s drew to a close the antislavery movement in England gained steam as literate blacks—many of them former slaves—became important advocates for their enslaved brethren.[18] Two friends, Quobna Ottobah

Cugoano and Olaudah Equiano or Gustavus Vassa, worked together to protect the rights of black people within Britain and to win rights for them in the colonies. Cugoano and Equiano also each wrote a book designed to convince Britons to outlaw the slave trade and move toward the abolition of colonial slavery. Equiano was the more polished writer, and evidence indicates that he helped with the composition of Cugoano's *Thoughts and Sentiments on the Evil and Wicked Traffic of Slavery and Commerce of the Human Species.*[19] Given this cooperation, the differences between the two texts stand out. Equiano's justly more famous book is a classic slave autobiography, offering a polemic against slavery while telling the story of an individual's life.[20] Cugoano's book largely avoids autobiography—he inserted an abbreviated author's biography following the table of contents in response to pre-publication readers' request that he "add . . . information concerning myself."[21] He offered instead an expository attack on the evils of slavery, including personal detail only in support of his polemic. Both men claimed the "African" identity that John Marrant pointed toward at the end of his narrative; like Gronniosaw, both reported having been born on the continent of Africa and enslaved by other residents of that continent; also, like Gronniosaw, both perceived themselves to have moved away from the selves they would have been had they remained in the lands of their births. Cugoano attacked the worldly evils of slavery in what scholar Vincent Carretta calls "quasi-biblical diction."[22] Equiano peppered his narrative with biblical and other literary allusions while writing in a more ethnographic style.[23]

The formal and substantive differences between the two books create a complementary temporal perspective on the authors' vision of the emergence of African identity in the eighteenth-century diaspora, revealing that they pushed the origins of African unity into the biblical past while projecting its culmination into a future ordained by God. Equiano's *Interesting Narrative* offered an individual example of the path to African identity. In the course of his autobiography he became an African, and his narrative voice encompassed both an ethnic "Eboe" (Igbo) and an African perspective.[24] Cugoano included traces of the same process in his text, but wrote throughout in his adult (and thus "African") voice.[25] Read together the two books condemned Atlantic slavery as both a secular wrong and a sacred sin, as both a violation of the natural rights of the peoples of Africa who were victimized by the slave trade and as an assault on a chosen people whose shared history reached into the mythic past. Each writer recognized the complexities created by the social and ethnic diversity of Africa for the emergence of an African identity, and together they turned to political activism to overcome barriers created by African diversity. While neither book, at its most obvious level, deals explicitly with African identity, together they offered a way for black people of the diaspora to unify as Africans in the struggle against slavery and racial oppression. Equiano's *Interesting Narrative* centered on a story of personal transformation that embodied in microcosm a plan for social transformation. Cugoano's text reversed that approach, alluding to the story of personal change while focusing on a plan for political and economic change.

Equiano began with names.[26] In many of the cultures of West Africa, a child's name was believed to influence the course of his or her life, and both Equiano and Cugoano used the name(s) under which they wrote to fashion authorial identity. Cugoano was named John Stewart (sometimes Stuart) by his first master, but he explicitly rejected that name in his narrative. He put only his "African name to the title of the book" and denounced the idea that blacks who sought baptism "should be deprived of our own personal name, or the name of our ancestors."[27] He wrote as an "African."

Equiano used his names to tell a more complicated story. He reported having been born in an Igbo village and named Olaudah Equiano before being kidnapped and sold into Atlantic slavery.[28] Two masters gave him western names before a third named him Gustavus Vassa, and he wrote the *Interesting Narrative* as "Olaudah Equiano, or Gustavus Vassa, the African," invoking in the very title of his book both his Igbo and "Christian" names. More to the point, it was Gustavus Vassa, not Equiano, that he modified by adding "the African," suggesting that his "African" identity resided in the name he was given by a slaveowner. The journey from Olaudah Equiano to Gustavus Vassa, the African, was neither final nor unequivocal, and by narrating it, he offered in microcosm the process through which he forged the "African" (and implicitly racial) identity from which he and Cugoano wrote.[29]

Equiano's remarkable life provided voluminous material for his *Interesting Narrative*. He visited or lived in Barbados, Martinique, Jamaica, present-day Nicaragua, Virginia, Savannah, Charleston, Philadelphia, New York, London, Plymouth (England), Falmouth, La Rochelle, Cadiz, Malaga, Oporto, and Smyrna. Finally, he opted for a more sedate life in England, marrying and raising a family while participating in London's growing and politically active free black community. As a leader of that community he wrote an autobiography that sometimes reads like a picaresque novel.[30] The narrative is punctuated, however, with key moments that the author sets apart from his adventures. These moments reveal the dynamic through which Equiano became an "African Christian," because they center on personal transformations and their effects on his sense of self. He described these events in a prophetic voice designed to call "Africans" to their destiny as a people.

Only by forging a sense of Christian unity and working together could good and oppressed peoples—sometimes "Africans," sometimes "blacks" or "sable races," and sometimes "Christians" of any race—overcome the wicked and achieve true freedom. That such cooperation is not, in Equiano's text, founded on naturally occurring alliances is hardly surprising given his claim to have been kidnapped and spirited away from his home village of Essaka by men whom Europeans would have considered his fellow Africans. He sought to create a sense of cohesion out of shared experiences of oppression, and he hoped to use that sense of affinity to achieve God's plan. In contrast to Sancho and Wheatley, this would entail reunifying an African people who had been dispersed and fragmented in ancient times.[31]

Some aspects of Equiano's emerging sense of kinship with other "Africans" are familiar from classic interpretations of American slave cultures.[32] For example, Equiano reported that he began to perceive things that he shared with other residents of Africa while moving from his inland home to the coast in the hands first of his kidnappers and then of a series of people to whom he was sold. Throughout the journey from his "own nation," he "always found somebody that understood" him until he arrived at the coast.[33] This created a budding if ambivalent sense of allegiance to Africa that he expressed when describing his conviction, as the ship weighed anchor, that he had not only lost all chance of "returning to [his] native country," but "even" lacked hope of "gaining the shore, which I now considered as friendly." This uneasy entente between an Igbo and an African (and implicitly racial) self continued during the Middle Passage, when he reported having learned enough to understand one of his "fellow prisoners" who was talking to one of his own "countrym[e]n," even though the two speakers "were from a distant part of Africa."[34]

The narrative continues along this familiar path when it moves from the author's incipient recognition that he shared something with other victims of the slave trade to a more explicit assertion of African diasporic identity. In the final chapter of his autobiography Equiano referred to "African complexion" without attention to differences like those he mentioned earlier among the darker peoples of Essaka and the "stout mahogany-coloured men" who lived "at a distance." By then he was filled with "pleasure . . . in seeing the worthy Quakers freeing and easing the burdens of many of my oppressed African brethren," and he spoke of Britain's planned colony at Sierra Leone as a philanthropic project "to send the Africans from" London "to their native quarter." He even agreed to "go with the black poor to Africa," which had now become his ancestral home and, by extension, the home of men and women from countless different villages like Essaka.[35]

The starting point for Equiano's journey to reach this understanding of himself as an "African" was a detailed ethnographic description of Essaka. This ethnography is, along with the account of his "true" conversion to Christianity, one of the narrative's most fully realized set pieces, and it explicitly and repeatedly compares Essaka with ancient Israel. The people of Essaka "practiced circumcision like the Jews," used "purifications and washings ... on the same occasions ... as the Jews," and governed themselves through "chiefs or judges" just as had "the Israelites in their primitive state." Igbos could hardly be considered barbarians by Christians who considered themselves the spiritual heirs of God's chosen people.[36] Equiano went beyond arguing by analogy that the Igbo were *like* the ancient Hebrews, endorsing the claim that black Africans descended from "Afer and Afra, the descendants of Abraham by Keturah his wife."[37] As children of Abraham, these Igbo chosen people could scarcely be thought unworthy of legal protection, especially once they accepted the "true" word of Christ.[38] Equiano's narrative of identity formation begins by asserting that Igbos and, by extension, members of other African ethnic groups were the tragically scattered descendants of an ancient diaspora.

Equiano elaborated on this image of his homeland through his representation of the relationship between the village of his birth and his later life. He did not summarize this relationship in a single sentence or paragraph; instead, he presented it implicitly through his description of Essaka. He began describing village culture with personal reminiscences, and naturally enough he used the first person ("our language"), but within the same paragraph he switched to the third person ("Their mode of marriage").[39] This recurs throughout the first chapter, and there does not appear to be a reliable pattern in Equiano's movement between the first and third person. Equiano created a narrative voice that belonged alternatively to a native of Essaka and to a man removed enough from Igboland to write as, to use an anachronistic term, a dispassionate ethnographer.[40] The *Interesting Narrative* contains both the voice of an Igbo, Olaudah Equiano, and that of a Christian African of the diaspora, Gustavus Vassa, the African.

Through stories of the Middle Passage, of the shared oppression of Atlantic slavery, and especially of his passage from an Igbo descendant of Abraham living in ignorance of Christ into a Christian African, Equiano's *Narrative* provides an account of the emergence of racial identity. But what makes the *Narrative* especially interesting is its complicated presentation of the path from "ethnic" to African identity. As the movement from first to third person suggests, Equiano's passage from Igbo to African was not the simple shedding of an ethnic past. Instead, he portrayed the local and ethnic identities that he found in various African and American societies as powerful forces shaping the nature of the protoracial identity that he sought to bring into existence. Evangelical Christianity was the medium that God provided through which individuals would achieve this new identity, and the shared oppression of Atlantic slavery provided the impetus pushing Africans of the diaspora toward salvation. Affiliative kinship forged through political and cultural activism would help reunify a people whose filiative kinship had long been forgotten.

Conversion did not purge Equiano's Igbo origins, nor, presumably, would it purge the ethnic origins of other peoples whose experiences as slaves prepared them to heed his call to become "African." Over the course of the *Interesting Narrative* Equiano expressed levels of kinship by using a variety of terms: countrymen, brethren, Ethiopian, African, Negroes, blacks, and sable people. Of these, at least one key term was used inconsistently: "countrymen" most frequently referred to his fellow Igbo or, by the same token, to other black people who shared an ethnic origin, but it could also refer more broadly to "my African countrymen," and sometimes he used the term in ways that defy attempts to clarify a precise meaning.[41] This loose usage, while hardly surprising in itself, points to a persistent tension in the second half of Equiano's story. Despite his general portrayal of an emerging diasporic identity, he continually brought African ethnicity back into play. Ethnic difference appeared in the text at times when Equiano was specifically attuned to cultural difference, as, for example when he "came to Kingston [Jamaica]," and "was surprised to see the number of Africans who were assembled together on Sundays. . . . Here each different nation of Africa meet and dance after the manner of their own country."[42]

What role did these invocations of ethnic difference play in the *Interesting Narrative*? Vassa the author was an "African," but if his personal transformation was to have a broader meaning, he had to confront the persistent significance of ethnic identities rooted in Africa, and make sense of the relationship between the ethnic and the diasporic. He sought to do that in the three central episodes that structure his account of life as a free man: his rebirth as a Christian, his return to the West Indies as an overseer, and his involvement with the first British expedition to colonize Sierra Leone.

Though Equiano was baptized into the Anglican Church while a young slave, his "true" rebirth in Christ came after he had purchased his freedom. After working for his former owner in America and then spending two sedentary years in London, he was "roused by the sound of fame" to join an expedition seeking a northern passage to India. The hardships of his Arctic experience caused him to "reflect deeply" on his "eternal state" and to resume his search for salvation. After studying the Bible and attending various Christian and Jewish services, he resolved to travel to Turkey aboard the *Anglicanai* and convert to Islam. His plans were cut short, however, when a friend whom he had recommended as a crew member to the captain of the *Anglicanai* was forcibly removed by a former master and transported back to a brutal death on the Caribbean island of St. Kitts. In an effort to save his friend, Equiano left the ship, contacted the prominent British abolitionist Granville Sharp, and disguised himself in whiteface to spy on the kidnappers. Equiano's first antislavery effort antagonized the captains of London ships plying the Mediterranean trade, effectively blocking his intention to reject

Britain and "saving" him from Islam. He had no choice but to renew his search for salvation within Christian traditions. Soon he was invited to a Huntingdonian Methodist love feast, and, after much struggle, "the Lord was pleased to break in upon [his] soul ... and in an instant ... the scriptures became an unsealed book." He then began to view "the unconverted people of the world in a very awful state, being without God and without hope."[43]

With the important exception of the providential role played by his anti-slavery activism, Equiano's was a conventional eighteenth-century Methodist story of rebirth in Christ.[44] To this account he appended the extended "Miscellaneous Verses: or, Reflections on the state of my mind during my first Convictions, of the necessity of believing the Truth, and experiencing the inestimable benefits of Christianity," a poem that explored the relationship between the universal promise of Christianity and the author's personal and communal history. He wrote of being kidnapped from his "native land," of struggling in the evil world in which he found himself, and of wondering why he had "not in Ethiopia died." In the glow of conversion these problems dissolved into the belief that "works can nothing do," and that salvation, as he quotes from Acts 4:12, "is by Christ alone!"[45] This solution remained central to Equiano's vision of his place on earth—in the famous engraving that adorned the frontispiece of the *Interesting Narrative* he holds a Bible opened to Acts 4:12.

But by portraying his native land as the biblical Ethiopia, he effaced African ethnicity in order to highlight a shared mythic past for all sub-Saharan African peoples.[46] This shared past accorded poorly with the life that Equiano had described on the continent of Africa, and the idealized denial of cultural difference proved unsatisfactory in the world in which Equiano lived after his conversion.

He never directly addressed that problem, perhaps because doing so would have complicated his antislavery message. He followed the account of his conversion, however, with a confusing and often-ignored incident that sheds light on the tension among his ethnic, religious, and racial identities. After a short voyage to Spain, where he defended English Protestantism in arguments with a Catholic priest, he agreed to serve as an overseer for his "old friend, the celebrated Doctor Irving," who had decided to build a plantation on the Mosquito Coast of present-day Nicaragua. Equiano explained this odd decision in explicitly evangelical terms: "I accepted of the offer, knowing that the harvest was fully ripe in those parts, and I hoped to be an instrument, under God, of bringing some poor sinner to my well-beloved master, Jesus Christ."[47] This effort to serve two masters, even two beloved masters, was to fail miserably.

Despite the language of Ethiopianism in Equiano's account of his rebirth, his story of his career as an overseer reflects his recognition of the

Figure 2.1. Frontispiece of Equiano's *Interesting Narrative*. The portrait is an engraving by Daniel Orme from a painting by William Denton. The Bible in Equiano's hand is open to Acts 4. 12, which reads "Neither is there salvation in any other. For there is none other name under heaven given among men, whereby we must be saved" [National Portrait Gallery, Smithsonian Institution/Art Resource, New York].

continuing power and importance of African ethnicity even as he struggled to find his place within the universal promise of Christianity. When he boarded a "Guinea-man" to buy slaves for the new plantation, Equiano "chose them all my own countrymen." His description of his experience on the Mosquito Coast dealt only cryptically with his ostensible purpose in becoming an overseer—proselytizing his "countrymen." He spent far more time describing the mestizo natives of the coast in terms that violated eighteenth-century notions of racial difference: a native prince reportedly referred to Equiano as one of "the white men," and Equiano himself included the Indians among the "sable people." Though he did not romanticize "living in this heathenish form," the confusing mixture of peoples did permit "merry-making . . . without the least discord . . . although it was made up of different nations and complexions." These stories should not, however, distract attention from the failure of his initial project. "All my poor countrymen, the slaves, when they heard of my leaving them, were very sorry, as I had always treated them with care and affection."[48] But whatever he had done to "comfort the poor creatures," he apparently made no progress evangelizing among them. Nor did his sojourn among them, however noble he believed his motives, offer a Christian path to a gentler form of slavery. Even the benevolent Dr. Irving replaced Equiano with a cruel white overseer who drove the Igbo men and women to try to escape in a large canoe. It overturned, and they drowned, a different sort of baptism than the one Equiano had envisioned.[49]

Equiano never returned to plantation America, but he did revisit and reinterpret his Nicaraguan experience while revising his *Narrative*. In the first four editions he described the slaves he helped Dr. Irving purchase simply as "my own countrymen." But beginning in the fifth edition he added the phrase "some of whom came from Lybia," an odd claim since Libyans were not generally victims of the Atlantic slave trade, but Equiano added a footnote to ensure that readers would recognize the metaphorical sense in which "his countrymen" were "from Lybia." He cited "John Brown's Scripture Dictionary, 1 Chron. I. 33" and "Purver's Bible, with Notes on Gen. xxv. 4" to document that "Apher, one Abraham's Offspring [*sic*], led an Army against Libya, and getting Victory, settled there, from whom his Posterity were called Africans." As Equiano reconsidered his experiences on the Mosquito Coast during his periodic revisions of the narrative, perhaps he realized that his willingness to serve as a slave driver seemed incongruous to some readers. He offered a way for them to understand his willingness to serve as Dr. Irving's overseer within the broader context of his struggle for "African" liberation.[50] Only through the shared experience of slavery and the affilliative sense of kinship that it fostered among its victims could people from Africa find Christ and desire unity. Through this process, Equiano hoped to dissolve divisions among sub-Saharan Africans and reestablish the unity that had been lost in ancient history. He failed in Nicaragua and discarded the notion that slavery offered a reliable path to his goal, but he did not abandon the larger project.

Equiano had found Christianity through slavery, but his experience on the Mosquito Coast led him to look for surer venues through which to spread Christ's message. He returned to London tired of the impositions that he had suffered at the hands of white men at sea and took a position in service to a former governor of an African trading fort.[51] Thereafter he stopped looking for a small community to whose needs he could minister and among whom he could evangelize and opted instead to write, travel, and speak as an itinerant prophet attempting to call an "African" people into being.[52] Or, as the rechristening of his "countrymen" as Lybians suggests he came to conceive of it, he sought to bring an "African" people back into existence. His goal was not purely or even primarily secular, for ethnic difference and native barbarity would be ended through conversion to Christianity. His religious and secular goals became so intertwined as to be inseparable.

Thus, in seeking ordination from the Bishop of London as a precondition for missionary work on the coast of Africa, he described himself as "a native of Africa" with a "knowledge of the manners and customs of the inhabitants of that country." This homogenization of African societies was not an aberration. When the bishop rejected his request for ordination, Equiano traveled first to New York and then to Philadelphia. Though he wrote little of New York, he quickly went to work in Philadelphia in support of his "oppressed African brethren." That term did not, however, refer to residents (or even natives) of Africa but to the largely Creole black people of New York and Philadelphia.[53] During this trip, Equiano played the evangelist, but the message he reported spreading was the secular message of African unity, a unity that rested on the same shared history of oppression that informed similar appeals in Wheatley's poetry and Sancho's letters. This shared history created affiliative bonds of kinship that tied him to his black brethren in Philadelphia, and tied them all to those suffering in southern and West Indian slavery.

When Equiano returned to London, he continued his quest to build these scattered sufferers into an African people. Finding that the British government had joined philanthropists to fund an expedition to send "Africans" in London to "their native quarter," Equiano became involved in the fledgling movement to send poor black residents of London to Sierra Leone.[54] His growing reputation among black Londoners and evangelical Methodists made him an attractive potential recruit for white supporters of colonization, and they contacted him when he arrived back in the city. Equiano's experience with the Sierra Leone Company proved disastrous as he uncovered layers of corruption and engaged in a struggle for authority that helped doom the initial expedition. He was dismissed before the ships set sail for Africa, probably sparing him an early death. Equiano salvaged his name and the money that he had invested, but he accomplished little for the expedition: the poor black settlers arrived inadequately provisioned at the beginning of Sierra Leone's rainy season and died in horrifying numbers.[55] Soon afterward the surviving residents of Granville Sharp's Province of Freedom were scattered along the coast when a neighboring Temne village sacked the colony.

Neither the failures of this specific expedition nor the personality clashes that led to his dismissal caused Equiano to lose faith in the project. British involvement in Africa remained an important part, but only a part, of the salvation he sought for his "African brethren." He worked to end slavery in the West Indies, and hoped that Britons, "because to them the Gospel is preached" would play a prime role in bringing an "auspicious era of extensive freedom" to "the sable people."[56] Like most British opponents of the slave trade, he believed that humane commerce could be fostered by the colonization of Sierra Leone and that it would help bring Christian "civilization" to the pagan residents of Africa. The more secular aspects of his plan cannot be separated from his personal religious transformation and the vision that it gave him of a Christian African people.[57]

But the African continent would not be *the* home of the Africans that Equiano sought to call into existence. He, after all, remained "Gustavus Vassa, the African" while living and working in England. And he gave no indication that, following emancipation, the freedpeople of the British West Indies should choose to migrate to Africa, nor did he suggest that his "African" friends in Philadelphia should desert the Quaker city for the land(s) of their forebears. Instead he envisioned a people who would respond to shared affliction by uniting under the banner of "true" religion in order to move beyond the ethnic differences that divided those living on the continent of Africa and, by so doing, fueled the slave trade. Given that this religion would be a Methodist version of the Protestant "church of England, agreeable to the thirty-nine articles" that might seem to have been a recipe for assimilation and for the disappearance of "Africans" into the universalistic pretensions of Christianity.[58] But Equiano did not expect that to happen, in part because he did not think Christian universalism a pretension. Furthermore, if ethnic pasts were to be superseded by a Christian present, they were not to be erased. They and the history of affliction and oppression that they helped to engender would remain a part of the African Christian present that would overtake them just as the sacred history in the Old Testament remained part of Christ's new promise.

Because the bulk of Equiano's narrative details the personal journey he traveled to arrive at his African identity, he only touched on his vision of an Africa transformed by commercial revolution into a suitable home for "Africans." In contrast, Cugoano wrote his polemic against slavery and the slave trade from a more straightforward and unchanging authorial perspective. As an "African" author he discussed many issues with parallels in Equiano's text: his early life in Africa, the way he was enslaved and sold, different biblical theories of the origins of African peoples. He, like Equiano, believed Christianity to be "True" religion, and, like Equiano, he looked to the creation of an Africa that would be Christian, "civilized," and "enlightened." He went into far greater detail than Equiano, however, regarding the prospects for a transformed home for Africans, the benefits such a transformation would bring to Britain, and the threat of divine vengeance that Britons faced should they block change by perpetuating slavery and the slave trade. Cugoano's text complements Equiano's attempts to forge a shared past for "Africans" by describing more specifically the projected future that would emerge from that past.

III

The questions surrounding issues of race, Christianity, and slavery that arose in the narratives of Gronniosaw and Marrant were answered forcefully in Olaudah Equiano's autobiographical account of becoming an African Christian. With his answer he introduced a narrative that built upon the affinities created by the shared oppression of the Atlantic slave trade to re-create a filiative connection among the peoples of Africa and their descendants that was rooted in biblical times. It was only at the conclusion of the *Interesting Narrative*, however, that Equiano explicitly moved beyond providing an individual model of an Igbo becoming African and presented a program designed to change Atlantic societies in ways that would foster the creation of an African people. He sketched a brief picture of this plan, but his friend and collaborator, Quobna Ottobah Cugoano, elaborated the plan in greater detail. Both of them looked to market forces under the auspices of a humane and godly English hand to create the conditions for the rise of a Christian African people.[59] Their advocacy of humane market forces rested, as did those of other antislavery thinkers, on a critique of the barbaric markets that had produced the Atlantic slave trade. By supplanting the slave trade, white antislavery thinkers had envisioned bringing Africa into Britain's benevolent commercial orbit. Equiano and Cugoano accepted this goal, but saw it as a stepping stone toward a more important development—the rise of the African people. Only in this way would the affiliative connections among the peoples of Africa's diaspora lead to the rediscovery of deeper filiative ties.

An initial step in projecting this history of commercial development onto Africa involved stories of the African slave trade, and several writers told stories in which early anglophone blacks confronted in the starkest terms the barriers they faced as they sought to forge an "African" identity. Those who had been born on the continent of Africa had to confront and make sense of having been enslaved by people Europeans called "Africans." The moment of enslavement, then, stands on several levels as the baseline from which the projection of a "commercial" African people into history begins. It was one of *the* key moments in the personal histories of those—like Equiano, Cugoano, Gronniosaw, and Venture Smith—who experienced it, and each was aware that his path toward becoming an author began with enslavement. In addition, the moment of enslavement stands in their texts as the epitome of the unjust and illegitimate market that had to be eradicated if Africa was to be transformed.[60]

None of this is to say that these authors portrayed their native societies as characterized by illegitimate market cultures. Instead each described his enslavement in ways that showed the local traditional market relations of his village to have been perverted or infringed upon in some way by trade with Europe and the Americas. Equiano, for example, described the traditional markets that he reported having frequented with his mother, markets that included what he believed to be a more legitimate trade in enslaved people: the "strictest account" was taken, he said, of the "manner of procuring" slaves, and only those who were "prisoners of war, or . . . had been convicted of kidnapping, or adultery" or other heinous crimes were "suffered to pass." The people of his native village, Essaka, did, in fact, enslave prisoners of war, but Equiano insisted that slavery in Essaka differed fundamentally from American slavery: "with us they" did "no more work than other members of the community," their material lives resembled those of free people, and they could own property.[61] Most other authors passed on describing traditional slavery in Africa, but several described their own enslavement and experiences as slaves in Africa in ways that complicate Equiano's picture.

Equiano, Gronniosaw, Cugoano, and the New England author Venture Smith all portrayed themselves as having been illegitimately enslaved. Equiano and Cugoano both reported having been kidnapped by marauding bandits; Gronniosaw joined a merchant traveling to the coast in hopes of seeing more of the world, only to find himself transformed into a commodity and sold into the Atlantic world; and Smith and his village fell victim to a "numerous army . . . instigated by some white nation" that attacked his people, tortured and killed his father, and took young Smith himself "and the women prisoners."[62] Some described time spent in traditional African familial slavery— Equiano, for example, described being sold to a goldsmith who had "two wives and some children, and they all used me extremely well"[63]—but most reported being brutally transported from their homes to the coast in response to market forces that pulled them into the Atlantic world. Whether victims of brutal armies, unscrupulous merchants, or evil bandits, each of these men portrayed an Africa in which the forces of international commerce had transformed men into monsters who cheated and stole without concern for right or wrong in their efforts to feed European and American demand. The slave trade subverted the supposedly civilizing force of commerce.

For Equiano and Cugoano, and for their project to call into existence an "African" people, the color of their enslavers raised important questions about the way European commerce combined with the cultural diversity of sub-Saharan Africa to hinder the rise of an "African" nation.[64] Equiano provided no physical description of his kidnappers, but he did note that he passed through "different nations" while being transported from Essaka to the slave-trading fort on the coast, and he referred to the traders responsible for his journey as "sable destroyers of human rights."[65] Cugoano demonstrated how much he thought was at stake in this question by approaching it indirectly. He first asserted that it "matter[ed] not" whether his kidnappers were black or white, but several pages later he acknowledged that it did, in fact, matter to him: "to the shame of my own countrymen . . . I was first kidnapped and betrayed by some of my own complexion."[66] Both men recognized and pointed out the role that European demand played in transforming Africa's slave trade, but the role of African residents in the trade highlighted the problems of an Africa perverted by contact with Europe but untransformed by Christian benevolence and legitimate commerce.

It was from their experiences within the Atlantic world economy that these authors learned of the supposedly beneficial effects of markets on people, though ironically the lessons of market beneficence were often taught most convincingly by white failures to respect the market's rules. Equiano again provided the most subtle and engaging picture of this process when he described his career as a petty merchant seeking to scratch out enough capital to purchase his freedom. On several occasions he paid a price for believing the market's conceit that each buyer or seller entered into exchanges as an equal whose personal qualities—race, wealth, religion—were rendered irrelevant by universal market forces. During the four years that he spent trading in the Caribbean while still a slave, he "experienced many instances of ill usage, and . . . [saw] many injuries done to other negroes" in their "dealings with whites." On one island all of his trade goods, as well as those of a black friend, were taken by white ruffians. When Equiano and his friend complained, their antagonists threatened them with flogging. Complaints to local authorities only brought a "volley of imprecations" and more threats.[67] Venture Smith had an analogous experience when, while still enslaved, he "hired out a sum of money to" a white man, only to have his creditor's brother break "open my chest containing" the note and destroy it.[68] In these and countless other cases, the authors accepted the rules of the market that had turned them into commodities and behaved in the way that the market dictated.[69] Their black skins, however, made them vulnerable to unscrupulous whites in Europe and the Americas, and they were denied the rewards that they had earned.

Despite these setbacks the authors of these early texts did use the market to gain their freedom. Through this process they reversed the earlier action of the market, purchasing themselves as commodities—as objects—on the market and transforming themselves into owners of commodities or subjects. Such a transformation could not be worked through the unfettered mechanism of the market: the laws that created the framework in which British Atlantic commerce proceeded did not recognize slaves' right to own property, so British law did not recognize the right of enslaved people to use money to purchase themselves.[70] Instead, slaves living in British polities or in the United States depended on their masters to grant them the privilege of owning property and the privilege of self-purchase. This requirement loomed over their attempts to win freedom. Even though Robert King had promised to sell Equiano his freedom when the slave acquired enough money to pay a previously agreed purchase price, Equiano remained anxious lest King revoke the promise. And Equiano claimed that King might have done so had he not been convinced to honor his word by the ship captain under whom Equiano had been serving. The market, then, provided a path along which the enslaved could pursue freedom, but so long as racism and the laws of slavery distorted the universal formal equality that was, in theory, the essence of market culture, the path remained unsure.[71]

On its simplest level, removing the barriers that hindered blacks from traveling that path freely meant abolishing slavery and the slave trade, and Equiano and Cugoano, as authors and political activists, sought to convince the British to take this step. But as Equiano's narrative made clear, many of the hindrances that blocked black progress resulted from racial prejudice as much as from slavery. Thus he continued to be physically threatened and economically cheated after he purchased his freedom, as did Gronniosaw and many other now-anonymous free people of color in Britain and the Americas. So long as Africa remained outside of the West's concept of history, so long as descendants of Africa remained a *nonpeople*, such oppression would continue and the beneficial effects of the market would flow unreliably if at all to blacks. Denied entry into the culture of the market, they would remain outsiders to the Atlantic market, subject at worst to being commodified as objects, and at best to struggling on the market's margins.

Cugoano and Equiano believed that overcoming these obstacles required the complete social and religious transformation of Africa's residents and of the peoples of its diaspora. Christianity was the key to this transformation, and virtually all of the early slave narrators hoped to encourage missionaries to spread the "Truth" of Christianity among the black peoples of Africa and the Americas. Such missionary activity would also require that Europeans recognize the ways that slavery and the slave trade violated the spirit of Christianity and thus that they begin to live up to the universalist promise of Christianity. As noted earlier, Equiano's *Interesting Narrative* provided an individual model of just such a transformation.

The future social transformation envisioned by these authors needs further elaboration.[72] Equiano and Cugoano developed an interpretation of the history of "African" people that inserted them into Western history. Christianity offered the shared past that they needed, allowing the authors to see the diversity of sub-Saharan Africa as rooted in an ancient diaspora that could be explained, ultimately, by reference to the Old Testament. The Bible also foretold a projected future of the sort that history requires, foreseeing a world in which Africans would come together as a Christian people to overcome their diaspora. But these authors also turned to the market and its capacity to transform society in order to project a secular future for "Africans" in the world of Western nation-states.

In and of itself, melding secular and sacred visions of national identity was neither unusual nor original. Great Britain and its colonies had nurtured an eighteenth-century tradition in which "freeborn Englishmen" saw themselves as both a commercial people and an "Elect Nation."[73] Many historians have analyzed the interpenetration of market relations and religious belief as, to use Richard Bushman's classic formulation, the children of Puritan New Englanders became Yankees.[74] But if many groups in the eighteenth-century English-speaking world saw themselves embedded in both biblical archetypal narratives and largely secular processes of social progress, each idiosyncratic combination of these idioms reveals much about those who created the mix. Such is the case for the historical vision that emerged among early black writers.

As noted earlier, Equiano offered only an abbreviated version of this projected future. Having called for support of missionary efforts in Africa and of the British colony at Sierra Leone, he turned to the need to integrate the peoples of West Africa as equals into the West's empire of commerce. This would involve the elimination of the "inhuman traffic of slavery," and its replacement by "a system of commerce . . . in Africa." Thus in a single sentence Equiano denied that the inhuman trade in people belonged in a legitimate commercial system, while appealing to Britons' greed ("the demand for manufactures would most rapidly augment") and sense of secular civilizing mission ("the native inhabitants would insensibly adopt the British fashions, manners, customs, &c."). Promising that merchants and manufacturers could do well by doing good, he assured them that a "commercial intercourse with Africa" would open "an inexhaustible source of wealth to the manufacturing interests of Great Britain." Abolition of the slave trade and the integration of Africa into England's commercial empire offered an "immense, glorious, and happy prospect—the clothing, &c. of a continent ten thousand miles in circumference, and immensely rich in productions of every denomination in return for manufactures."[75] Intent on winning the political support of British merchants and manufacturers, he did little to specify the way Africa and Africans would be transformed by this market revolution. Instead he borrowed a vision of commercial transformation that had been enunciated by antislavery thinkers earlier in the century.[76]

Cugoano was more explicit than Equiano, offering a vision of the transformation of Africa that appears to have drawn explicitly on Great Britain's settler societies in the Americas. He shared Equiano's belief that the first step was to stop Europe's illegitimate exploitation of Africa, and he argued that this could only happen if the slave traders' misrepresentations of the "character of the inhabitants on the west coast of Africa" were countered and the slave trade abolished. If "noble Britons" were to accomplish this change and begin to deal with West Africans "in a friendly manner," then learning and commerce would transform the coast. "As the Africans became refined and established in light and knowledge, they would imitate their noble British friends, to improve their lands, and make use of that industry as the nature of their country might require," bringing far more wealth to England than could slavery. Africa, then, "would become a kind of first ornament to Great-Britain."[77] Enlightened through Christianity and secular learning, civilized through commerce and industry, Africa and Africans would rise as fully equal participants in the West's narrative of universal history.

Doing so entailed both accepting the culture of the Atlantic world market and being accepted into it. Olaudah Equiano and Quobna Ottobah Cugoano supported missionary programs that they believed would bring the residents of West Africa willingly to the culture of the market. Such a transformation for Africa was worthwhile not only because it would end the iniquitous traffic in human beings, but also because Equiano and Cugoano both implicitly accepted Enlightenment historical ethnography, which understood human societies to pass through set stages of progress, and both believed African societies to exist at more primitive stages of development than those that prevailed in Europe and the settler societies in the Americas. Both men insisted, however, that European exploitation of Africa violated the rules of the market and the bounds marking off the civilized from the savage or barbaric.[78] Integrating Africa into the market would, at once, raise Africa out of primitivism, help create Africans as a people, and further the progress and civilization of Great Britain specifically and of mankind more generally. Just as the masters of several of these authors had, by granting them the privilege of self-purchase, permitted them to transform themselves from object to subject, so Britain, by fostering the commercial development of Africa, would permit the peoples there and in the diaspora—"Africans"—to transform themselves into a people and to take their proper place on the stage of world history. The individual elements of this commercial vision reflected conventional if advanced enlightened social theory, but Equiano and Cugoano were the first to use it to project a rising African people.

The analogy between individual manumission and the liberation and creation of a people, however, cut in more than one direction. Equiano and Cugoano, the two authors who explicitly participated in this discourse, could be understood to be asking for British charity toward Africa and Africans, but that is a distorting simplification. While Equiano expressed gratitude toward Robert King, the master who manumitted him, he made it clear that freedom came from something more fundamental than King's benevolence. Equiano had sought commercial success in order to be ready to exploit the chance for freedom when God presented it, but he explained passing up an earlier chance to run to freedom by insisting that if God wanted him to become free, He would offer a legal and legitimate path. Thus, King offered Equiano his freedom not only out of benevolence but also because it was part of God's plan.

Equiano and Cugoano were equally certain that the rise of an African people was part of God's plan, and thus their request for British aid implied a cost should the British fail to live up to their obligations. Commercial development was, after all, a universal law only because God made it so, and should those in power on earth fail to follow divine prescription, then there would be a price to pay. Equiano, clearly the voice of conciliation in the collaborative project of the two men, left the threat of vengeance unspoken in his narrative, but his friend Cugoano was explicit. Should the British block the divinely mandated march of progress on earth, should, in other words, Europeans turn their backs on God's benevolent plans for "Africans" and the rest of mankind, then a just God would punish the wicked offenders:

> O ye inhabitants of Great-Britain! To whom I owe the greatest respect, . . . tho' many things which I have written may seem harsh, it cannot be otherwise evaded when such horrible iniquity is transacted: and tho' to some what I have said may appear as the rattling of leaves of autumn, that may soon be blown away and whirled in a vortex where few can hear and know: I must yet say, . . . that the voice of our complaint implies a vengeance.[79]

Africans would be brought into existence as a people, either in man's time through their incorporation into the culture of the market, or in God's time when true justice would be brought to the world.

Cugoano forthrightly asserted that it was "the incumbent duty of all men of enlightened understanding, and of every man that has any claim or affinity to the name of Christian" to work for abolition.[80] Throughout *Thoughts and*

Sentiments he mixed appeals couched in the rationalist language of natural rights with threats issued in the name of an avenging God, and in doing so, he developed a vision of human history and of Africans' place in human history that steered unevenly between the prospect of unlimited progress through secular enlightenment and the threat of divine intervention to bring secular history to an end. England's future, and with it the future of the West, depended on how enlightened Britons responded to the evils of slavery.

Cugoano did not pursue either the progressive or apocalyptic strain of thought systematically, so any effort to untangle the relationship between these two approaches risks conveying greater clarity than he offered. Cugoano believed that God intervened actively in human affairs, for he credited divine aid for much that happened to him. Such belief did not, of course, bar him from seeking secular enlightenment; while the dense tissue of biblical citation and allusion shows that he often read the Bible, he also "sought to get all the intelligence" he could find about "the state of my brethren and countrymen in complexion," and he thanked God for allowing him to gain "some little learning." Like most British Methodists (whether Huntingdonian or Wesleyan), he perceived no contradiction in simultaneously believing in progress through human agency and in ongoing divine action on earth.[81]

Both strains of belief informed Cugoano's critique of slavery. He went to great lengths to denounce biblical defenses of slavery and of racism, engaging in an innovative bit of typological reasoning to explain why the existence of slavery in ancient Israel should not be read as divine approval of the institution, and why black skin could represent evil without making black people themselves evil.[82] Such analysis was not alone sufficient. He also insisted that "the light of nature, and the dictates of reason, when rightly considered, teach . . . that no man ought to enslave another." Thus, the "learned" could choose either "revelation [or] . . . reason for their guide." Either way, slavery was simply wrong.[83]

And England was paying the price for that wrong. Cugoano's list of the corrupting influences eating at the nation's vitality would have made a "country" politician proud. The empire in which ignorant Britons had such pride had "sunk [the nation] into a world of debt" that required ever higher taxes. That debt had created a "sluggish deadness over the whole realm" that was clogging "the wheels of commerce" and draining "the money out of the nation." Cugoano thought "all stock-jobbing, lotteries, and useless business ha[d] a tendency to slavery and oppression." If Britons continued to carry "on that horrible and wicked traffic of slavery" it would "at last mark out the whole of the British constitution with ruin and destruction," and lead "the most generous and tenacious people in the world for liberty" to be "reduced to slaves." Cugoano built upon the hope developing among

Britons that antislavery activism could, in the wake of the American Revolution, reestablish England's status as a liberty-loving nation.[84]

Lest anyone mistake the appearance of general prosperity for security from these dangers, Cugoano invoked a warning drawn from sacred history. "Had one been among the Canaanites a few years before the Israelites entered their country, or in Babylon a little before Cyrus encamped against it, he would have beheld a people in a state of great worldly prosperity, and in much security notwithstanding that the judgments of God were ready to seize upon them." This warning provides the key to Cugoano's melding of sacred and progressive history. Like Equiano, he hoped that England would turn away from slavery and the slave trade and foster the development of Africa and of Africans in America. Like Equiano, he insisted that Britain would benefit economically as well as spiritually if it acted justly. If only England were to live up to its obligations as a civilized nation to extend "Christian government" and the "blessings of liberty," then "every thing would increase and prosper at home and abroad, and ten thousand times greater and greater advantages would arise to the state, and more permanent and solid benefit to individuals from the service of freemen, than ever they can reap, or in any possible way enjoy, by the labour of slaves." If, as he added, Africans ceased to be victimized by "such religion as the philosophers of the North Produce," and were offered their rightful place in a projected history of human progress, all would be well.[85] His oppressed brethren would continue to come together, to feel an affiliative tie to one another, and Ethiopia would ultimately stretch forth her hands unto God to recreate the filiative unity of biblical times.

Cugoano offered a succinct program that the British state could follow to achieve this hopeful future. The English should begin with a period of mourning and fasting during which they should confront the evils they had visited upon "Heathen nations" and "poor Africans." Then they should abolish both slavery and the slave trade, and seek to convince other European nations to do the same. This should be followed up with naval patrols along the coast of Africa to stop slave trading by Europeans who refused to stop voluntarily. In addition to playing God's policeman on the slave coast, Britons in the Caribbean should begin a program of instruction for blacks who had been held in ignorance by slavery, and the treatment of bound laborers should be regulated during a brief necessary transition to total freedom.

Finally, Cugoano endorsed a "back to Africa" program that fits much better with Equiano's vision of an African identity than did the plan for the Sierra Leone colony.[86] Cugoano did not call for Africans in England or America to be sent indiscriminately back to a single colony. Instead he called for British Christians "to make enquiry concerning" newly freed slaves' "friends and relations in Africa." Freed people who made "progress in useful learning and the knowledge of the Christian religion" could return to their home villages "fit for instructing others."[87] As this process progressed, Africans would become "refined and established in light and knowledge, they would imitate their noble British friends, . . . improve their lands, and . . . become a kind of first ornament to Great-Britain for her tender and compassionate care of such a set of distressed poor ignorant people." Anticipating Equiano, he insisted that England would soon earn ten times more from humane commerce than it did from the slave trade.[88]

Should Great Britain reject its historic role, should it continue to exclude Africa and Africans from the progressive course of Western development, then human history would be cast into a different mode. God had ordained that the peoples of Africa should be brought to the "Truth," and England was appointed to redeem itself for previous iniquity by doing that work. Like any prophetic voice calling on men to do God's work, Cugoano warned of the cost of failure. He closed *Thoughts and Sentiments* by warning his British readers that if his voice was

> not hearkened unto, it may yet arise with a louder voice, as the rolling
> thunder, and it may encrease in the force of its volubility, not only to shake
> the leaves of the most stout in heart, but to rend the mountains before them,
> and to cleave in pieces the rocks under them, and to go on with fury to
> smite the stoutest oaks in the forest; and even to make that which is strong,
> and wherein you think that your strength lieth, to become as stubble, and
> as the fibres of rotten wood, that will do you no good, and your trust in it
> will become a snare of infatuation to you!

Like the God of the Old Testament, the God of African Christians could and would destroy the enemies of his newly chosen people, and doing so would entail the destruction of the progress and enlightenment in which the British took such pride.

IV

Equiano and Cugoano may not have agreed on everything, but they worked together to fight slavery, and each sought to create an identity for residents of Africa and peoples of the African diaspora that could help in that fight. They struggled to do that using philosophical and religious languages that had, during the preceding two centuries, placed "Africans" outside of the great projects of Western subject formation that were so central to the

Enlightenment. The logic of this situation, combined with the fact that Equiano and Cugoano both came to "enlightenment" through Christianity, led to internal contradictions in the ways they placed Africans in time. From a broad perspective, Western culture was moving from seeing humans as the objects of God's action to seeing them as the subjects of their own history, and thus from placing humans in God's eschatological time to believing them to be engaged in the infinite production of progress.

Cugoano and Equiano collapsed these two perspectives. In their post-millennial optimistic moments, they foresaw a world in which Europeans worked to bring God's justice to earth by fostering the creation of an African people—in Africa, Europe, and the Americas—that would take its place among the rising peoples of the world. As devout Christians, Cugoano and Equiano presumably believed that such a history would further the peaceful return of Christ to earth, and the gentle transition from human to sacred time. Conversely, should Europeans neglect their responsibility and choose instead to continue to oppress the "poor Africans," then the God of the Old Testament and of Revelations would intervene to save his enslaved chosen people.

Equiano and Cugoano were not unusual in combining Enlightenment rationalism with Christian millennialism. The combination that they developed, however, is important. It held open the alternative possibilities that humans would achieve God's justice through progressive reform, or that God would visit the apocalypse upon his evil children. By casting Africans' origins both into the mythic past of a chosen people and into the historical past of shared oppression, by embracing the basis of both filiative and affiliative African identity, Equiano and Cugoano held open two paths; one led toward revolutionary activism fueled by God's favor, while the other pointed toward secular reform rooted in progressive history. If the first path was followed, an African people divided by an ancient diaspora would be reunited in sacred time as a chosen people; the second path would produce a commercial African people united as a metaphorical nation whose modern diaspora encompassed Africa, Europe, and the Americas.

3

An African Homeland?

African Institutions and Emigration in the 1780s and 1790s

Historians often note that no one lives a "typical" or "representative" life, but the experiences of Ignatius Sancho, Phillis Wheatley, Olaudah Equiano, and Quobna Ottobah Cugoano stand out from those of most victims of Atlantic slavery. To what extent did their ideas about African identity reflect or resonate with those of their black contemporaries in the English Black Atlantic? Answering questions of this sort is difficult in the best of circumstances—this is why scholars often discount arguments about "typicality"; given the small number of blacks who had access to the books written by black authors, one might be tempted to suspect that, however interestingly Equiano and the others responded to the challenges of forging an African identity, their theories belong on the margins of late eighteenth-century black life. That the *Interesting Narrative* went through nine British editions and appeared in pirated form in New York, Holland, and Germany during Equiano's lifetime offers evidence of its importance for the reading public, but most members of that public were white, and most blacks remained excluded from it.

If, however, the direct influence of Equiano and Cugoano on their black contemporaries may have been limited and is almost certainly beyond recovery, there are clear indications that black people living in different parts of North America stretching from Georgia north to Nova Scotia addressed questions about African identity in complementary ways. The most obvious indication that this might have been the case lies in the sudden appearance of many self-styled "African" institutions during the last quarter of the eighteenth century. African Baptist churches arose independently in Williamsburg, Virginia, and Savannah, Georgia; an African

Masonic Lodge was formed in Boston; and other African fraternal organizations, most notably the African Union Society of Newport, Rhode Island, appeared in northern towns and cities

These self-styled "African" institutions developed as energetic local organizational centers for black communities in ports up and down the Atlantic seaboard, but, as indicated by their separate and broadly simultaneous decisions to label themselves "African," their horizons extended beyond the local.[1] The African Baptist Church of Savannah, founded during the Revolutionary War, not only ministered to the spiritual needs of low-country black Georgians, it also became the home congregation for Baptist churches throughout much of the black Atlantic. At about the same time, Prince Hall founded the African Masonic Lodge as a fraternal organization for black Bostonians, and soon the African lodge began chartering locals in other northern towns. Blacks living in Newport and Providence, Rhode Island's two largest ports, formed "African" fraternal organizations that remained local in their organization, though their officers carried on correspondence with blacks in other American towns and with others in the broader Atlantic world. The artisans and laborers who joined these various African organizations confronted the same issues when asserting an African identity as had London authors like Equiano. Like those discussed in preceding chapters, they began to articulate collective histories as "Africans" that confronted and engaged with the complicated questions that arose out of the roles that ethnic conflict played in the Atlantic slave trade. Only in this way could they make sense of how to think of the peoples of Africa and the diaspora as a people. Their interest in these questions undercuts any suspicion that discussions of African identity at the turn of the nineteenth century were the province of a small cadre of literary figures; understanding what it meant to be African in the modern world engaged many black people throughout the English-speaking Atlantic.

I

Few towns would have seemed less likely to produce an important transnational movement than Revolutionary Savannah. Given the indifference of eighteenth-century lower southern whites to the Christian conversion of those they enslaved, it is even more surprising that the movement that emerged out of Savannah took the form of an "African" evangelical Christian church. The chaos of the Revolutionary War, however, created conditions out of which an exceptional group of charismatic black preachers founded the African Baptist Church of Savannah. After the war most members of the church remained in Georgia, but others, who were evacuated with the British, founded black Baptist churches in Canada, Africa, and the British Caribbean.

The transatlantic revival known as the Great Awakening influenced deep southern colonies less fundamentally than it affected New England and the Middle Colonies. Still, George Whitefield, the British evangelist who helped spark the Great Awakening, made several trips to Charleston and helped found an orphanage in Savannah, and the young John Wesley, founder of the Methodist movement within the Church of England, spent two years in Georgia during the 1730s, an experience that influenced his belief that slavery was sinful. While in Charleston, Whitefield converted John Marrant to Huntingdonian Methodism. Marrant participated in the black Huntingdonian community in London that included Equiano and Cugoano, and he did evangelical work in Nova Scotia and Boston, linking black communities there to Equiano's London.[2] On the whole, however, the difficult work of spreading Christianity through deep southern slave quarters fell not to Whitefield or even to Marrant, but to a small group of obscure itinerant white ministers, and especially to their black converts. These preachers traveled the swampy lowlands and poorly developed upcountry and often had to brave the hostility of planters who realized that slaves could develop antislavery interpretations of the Bible.[3]

Despite barriers that the planters erected, black and white preachers combined to ignite a series of conversions along the Savannah River during the 1770s, allowing evangelical Christianity to develop a toehold among low-country blacks. The first missionary outreach to target slaves explicitly took a much more radical turn than its white sponsors had intended. In 1774, Selena Hastings, the Countess of Huntingdon and leader of the religious group that had sent George Whitefield to preach in America, became concerned about the spiritual welfare of the slaves whose labor sustained an orphanage that Whitefield had founded in Savannah. David Margate, a young man of African descent, was completing his training at Trevecca College, the Huntingdon Connexion's seminary in South Wales, and Hastings chose him as the perfect messenger to preach to those slaving to support the Connexion's philanthropic efforts in Savannah. Presumably, neither the countess nor others who participated in the decision to send Margate to the Lower South realized that he had developed a strong sense of racial identity and a deep aversion to slavery.[4]

Margate arrived in Charleston in January 1775 and immediately began speaking in ways that whites found dangerous. By the time he settled into Bethesda, the Savannah orphanage, his idiosyncratic approach to life and to his calling began to constitute a direct threat both to orthodoxy at the orphanage and to the slave system of the Lower South. His fellow missionaries were troubled by his belief that God wanted him to "take a Negro woman in [the] house to be his wife," even though she was already married to another enslaved man. This hinted at a degree of antinomianism—the belief that those who experience salvation are exempt from human law—that would reappear among later black Christians who escaped from Savannah, but it paled in comparison to Margate's other challenges to the social order. From the pulpit he informed both black and white listeners that slaves were part of God's chosen people and that "God would send Deliverance to the Negroes, from the power of their Masters, as He freed the Children of Israel from Egyptian Bondage." William Piercy, the director of the orphanage, concluded that Margate's pride made it impossible for him to "bear to think of any of his colour being slaves."[5] Whites beyond the orphanage reacted quickly to Margate's radical preaching, seeking to "pursue, and hang him," and his Huntingdonian sponsors barely managed to spirit him out of America before vigilantes could act.[6] Unfortunately, no surviving evidence reveals how blacks responded to Margate's preaching, but it is suggestive that Savannah soon became a hotbed of "African" evangelical activity.

The leaders of this evangelism were not Huntingdonian Methodists, but a group of black men who would found the African Baptist Church of Savannah before going on to lead black Baptist movements in Jamaica, Nova Scotia, and Sierra Leone. George Liele may have been the most important of these Baptists. A Virginia-born man, Liele had been sold into the Deep South when young. In 1773, while attending church with his Baptist master, Henry Sharpe, in the Georgia upcountry, Liele displayed a calling to preach, and his pious master manumitted him so that he could pursue that calling unencumbered by bondage. Liele then began to travel and preach throughout the area, helping to convert several of the key figures in the spread of the Baptist faith in the black Atlantic. They included another Virginia-born man, David George, who would travel to Nova Scotia and Sierra Leone; Andrew Bryan, who would lead the Savannah church after the American Revolution; and Jesse Peter, who founded an African Baptist Church in Augusta, Georgia. Liele himself built a successful church in Jamaica after the war.[7]

The chaos attending the American Revolutionary War in the Deep South permitted these men to travel, preach, and organize churches, first in Savannah and then throughout the Atlantic. First, the war created worldly opportunities. The British invaded Georgia and held Savannah from 1778 until they evacuated the region in 1782. While there the British army offered a real if uncertain haven to runaway slaves, and many took advantage of its presence in the low country to escape by running to its headquarters in Savannah or Charleston. David George and George Liele were among these,[8] and while in Savannah they continued to preach, converting and baptizing Andrew Bryan among many others. When the war ended and the British Army withdrew, many blacks left with it. A few, including Liele, went to the British Caribbean and joined the free colored communities on those islands. Others, like George, joined several thousand Black Loyalists who immigrated to Nova Scotia. They left behind, however, many black people whom they had converted to the Baptist faith, and it was those people who raised Savannah's African Baptist congregation on the foundation that Liele had built.

Bryan, the most important black religious leader who remained in Savannah after the war, began exhorting black followers almost immediately after Liele left for Jamaica. He started in a barn on his master's plantation, and as his reputation grew the increasing crowds of worshippers brought hostile attention from neighborhood planters. He continued exhorting in the face of this opposition—opposition that included a brutal beating—until 1788, when he was ordained by a white preacher. Bryan then founded the First African Baptist Church of Savannah, which grew to include more than 800 members by the turn of the century. Soon the Second African Baptist Church of Savannah was formed.[9]

Little surviving evidence sheds light on what made these early churches "African" in the minds of their members. They were, of course, churches of black congregants, and "African" may have been a simple racial descriptor. More likely, Liele and then Bryan preached about the kinship of African peoples and the biblical history of blacks in terms that paralleled those that their friend and former colleague David George would use when portraying his Nova Scotian congregation as both chosen people and participants in a universalist church (see chap. 4). Without a record of their sermons or contemporary descriptions of their preaching, there is simply no way to know.

What can be known is that preachers from Savannah maintained their connections with one another as they moved out across the Atlantic to spread their vision of the gospel among enslaved and free black people throughout the Anglophone world. Liele, who was instrumental in bringing these other figures to the Baptist faith, maintained contact with his former followers. While founding his Baptist church in Jamaica, he stayed in written contact with George in Canada and then in Africa, and with Bryan in Savannah. Unfortunately, their letters have not survived, but Liele and George both mention their correspondence in letters they wrote to John Rippon, the chief London coordinator of British Baptist evangelical efforts throughout the world. The letters to Rippon were designed to raise money for missionary work, so they focus on the spread of the Word to blacks in each of these locales and make much of the doctrinal orthodoxy of the black correspondents. Rippon published edited versions of the letters—the only versions that have survived—in annual reports on world Baptist missionary efforts that targeted British Baptist philanthropy.[10]

What bound these men to one another, to the Baptist Church, and to their African brethren, despite their geographic dispersion? First, as illustrated by their reports to Rippon, they considered themselves part of a universal Baptist movement bounded by neither nationality nor race. At the other extreme, as men who had shared the life-changing experience of conversion and had been born again together as Christian believers, they formed a small brotherhood that neither time nor space could separate.[11] They believed themselves to have been reborn in Christ, and their common history stretched back to their individual beginnings as saved souls. Their sense of allegiance to other black people was more complicated. They founded and preached to black churches but also welcomed white worshippers once they became ministers—Liele, George, and Bryan all wrote of white participants in their services. Some part of their decision to bring the Word to blacks may simply have reflected an astute reading of their best opportunities for evangelical activity, though George Liele's claim that his "obligations to God" led him to "instruct the people of my own colour" suggests more than mere expedience.[12] Although these Baptists believed all men to be potential brothers in Christ, their churches and their movement were self-consciously black and African, presumably because as blacks living in the Atlantic world, they faced common difficulties.

African Baptists in Savannah probably shared some version of the belief in blacks' status as a chosen people that Margate had espoused in 1775 and that George would proclaim after he left Georgia, but they rarely had to confront the implicit tension between chosen-ness and universalism. White racism and blacks' desire for social and cultural autonomy produced a growing tendency toward segregation throughout American evangelical churches following the American Revolution.[13] As self-styled "African" people joined in gathered churches and used the language of the chosen people, few felt any need to clarify the presence or absence of a racial dimension to the chosen. When circumstances dictated that African Baptist preachers address this tension, they set forth universalist visions of God's people—David George once claimed that "all of [his] people" thought of London as "home" and looked to white religious leaders in London for guidance. When, however, his all-black congregation later sought to escape the oppression it faced in Nova Scotia, the congregants invoked the language of Exodus to describe their migration to Africa, drawing on their special status as a perfect church to defend their communal prerogatives.[14] The brethren who remained in Savannah left fewer traces of their attempts to think through their kinship and affiliation with all "Africans" and with all Baptists, and thus of what made their church "African."

If the best documentation that we have of what these men *said* about Africa—and that evidence is not very good—provides no proof that they looked to a biblical or mythic shared past on the coast of Africa, the lives that they lived fit into a way of perceiving the world that shared much with the black discourse on Africa that can be documented in Britain and the northern United States. That fit suggests that black people living in the slave South engaged in efforts to understand their relation to Africanness through imperfectly defined combinations of affiliation through shared oppression and fleeting allusions to a more fundamental or filiative mythic unity, and they began to conceive of themselves as a chosen people, a way of approaching kinship that helped bridge the distance between filiative and affiliative narratives.

II

While blacks in South Carolina and Georgia were founding an African Baptist movement that would spread to Canada, the Caribbean, and Africa, a group of free black workingmen in Boston founded what would become the most influential secular fraternal organization in African America— African Freemasonry. Like the African Baptists in Savannah, Prince Hall and those who joined him to found Boston's African Masonic Lodge built a fundamentally new "African" movement on a preexisting institutional foundation. Within that movement they asserted emotional, mythical, and genealogical links to the continent of Africa and its peoples.[15]

Freemasonry had developed into a transatlantic fraternal movement during the eighteenth century, and its popularity in the new United States made it one of the most important social and cultural institutions in the early republic. Freemasons combined secrecy and exclusivity with an ecumenical vision of the Supreme Being as a great architect, and they projected a history of the "craft" of masonry far back into the ancient and biblical past. Freemasons—"brothers in the craft"—looked to Egypt and ancient Israel to find the first earthly architects and saw themselves as the inheritors of the sacred and architectural mysteries surrounding the building of the pyramids and of Solomon's Temple. Throughout the eighteenth-century English-speaking world, Masons developed an organization whose members withdrew into the semisecrecy of their lodges to proclaim the brotherhood of all men, to pursue benevolent commerce, and to espouse natural rights ideologies. Freemasonry won the allegiance of Benjamin Franklin, George Washington, and other Founding Fathers, as well as many merchants and professionals in the towns and cities up and down the Atlantic seaboard. These American Masons felt fraternal kinship with Masons in England, the West Indies, and the rest of the Anglophone world. Ultimately,

Freemasonry elicited enough hostility in the United States to fuel an Anti-Masonic Party and an oppositional political movement during the antebellum era.[16] Remarkably, given these white Masonic traditions, African Freemasonry—eventually Prince Hall Freemasonry—became the largest and most geographically extensive secular organization in nineteenth-century black America. George Washington may have been the father of the country and the most famous early American Mason, but Prince Hall was the father of African Freemasonry, leading a movement that expressed and fought for the interests of northern free black people.[17]

Parts of the early history of African Freemasonry remain obscure. Some early writers claimed that Hall was born in the British Caribbean, perhaps in Barbados according to an unsubstantiated assertion by one early Masonic historian. At least one historian has speculated that he was born in Africa. It is more likely that he was a native of New England, but if not, then he had moved to Boston by the end of the Seven Years War and was living there by the beginning of the imperial disputes about taxation and representation that would culminate in the movement for American independence.[18] He established himself as a leatherworker and caterer, and, for reasons that have not survived, he felt drawn to Freemasonry and sought to join a local all-white lodge. Its officers rejected his application.

In 1775 he and a small group of black friends met an Irish soldier who, perhaps because he had met black Masons when stationed in the British Caribbean, accepted their aspirations to join the craft and brought them into his military lodge, where they were initiated as Masons. They began meeting in Boston, but the town's Grand Lodge refused repeated requests for a charter. In the mid-1780s, Hall gave up on the Boston Grand Lodge and petitioned London's Grand Masonic Lodge, which issued a charter to African Lodge No. 459. In short order, Boston's African Lodge gained local prominence, and then began extending its sweep by chartering African lodges in Providence, Philadelphia, and then other northern cities. Throughout the 1790s Hall assiduously maintained ties with the London Lodge, remitting contributions to its charitable fund while passing along news about American masonry.[19] Finally in 1827, two decades after Hall's death, the African Masonic Lodges of the United States declared their independence from the London Lodge, renaming themselves in the founder's honor as the Prince Hall Masonic Lodges.

Throughout the 1780s and 1790s, Lodge No. 459 met in Boston at Prince Hall's leather shop at the sign of the Golden Fleece. Hall quickly gained white Bostonians' recognition as one of the most prominent black people in the city, inspiring some to claim that he was not just a prince in name, but was descended from African royalty. One prominent white townsman believed that Hall's stature extended to others in the craft, rendering membership in the African Lodge something that could set someone several steps "above the common blacks" of the town.[20]

That status was based, in large part, on African Masons' perceived respectability. Hall had fought in the American Revolutionary War, and when in 1786 western Massachusetts farmers rallied behind Daniel Shays to demand an end to farm foreclosures, Hall wrote to Massachusetts governor James Bowdoin volunteering to help put down the rebellion.[21] Hall sought to establish African Masonry as a bulwark to ordered liberty, and his offer was consistent with the basic duties of a Mason that he presented in a speech at his lodge's annual feast in honor of St. John the Baptist in 1792: Masons, he insisted, "must be good subjects to the laws of the land . . . giving honour to our lawful Governors and Magistrates," and foregoing participation in "any plots or conspiracies or rebellion."[22] From its inception, African Freemasonry was an organization of respectable and established black men, and Hall and his followers, like their white Masonic brothers in the craft, advocated positions on most political and religious issues that remained within the mainstream of elite opinion.

Members of African Lodge No. 459 parted ways with respectable white Boston, however, over issues involving race and slavery. Slavery had never been a dominant institution within New England, but recent scholarship has shown that slaves and slavery were more important to the region's history and culture than was once thought.[23] The movement for American independence encouraged many to question whether slavery belonged in free republics, and black New Englanders capitalized on these doubts by pushing for fundamental changes in their status. As early as 1773 a substantial group of free black New Englanders went much farther, petitioning for aid in escaping from American racism and moving to "some part of the coast of Africa."[24]

Hall and many of his brother Masons took up this call in 1787 with a remarkable petition of their own. Condemning white racism while expressing loyalty to and admiration for American "civilization," they issued a lengthy request for aid to emigration, a call that expressed the complicated and sometimes contradictory senses of allegiance to Africa and African identity that would later reappear in Hall's published statements.[25] The early petition began by rooting a common identity among black people in their relatively recent shared history of enslavement—"we or our ancestors" were "brought from Africa and put into a state of slavery in this country"— and in the experience of white racism that relegated them and their children to "disagreeable and disadvantageous" lives in America. Later, however, the petitioners looked farther back in time and to a more distant place by invoking a shared homeland with other African people. Twice the petitioners referred to Africa as their "native country"; three times they described immigration as a "return" and only once as a "remove"; twice they called natives of the West African coast their "brethren." Such expressions of kinship moved beyond metaphorical claims to friendship and entered the realm of nature when the petitioners asserted that Africa's "warm climate" was "more natural and agreeable" because it was the climate "for which the God of nature" had "formed" them. When they took this turn to natural history by defining immigration as a return to a homeland naturally suited to black people, the petitioners moved from an explicitly affiliative assertion of racial kinship to an implicitly filiative one.

The return they envisioned would be controlled by blacks and largely independent of whites: they intended to choose representatives to travel to the African coast and procure rich but uncultivated land from native leaders. Once they acquired clear title to land, they would invite other blacks who were "disposed" to join them. The settlers would form a "civil society" based upon a "political constitution" and including a "religious society" led by "blacks ordained as . . . pastors or Bishops." In a vision that anticipated the more fully elaborated one that Equiano and Cugoano were beginning to articulate an ocean away in London, these settlers hoped to civilize and enlighten their "heathen brethren," saving their souls from the "prince of darkness" by spreading the word of Christ. Commerce would be the handmaiden of religion in this process of transformation, and the investment that the petitioners asked white residents of Massachusetts to make would be "over-balance[d]" by the wealth produced by "mutual intercourse and profitable commerce" between the United States and Africa.[26]

The sense of a natural or filiative kinship among all people of African descent is unmistakable, as is the petitioners' pride in being "civilized" by virtue of being culturally Anglo-American. The resemblance between this plan and Britain's seventeenth-century colonization of New England is obvious and unlikely to have been coincidental; indeed, the petitioners elaborated their plan for a constitutional republic in a document that opens with an explicit reference to "the new constitution" of Massachusetts.[27] Like Equiano and Cugoano, these petitioners saw emigration as a way to escape from white racism, while bringing Africa out of an age of darkness and into a legitimate and mutually beneficial commercial relationship with the West. In this petition they asserted a rich if somewhat confusing combination of identities. The essentialist kinship with other Africans that is based in natural history sits comfortably beside the diasporic kinship among blacks whose roots lie in shared oppression. Their experience among Europeans and white Americans in the diaspora had, according to the petition, afforded black Americans the chance to acquire religious and secular knowledge that would help them transform the Africa to which they hoped to "return." Embracing both aspects they perceived in themselves—one that we might call essential and the other cultural, one rooted in natural history and the other in relatively recent social history—would allow them to save Africa while benefiting America. Though this brief petition did not offer a clearly articulated process though which "Africans" would be created from the pagan residents of their Old World homes, it did project a history of colonization that drew on many of the sources that informed Equiano's *Interesting Narrative*.

III

At roughly the same time that Hall was building the African Masonic Lodge in Boston and George Liele was initiating the religious movement that created the African Baptist Church of Savannah, black residents of Newport, Rhode Island, formed a self-styled "African" self-help organization. The African Union Society of Newport was one among many benevolent societies created by blacks in northern cities, and it resembled the others in ways that extend beyond its name. Most were formed to ensure respectable funerals for their members and to facilitate the education of free black children.[28] Newport's African Union Society pursued these conventional goals, but it went further, also participating in early black emigrationist movements. Due to the peculiarities of Rhode Island's history in the slave trade, several leaders of Newport's black community and of its African Union Society were African-born men who approached "African" identity and the complexities of African ethnicities from a different starting point than did Prince Hall or Andrew Bryan.

Newport's prominence as a North American center of the African slave trade helps explain why Rhode Island became home to one of New England's highest concentrations of enslaved people.[29] Some of the slaves who ended up in Rhode Island had been taken from Africa as children, but because they were too young to bring good prices in the Caribbean, or perhaps because they became favorites of captains of slavers, they were brought "home" to Newport when the slave ships finished their voyages. There the young slaves went to work in Rhode Island's mixed farming economy.[30] Though there is no reliable estimate of the proportion of Newport slaves who were African-born, this pathway to the port resulted in a steady if small flow of African-born people into the region, helping to explain why several important leaders of Newport's Free African Union Society were natives of Africa. These West African origins influenced their approaches to African identity.

The Society itself grew out of networks that were created when several white Newport religious leaders began evangelizing among area slaves. The first and, in many ways, the most important of these figures was Sarah Osborn, an impoverished woman who taught school and led informal prayer meetings at her house. During the 1760s Osborn was holding prayer meetings six nights a week with a combined attendance of up to five hundred people. One night each week she worshipped with an average of about seventy black residents of Newport. Among her black followers were Obour Tanner, Phillis Wheatley's friend and correspondent, as well as two men who would become central figures in early emigration efforts and in the formation of the African Union Society—Newport Gardner and John Quamine. Osborn suffered from a degenerative illness that ultimately forced her to give up her prayer meetings, but Samuel Hopkins and Ezra Stiles, two white ministers, sought to continue the work that she had begun among the town's enslaved and free black people. During the 1770s they began to envision a plan that extended beyond Newport.[31] By converting African-born men and then freeing them to travel back to Africa to spread the gospel, they hoped to take advantage of the evil of slavery to bring "enlightenment" to the "dark continent." The missionaries hoped to transform and Christianize Africa and believed that such a transformation could be most easily effected if the missionaries were adults returning to ethnic cultures they had known as children. Prior to the outbreak of the American Revolution, Ezra Stiles, the future president of Yale College, had chosen two African-born men— John Quamine and Bristol Yamma—to pioneer this project of return and redemption, but the war redirected the interests of Stiles and Hopkins, stalling the project.[32]

In the wake of the Revolution, black residents of Newport assumed leadership of this project. Sometime before 1787 they formed the African Union Society of Newport, and in January of that year they began reaching out to invite others to help pursue their "earnest desire of returning to Affrica."[33] Perhaps because they lived in a port and thus interacted frequently with people throughout the Atlantic basin, members of the Union Society immediately sought to build a broad network of black people in support of their plan. In 1787 they wrote to prominent blacks in Boston, Providence, and Philadelphia to encourage cooperation and to drum up support for a return. Only by bringing together all of their "brethren in affliction" could they hope to build a movement that would benefit blacks throughout the Americas and Africa. Perhaps as a result of their correspondence with Prince Hall and other black Bostonians, or perhaps simply because they drew on common sources, their plans echo some of the earlier petitions.[34]

As might be expected, given white ministers' roles at the beginning of this impulse toward emigration, some in the Society feared that whites might control both emigration and the colony in Africa. Though Stiles and Hopkins drifted into the background after the Revolution, the British were in the process of founding the colony of Sierra Leone, providing a focus for discussions of emigration while raising questions about African American settlers' legal status within a British colony. Concerns about citizenship and autonomy were exacerbated by the enthusiasm of William Thornton, the son of a Caribbean planter, who became convinced that emigration to Africa would solve the problems of slavery in the Americas. He pledged to send the slaves that he inherited to Sierra Leone and then worked to further the movement, visiting local groups like the Union Society and linking them to broader currents of international antislavery.[35] Black Newporters decided they could take advantage of Thornton's promotional efforts while minimizing the danger of falling under the sway of whites or indigenous Africans by sending local representatives to find and bargain for land—as Boston petitioners had earlier said they would.

In 1789 Anthony Taylor, the president of Newport's African Union Society, and Salmar Nubia, the Secretary, wrote to "all the Affricans in Providence" to invite their nearby "brethren in affliction" to join the Union Society. Taylor and Nubia expressed little hope for blacks' prospects in the United States and despaired over the lives of slaves in the West Indies. They were equally distraught over the "heathenish darkness and . . . barbarity" that led their "brethren, the Nations of Affrica" to be "so foolish and wicked as to sell one another into slavery." Taylor and Nubia asked Providence blacks to accept the Society's rules as a model and form an affiliate that would help "effect" black people's "return to their own country . . . where they may be more happy than they can be here."[36] Such happiness would only come, however, when immigrant blacks built transforming civilized settlements on the African coast.

This brief letter hints at a sense of African identity much like that which Olaudah Equiano and Ottobah Quobna Cugoano were then articulating more fully in London. Taylor and Nubia believed Africans to be brethren in affliction, but they recognized the fissures dividing this family; after all, it included both the slave trading "Nations of Affrica" and their victims who had been "transported to a Land of Slavery." This language invokes both an affiliative sense of racial kinship based on shared oppression and a latent, if too often violated, filiative or essentialist tie among all black people, though it does not explain the basis for filiative kinship. Newport's blacks saw the hand of God in the growing support for emigration, believing that a "return" would contribute to the welfare of blacks in America and Africa, presumably in part by introducing Christianity to the "heathens" on the continent and weaning them away from their "foolish and wicked" wars. Such a movement would begin to subsume indigenous ethnic divisions in a broader African unity, thereby forging a sense of unity among members of what the African Union Society repeatedly referred to as "the African Race."[37]

Boston blacks responded to the Newporters' solicitation by proposing that all towns with blacks interested in "returning" to Africa should send "some of our own Blacks" to find and negotiate with indigenous leaders for suitable land on which to settle. Newport's African Union Society endorsed the idea but claimed that "poverty" would prevent its participation. The Providence Society's efforts were, however, entirely in keeping with black Newporters' expressions of allegiance to their African "brethren."

The possibilities for emigration from the United States to West Africa appeared to be growing exponentially at the very moment that black New Englanders were discussing a move. Granville Sharp's disastrous Province of Freedom, the colonizing expedition from which Equiano had been fired, had initiated sustained interest on the part of English antislavery activists in a free black African colony. Black Newporters and their white allies, including William Thornton, were aware of, and responding to, the efforts of Sharp and others in England.

IV

The movement of London's "Black Poor" to the Province of Freedom did not begin in England. It began in the plantation South during the American Revolution, and occurred within the context of the booming late eighteenth-century Atlantic slave trade that had carried African peoples far beyond the Caribbean and Brazilian centers of the New World plantation complex, ensuring that small but significant populations of black people lived in the farthest reaches of European trade and settlement on the eve of the Revolution. Africans or their descendants lived in Holland, France, Russia, and Germany, in Spain and Portugal, as well as in Great Britain. Black slavery also existed in all of Britain's eighteenth-century colonies—in Nova Scotia as well as in Jamaica—and enslaved and free black people played important economic and cultural roles even in societies in which their numbers were small.[38] The American Revolution created a diaspora of roughly 9,000 blacks from North America—especially from Virginia and the Carolinas—to various parts of the British Empire, further broadening and deepening the black presence in the English-speaking world.[39] That this diaspora was unplanned and unintended only intensified its effects on places like London and Nova Scotia that suddenly became home to far more black people than ever before.

This scattering of former slaves happened because the Revolution created conditions in which many black Americans could escape. For the first time, whole families, sometimes even whole communities, managed to flee bondage together. These opportunities arose out of the exigencies of war and in response to a series of strategic decisions made by British commanders. The best known of these was Virginia governor Lord Dunmore's famous offer of freedom to the slaves of rebel masters who escaped and helped compel rebellious white Virginians to submit to royal authority.[40] Dunmore's proclamation created a precedent that other British commanders found expedient to follow, and enslaved blacks ran from their masters to join British armies throughout the war.[41]

The fate of many of these black escapees is depressing.[42] Some died in battle. Many, including some who joined Dunmore, succumbed to diseases like smallpox that often devastated American-born soldiers in military camps.[43] Still others served the British faithfully throughout the war, only to be sold by their erstwhile liberators into Caribbean captivity when hostilities ended. Within the context of an eighteenth-century imperial war, however, the injustices visited upon black loyalists are less surprising than the fact that some British officials, especially General Guy Carleton, took seriously their armies' pledges to the formerly enslaved men and women who had served the king.[44] These Britons refused to countenance either the unofficial slave trade to the Caribbean or American attempts to reclaim human property. Carleton, who oversaw the evacuation from New York City, the final British stronghold in the new United States, ignored George Washington's demands that the black men and women who had won their freedom be reenslaved. Instead, Carleton moved approximately 3,000 black men, women, and children to Nova Scotia, where they were to be given land and freedom.[45] Most of the "Nova Scotians" who would later move to Sierra Leone came from this group. Other Black Loyalists, as well as a number of slaves taken to England by their white Loyalist masters, ended up free and struggling on the streets of London.

Granville Sharp's Province of Freedom was intended to offer both a safe haven and the prospect of productive lives to these seemingly abandoned black Londoners. The initial expedition failed miserably as a result of several mistakes that could and should have been avoided: poor planning and bad luck brought the settlers to Africa at the wrong time of year, and corruption left them without the provisions intended to help them survive their first few months. Notwithstanding these logistical problems, the settlers' experiences on the coast of Africa highlighted problems that would persist in future efforts to settle freed slaves on the continent.

On the most basic level, the region at the mouth of the Sierra Leone River proved to be far less hospitable for people raised in temperate American climates than either Sharp or the settlers had been led to believe. The ships carrying the Black Poor landed in May 1787 on the shore of a beautifully inviting peninsula. Mountains gave way to rolling hills that descended down to the shore of Frenchman's Bay, the whole covered with thick vegetation that seemed a sure indicator of rich soil. Unfortunately, June brought the rainy season with torrential downpours and periodic tornadoes, combined with brutal heat that sapped the enthusiasm of those fortunate enough to survive the endemic malaria and yellow fever. Notwithstanding the claims of British promoters of African settlement like Henry Smeathman, the soil was ill suited for the crops the settlers knew how to cultivate. Leopards snuck into town from the surrounding jungle to prey upon the settlers' pets, and swarms of voracious ants devoured anything that failed to get out of their paths. A discouraged Abraham Elliot Griffith reported to Sharp, his friend, teacher, and patron, that the settlers found Sierra Leone so inhospitable that it was a "very great pity we ever came to the country."[46]

Nature did not pose the only challenges faced by the settlers, for Sierra Leone was an active slave-trading region. A few miles upriver from Frenchman's Bay lay Bance Island, home to a thriving British slaving fort; Gambia Island, a rudimentary French slave depot, was a bit farther up the Bunch—a tributary river.[47] Sharp's Province of Freedom was, of course, supposed to undercut the slave trade by providing an example of the prosperity that free labor and legitimate commerce could produce, but the slave trade affected the nascent colony far more than it affected the trade, and it did so in a way that foreshadowed tensions that would trouble relations among black American colonists and the native residents of Africa during the next few decades. Like many coastal peoples, the local Koya Temne participated in the slave trade, and one headman, King Tom, responded to a dispute with the colonists by seizing two settlers and selling them back into slavery. This terrifying story was merely prologue to the decision of another headman, King Jimmy, to destroy the settlement in retaliation for a dispute with slave traders and the Royal Navy.[48]

King Jimmy's sacking of Granville Town, the name the Black Poor had given to their nascent village, would prove to be the first of many tense encounters between colonists and natives, but it would be misleading to say that it set a firm pattern. In the wake of the town's destruction, the sixty or so surviving settlers scattered in search of safety. A number moved to Bance Island and went to work for slave traders, a development that horrified Granville Sharp and other London abolitionist supporters of the colony. Others tried to scratch out their subsistence on a plot of land close to Bance Island but under the protection of a Temne headman named Pa Boson. Still others joined Abraham Elliot Griffith, who had moved farther upriver to the town of Robana to live with and ultimately marry into the family of Naimbana, the paramount king of the Koya Temne. Griffith translated for Naimbana during negotiations with Britons and served as a cultural broker among the Temne, the British, and black settlers from America.[49]

His success carving out a life and a role at Robana represents the more benevolent possibilities for relationships among natives and newcomers.

Neither Griffith's presence at Naimbana's court nor other settlers' labor at the Bance Island slave fort altered King Jimmy's success in erasing Granville Sharp's Province of Freedom from the coast of Africa. Sharp was discouraged, but he did not give up on creating a colony of freedom in West Africa. The enterprising abolitionist ultimately convinced a group of wealthy evangelical businessmen, led by the banker Henry Thornton, to form the private Sierra Leone Company, and to invest enough capital to found a proper colony. Thornton and other members of the famous Clapham Sect had deep enough pockets to create and support a West African colony of former slaves, but black Londoners were not eager to follow in the footsteps of Sharp's previous colonists, so the company's directors had to look elsewhere to find settlers.[50] They turned to unhappy Black Loyalists who had settled in Nova Scotia.

Things had not gone well for the freed people whom General Carleton had taken to Nova Scotia during the evacuation from New York. Far more white than black Loyalists escaped to Canada, and the previously tiny province was overwhelmed by the addition of roughly 30,000 newcomers who arrived in 1783. All expected free land grants. All sought public support. Unjustly, if all too predictably, Nova Scotian authorities gave lower priority to the needs of Black Loyalists, who were settled in a number of dispersed and mostly segregated communities in the province: officials stinted on the provisions that the British government had promised and were slow to distribute the land that had been guaranteed.

As a result, the black refugees found themselves falling back into a state of dependence. Archaeological evidence suggests that some had to survive their first brutal Nova Scotian winters in "shelters" that consisted of nothing more than five-by-five foot holes dug into the ground with makeshift roofs constructed over the top.[51] Literary evidence shows that many were forced into exploitative sharecropping relationships with white Nova Scotians, and that some were reenslaved. Blacks claimed that "Whites seldom or ever pay[ed] for work done," and some white Nova Scotians hired blacks to work, promising "so much pr. day," only to pick a fight in the late afternoon when the work was "almost finished," so that they could haul the black worker before a justice of the peace. The black "offenders" were then punished by having their pay withheld.[52] Nova Scotian officials also denied basic political rights to black settlers and passed criminal and other ordinances that discriminated on the basis of race.[53] In response, the Black Loyalists began to separate from their oppressive white neighbors. They built black townships, the largest of which was called Birchtown, seeking to help one another through the hardships that they faced.[54] Their communities offered fertile ground for evangelical preachers; in the course of the Black Loyalists' first decade in Nova Scotia, Baptists, Wesleyan Methodists, and Huntingdonian Methodists each grew rapidly behind charismatic black leadership.[55]

David George, having escaped the threat of reenslavement in Georgia by evacuating with the British troops following the Revolutionary War, built a thriving black Baptist congregation in the town of Shelburne, which he used as a base for missionary outreach to Black Loyalists scattered throughout Nova Scotia. George preached to whites and Indians as well as blacks, but his success building a unified black Baptist movement stimulated white attempts to intimidate him into silence, and his followers would prove their unity when offered the chance to immigrate to Sierra Leone. Wesleyan Methodists constituted the largest denominational group of Black Loyalists, and they, too, coalesced behind a charismatic preacher. "Daddy" Moses Wilkinson, a former slave from Nansemond County, Virginia, had joined Dunmore's Ethiopian Regiment at the beginning of the war. Camp life took a toll on Wilkinson, leaving him blind and physically infirm, but it had done nothing to calm his fiery preaching. Boston King, who had escaped from slavery in South Carolina, reported that Wilkinson's words had knocked his wife to the floor and left her crying "out for mercy," and King himself soon experienced the call and joined the Methodists. Following his conversion, but before Sharp sponsored the "Black Poor's" expedition to Sierra Leone, King had already begun to "commiserate" with his "poor brethren in Africa," so there is little wonder that he would support his congregation's decision to follow Moses Wilkinson and sail from Nova Scotia to Sierra Leone in 1792.[56]

Baptists and Methodists had dominated the Great Awakening in the South and the efforts it spawned to convert southern slaves prior to the Revolution, so powerful preachers like George and Wilkinson found audiences prepared to receive their messages once the Black Loyalists arrived in Nova Scotia. Wilkinson almost surely arrived in Canada with a sizable following.[57] The third denominational group that came together in the inhospitable North—the Huntingdonian Methodists—lacked a similar institutional base among black Southerners, so its growth is even more directly tied to the efforts of a charismatic preacher. John Marrant sailed from London to Nova Scotia in 1785, embarking on a three-year mission, during which he worked tirelessly and successfully to create a Huntingdonian church among the Black Loyalists. His valuable journal of his time in Nova Scotia records the physical hardship that he endured, and his doctrinal disputes with Moses Wilkinson and other Wesleyan Methodists, as well as his spiritual triumphs. He transcribed only one full sermon, but the literary scholar Joanna Brooks provides a remarkable reconstruction of the message that he offered to his audiences in Nova Scotia by analyzing the scriptual passages upon which he preached.[58]

Although Marrant made a point of preaching to diverse people who ranged from white Roman Catholics to indigent Native Americans, he offered a special prophetic vision to the black congregation that he gathered at the black settlement of Birchtown.[59] He came to them as a fully ordained minister under the aegis of the Countess of Huntingdon, but his true authority was greater still. He arrived as a Moses coming to call God's new chosen people into a gathered congregation. In the absence of the actual sermons, one must make educated guesses about the future that he projected for the people he called together, but, as Brooks points out, Isaiah 60, the verse upon which he preached a Christmas sermon in 1785, foretold "the appointed emergence of a 'strong nation.'"[60] Whether he conceived of the ties binding that nation together in filiative or affiliative terms remains unclear in his *Journal*, but when he left Nova Scotia he traveled to Boston to become chaplain to Prince Hall's African Masonic Lodge. A sermon he gave there dealt with some of these questions and will be discussed later.

Marrant's *Journal* provides an interesting glimpse at a theological principle that Baptist, Wesleyan, and Huntingdonian Black Loyalists seem to have shared, a principle that all would carry across the Atlantic to Sierra Leone. Throughout his time in Nova Scotia Marrant characterized the Wesleyan Methodists as the "Arminians," underscoring one of the fundamental issues dividing the predestinarian Huntingdonians from the followers of John and Charles Wesley, who were inclined to believe salvation remained open to all.[61] When Freeborn Garrettson, a white Methodist circuit rider who sought to counter Marrant's success, described the beliefs that made Marrant so dangerous, however, he focused on a related but different issue. Garrettson was most troubled by Marrant's antinomianism, his belief that "the sins of the body did not affect the union of the spirit with God," and thus that violating moral precepts had no effect on one's salvation.[62] The same belief prevailed among Wilkinson's Methodists and George's Baptists. Members of all three groups saw themselves as gathered communities of God's chosen, and each group organized to worship God and to defend their rights. They came to doubt the promises of white residents of Nova Scotia, but none left any evidence of doubt about the righteousness of their communities of faith.

By 1790 some had grown so disillusioned by white Nova Scotians' racism that they pooled their resources to send a representative to London to seek relief from the Crown. Thomas Peters, the man they sent, was probably born in what is now Nigeria. He had escaped from slavery in Wilmington, North Carolina, at the beginning of the Revolution and served the British Army as a "Pioneer" until peace was declared, at which point he evacuated from New York City to Nova Scotia.[63] Once there, Peters settled in an all-black community called Brindley Town outside Digby in Annapolis County, but when he and his neighbors were repeatedly denied the land grants that they had been promised, he moved to St. John looking for work to support his family. He and other blacks in Annapolis and Halifax counties finally became so frustrated by the refusal of local officials to honor governmental promises that they decided to appeal directly to London. Peters took passage to England with a petition signed by the heads of more than 100 families; it reminded the Crown of the service the Black Loyalists had given during the war and of all that they were still owed. The petitioners had gone to Nova Scotia "under the Promise of obtaining . . . Lands and Provision," but neither land nor provisions appeared to be forthcoming. Some wanted to remain in North America, so the petitioners asked the Crown to force local authorities to distribute "their due Allotment of Land." Others had lost hope that they could ever build meaningful lives in the Canadian cold and appealed to be sent "wherever the Wisdom of Government may think proper to provide for them as free Subjects of the British Empire."[64]

The petition did not mention Africa, but Peters arrived in London as Granville Sharp's wealthy friends and associates were incorporating the Sierra Leone Company to revitalize the remnants of the Province of Freedom.[65] The board of directors, led by Henry Thornton, did not share Sharp's vision of a colony composed exclusively of black settlers "returning" to Africa, but they were committed to a society in which all people, regardless of race, would be treated fairly and equally. The new directors hoped that such a colony could develop trading relationships with natives of Africa and then grow into more than a mere commercial enterprise by becoming a model of Christian civilization that could transform the continent through its example.[66]

Peters's arrival offered a seemingly perfect source of settlers for the Company, and the Company's plans seemed to mesh providentially with the aspirations of the Nova Scotians. After meeting with Peters, the Company directors invited him and his followers to move to their new colony and asked the British government to foot the bill for transporting those who chose to leave Nova Scotia. The Company hired John Clarkson, younger brother of the famous abolitionist and board member Thomas Clarkson, to follow Peters back to Nova Scotia in order to recruit and organize emigrants. This began a long and complicated relationship between John Clarkson and the Nova Scotians.[67]

V

It might seem remarkable that black people living in quite different social settings in Georgia, Boston, Nova Scotia, and Rhode Island all participated in a shared discourse on Africa and Africanness. Even more surprising, these disparate American blacks wrote and spoke in terms congruent with the discussions of Africa being carried on simultaneously by Equiano and Cugoano across the Atlantic in London. They did, of course, say different things, but all engaged with questions of African history and with the uncertain roots of a common African heritage. The racial identities they asserted often displayed unresolved tension between an affiliative vision of African unity that began at the moment of enslavement and emerged through the shared oppression experienced by people swept into the African diaspora, and a historically deeper filiative vision of African identity rooted in different narratives of the ancient, natural, or biblical past. These common lines of thought can be partially explained by the pervasive influence of slavery and the slave trade on blacks in Britain and the Americas. Recent scholarship revealing the presence and influence of black mariners throughout the Atlantic also helps explain why blacks living in far-flung ports thought in such similar terms.[68] The life of John Marrant, the Huntingdonian missionary to Nova Scotia, provides an unusually vivid illustration of the ties that could bind blacks living in the shadow of southern slavery to their free brethren in the North and elsewhere.

Marrant had been born free in New York. While still a boy, his family moved to Charleston, South Carolina. He is best known for the narrative that he published about his experiences in captivity to the Cherokee on the southern frontier, and it was in that text that he told of hearing and being converted by George Whitefield's preaching, of traveling to Britain as a mariner, and finally of his intent to go to Nova Scotia to preach to the Black Loyalists. He worshipped, preached, and published in the London circle of the Countess of Huntingdon, the group that had sent David Margate to Whitefield's Savannah orphanage and included Equiano and Cugoano. After building the Huntingdonian church that would help galvanize a black Nova Scotian exodus to Sierra Leone, Marrant traveled to Boston where he joined and preached to Prince Hall's African Masonic Lodge. In short, Marrant epitomized the diasporic identity that the subjects of this chapter strove to forge. His life and evangelical work linked North to South, the free to the enslaved, and London's black literary culture to the world of American "African" institutions. Marrant's biography helps demonstrate why black people living in such diverse settings during the 1780s and 1790s thought in such similar terms about the challenges and meanings of African identity.

In a sermon delivered to the African Masons on June 24, 1789, Marrant offered an understanding of the place of African Masons in the grand history of speculative Freemasonry, and a vision of African people in God's plan. In the process, he explained African identity more clearly than he did in his *Journal*. His sermon brings together many themes present in the thought and actions of his black contemporaries, while exemplifying the way that invocations of blacks as a chosen people could mediate the unresolved ambiguity about filiative and affiliative conceptions of kinship among all black people.[69] Marrant sets up the sermon by offering a sharp but unsurprising reminder of the harsh world that faced black people in late eighteenth-century Boston. He then set out to prove that Freemasonry was ancient, and that "Africans" had a right to be Masons, and, as such, a right to honor, freedom, and general acceptance.[70] He pursued the ancient pedigree of Freemasonry by turning to the Bible and declaring Cain and his children to have become the first human architects when they traveled east from Eden to build a city. There followed a standard narrative of Masonic history in which Marrant discussed the wondrous buildings of Babylon and the glories of Solomon's Temple.[71] This conventional sketch of fraternal history took its special meanings from a social context in which many whites denied black people the right to claim a shared Masonic heritage.

Marrant embraced but subverted the biblical explanations of black people's origins that some whites used to argue for black inferiority. He did this by tracing the genealogy of "Ethiopians" (or "Cushites") from Cain down through the sons of Ham, and into some of the more than 100,000 Masons whom he said participated in the building of Solomon's great Temple. He turned the tables on whites who focused on the curse of Ham, however, by describing instead the signal contributions that these biblical black people had made to the building of great cities and to the development of mathematics and other forms of useful knowledge. All of this was offered to support the proposition that God would visit harsh judgment on any nation that dared "tyrannize" the "lives or liberties" of its fellow men.[72]

In pursuit of this antislavery message, Marrant presented an ambiguous picture of black people as an essentially distinct nation within a Christian universalist family of mankind. He insisted that among the multitude of Masons working on the Temple were people "of different nations and different colours, yet" they were able to work and live "in perfect harmony among themselves, and [they were] strongly cemented in brotherly love and friendship." He looked forward to a day in which African Masons would once again be accepted and "have a free intercourse with all Lodges over the whole terrestrial globe."

Marrant used Christ's call for universal love within the context of communal cohesion—the text of his sermon was "Be kindly affectioned one to another, with brotherly love, in honour preferring one another" (Rom. 12:10)—to remind African Masons of their legitimacy while condemning white Masons who rejected their black brothers. Blacks were part of a universal family tree, but their branch had been separate and distinct from the earliest periods of sacred history. To be an "African" was to share with other black people an ancient identity that encompassed glory as well as oppression. African Masons were charged with the responsibility to resuscitate that identity in the face of white racism. The study of ancient history uncovered "some of the Africans" who excelled in humanity, learning, and eloquence, and awareness of that history should remind everyone—especially whites who were currently free of slavery—that every "nation on earth" had "at some period" suffered slavery.[73] Africans, a chosen people, should and would rise again through Christianity. In this sense, Marrant's sermon encompassed at once the projects of Prince Hall, those who participated in the southern "African Baptist" movement, and the members of the Newport African Union Society.

Marrant invoked several texts in his address. Like Equiano in London, Hall in Boston, Gardner in Newport, and his doctrinal rivals in Nova Scotia, he was deeply Christian and sought the origins of black people, as he would have sought the origins of other racial groups, in the Bible and in texts that shed light upon biblical times. We will never know whether George, Liele, and Bryan engaged in the same search through classical historical texts, but each was equally inclined to understand the world through the Bible and to see himself and his community—however "race" defined that community— as a community of the book. This has sometimes been obscured in modern scholarship because of the high rates of illiteracy that whites sought to maintain among blacks, especially in plantation regions, but the work of all of those discussed in this chapter brims with biblical citation, and Marrant and Hall go considerably farther by citing historians from the classical era.[74] That Marrant mentioned them in the text of his sermon underscores the authority that learning and literacy carried among his listeners. As many blacks throughout the Atlantic basin converted to Christianity—especially to Protestant churches that focused on biblical authority—they increasingly engaged in a search for ancient biblical roots to their African identity. This yearning for a filiative or essentialist basis for racial identity either complemented or remained in tension with what all of these thinkers saw as the temporally shallower affiliative roots in secular history.

VI

The organizations examined in this chapter must stand for dozens of contemporary "African" social institutions whose records have not survived or whose interpretations of African identity remain obscure in the surviving records. One cannot, of course, be sure that the members of these silenced organizations approached these questions by exploring the nature of

African history or, if they did, that their interpretations shared the creative tension between filiative and affiliative senses of unity that played such important roles in the thought of Savannah Baptists, members of New England fraternal organizations, and emigrants to Sierra Leone. Nonetheless, for all that remains obscured by missing records, we do know that black Americans from Savannah north to Nova Scotia and east to London came out of the American Revolution with heightened hopes for liberty and with a growing conviction that black liberty in Anglo-America would become more real when "Africans" united as a people, overcame the ethnic hatred that helped fuel the slave trade in the Old World, and spread faith in Christ as a unifying force among the enslaved in the Americas and the indigenous enslavers on the coast of Africa. When Marrant's appointed successors among Nova Scotia's Huntingdonians—Cato Perkins and William Ashe—joined David George and Moses Wilkinson to lead their respective gathered communities on an exodus to the promised land of Sierra Leone, discussions of the meanings of African identity and the future of an African people took on greater immediacy within the black Atlantic.

4

Out of America

Sierra Leone's Settler Society and Its Meanings for
"Africans" in America

When Thomas Peters asked the British government to provide a new
home for the Black Loyalists living in Nova Scotia, he helped set into
motion a train of events that would deepen and complicate black discussions of African identity. More than 1,000 Black Loyalists would settle
in Sierra Leone. Having decided to live in Africa, they would call themselves "Nova Scotians," and through their struggles with one another,
with white Sierra Leone Company officials, and with the Koya Temne
people who surrounded their settlements, they would attempt to put
into practice the transformative project of African identity that Equiano
and others had theorized. Their efforts attracted the interest of black
Americans who believed themselves to be "Africans"—including Prince
Hall and his followers and the members of Newport's African Union
Society.

From 1790 until 1820, the Nova Scotians living in Sierra Leone experienced twists and turns that make for an intrinsically fascinating story, but
the importance of that story to early black discussions of African identity
does not rest solely on its interest. Their effort to build lives in Africa
served as a touchstone for many blacks seeking to think through or enact
a project of diasporic African identity formation. A crucial step in that
project began when Captain John Clarkson traveled from England to
Nova Scotia in order to recruit settlers for the Sierra Leone Company. In
Canada he found cohesive, well-organized communities of Black
Loyalists eager to take the lead in settling, Christianizing, and "civilizing"
West Africa.

I

Clarkson arrived in Canada in the fall of 1791 to discover the Black Loyalists living in conditions even worse than he had been led to expect. Many had escaped formal bondage in the United States only to find themselves pushed through legal and extralegal means into dependence so complete as to approximate another form of slavery. Clarkson, outraged by these conditions but also anxious lest he give the false impression that Sierra Leone offered an easy alternative, emphasized the difficulties inherent in founding a new society and the hardships that all would face. He warned any who would listen that the only things he could promise were free and unencumbered land for anyone willing to work it, and social and legal equality for all willing to cast their lot with the new colony.[1] As it turned out, he promised more than the Company would deliver.

The black settlers Clarkson found when he arrived in Nova Scotia had been struggling for nearly a decade against apathetic officials and hostile white neighbors. They had forged tightly bound denominational communities that sought to understand their collective role in God's divine plan.[2] During the final years of the 1780s when evangelist John Marrant had spearheaded the rapid growth of Huntingdonian congregations, conflicts among black followers of different confessions sometimes became heated, but by the time Marrant left the province in 1789, black Christians of different denominations seem to have reached a kind of equilibrium. Clarkson found unified congregations that made communal decisions about whether to accept his offer of transportation to Sierra Leone and who envisioned a collective future in Africa.[3]

Potential settlers did express concerns to Clarkson. Having survived southern slavery and then life in the British Army only to find new but depressingly familiar forms of oppression in Nova Scotia, they sought assurance that things would be different in Africa. Examples of illegal reenslavement occurred even in Nova Scotia, so they were particularly anxious about the prospect of living in the middle of an active slave-trading region. Given their struggles to win land claims in Canada, they also needed more confidence in the sincerity of the Company's promise to distribute land. Many badly wanted to leave behind the cold winters, poor land, and white exploitation that shaped their lives in Nova Scotia, but they had to be convinced that Sierra Leone offered something better, if not for themselves, then for their children.[4] Clarkson traveled through the Maritime Province's rugged countryside during the winter in order to speak with as many potential emigrants as he could, and he approached them with respect. He promised land, legal rights, and social equality to those who were willing to work, speaking directly to the settlers' deepest aspirations and to their bitterness over what had previously been denied.

Potential settlers' confidence in Clarkson's good intentions grew when he began outfitting the ships on which they would travel. He inspected each ship and all provisions, making sure that those who traveled to Sierra Leone would be comfortable and well supplied while en route, and ensuring that they, unlike the "Black Poor" who had been sent out to Sharp's "Province of Freedom," would have adequate food during their first months in their new homes. He strove to surmount legal problems that threatened to force some emigrants to leave family members behind, once risking becoming an accomplice in a criminal act in order to help parents protect their son from the white man to whom the child was apprenticed.[5] In all of these ways Clarkson assured those who were predisposed to emigrate that he could be trusted as an agent, but one must look beyond his actions—beyond him—to understand why so many black Nova Scotians decided to go to Sierra Leone.

Those who chose to emigrate were not simply escaping material deprivation. Though most Black Loyalists suffered poverty and hardship in Nova Scotia, a small number had gained economic footing by 1792, and the relatively well-off often led the exodus.[6] Clarkson emphasized the difficulties emigrants would face in Africa, and he tried to help them liquidate their property fairly, indicating that some had acquired a basic level of economic independence in Canada.[7] These Nova Scotians did not move to Sierra Leone out of a naive belief that pioneer life in Sierra Leone would be easy or materially abundant, but out of the hope that it would offer their children the prospect of better lives. Understanding their decisions involves untangling this deceptively simple hope: what did the settlers envision when they projected a bright communal future in Sierra Leone?

The complexities of the settlers' aspirations can be obscured by the part of that bright future that involved age-old hopes for family security. The key was freehold land. The settlers had come to Nova Scotia believing that they would be given substantial grants of land on which they could build farms and sink stable roots. They had assumed that their children would inherit and develop those farms, building strong and prosperous families and communities. Instead, as Clarkson reported, "the greatest part have never been in possession of more than one or two acres."[8] Like so many freedpeople throughout the Americas, from Haiti in the 1790s to Jamaica in the 1840s to the rural American South in the 1870s, these men and women sought liberty and independence through the ownership of small farms and the control that would give them over the commodities they produced. Presumably they, like other freedpeople before and after them, hoped to use the market to establish a reasonable standard of living without becoming fully enmeshed in, and thus dependent upon, market relations.[9] When these hopes proved unattainable in Canada, many decided to cross an ocean to pursue their goals. Clarkson understood the settlers' desire for land, and, shortly before leaving for Africa, expressed tragically premature satisfaction that "on my arrival in Africa, I shall find that the Surveyor has marked out" the settlers' "allotments of land."[10] Despite Clarkson's best efforts, the Nova Scotians would never see this basic expectation fulfilled.

Land, however, was just one part of an expansive communal vision that informed settlers' hopes for the African society they planned to build. Politics also played a role, and Clarkson's place in the future colony became an issue. Thomas Peters had first convinced the Crown to support the Black Loyalists' relocation to Sierra Leone, and on his return to Nova Scotia he had prepared the ground for Clarkson's recruiting efforts. While in London, Peters made little of racial difference when explaining his followers' desire to escape Nova Scotia; doing so could only have alienated the public officials whose aid he hoped to enlist. Black leaders of the emigration movement spoke more openly about racism in Nova Scotia, and Clarkson proved an ideal ally in America. He was outraged by the injustices he witnessed and had both the courage and the connections to confront those oppressing the Black Loyalists. After organizing the settlers' transportation, and initiating a process of settlement, he planned to return to his fiancée in England while the Black Loyalists built their own futures in Sierra Leone.[11] Those Clarkson recruited should "look up to" him as "their friend and protector." In return, he would "see that" they received "their proper allotments of land" when they arrived "in Africa."[12] Then he would go home, leaving Peters and the other settlers to pursue their social and political ambitions.

More than 1,100 Nova Scotians accepted Clarkson's offer to take free passage and help jump-start the colony in Sierra Leone. The two largest black settlements in the Maritimes—Birchtown and Shelburne—each contributed about 500 settlers, with close to another hundred coming with Thomas Peters from Annapolis and New Brunswick. Another sizable group came from Preston, near Halifax.[13] As had been true of the evacuees from New York at the end of the Revolutionary War, but to an extent rare among early colonization expeditions, the settlers traveled in family groups, including men and women as well as the very young and the very old. The Nova Scotians also joined the expedition in congregational communities, though the exact breakdown of each group is difficult to determine. Moses Wilkinson's Wesleyan Methodists, the largest group, comprised a majority of the immigrants; the Huntingdonians, led by Ashe and Perkins, and David George's Baptists completed the contingent.[14]

Denominational splits would shape settler politics in Sierra Leone, but they did not produce rivalries while Clarkson was recruiting and organizing the move from Nova Scotia. Baptists, Wesleyans, and Huntingdonians all understood their migration through the metaphor of an exodus to a promised land. The society they planned to build would serve as something akin to what English Puritans settling in seventeenth-century America had called a City on a Hill. The civilized and Christian foothold that they would establish on the slaving coast of Africa would reveal the hypocrisy of American slavery, while showing indigenous residents of Africa how wealthy, happy, and secure they could be if they rejected the slave trade in favor of commerce in legitimate commodities. Accomplishing these ends would require secure title to freehold land, and the guarantee of basic political, religious, and civic freedom. Baptists, Wesleyans, and Huntingdonians all believed Clarkson's assurance that they would enjoy these fundamental rights.

Each group pursued those rights through strategies that grew out of their communal histories. Their spiritual leaders had turned to Christianity while living in the southern plantation colonies, but the circumstances surrounding their conversions, the conditions in which they had worshipped in the South, and their experiences as free black Britons during and after the Revolutionary War all shaped the latitude each group would grant white Company officials and the limits of their trust of white authority. David George's Baptist church grew out of the African Baptist Church movement in Savannah, a movement with a history of cross-racial alliances and one in which white patrons had fostered and protected black religious autonomy. George led his congregation's exodus to Africa as part of an international and transracial missionary movement to spread the gospel to the benighted throughout the world. While living in Sierra Leone, he referred to London as "home" and reported that "almost all our people, in different parts, call it so."[15] Neither George nor his followers were duped by the Company, but their vision of Sierra Leone's future complemented the Company's plan for a multiracial, commercial British society. Moses Wilkinson's Methodists emerged out of a comparable biracial movement in Virginia, and many Huntingdonians had turned to Christianity in response to the preaching of John Marrant, a product of the chapels and movement that had inspired Phillis Wheatley, Gustavus Vassa, and Quobna Ottobah Cugoano. While in Nova Scotia, however, both the Wesleyan Methodists and the Huntingdonians had been accused of apostasy by Freeborn Garrettson, an influential Methodist leader. His attack on the spiritual foundation of their communities, an attack that Garrettson had based on a claim to superior scriptural knowledge and ecclesiastical authority, may well have predisposed them to greater vigilance against putatively benevolent white authorities than the Baptists.[16] They had not crossed the Atlantic to follow, once again, the orders of white people. These dissidents did not publicly enunciate a vision of Africa for black people during the buildup to emigration in America, so it is difficult to know when that vision developed. Perhaps they would have been willing to live as equals with whites in the colony had that been a real possibility, but given all they had experienced as slaves and refugees, many must have been deeply skeptical about such promises.

Another smaller group of prospective colonists brought a different set of expectations to the decision to emigrate, for they had been born in Africa— several in the Sierra Leone region. Thomas Peters was the most prominent native of Africa among the Nova Scotians, but he was not alone. One man explained to Clarkson that he knew well that returning to the region of his birth would involve hard work in hot weather: "Massa, me can work much and care not for climate; if me die, me die, had rather die in me own country than this cold place."[17] Most emigrants were going to a country they planned to make their own rather than returning to the land of their birth, but whether they envisioned the new society as metaphorically or historically theirs, such settlers had no intention of traveling across the Atlantic to live and work under the direction of white people.

Surviving evidence does not speak clearly, however, to whether George's Baptists, the smallest of the three groups of settlers, recognized that their vision of a multiracial society clashed with the more racially exclusive vision that was emerging among the two Methodist denominations under Thomas Peters, Cato Perkins, William Ashe, Cato Anderson, and Moses Wilkinson, or vice versa. Black Nova Scotians lived in settlements organized around their congregations, and they remained in relatively insular denominational communities while traveling to Sierra Leone. Several petitioned Clarkson and the Company for the right to be able to "be as nearly connected" to their American neighbors "as possible when the tract or tracts of land" were "laid out" for their new homes. Clarkson faced sizable logistical problems organizing more than 1,000 emigrants and sought to take advantage of this preexisting social organization by appointing and working through one representative from each denominational group.[18] This principle of community representation fit the settlers' expectations and may have kept the different groups of settlers from realizing that they sought different ends in Africa. Or perhaps settlers chose to downplay their differences as long as possible. Regardless, the disagreements would emerge and play themselves out on the ground in Sierra Leone as the settlers built a new society. When that happened the Christian visions of a better society that informed the settlers' decisions to move to Africa endowed seemingly minor disputes with cosmic importance. The Nova Scotians would find it as hard to compromise with one

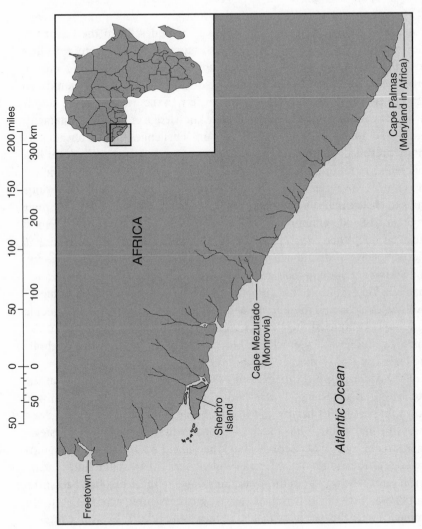

Map 4.1. A Map of the west coast of Africa from the northern boundary of present-day Sierra Leone to the southern boundary of present-day Liberia.

another over alternative interpretations of God's plan for their chosen land as had the Puritans before them and as would Zionists after them.

II

Just before sailing, Clarkson had received a request from the Company directors that he stay on in Sierra Leone to superintend the colony as its first governor, so he and the settlers would not only work together to complete their escape from captivity in the old world—their exodus—they would also need to cooperate in building a godly society in the new promised land.[19] As they might have expected, given their knowledge of the Old Testament, this would not be easy, but regardless of any challenges that lay ahead, harmony prevailed throughout the passage across the Atlantic. Clarkson had succeeded in finding seaworthy boats and supplying them with sufficient food for the voyage, and he had interceded with the captains of the various ships to ensure that sailors, infamous among contemporary blacks for their irreligion, would neither mock the Nova Scotians' piety nor subject them to racial taunts. When the ships all arrived safely, the deeply religious settlers shared a sense of divine deliverance with the equally pious Clarkson, disembarking and joining their governor onshore to sing a hymn proclaiming that "the Year of Jubilee has come/Returned ye ransomed sinners home."[20] Nothing could sound more natural to modern ears. These "African" people had finally completed their escape from thralldom to various pharaohs in America, and now they proclaimed the arrival of the Jubilee while celebrating their "return" to mother Africa.

They decided to erect their town—Free Town (soon Freetown)—at the site that Granville Sharp's "Black Poor" had originally chosen for Granville Town, in part for its beauty and in part because they could and did claim prior title to the land. Thus the Nova Scotians disembarked on the western, or upstream, side of St. George's Bay, the second major bay on the southern edge of the mouth of the Sierra Leone River. The trees and thick underbrush ran all the way from the mountains down to the shore, but, before the month was out, the settlers had cleared a twenty-three acre site atop "an eminence near the beach" to catch the "sea breezes" that blew in at "ten or eleven o'clock" each morning. Immediately to the east lay the Temne town of King Jimmy, the headman who had sacked Granville Town in 1789; about three miles to the west of the Freetown site, at Fora (now Forah) Bay, the survivors of the first expedition had moved back downriver from Bance Island and Robanna to build a new Granville Town. This formed the new colony's early western border.[21]

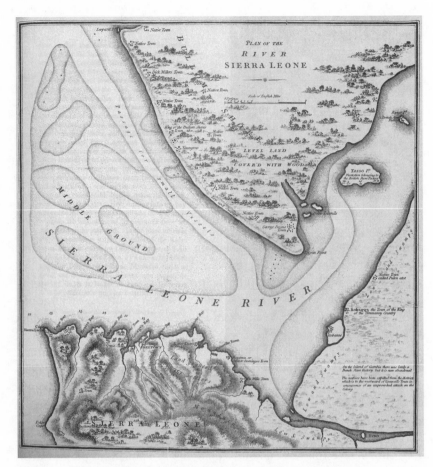

Figure 4.1. "Plan of the River Sierra Leone," from Thomas Winterbottom, *An Account of the Native Africans in the Neighborhood of Sierra Leone* (1803). This map shows the location of Freetown, Granville Town, Pirate's Bay, and various Temne settlements surrounding the colony. Bance Island, home to a British slaving fort, is located upriver in the top right corner of the map.

Given the history of trouble with King Jimmy, Clarkson began immediately to pursue a delicate strategy of projecting strength while offering friendship to the surrounding Temne. King Jimmy was understandably nervous about the appearance of a flotilla of boats disgorging well-armed and supplied settlers. Clarkson sought to take advantage of his anxiety, and to allay it a bit, by crossing the bay to pay an informal visit soon after arriving. The villagers wore loincloths, sometimes with a shirt, but the "king was dressed in an old naval captain's uniform"—presumably a gift from a slaver. Clarkson expressed no surprise at King Jimmy's appearance, and it seems reasonable to assume that he expected native Africans to reflect their centuries of engagement with Europeans. He had, after all, spent much of his young life at sea.

It is less obvious what blacks born in America, who understood themselves to be participating in a mission to civilize savages, might have made of the arrival of Naimbana, the paramount king of the Koya Temne, when he responded to Clarkson's invitation to visit the fledgling settlement at Freetown. Clarkson had sent the *Lapwing*, a Company vessel, to Robanna to transport the king, and Naimbana disembarked wearing "a sky-blue silk jacket with silver lace, striped cotton trowsers, ruffled shirt, green morocco slippers, a cocked-hat with gold lace, and a white cotton cap, for which a large old judge's wig was afterwards substituted. He had a belt round his neck from which hung the figure of a lamb bearing a cross set with rays formed of paste." This was not the ignorant, naked native the Sierra Leone Company placed on its coat of arms, and, notwithstanding the natives of Africa among them, it seems unlikely that Naimbana embodied the ignorant savage that most Nova Scotians had envisioned civilizing. That the one son that he was sending to be educated in England was balanced by another whom he had sent to France to learn Catholic ways, and a third entrusted to local Muslims for an Islamic education underscores the cosmopolitanism of the slave-trading elite of the African coast—something the Nova Scotians might have found disconcerting.[22] The settlers' immediate problems had less to do with the Temne, however, than with a series of troubling disagreements with the Sierra Leone Company.

The root problems were structural. The Company consisted of wealthy Englishmen investing large amounts of money in a philanthropic endeavor; the settlers were poor African Americans investing their lives in a utopian vision. Disagreement over who should control the colony may have been inevitable. While recruiting in Nova Scotia, Clarkson had promised freehold rights to land and political equality to any who went to Sierra Leone, but the Company would later insist that settlers pay quitrents—annual fees that each settler would pay to retain the right to his or her land—and it would reserve ultimate political control for whites sent out as Company officials. The resulting disputes wracked the colony throughout the 1790s.[23] Modern sympathies flow naturally to the Nova Scotians, but the vehemence of the dispute and, more important, the variety of settler responses only make sense if the Company's position is understood.

Henry Thornton, the chairman of the Company's board of directors, made that case in a private letter that Clarkson received just before leaving for Africa. The British investors were "at the expense of governing . . . , setting up a factory [trading fort], and giving even a premium of a free Passage, and provision to the first settlers." He thought it only "reasonable" that they "should have the profits of trade" rather than letting "private traders . . . [draw] to themselves all the advantages of . . . [the Company's] protection and political establishment." This sounds callous and selfish, and it is only partly true: the British government paid for the Nova Scotians' passage to Freetown. Nonetheless, the directors raised the enormous sum of £200,000 to support the colony, and, though they would often act badly in the coming years, they invested generously in the Nova Scotians' material well-being. Unfortunately, in return for this investment, they believed that the settlers should behave more like grateful freed clients than freeborn subjects of the Crown.[24]

Thornton's insistence on revenue, and thus on the quitrent, cannot be separated from his "humanitarian" goals, for the demand for quitrents came in a discussion of how to achieve philanthropic ends, and one key was the scope of the project: "the scale of our establishment could not be at the outset smaller than it is, if we are really to make a thorough tryal whether Africa can be cultivated by labourers enjoying the advantage of a free British Government."[25] Revenue was crucial for this. Many Nova Scotians contested the Company upon learning of its intentions, but they faced a board of directors that believed it acted in the settlers' best interests.[26] Some settlers were convinced—sometimes.

The first disagreements arose over twinned questions of settler access to land and the relations between residents of the colonies and the corrupting (in Clarkson's eyes) influences that impinged on the colony from all sides. The Nova Scotians were frustrated to find that no plots of land had been laid out prior to their arrival, but they set about building shelters and clearing land without the desired assurance of legal title to freehold land. Early on a Methodist leader, Nathaniel Snowball, built his house on waterfront property that the Company decided to reserve for official purposes. When Snowball refused to move, Clarkson mediated an agreement that permitted the community leader to remain in his house until "the place it occupied was really wanted," after which he was promised the "benefit of the present crop in the garden" and "assistance in pulling . . . down and erecting his new hut," as well as ten dollars in compensation. He accepted the settlement, but the dispute intensified the Nova Scotians' growing "want of confidence in . . . the directors" and their "jealousy of the white people."[27]

Distrust was exacerbated by Clarkson's effort to insulate settlers from their environment. The Company deliberately placed its colony in the heart of an active slave-trading region in the hope that it would offer a prosperous model to the Koya Temne and other surrounding peoples. The history of the Black Poor in Granville Sharp's Province of Freedom suggested that without precautions the slave traders might corrupt and destroy the colony rather than be converted by it. Not only had the colony been sacked by a

Temne headman as a result of a dispute with a British slaver, but some surviving settlers had become involved in the slave trade. In fact, among the first criminal complaints in the new colony was one in which one of the "old settlers," as they came to be called, was charged with enslaving and selling another survivor of the first expedition. Clarkson distrusted the "old settlers" and initially tried to prohibit them from entering Freetown. He hoped that by preventing sailors from commercial ships—generally slavers—from entering the colony, where they could "unsettle the minds of the Nova Scotians, and mix their morals," he could limit the Nova Scotians' exposure to the forces that had corrupted their predecessors.[28]

Clarkson's efforts were well meaning and his willingness to discuss his decisions with dissenting settlers won him loyal supporters, but Clarkson's paternalism also fueled discontent. After all, Thomas Peters had established his leadership in Nova Scotia before Clarkson appeared, and he had expected Clarkson to leave the settlers in Sierra Leone and return to his life and fiancée in England. When Clarkson decided to remain in Africa as governor of the new colony, Peters moved to establish both his own authority and the settlers' right to participate in their own government. The dispute came to a head during the first month in Sierra Leone, when "the Preston people" secretly warned Clarkson that Peters sought to take over the colony and promised "to stand fast by your Honor."[29] Clarkson called the settlers together to confront Peters and discuss the reciprocal rights and obligations of the Company and settlers.

Peters's true plans remain murky. Clarkson accused him of leading a coup, but several of Clarkson's friends among both settlers and Company officials insisted that his goals were less radical. Perhaps Peters did intend to "get himself at the Head of the People" and drive "all the Whites out of the place," as Clarkson contended, but it seems at least as likely that company official James Strand was right that Peters wanted recognition as the blacks' "Speaker general," a position he might well have expected.[30] If Peters envisioned building an exclusively black settlement at Freetown, he had moved farther and faster than many he counted on as followers. He rallied significant support, as evidenced by a petition with 132 settlers' signatures, but some backed him without any intention of challenging Clarkson. David George, for example, signed, but he would prove to be one of the Company's most steadfast black supporters throughout the 1790s, and Clarkson credited him with the "firmness to preach against Thomas Peters's Conduct" despite being "threatened with assassination." Clarkson's faith in the support of George's Baptists led him to fear that his showdown with Peters would cause additional "misunderstanding between the Methodists and Anabaptists."[31]

Peters backed down when Clarkson confronted him before the assembled settlers, and then the governor undermined his rival in conversations with

settlers over the next few weeks. He was aided when an all-black jury convicted Peters of breaking into the chest of a recently deceased settler and
stealing money and food that should rightfully have gone to the deceased's
orphaned children. Peters died shortly thereafter. Clarkson's triumph over
him reveals divisions among the Nova Scotians as they tried to sort out their
expectations in their African homes. Some settlers, especially those who worshipped in Wesleyan and Huntingdonian chapels, moved quickly to assert
black settler power and began to oppose the authority of white Company officials. Clarkson may have imagined Peters's desire to run whites out of the
colony, but his rival did seek to wrest authority away from officials appointed
by London and to vest it in the chosen representatives of the settlers. So long
as this desire was expressed in moderate terms, Peters could mobilize support
even among those settlers most loyal to the governor.

By portraying Peters as intent on expelling all whites and severing ties
with London, the governor marginalized his rival and sought to leave him
"almost universally despised" among the other settlers.[32] Clarkson could do
this because the settlers knew he was honestly committed to distributing
land and building consensus among the settlers. He also won support,
because, perhaps in response to Peters's challenge, he granted the Nova
Scotians more political rights and influence than black people enjoyed in
any other white-controlled polity. The black jury that convicted Peters was
no aberration and black Nova Scotians served as constables—the primary
law enforcement officers in the colony—and bore arms in defense of
Freetown. Peters's fall did not settle underlying tensions over who controlled the colony, but it does illustrate the real, if, for many, insufficient
rights that settlers enjoyed in Sierra Leone.

Clarkson's political and diplomatic skills prevented those tensions from
coming to the fore for the rest of his tenure as governor. Other conflicts certainly arose, but because the settlers believed him to have their best interests at heart, and probably because they trusted that his recognition of their
rights would grow over time, they rallied behind his leadership and began
constructing buildings, planting gardens, building wharfs, and laying the
necessary physical infrastructure for a new colony. They worked for wages
and goods provided by the Company's store, so London investors' support
proved crucial. Clarkson strengthened the hand of his moderate allies
through sensitivity to the former slaves' "extreme suspicion of white people." He "implored" them to overcome that suspicion and sought to give
them reason to do so.[33] By the end of the first summer in Africa, Clarkson
saw cause for optimism: "The gardens of the settlers begin to look very
pleasing, . . . and [furnish] the officers [of the Company] with many vegeta-
bles, especially cabbages, besides satisfying their own wants. . . . In many of
the houses of the settlers are seen great quantities of beef and pork that they

have saved out of their allowance, and hung up along the ridges of their houses to smoke, as provisions for the time when they first go upon their lots of land."[34] Neither he nor they yet realized how difficult it would be for them to get that land.

Clarkson was recalled to London for consultation with the Company's board of directors at the end of 1792, but he left with the assurance that William Dawes, his replacement, and Richard Pepys, the Company surveyor, would finish surveying and distributing the settlers' lots within weeks of his departure. Unaware that the board would dismiss him in London, in part for preferring the settlers' interests to the Company's and in part for suspected Jacobin sympathies, Clarkson assured the settlers that he would return and that they would soon receive freehold claims to their promised land. Unfortunately, neither Dawes, nor Zachary Macaulay, Dawes's newly arrived counselor and eventual successor, shared Clarkson's commitment to or fondness for the Nova Scotians. When Clarkson left, they stopped surveying lots for the settlers and began building a fort.

The Nova Scotians would look back on John Clarkson's tenure at Freetown as both a golden period and a lost opportunity to build the society they had envisioned. Of course that first year had not been characterized by perfect consensus; some Nova Scotians probably sought from the first to build an autonomous black society in Sierra Leone. However different the promised lands envisioned by Baptists, Wesleyans, and Huntingdonians may have been, all appreciated the chance to pursue their visions while working with a governor who genuinely respected and listened to them. From a material perspective, the colonists and the governor had, in fact, made remarkable strides. Freetown consisted of twelve streets that had been carved out of the thick vegetation, three that ran parallel to the shore and nine that crossed them and went inland toward the mountains. The street running closest to the water included a small cluster of public buildings, which had been sent out in prefabricated frames from England, and the settlers had raised their small dwellings, as well as a schoolhouse and several churches.[35] The Wesleyan Methodists almost surely chafed at the amount of power Clarkson retained for Company officials, but their regard for Clarkson would grow markedly once they experienced life with his successors.

III

The failure of the Company's new regime to distribute land to the settlers created immediate dissension, which Dawes and Pepys tried to quash by casting aspersions upon Clarkson.[36] Settlers responded in writing to

Clarkson, reminding him that he had "prommised the People . . . that every Lot of Land shoud be given them within a fortnight" and asking his advice on how to make the new Governor honor that pledge.[37] Over the course of 1793 it became evident that the very real conflicts over land provided flashpoints for even more fundamental disagreements. For Dawes and Macaulay, Freetown was a Company town to be run so that shareholders could eventually make a return on their investment. The settlers, having wagered their lives on the colony, believed that their interests should supersede those of London investors and that their perceptions should be taken into account in governing the colony.

Dawes and Macaulay both held antislavery convictions and were, relative to most of their white contemporaries, committed to racial equality. Dawes had served as a Marine lieutenant at Botany Bay, and brought both an ethnographic interest in "primitive" natives and an authoritarian streak to Sierra Leone. As a very young man, Macaulay had worked as a manager of a Jamaican plantation where he gained a participant's knowledge of slavery's brutality and injustice. A religious awakening had saved him from the bottle and endowed him with unshakable confidence in his beliefs, but it had done nothing to soften the former plantation manager's own authoritarian streak. Both men enjoyed close ties to the evangelical Clapham Sect, whose leader, Henry Thornton, presided over the board of the Sierra Leone Company.[38] As a result, they enjoyed the full faith and support of the Company. Dawes and Macaulay believed that the true interests of the Nova Scotians and of Africa coincided with those of the Company, and neither showed much respect for the conflicting opinions offered by the Nova Scotians.

Each side developed an institutional base. The governor and his council enjoyed almost unlimited legislative and executive power within Sierra Leone, but sheer numbers would have forced them to consult the settlers even if they had not been ideologically predisposed to do so. Happily, even the least appealing leaders sent out from London recognized the need to grant settlers a role in their own government. Shortly before leaving Africa, Clarkson had proposed a rudimentary administrative structure based on Granville Sharp's original plan for representation in his Province of Freedom. Dawes and Macaulay instituted that plan, dividing the settlers into "Tythings" of ten families, each of which was to choose a Tythingman, and instructing each ten Tythingmen to elect a Hundredor "to act as head Constable" over those ten Tythings.[39] Within five months the Tythingmen and Hundredors had moved beyond administering rules and proposed a law to the governor and council.[40] This protolegislative structure afforded the Nova Scotians a collective voice in the colony.

Little evidence survives of the settlers' discussions during the run up to this election, but some moderates clearly sought to counter the influence of their disaffected colleagues by arguing that Dawes, Macaulay, and Pepys acted contrary to the wishes of the Company directors. As the situation became increasingly contentious, the settlers decided to send emissaries to the Company to clarify the directors' expectations, and in June 1793, Isaac Anderson and Cato Perkins sailed for London with a petition expressing the Nova Scotians' hopes and disappointments.[41] They couched their complaints in the language of deference, thanking the directors for all they had done, and assuring them that the settlers wanted to do anything in their "po[w]er . . . to help your . . . good intentions." They were, however, "forced to trouble" their patrons so that their "eyes as well as ours may be open." They sent thanks to and for Clarkson, while presenting a virtual bill of indictment against Dawes. He prevented them from trading, except with the company store, which charged "extortionate Price[s]"; he took advantage of the Company's monopoly on employment to pay "what wages" he "pleace[d]"; he played favorites among the settlers and treated others "just as bad as if . . . [they] were all Slaves"; he refused to distribute land, thus preventing the settlers from supporting themselves and costing "your Honrs a great deal of Money." In short, the Nova Scotians were not being "treated as Freemen," and only "the fear of God" led them to support the Company "until . . . [they could] know from your Honrs what footing . . . [they were] upon." The petition was signed by the "Hundreds and Tythings and Preachers of the Gospel . . . in behalf of all the Setlers in this Place."

The directors ignored this thinly veiled threat and treated Anderson and Perkins with almost open contempt. They met the representatives briefly, but refused to answer the petition or even to help Perkins and Anderson contact Clarkson.[42] Perkins and Anderson complained of being sent "back like Fools," and warned Clarkson that "the Company . . . [would] loose their Colony" if the directors continued down this path, for "nothing kept the People quiet but the thoughts that when the Company heard their Grievances," it would redress them. If "the company [did] not see Justice done to us they [would] not have Justice done to them."[43] Not surprisingly, relations between the Nova Scotians and the Company continued to deteriorate after Perkins and Anderson returned to Freetown.

When they got back, they learned that Dawes had returned to England, leaving Zachary Macaulay in charge. The new governor was a rigidly authoritarian Christian who, while serving on the governing council under Dawes, had expressed disgust at the religious practices of Methodist settlers. He ridiculed their belief that "dreams and visions and the most ridiculous bodily sensations" provided "incontestable proofs of their acceptance with God and of their being filled with the Holy Ghost." His discomfort with the sensuality of the Nova Scotians spirituality made him uneasy when one woman who was, in his eyes, "by no means remarkable for the unblameableness of her life and conversation," dreamed that "the spirit of God came up into" her "nostrils as a warm steam" while she lay in bed. This incident foreshadowed later trouble he would have with the settlers' sexuality.[44] Less than a month later he described a meeting among the settlers with open disgust:

> Some Methodist Preachers returned this morning from Granville Town, greatly rejoicing in the work which God was carrying on there. . . . On inquiry I found that the wildest extravagances had been committed there. People falling down as if dead and remaining in a trance for some time. Others bellowing with all their might pretended that the Devil overpowered by the preaching of the word but unwilling to leave them was wrestling with their spirits. Altho I trust that in Gods hands any Instrument may be useful in accomplishing his work, yet I have my fears that evil may follow this violent enthusiastic spirit excited chiefly by [Henry] Beverhout. Granville town is already torn by *domestic* dissensions and I am told that their [discussions?] are attended with great rancor.[45]

Macaulay's contempt for the evangelical religious cultures that the settlers had brought from America hampered his attempts to govern, strengthening instead the hand of settlers arguing that this colony on the coast of Africa should be exclusively for "Africans." If the Company broke the original social contract, if it failed to distribute freehold land and to treat the settlers as free men, then, these increasingly separatist settlers believed, it forfeited its claim to the Nova Scotians' loyalty.

Others among the Nova Scotians retained faith in the Company and continued to work under the aegis of the governor and council. In the fall of 1793 several settlers accepted official positions and generous salaries from the Company. Many probably felt their faith was justified when Dawes and Macaulay dismissed Captain William Davis from the Company's service on a complaint lodged by Tythingman Richard Crankapone that Davis had bought "two boys whom he . . . held as slaves."[46] Other settlers had become so unhappy by then, however, that they had bought land from a local Temne headman and moved outside the colony's bounds.[47]

The origins of this independent settlement do not appear to have been separatist. When surveying the economic successes of the settlement before returning to England, Governor Clarkson had noted "a new settlement" to the east of Freetown, consisting of "five or six families, who have bought their ground from" King Jimmy. Perhaps these settlers had moved away because they had tired of waiting for land from the Company or out of dissatisfaction with the land available in the colony, but Clarkson did not see their small settlement as antagonistic. Macaulay may have imputed antagonism that was not there when he complained that settlers had "quitted the

Colony and settled themselves without its boundaries," but whatever the intentions of the breakaway faction in 1792 or 1793, their experiment living as a free community under the aegis of a Temne headman would become an important alternative when some of their fellow Nova Scotians tired of living under oppressive British governors.[48]

The underlying tensions among settlers first pushed to the fore when Acting Governor Macaulay failed to defuse what should have been a minor incident. In 1794 Alexander Grierson, a veteran slave trader who had lost his ship to a wreck, was waiting in Freetown to transport Company papers back to Liverpool.[49] While in the colony Grierson became angry with a group of settlers and described what he would do to them if "he had them in the West Indies." Robert Keeling and Scipio Channel, reminding Grierson that he was not in the West Indies, "excited a mob" to insult the good captain. Channel then tried to "knock the said Captain Grierson's brains out with a hammer."[50] Macaulay, ignoring the Nova Scotians' understandable anger in the face of provocation by an inveterate slaver, decided to ensure that "strangers should be protected from violence" by punishing "all riotous and disorderly conduct." Rather than trusting a jury to convict Keeling and Channel, he and the council unilaterally suspended them from the Company's service, leaving them unemployed and without any means of support. The Hundredors and Tythingmen immediately protested the dismissal of the two men, as well as other Company policies, and threatened to resign.

Macaulay acted swiftly and characteristically to exacerbate the problem. He insisted that "no one, within the Colony" had "a right to censure the Governor and Council," and even denied that the Hundredors and Tythingmen enjoyed the right "to quit their Offices." On Friday, June 20, Channel and five friends confronted Macaulay to ask for an explanation and, finding it unsatisfactory, "insult[ed] and abuse[d]" the governor and, he claimed, "even threatened" his life. Lewis Kirby and Simon Johnson, two of Channel's friends, then severely beat Richard Crankapone, a settler who had been appointed marshal of the town and remained loyal to the Company. Crankapone was not alone in his commitment to the governing council, for after ordering all white employees to report to the governor's house for service, the council asked David George to mobilize other "well affected" settlers—presumably members of his Baptist congregation. The next evening, disaffected Methodists engaged in "several acts of violence" and marched toward the "Governor's Gate," but they turned back. By Sunday morning, June 22, the situation calmed, and Macaulay took advantage by publishing a "remonstrance pointing out to the People" their "Folly and madness."

The proclamation combined an appeal to the Nova Scotians' idealism with open threats to any who continued to challenge the government. Macaulay asserted the disinterestedness of Company officials who "as Individuals" had "little to lose" should the colony fail, but who hoped not to see the settlers "reduced to the Situation of the Natives" and thus in danger of finding themselves "doomed to groan chained in the Hold of a Slave Ship" before living out "a miserable life under the Smart of a West Indian Whip." The echo of Grierson's threat is unmistakable. Nor, Macaulay warned, would the cost of disobedience to "the Authority of the Laws" be purely secular. Failure to submit would also implicate the settlers in the "*overthrow* of *God's Altars* in this place, and ... of all those fair prospects of civilizing Africa which are now opened to us." Those contesting the government would see Africa's "miseries encreased" and the continent's "hope of rejoicing in the salvation of God" destroyed. The governor and council invited dissatisfied settlers to take free passage back to Nova Scotia, but insisted that those who chose to stay must accept the legitimacy of the government's actions prior to the "Riot" and realize that terminating people from the Company payroll was "a right which belong[ed]" to the governor, and one "which he *will* always exercise." No one returned to Nova Scotia, and the immediate trouble subsided.[51]

George's Baptists supported Macaulay, while the Methodists led the opposition. As tensions began to dissipate, leading Methodists sought reconciliation, but Macaulay's response deepened the wounds rather than healing them. Moses Wilkinson, the Wesleyans' blind patriarch, approached the governor for "advice on the subject of the division that had taken place among the Methodists."[52] Unable to resist "telling the old man a little wholesome truth," Macaulay undercut this peace mission by insisting that the settlers displayed such "serious faults in their conduct as a xtian [Christian] society" that no "sincere and pious xtians" could live with them. Macaulay helpfully offered a bill of indictment that underscores the deep cultural divisions separating Company officials from the settlers, especially the Methodists. He complained of the Methodists' "discontent and rebellion" and tied their political dissent to religious heterodoxy: Wilkinson's Methodists tolerated "notoriously irreligious lives" without censuring the members who lived them; they flouted the "laws of the Colony"; they blocked the imposition of "the discipline required by the Methodist rules." Finally, they refused to welcome John Clarke, one of the Company's preachers, for what Macaulay considered a petty cause—simply because Clarke "called them, what in truth they were, a rotten society."[53] Company officials faced down the uprising of 1794 much as Clarkson had faced down Peters in 1792, but unlike Clarkson, Macaulay showed neither the ability nor the inclination to redress the grievances that lay behind the "riots." Instead, he grew increasingly intolerant of the antinomianism that he saw behind the Methodist (and, increasingly, other) settlers' vision of an African colony exclusively for "Africans" or "blacks."

Three months later, a different challenge arose. On September 28, 1794, a French fleet entered the harbor and attacked the colony, bringing the wars of the French Revolution to Freetown.[54] Macaulay chose surrender as the safest course of action, and French sailors occupied Freetown for about two weeks, looting all that they could consume or carry. Colonists pulled together in response to the attack. Black settlers withdrew from town and occasionally ambushed French sailors who ventured into the surrounding bush. Macaulay walked among the settlers outside of Freetown and was "gratified by the warm congratulations of the Settlers on our health and safety." In short, while the French remained in the colony, the settlers "behaved with kindness to all" Company officials, and there was "no instance of any of them, even of those who were most disaffected, showing a disposition to insult any of us."[55] The governor quickly transformed these glimmerings of harmony back into dissonance, strengthening many settlers' conviction that the colony should be run by and for "Africans."

During the French occupation, some Nova Scotians stole into Freetown at night to liberate items the French otherwise would have stolen. In Macaulay's words:

> They had saved a good deal of rice and molasses, and also rum, which
> I gave them to understand should not be claimed; but that everything else,
> belonging to the Company, which they might have saved, I should think the
> Company entitled to. Great quantities of lumber had been removed by
> them in the night time to their own yards. They had stript off and removed
> the lining of many of the houses, and the frame of the old hospital was
> almost entirely saved. They had also saved two or three of the Company's
> boats, and a great quantity of ironmongery.

Macaulay, exhibiting his characteristic subtlety and sensitivity, assembled the Hundredors and Tythingmen to announce that "no one . . . could expect future aid who did not faithfully restore all the Company's property in his possession." When the settlers' representatives raised objections, he "told them that I had made up my mind that they were in justice bound to restore the Company's property now, as much as if they had assisted in rescuing their neighbours' furniture from fire."[56] He decided this, of course, before speaking to the settlers' representatives.

The Nova Scotians, having served the colony loyally and bravely during the French attack, had no intention of bowing to Company officials. Macaulay thought the Methodists particularly culpable and claimed that they became angry and were "ready to fly in ones face if he should call" what they did "by the appropriate names of theft and robbery."[57] Had the Methodists been the lone supporters of a right to salvage, however, then Macaulay would have found far more than the 120 settlers willing to sign the pledge he required of anyone seeking employment, access to schools, or medical care from the Company.

Distraught Methodist settlers wrote to Clarkson complaining that they used to call their new home "Freetown but since your Absence We have a Reason to call it A town of Slavery." They saw the French attack as God's response to the "tyranny and oppression" displayed by their "Barbarous Task Masters," and they contested Macaulay's account of their behavior. They had recovered only "a few [wooden] Boards and one little Notion A Nother," which they claimed by right of salvage. Those rights notwithstanding, they insisted that had "the Superintendent had the lest Consideration to come and Ask Us in a fare Manner if we will Bestow these things to the Company—God only knows we would give it up with all Respect—but instead of that he came With that Empression to tell us if We did not give them up we shold never be Emply'd in the Comp's Work nor not any more to be look'd upon but shall be Blotted Out of the Company's Book."

Macaulay returned to England in 1795 for a vacation, taking a letter of complaint addressed by the settlers to the Company directors and leaving behind a colony in which more settlers were opting to move into native villages or to negotiate with headmen for communal land outside Freetown. Even some of those who remained in Freetown had hired their own teacher and set up an independent school for their children.[58] Macaulay might blot them out of the Company's book, but he could not overcome their faith in God's Book and in God's assurance that their congregations had been promised land and equality in Sierra Leone.

When Macaulay returned from London, he resumed his unintentional work of alienating the Nova Scotians. Perhaps misled by "crowds of Settlers who hailed [his] return with the appearance of the liveliest joy," he called together the "Hundredors and also . . . the heads of the disaffected party" to inform them that the directors had rejected the claims in their letter, and worse than that, they had resurrected an old problem by demanding that the settlers begin to pay quitrents to the Company. Macaulay offered forgiveness and a fresh start to those who would pledge loyalty and make "restitution of the property plundered by them at the time of the French visit."[59] The accused, perceiving the situation and the need for forgiveness differently, turned back to John Clarkson in London to make their case. James Liaster (or Lester) complained that the Company had taken "all of my property land and house Only On Suspetion that I had some Goods when they gave up the Colony to the French in A most Scandolas Manner." Liaster joined a group of his fellow Methodists who so distrusted the Company that they decided to leave the colony. They accepted land "freely Given" by "Prince George Jemmy Queen." The secessionists—and unlike the earlier group, these clearly were secessionists—took up land at Pirate's Bay, a bit east of the first breakaway village, and appointed Nathaniel Snowball, Luke

Jordan, and Jonathan Glasgow their leaders. Modeling themselves on "the Ezerlites," they left continuing their exodus by leaving Freetown.[60]

If, however, this second exodus in a decade looks like a final flowering of a separatist vision, that separatism was hardly pure. Secessionists went beyond justifying themselves to Clarkson, and expressing affection for their former leader; several pleaded with him to return, and three settlers—James Liaster in one letter and James Hutcherson and Mosis Murry in another—sought to convince him to return to lead them "as Mosis and Joshua" had led the "Children of Esaral to the promise land."[61] They were determined to escape from the Company and the leaders that it had placed over them; they perceived the threat of the Company through the profoundly racialized concepts of slavery and liberty; nonetheless, at least some continued to look to John Clarkson, who had honestly sought to settle them on freehold farms and had governed with them through consultation and consent, as the man most able to lead them to an African promised land. It was an unusual form of black separatism that looked to a white Moses to lead the exodus, though they may well have been assuming that, like the biblical Moses, Clarkson would be taken before they entered their promised land.

This effort by a small group of Methodists to escape from the suzerainty of the Company initiated several years of quiet hostility in which different Nova Scotian congregations struggled alternately to reform conditions within the colony or to forge relationships with natives that would allow them to escape the Company's control. By 1797 the settlers had coalesced into four major groups: the Baptists under David George, whom Macaulay estimated to include about 60 followers; the main group of Wesleyan Methodists under Moses Wilkinson, estimated to number about 200; a splinter Methodist group of about 70 centered at Granville Town and including many at the Pirate's Bay settlement, led by a dissident white preacher named John Garvin and by settler Henry Beverhout; and a Huntingdonian congregation of about 70 led by Cato Perkins.[62] The congregations sometimes cooperated and sometimes struggled with one another as each sought to find its way, and some Methodists moved back and forth between the congregations led by Wilkinson and Garvin. The Baptists remained the most amenable to Company policy and the Wesleyans remained the most consistently inclined to oppose it, but Zachary Macaulay managed to pick fights with everyone. The resulting disputes forced settlers to articulate their sometimes common, sometimes divergent visions of their African futures.

Some were tempted to seek a communal future under the authority of Koya Temne headmen rather than a British governor, but occasional incidents called the compatibility of Nova Scotian dreams and Temne ways of life into question. In the years following the French invasion, the colony developed economically, as settlers built boats, raised livestock, and expanded trade with native villages.[63] Increased contact did not always produce harmony. In late 1794 inclement weather forced three settlers trading on the Rio Nunez to go ashore unexpectedly, where they were seized by "natives" who "reduced them to slavery." A few months later a dispute arose when one settler accused another of stealing money and forced her to submit to a Temne judicial test called the "ordeal of fire." A "hot iron" was applied to the skin of the accused, and "being burnt [was] considered . . . sufficient proof of . . . [her] guilt." Nova Scotians also accused natives of rustling livestock and enticing male settlers into adulterous liaisons in order to collect monetary damages.[64] Slavery, robbery, cattle rustling, and adultery were all familiar to the settlers long before they arrived in Sierra Leone, but in each of these cases, a major dispute arose because seemingly routine conflicts became entangled with incompatible senses of justice. Some settlers continued to pursue a rapprochement that would have allowed them to live under the Temne, but many began to suspect, perhaps with cause, that their Temne neighbors saw black American settlers less as racial brothers than as foreigners whose lack of local knowledge left them susceptible to being conned.

Most Nova Scotians remained in Freetown, where they fought with Company officials over basic political questions involving representation and authority. Early governors of Sierra Leone relied on the Company in London for their legal authority, but each had to earn actual authority in their daily interactions with settlers. Macaulay realized this, and though he had, even by his own estimation, a "severe disposition," he sought to win the settlers' consent by working with the Tythingmen and Hundredors.[65] The settlers' representatives had long since assumed informal legislative responsibility by recommending laws to the council, and toward the end of 1796 Macaulay, hoping to strengthen the colony's defenses, drafted a constitution that would have transformed these informal bodies into a legislature. When in December of that year the settlers elected representatives that the governor found unacceptable, he suspended plans to implement the constitution.[66]

This refusal to accept the outcome of the election exacerbated racial divisions and angered the settlers.[67] Macaulay's unease had begun before the vote was taken, when he heard that, in retaliation for the oppression the settlers had experienced under slavery, Ishmael York and Stephen Peters had been "busying themselves in persuading the people not merely not to choose whites for their representatives, but to prevent whites from voting." Whites voted, but the overwhelmingly black electorate chose Tythingmen and Hundredors whom Macaulay characterized variously as "factious," "pestilent," "void of principle," and "hairbrained," while describing the body of representatives as "disposed to thwart every measure" recommended by the Company "merely because it originates with Europeans."[68] Even Macaulay's own journals suggest that a different dynamic animated the dissident settlers.

The Nova Scotians, after all, corresponded with the "European" Clarkson, asking his advice and trying to convince him to return to Sierra Leone. In addition, the "most unmanageable and perverse" among the newly chosen representatives had called on Macaulay immediately after winning the election, and, after politely apologizing for "troubl[ing] your honour," had asked for clarification about the "new *Consecution*."[69] That Macaulay could not resist including—and underlining—his condescending phonetic rendering of the settlers' pronunciation in his journal shows his contempt for the dissident colonists. His resulting rigidity strengthened the most radical among the Nova Scotians.

His superiors in London made the situation even more difficult by ordering him to insist that quitrents be paid, a demand that galvanized settlers' opposition. To the Nova Scotians, the Company's insistence that they pay rent each year for every acre of Company land that they claimed constituted a fundamental betrayal. Clarkson had warned that life in Sierra Leone would be hard, but he had promised freehold farms. If land did not belong to the settlers "without paying a shilling per acre" each year, then, in the settlers' words, it would "never be ours, no not at all." Should the directors really want to enforce such a ruling, the settlers would appeal to the Crown in London or, failing that, to "the Kings of this country."[70]

Perceived threats to the Nova Scotians' religious autonomy stimulated further dissent. At the same time that Macaulay was discussing possible constitutional changes in the colony, he sent the Tythingmen and Hundredors a proposal to formalize the civic status of the marriage ceremony, thus removing it from the purview of the clergy. His plan elicited opposition from "one or two preachers" among the Tythingmen whom he thought "very tenacious of . . . religious rights," but both bodies initially approved the measure. When, however, word of the plan spread through the colony, significant opposition arose from an unexpected source. David George, the settler most frequently lauded for loyalty to the Company, sought out "the most disaffected of the Methodist leaders" and convinced them that the marriage law was simply a preliminary step toward "shutting up the meeting houses." George vowed to "resist such acts even to blood." The two congregations of Wesleyan Methodists responded with a formal remonstrance to the governor, a document that 128 settlers signed. For a moment this dispute over the marriage law threatened to blow up into something comparable to the 1794 rebellion, but Macaulay had no designs on the meetinghouses, so it blew over.[71]

The settlers' behavior in the wake of the fight over who should preside over weddings reveals that the different factions' conceptions of their settlements shared more than their often-differing political stances might lead one to believe. The Methodists' letter of protest asserted loyalty not to the

Company and its governor, but to "the Governor of the universe, whose we are and whom we serve." The signers were "Dissenters . . . and as such . . . a perfect Church" without any need of a "worldly power . . . [to] perform religious ceremonies." Macaulay easily convinced them that the attempt to regularize marriage as a civil rather than religious matter involved no "invasion of their religious rights"—it was, after all, a fundamental tenet of Protestantism—but this did not alter their sense of themselves as visible saints sanctified by God.[72]

Eight months later Macaulay engaged David George in an extended discussion rooted, in part, in surprise at the role that George had played in the marriage dispute, and, in part, in a series of moral failings of which Macaulay had judged George's Baptists guilty. The governor warned of "capital errors of the Antinomian kind which lay at the bottom" of the Baptists' shortcomings, before didactically using Socratic dialogue to make his point. George agreed that the "written word" must constitute the "rule of our faith," so Macaulay pushed him to reject the "mischievous effects of . . . dependence on inexplicable mental impressions and bodily feelings," and to recognize that evils like drunkenness and "unchastity" resulted from the "abominable doctrines" that George sometimes preached. Macaulay denounced George's claims from the pulpit that "prayer and instruction cant convey grace," while confronting his supposed friend with "passages which lay most directly against all who should pervert the good ways of God and murder by their teaching precious and immortal souls." Yet even when being accused of soul murder, George held tenaciously to his "favourite proposition," by insisting that "those who are once" saved "can never be deprived of their interest in him by the greatest crimes." George's Baptists, like Wilkinson's Methodists, were a sanctified people and a perfect church. Mere secular authorities could not question them. This powerful communal identity as chosen people was as strong among the colony's seemingly moderate Baptists as it was among "Lady H's Methodists" or the "mad Wesleans."[73] Congregations might differ about specific issues, but all saw Sierra Leone as a land promised to godly communities.

Macaulay found these qualities annoying, because they offended his own religious certainty and interfered with his administration of the colony. He found the settlers' leaders unreliable, because of the communal nature of the Nova Scotians' decision making. They had made consensual decisions to leave America, and they continued to work through consensus while living in Africa. Macaulay might badger David George into doubt about his antinomianism, but George's congregation would bring its preacher's beliefs back into line with their own. Earlier, the governor had convinced Nathaniel Snowball and Luke Jordan to agree that quitrents were justified, but he knew enough to expect them to yield to their followers' opinions when they returned to the community.[74] He might "procure . . . unqualified assent" in private from another Hundredor about the quitrent, but "no dependance was to be placed on his fairly representing . . . [Macaulay's] sentiments" to his constituents.[75]

These conflicts all involved a tension between the settlers' notions of representation—notions rooted in their own communalism, as well as in their American experiences—and Macaulay's English notions. The Nova Scotians' leaders were of the people they led and they could not make commitments that outstripped the willingness of their followers to support them.[76] This weakened the power of Macaulay's elite background: he might overwhelm individual adversaries in conversation, but unless the community believed that he was winning on the merits rather than through debating tricks or educational privilege, he had accomplished nothing. The settlers' representatives could not, on the other hand, move too far out in front of their followers without losing their authority, as would be proven in the final conflict of Zachary Macaulay's administration.

When Macaulay refused to enact the proposed constitution with the newly elected representatives, the Hundredors and Tythingmen moved outside of official channels. In the fall of 1797, with the next round of elections approaching in December, they convinced two-thirds of the settlers to sign a document authorizing them to act "without limitation in behalf of their rights."[77] Having acquired a claim to authority based on popular sovereignty, the shadow government called on the settlers from all denominations to renounce their grants of Company land until the quitrents were rescinded. They convened an extralegal court outside of Freetown, and summoned settlers who had accepted Company land to demand that they relinquish their grants. These settlers—presumably most were Baptists—rejected the court's threats as well as its characterization of their enslavement to the Company; they opted instead to stand up to the Hundredors and Tythingmen's threats by reporting on the court's activities. Macaulay promised to defend their land and lives and mobilized for another rebellion.

He had reason to believe that the threat was more serious than in 1794. Settlers loyal to him warned that Isaac Anderson had led a delegation to the Temne king Firama to "solicit . . . his help" in preparation for an attempt to achieve what some had "fondly cherished . . . since the foundation of the Colony, viz., throwing off the jurisdiction of the Company's servants." Macaulay believed the rebels would then rule Freetown through "a kind of Dictator . . . assisted by a council . . . in the manner of the Natives." It seems more likely that the Hundredors and Tythingmen envisioned the kind of collective decision making through elected leaders that their communities had used since before leaving America, though how they would have reconciled their conceptions of communal authority with Temne political traditions remains unclear.

At any rate, the potential insurgents quickly learned that they could not achieve their plans without deeper support than they enjoyed. A modest show of force on the part of the Company convinced the settlers to disavow "all intention of violence" and discontinue the "new instituted Court."[78] In the next election, three months later, the sitting Hundredors and Tythingmen tried, once again, to win support for their separatist agenda, but the "majority of those chosen" were, in Macaulay's estimation, "good men."[79] The separatist tide had receded, at least temporarily. Having waited for a legislature that he liked, the governor accepted its resolutions "respecting the forming two Chambers," and the appointment of a committee to consult with him regarding "regulations . . . for the general good."[80] The separatists, leery of the governor's intentions and unwilling (or unable) to win the aid of Firama, appealed to the captain of a Royal Navy ship in Freetown's harbor to intervene.[81]

The captain refused, and the tensions remained unresolved. The moderate newly elected Hundredors and Tythingmen chose not to challenge Macaulay openly during what turned out to be his final year in Sierra Leone. Even within Freetown itself, however, where Macaulay's political ascendancy was relatively uncontested, the settlers openly rejected his vision of a good Christian society. Perhaps unsurprisingly, the prudish governor was most perplexed by Nova Scotian women's instrumental attitudes toward sex. He could not understand how women who believed themselves to be sanctified could engage in prostitution with sailors from ships that docked in the colony's harbor, and he was particularly troubled when his young male protégé began stealing from the Company store. Upon investigation he learned that "a number of women . . . some married and some unmarried had been . . . enticing youths of 15 or 16 to their houses" and convincing them to pursue "villainous schemes" in return for "ministering to their wants."[82] Incidents like these had inspired Macaulay's earlier attempt to argue David George out of his "antinomian" beliefs, and to convince him to impress upon his congregation that they "could not be sure of . . . election unless" they were "following holiness in squaring" their conduct with the "word of God," but George and the Baptists followed their own counsel on these matters.[83]

By 1798, when Macaulay returned to England for good, he left a colony that had made enormous material progress. Few new societies have managed, in the course of six short years, to build multiple schools, public buildings, and meetinghouses. Freetown had a functioning court system, licensed taverns, and a rudimentary but vibrant system of representative government. The Nova Scotians had moved out of the small thatched huts they had lived in for the first few years, to build thirty foot by fifteen foot "wooden buildings" with wooden floors and shingled roofs that were "divided into rooms by partitions, and raised two or three feet from the ground."[84]

A View of Free-town on the River Sierra Leone?

Figure 4.2.   "A View of Free-town on the River Sierra Leone," from Thomas Winterbottom, *An Account of the Native Africans in the Neighborhood of Sierra Leone* (1803). The company fort is the structure built on the highest hill; various Company buildings and settler houses are portrayed closer to the shore.

Much of the colony's success was predicated on continuing heavy subsidies from London investors, but the successes were real. Notwithstanding divisions among settlers and deep divisions between some settlers and the Company—divisions to which we will return—the colony at Sierra Leone offered good grounds for hope to black Americans who were either considering emigrating to Africa or engaged with the project of creating an African people.

IV

Blacks in North America continued to explore the meanings and implications of Africanness while the Nova Scotians struggled to achieve true liberty in their African promised land. New England activists had been actively engaged in discussions of African identity and the possibility of immigrating to Africa prior to Sierra Leone's founding. Events in Freetown did not radically alter the terms of these discussions, in part because Freetown was settled according to broad principles that many "African" theorists shared. The desire to bring Christianity and civilization to the "heathen savages" of Africa had, after all, informed the plans of Olaudah Equiano, John Marrant, and Prince Hall, as well as those of their white allies like Granville Sharp, Samuel Hopkins, and John Clarkson. The same goals inspired the Nova Scotians. The African Masons in Boston and the Rhode Island African Union Societies searched for abstract ties binding Africans together as a people at the same time that Nova Scotians struggled with the possibilities of making such ties concrete.

Prince Hall did not discuss Sierra Leone in his surviving speeches from the 1790s. In some ways, this seems odd. John Marrant, after all, built the Huntingdonian congregation in Nova Scotia and contributed to the theology that inspired that congregation's exodus to Africa just before he traveled to Boston, where he offered the same nationalist vision to enthusiastic members of Hall's African Lodge. If, however, Hall made no specific mention of Sierra Leone—at least no surviving mention—he did seek to build upon the foundation that Marrant's sermon to the Masons had provided. In two "Charges" to his African Masonic Lodge—one in 1792 and the other in 1797—he explained the responsibilities of African Masons, rooting that responsibility in their proud heritages as both Masons and Africans.[85]

The first Charge (1792) has the quality of catechism. Hall enjoined good Masons to believe in the Almighty, to remain loyal to their country and to their lodge, and to embrace the entire family of mankind. But even when restating conventional political and ethical values, Hall's position as a black man speaking in a country committed to racial slavery produced less predictable riffs on well-worn homilies. Like most good Americans of his time, Hall often turned to the Bible to support his claims, but unlike many of his white contemporaries, he paid close attention to the ways in which an eighteenth-century sense of racial difference could be read back into scripture. It was not enough to ask his followers to display "love and benevolence to all the family of mankind"; he called on African Freemasons to help their fellows "let them be of what colour or nation they may." To buttress this obligation he pointed out that "a blackman" had shown compassion to Jeremiah, and he invoked the parable of the Good Samaritan to remind his listeners that Christ had found benevolence and goodness in the despised among the peoples of the Holy Land.[86]

He then broadened his approach to black history by providing a specifically African twist to what could have been a simple, and classically Masonic, universalist appeal when he listed "reverend fathers for . . . imitation." These included Tertullian, Augustine, and Fulgentius, three early church fathers from North Africa whose contributions to religion and civilization he lauded. African Masons' glorious history of service and sacrifice did not stop with the fall of Rome. Hall traced the Knights of Malta to an "order of St. John" that had fought the "Turks" during the crusades, insisting that Africans were surely members of the order. As Masons, and as Africans, and as members of an order honoring St. John, he wove together for his listeners intertwining strands that formed an inspirational shared history.

Hall's second Charge (1797) continued to present the history of Africans, while offering more explicit and potentially controversial attempts to link African Masons' ancient illustrious past to the contemporary world of the late eighteenth century.[87] He likened slave traders to the immoral merchants described in the book of Revelations, before pointing out that Moses' wife was Ethiopian, meaning that crucial advice that the prophet received from his father-in-law, Jethro, redounded to Ethiopia's credit. Hall further insisted that Jethro was a Mason, and noted that Jesus' apostle Philip welcomed an Ethiopian eunuch, just as Solomon had welcomed the Queen of Sheba (a "female mason" if "ever there was" one).

This invocation of a distinguished black biblical history informed Hall's reinterpretation of Africa's modern difficulties; while whites often saw the contemporary state of the continent as a sign of Africans' innate inferiority, Hall used it to remind his listeners of the inevitability of historical change and the certainty that current conditions would not remain unchanged forever.[88] In a complicated juxtaposition, he praised black Bostonians for their patience in the face of day-to-day racism, but then invoked the threat of violent revolution by encouraging them to recall what their "African brethren" had done six years earlier "in the French West-Indies." His attitude toward conspiracy and rebellion appears to have changed in the five years between his two published Charges, a change that became stark when he summarized the struggle that was then becoming the Haitian Revolution: "Thus doth Ethiopia begin to stretch forth her hand, from a sink of slavery to freedom and equality."[89]Coincidentally, Hall's choice of an increasingly autonomous black polity in St. Domingue, rather than the civilizing project centered at Sierra Leone, as the site of the initial fulfillment of the psalmist's prophecy, mirrors the separatist sentiment then gaining ascendancy among the Nova Scotians living in Freetown.

Hall's changing understanding of resistance to slavery and white prejudice occurred in the context of his consistent embrace of kinship with black people across time and space. All blacks were brothers, whether the church fathers of the late classical period, the Ethiopians of the Bible, the revolutionaries of St. Domingue, or the "African kings and princes" who destroyed their "peaceable kingdoms" to participate in the slave trade. As brothers, all could accomplish much so long as they feared and obeyed God. All either did or should love and respect their fellow man. In this regard, Hall's vision was universalist: "give the right hand of affection and fellowship to whom it justly belongs; let their colour and complexion be what it will." Let people's "nation be what it will," Hall said, they remained "brethren," and no Mason should deny this as did false white Masons who excluded blacks. At the same time, however, a rhetoric of kinship infused his invocation of black historical and biblical exemplars. Underdeveloped and sadly unreliable affiliative ties bound all humans together, and African Masons, like all Masons, should long for the day when true human fraternity would be achieved. The ties that bound Africans to one another, however, were filiative, as well as affiliative, and stretched back to the first exodus.[90]

Black activists in Rhode Island also continued to explore their ties to Africa, but, unlike the Masons, they engaged directly and explicitly with Sierra Leone. During the early 1790s, the Newport and Providence African Union Societies had begun to discuss how to implement their vague plans to leave the United States and help Christianize and civilize Africa. In 1794, members of the Providence Society lost patience and stopped waiting for their colleagues in other cities; they chose one of their members, James McKenzie, to visit Freetown in order to discern how best to proceed. Providence blacks invited other towns to choose envoys to travel with McKenzie, but when none moved quickly enough, McKenzie sailed on his own, arriving in Freetown in January 1795. A letter addressed to Governor Zachary Macaulay endowed McKenzie with "full power to transact, bargain, and agree to any thing Respect'g our Emmigration." McKenzie's impressions of Freetown have not survived, and he failed to achieve what he and his Society had hoped: Macaulay promised that the Company would accept and settle up to twelve Rhode Island families on the Bullum Shore (on the north shore of the Sierra

Leone River across from Freetown), but only if the emigrants arrived with certificates of good character signed by Samuel Hopkins and one other "respectable Clergyman," as well as the president of the Rhode Island Abolition Society. Macaulay then wrote to Hopkins, presumably behind McKenzie's back, asking him to screen out religious enthusiasts and anyone who had been seduced by "speculative infidelity."[91]

Macaulay's implicit anxiety that black Americans might seek to overwhelm Britain's colony was reasonable, given his struggles with the Nova Scotians and the ambitions of Rhode Island's black emigrationists. While McKenzie was in Freetown, the Newport Society proposed the calling of an assembly of representatives from the "free people of colour in every Town in this State" to draft a petition seeking state aid for emigration to Africa, and also to "determine how many men shall be sufficient to send to . . . the coast of Africa." Macaulay was ready to welcome a small group of skilled, literate, and religiously orthodox immigrants who would help to bolster Company control of Sierra Leone, but members of Newport's African Union Society envisioned something else. Looking to "the God who did promise the children of Israel" that he would "'gather them from the North Country and all the country wherein they have been scattered and will carry them to their native country,'" they hoped to "gather" black people "from all the country and carry" them to an African promised land.[92] The Sierra Leone Company's modest offer to accept twelve immigrant families must have seemed irrelevant and perhaps insulting in the context of the large-scale migration that the African Union Society envisioned.

The impetus toward a large "return" of black Newporters (and others) to Africa went off track by the mid-1790s, but the Union Society continued to conceive of itself as "African." The unity that its members sought to foster within "the African race" had multiple and almost contradictory sources. It was based in part on a belief in an essential racial unity. The failure of indigenous Africans to recognize and act upon that unity had helped create the slave trade and thus the shared oppression that had made "brethren in affliction" out of diasporic members of "the African race." Those who returned from America would defeat the heathenism that blighted Africa by spreading "true" religion. Given the Newport Society's plan for a statewide black assembly, black Newporters presumably planned to bring republicanism to Africa as well, something that would have bolstered the Nova Scotians in their contest with the Company.

As Christian universalists, emigrationists wanted to spread the word of God to the "pagans" on the continent. As former residents of African societies, they longed to raise "the Nations in Africa" out of the "heathenish darkness and barbarity" that had led them to be "so foolish and wicked as to sell one another." They spoke of Africa as a land of nations, and they recognized the importance of gaining clear and recognized title to land before traveling, so that they could transform the continent from a secure base. This made Sierra Leone seem providential. Members of the Union Society were committed to spread "the Gospel . . . to all the Nations in Africa" so that "the light of it [would] spread over all the World." In this way members of the "African race" would "become *a part of* his Chosen people" (my emphasis) and prosper on earth while preparing to enter "the Heavenly World, with Abraham, Isaac and Jacob," but also with "the Saints and holy Prophets."[93] Through conversion and "civilization" Africans would fulfill their destiny as a race and a people while simultaneously assuming their rightful place within the universal (and thus nonracial) church.

Neither Prince Hall's African Masons nor the African Union Societies ever moved to Africa. As Prince Hall's two "Charges" show, however, "Africans" in the United States could and did persist in studying and interpreting their links to the peoples and history of Africa without talking about emigration. As the 1790s progressed, both the Masons and members of the Union Societies formulated narratives that represented "Africans" as true "blood" kin. The conflicts that arose in Freetown did not push the Nova Scotians to tell stories about their collective pasts—the kinds of stories that reveal filiative and affiliative narratives—but racial separatism continued to grow in Sierra Leone during the final years of the century.

V

Racial separation in Sierra Leone was not synonymous with dissidence—all settlers expressed some dissatisfaction with Company rule, but not all were separatists—but the two certainly reinforced each other. Moses Wilkinson's Wesleyan Methodist congregation remained at the center of settler radicalism—though the Huntingdonians increasingly joined them there—and it was from the Wesleyans that the secessionists led by Nathanial Snowball and Luke Jordan originated. They formally broke away from the Company and moved to land that Temne headman King Tom gave them at Pirate's Bay, but they did not break away from their coreligionists who remained behind. The secessionists stayed at Pirate's Bay, so they must have found ways to reconcile living under the Temne with their commitments to individual freehold landownership, electoral government, and the project of "civilizing" Africa. Zachary Macaulay's reports, letters, and journals provide the fullest surviving descriptions of settler life during this period, and he did not record the successes of those who fled his rule. He did, however, report some of their problems, and though the problems that he recorded do not represent "normal" life at Pirate's Bay, one incident provides an entry into the conflicts that arose and the choices that the Nova Scotians had to face as they sought to pursue their collective dreams of building communities that would civilize and transform their promised land.

In January 1799 Macaulay reported "extraordinary transactions" in what he disdainfully labeled the "petty Settlement in Pirates Bay." The "Spirit of God" had come to Sally Cooper in a dream and told of a "great treasure" that "lay hid in a field at a small distance from her house."[94] She decided not to tell her husband, but she did mention her dream to Jane Marshall, her friend and neighbor, perhaps in part because Marshall's "own father had" reportedly "found a treasure in the same way." Cooper and Marshall went to their Methodist class leader, America Talbot, who inspected the site but insisted that no one dig the treasure until they could inform Nathaniel Snowball, who was both their preacher and the settlement's governor. Snowball was traveling, and when he returned, he and Talbot dug in the appointed spot but found nothing; Jane Marshall then protested, reporting that Talbot had taken advantage of Snowball's absence by secretly removing "the money" on the first night after she and Cooper had told him of the dream. Cooper's husband, perhaps peeved at having been excluded for so long, demanded and got a trial, but apparently jury trials were not the norm at Pirate's Bay, and few suspicions were allayed when Snowball acquitted his friend. Cooper's husband then turned to King Tom, the local Temne ruler. King Tom seized Talbot and issued a ruling that was cleverly rooted in local notions of collective village rights: "The Money he was sure was among them. He would leave it to them to settle the individual who had it. But they must pay him jointly the sum of 700 Bars, he having a right to" 40 percent of all treasure. However Snowball and his followers conceived of their ties with their Temne neighbors and landlords—filiative, affiliative, contractual—the incident must have reminded them of the cultural gulf that remained far from bridged.

Just two months later a similar clash between American experiences and native beliefs arose. Settler Frank Peters had been born near Freetown. Upon emigrating from Nova Scotia he had found his "mother and relations" and "separated himself entirely from the Colony . . . resuming the Native dress manners and language."[95] His attempt to return home proved disastrous. When Prince Tom fell prey to malign spirits and injured himself with an ax, he cast about for the responsible party. As an outsider, Frank Peters was "marked out" as "guilty" and sentenced to enslavement, so he was seized, bound, and carried to the coast. Luckily, his ties to the Company frightened off European traders at Pirate's Bay and Bance Island, buying him time to break his fetters and make "his way into the Colony." Macaulay hoped this incident would increase the settlers' "distaste" for "going among the

Natives," but it did nothing to alleviate the problems that drove many Nova Scotians to contemplate such a move. The presence of slave traders at Pirate's Bay underscores the limited economic options facing settlers who left the Company's book at Freetown, and thus helps explain why most dissident settlers remained in Freetown to pursue their rights.

Zachary Macaulay escaped these problems by moving back to England in April 1799, but the tensions roiling the colony did not go with him. John Gray arrived to replace Macaulay, bringing instructions to begin collecting the quitrent once and for all, instructions that immediately strengthened the separatists. During the next year and a half under the brief administration of Gray and then of Thomas Ludlam, the consensus among the settlers moved steadily against the Company, emboldening some Nova Scotians to articulate and pursue their vision of a Sierra Leone in which the Company would be just that—a trading company—and the settlers would form a self-governing society. The separatists' ascent began, as it had in each previous cycle, with annual elections in which "almost every friend of the Government among the Hundredors and Tythingmen was thrown out" of office.[96] The new legislature moved quickly to institutionalize power before anger over the quitrent cooled.

The separatists' first salvo involved an effort to strip judicial power from Company-appointed whites. In February 1800, the Hundredors and Tythingmen complained that they could not "get justice from the White people," a problem that they sought to remedy by appointing James Robinson, one of their own, as judge and another, John Cuthbert, as justice of the peace to "sit in judgment" of all blacks brought before the local court system.[97] Ludlam, now governor, responded that the settlers lacked the expertise necessary to serve as judges; Sierra Leone's black juries provided what would have to remain an adequate check within the judiciary until the settlers' children gained the education that judges needed. At any rate, the Company was waiting for the Crown to regularize the colony's judicial system, and in this, as in all else, the king would decide. Ludlam acknowledged that more than judicial power was at stake, by addressing those who claimed to be "*Africans*" and thus, "being in their *own* country," to be free of any obligation "to obey the King and laws of England." These professed "Africans" risked being sent to England and tried for "high treason."[98]

That fall, the Hundredors and Tythingmen, undeterred by Ludlam's threat, took the decisive step. On September 3, 1800, they met in extralegal session—"out of doors" according to the political traditions within which they were working—to pass laws to govern the settlers of Sierra Leone. A week later they posted the laws on the door of the settler Abram Smith.[99] Their manifesto quickly disappeared from the door, but two weeks later they put it back up, and this time it galvanized the colony. Most of their laws sought to implement a vision of a cooperative moral economy; they set maximum prices on basic foodstuffs, prohibited theft, and protected spouses in cases of desertion. The more radical agenda was not, however, shortchanged. The document closed by declaring that "all that come from Nova Scotia, shall be under this law or quit the place." It acknowledged that the "Company's affairs" would be the province of the governor and council, but insisted that this would have nothing "to do with the Colony." The separatists underscored the distinction between the Colony and the Company by asserting their right to exclude future immigrants. Company agents should stop admitting "strangers [presumably whites] into the colony," a formulation that puzzled white authorities who asked how one group of settlers who had been admitted to the colony could preclude authorities from "admitting others."[100] The Nova Scotians, however, never saw themselves as a mere "body of settlers" who had been "admitted." They were the chosen people of the promised Freetown.

Separatist Nova Scotians' belief that Sierra Leone was their colony not only influenced their preferred policies regarding new immigrants, it also informed their general response to the Company. They viewed any settler who sided with the governor as a traitor acting "against this law" and subject to a £20 fine. Like those who led England's thirteen American colonies to independence, the Hundredors and Tythingmen rooted their collective authority, and the authority of their laws, in transcendent powers, insisting that the settlers' law be obeyed because it was "just before God and Man." The new laws did not take the form of a declaration of independence, and those who promulgated them may have hoped that Company authorities would choose not to treat them as such, but declaring independence was, as Company authorities realized, the effect of the law.

Governor Ludlam saw this "overt act of sedition" as a "crisis . . . which would determine whether the Company's Government was to be annihilated" and replaced by men of "desperate fortunes and profligate morals."[101] He mobilized white officials and the Nova Scotian settlers who remained loyal to the Company, arming and organizing them to defend the Company compound in Freetown. At the same time the council summoned the leaders of what they now saw as a plot. When neither James Robinson, the head of the Hundredors, nor Nathaniel Wansey, the chairman of the Tythingmen, kept their appointment, the governor and council sent Richard Crankapone, who served as the marshal of the colony, with an armed party of supporters to surprise the separatists' leaders then meeting in a house in Freetown. Violence broke out as James Robinson and Anzel Zizer, another rebel leader, were arrested and at least three others, including Wansey, were injured but escaped into the countryside.[102] Wansey and Isaac Anderson rallied their supporters in Granville Town and entered what Ludlam called "a state of open rebellion"; they cut Freetown off from the hinterland and began receiving "hourly supplies" from both the town and the surrounding countryside.

As the two sides moved toward open battle, Adam Jones, Cato Perkins, and John Cuthbert approached the governor and sought to mediate. Ludlam rejected their overtures, judging them "biased in favor of the rebels" because they had no intention to help "strengthen the authority of Government." At least two of the delegates did indeed have close ties to the rebels—Cuthbert had been their choice to serve as justice of the peace, and Perkins was the head of the Huntingdonian congregation, many of whose members were rebels—but that would seem a given for a peace delegation. They may have been sent because the rebels feared they had overplayed their hand: Ludlam would later report that Adam Jones, for example, though a "determined and vigorous" opponent of the government, had split from the rebels over "judges and justices," and that the "Westleian Methodists" had found the Huntingdonians too extreme and had failed to rally to their side.[103] If, however, the Huntingdonians had moved beyond the Wesleyans and some settlers were drawing back from rebellion, Ludlam thought others were flocking to the rebels' banner. Anderson and his troops may have had a good chance of winning and establishing, at least in the short run, an independent black colony in Sierra Leone. Luck, however, was with the Company.

Just as an attack on the Company compound was looming amid rumors that neighboring Koya Temne might support the rebels, a ship transporting Jamaican Maroons from Nova Scotia to Sierra Leone with an escort of forty-five British marines pulled into the harbor.[104] Both the marines and the Maroons agreed to join the governor in "reducing the Rebels to obedience," and, after failing to receive an immediate answer to an ultimatum demanding that the rebels surrender, the troops in support of the Company attacked. The rebels were quickly routed. More than thirty men were captured and an unspecified number escaped and sought refuge with the Temne. The Company set up military courts presided over by Lieutenants John Sherriff, Lionel Smith, and U. D. Tolley, the commanders of the ship and troops that had helped repress the uprising. Thirty-three men were banished from the colony, most for life, and sent to other British outposts in Africa. Two people, Isaac Anderson and Francis Patrick, were hanged. A few, including Nathaniel Wansey, remained at large, taking up residence in Temne towns and attempting with some success to convince native leaders to attack the colony.[105] The effect of the Rebellion of 1800, however, was deeper than a catalog of punishments might suggest.

Among those exiled from Freetown were many of the most devoted and successful farmers among the settlers, and even those agriculturalists who remained loyal to the Company "quitted their lands and suffered their farms to fall to ruin" rather than pay the dreaded quitrent. The resulting commercial orientation of the persisting Nova Scotians did not fit the original vision of a society in which free black farmers would be settled securely on their own land. The addition of a large group of Maroons undercut the easy identification of the colony with the Nova Scotians, especially given the tension that carried over from the Rebellion.[106] Of course the Nova Scotians themselves had never been united in their vision of a new society, but they had shared a sense that the colony was a sacred communal endeavor and that their futures were linked to one another. The Maroons never shared the Nova Scotians' religious errand.

Robbed of the sense of mission that inspired so much activism during their first decade in Africa, the Nova Scotians settled into a less unusual experience as colonizers. Most stayed in Freetown. Others moved to slaving forts to engage in commerce. Many seemingly forgot their antislavery commitments, purchasing native children under the thinly veiled guise of "apprenticeship."[107] As the colony's government became more firmly institutionalized—the Crown took over Sierra Leone in 1808—new governors often considered the Nova Scotians to be the colony's least valuable settlers. But the memory of the initial errand persisted.

In 1827 Parliament sent a commission to investigate the perceived failures of the colony at Sierra Leone. The commissioners recorded depositions from three Nova Scotians—John Kizell, Eli Aikin (sometimes Ackim), and Lazarus Jones—each of whom recalled the idealistic beginning of his time in Africa, and each of whom recounted a similar, though not identical, litany of white betrayal. All three contrasted the African society that they had projected from Nova Scotia—a society in which they would be granted adequate land and in which they would finally receive the rights that Englishmen and Americans took for granted—with a society in which they discovered that there was "plenty of law but no justice."

John Kizell closed his narrative of the history of the Nova Scotians by noting that the Crown and Company had failed to honor Clarkson's assurance that the "Noviscotian and the white should be as one." Instead they "set a parcel of white and mullater boys . . . as majistrates," leading "our children to scatter from one place to another." How, he asked, could any colony "prosper when her inhabitants [were] trodden under foot and . . . scatter[ed] from one place to another." The exodus had ended in another diaspora.

These dispersed Nova Scotians had believed themselves called to travel in godly communities to a promised land. They had hoped to start stable family farms that would anchor a Christian civilizing mission to Africa and redeem the Dark Continent by ushering it into the world of enlightened peoples. In the process they hoped to find the freedom and prosperity that should have been their birthright in America. Not all had seen their mission in racially exclusive terms, but some had, and betrayals by white officials had convinced increasing numbers that their new land could only reach its promise if they escaped from the slavery whites repeatedly imposed in different forms. According to Ludlam, they had come to believe that Africa must become the country of "*Africans.*"

The Nova Scotians lost that struggle. They gave up dreams of prosperous agricultural villages and cohesive communities spreading the Word among the heathen surrounding them. It is hard to say that they became less American than they had been. Their turn to commerce and embrace of slavery reflected values and behaviors that were as deeply rooted in the American societies from which they had escaped as were the communitarian visions that had earlier inspired them. Nor should one romanticize the prospects that would have faced them had luck been on their side in the Rebellion of 1800, for it is difficult to imagine a future that would not have involved either a return to slavery or a turn to the slave trade for a small, unaffiliated settlement of black colonists living in a slave-trading region. Their attempt to constitute themselves as an African society at Freetown stands, however, as a revealing moment when the religious cultures rooted in the creolizing slave cultures of North America inspired an attempt to build a transforming "African" society in the Old World.

The less-than-inspiring events that culminated in 1800 probably help explain why Sierra Leone and the Nova Scotians lost prominence in black North Americans' assertions of African identities during the final few years of the eighteenth century and the first few years of the nineteenth, though Macaulay's unwelcoming stance toward future American immigrants may also have played a role. The setbacks in Sierra Leone did not discourage blacks in the United States from discussing what it meant to be "African." It would not take long for those discussions to circle back to Freetown and the Nova Scotians.

5

Becoming African in the English Atlantic

Politics, Religion, and Emigrationism at the Turn of the Nineteenth Century

During the 1790s, as the Nova Scotians' struggles in Sierra Leone moved toward their climax, and black activists in Massachusetts and Rhode Island offered increasingly elaborate discussions of what it meant to be an "African" in the diaspora, black leaders in mid-Atlantic Methodist churches took the first steps toward founding what would become the first black Christian denomination in the United States. Black ministers in Philadelphia and Baltimore led their followers into separate "African" congregations, and African churches in those towns and elsewhere became community centers in which newly freed black people struggled to protect and extend their own hard-won liberty, while contributing to the broader Atlantic struggle against slavery. As they built African churches, advocated in favor of state emancipation laws, and celebrated the end of the Atlantic slave trade and other victories, they offered the growing free black populations of Baltimore, Philadelphia, and New York ways to understand themselves as Africans in America.

Hindsight casts a depressing light on race during the early republic. The emancipatory march that emerged out of the American Revolution began to grind to a crawl with the halting and compromised gradual abolition laws passed in New York (1800) and New Jersey (1804). Slavery was becoming more deeply entrenched in the southern United States as the invention of the cotton gin and the opening of the Old Southwest to plantation agriculture undercut hopes that the institution might die of natural causes. Partially in response to these developments, white racism intensified and began morphing into its increasingly noxious nineteenth-century form. While historians differ over how profoundly the liberatory spirit of the American Revolution challenged slavery, almost all agree that the challenge had begun to recede, at least in the short term, by 1800.[1]

Those living through those decades could not, however, have known that the forces of racial reaction would emerge triumphant. For many free black Americans who had witnessed and benefited from the decision of state after northern state to opt for emancipation, those were justifiably hopeful years.[2] They saw the enslaved people of St. Domingue forcibly claiming their liberty and fighting off some of Europe's most powerful armies in order to secure that liberty.[3] They saw one slave power, France, abolish slavery entirely, if temporarily, and they saw two major slaving nations, Great Britain and the United States, outlaw the transatlantic trade in African bodies.[4] Free black leaders recognized the powerful forces arrayed against black liberty, but they believed themselves to be fighting on the side of God—and of history as well.

This optimism developed simultaneously along sacred and secular lines, and writers, speakers, and activists who worked under its influence began to project a collective future for African people. They did not all agree on the nature of that future—whether it lay primarily in the United States, on the coast of Africa, or perhaps someplace else—nor did they share a single definition of themselves as a people. As the new century progressed, however, black leaders in Baltimore and Philadelphia cooperated as leaders of an increasingly coordinated religious movement that gradually assumed de facto leadership of the African church movement throughout the new nation. As this was happening, Paul Cuffe, a black Quaker ship captain and merchant from coastal Massachusetts, decided to devote his final years to social activism and racial uplift. In alliance with self-styled African leaders throughout much of the Northeast, he sought to create and cement commercial and religious ties between blacks in the United States and residents first of Sierra Leone and then of all of western Africa. Cuffe's vision of a rising African people and nation helped galvanize black leaders throughout the United States to deepen their commitment to the advancement of all "Africans."

I

The story of the rise of separate churches among free black people in the North following the American Revolution—especially the rise of the African Methodist Episcopal Church (AME)—is one of the most frequently told in African American history.[5] Events that occurred in Philadelphia between the 1790s and 1820 have overshadowed the process of separation as it occurred in Baltimore, New York, Boston, and other places. The reasons are clear. First, Richard Allen's canonical account of the origins of the separate church movement in Philadelphia became emblematic of the dynamics that fueled the African church movement in different places and within different denominations; second, Philadelphia became the organizational hub of the AME, which emerged, under Allen's leadership, as the most important separate black denomination in antebellum America.[6]

The story begins in the 1770s, when itinerant evangelicals began to make concerted efforts to reach and convert enslaved blacks, especially in the Chesapeake. Richard Allen of Delaware, an early enslaved convert to Methodism, quickly attracted the attention of the most important white leaders of the denomination including bishops Thomas Coke and Francis Asbury.[7] After acquiring his freedom, Allen established his independence by declining Asbury's request that he travel and preach in the South, instead moving to Philadelphia hoping to win souls for Christ and also, presumably, to enjoy the relative freedom that the Quaker city accorded black people. Once there, he joined St. George's Methodist Church, which is probably where he met Absalom Jones, an older man who had also been a slave in Delaware before moving to Philadelphia and gaining freedom. Jones had been converted by old-line Anglicans but had begun worshipping with the Methodists at St. George's after moving to the city.

Jones and Allen soon began working together to organize Philadelphia blacks into the Free African Society, and they helped raise money for improvements to St. George's building. The completion of the new construction precipitated what is probably the most famous incident in early African American religious history. In the fall of 1792, black parishioners entered the expanded church for Sunday services only to be directed toward segregated seating in the new gallery above the main floor. When they went to a different section of the gallery, an usher ordered them to move. The black parishioners were on their knees praying at the time, and when the usher tried to pull Absalom Jones to his feet before he could finish, Jones famously replied, "Wait until the prayer is over, and I will get up, and trouble you no more." When the prayer ended, Jones and Allen led their followers "out of the church in a body," and the white congregation was never again "plagued by" its black former parishioners.[8]

This event initiated the separate church movement in Philadelphia. Most of those who walked out chose to leave the Methodist Church entirely, aligning with Episcopalians to form the St. Thomas African Church. They asked Allen to lead them, but he refused to leave the Methodist Church to serve as their pastor. Absalom Jones also favored the Methodists, but broke that tie for his followers when Bishop William White ordained him America's first black Episcopalian priest. Jones led St. Thomas for the next twenty years, eventually coming to be known as the unofficial "Black Bishop of the

Episcopal Church."[9] Meanwhile, Allen rallied black Methodists and founded the Bethel African Methodist Episcopal Church, becoming the first pastor of a new, separate black congregation within the Methodist Episcopal denomination. Together Jones and Allen assumed leadership of Philadelphia's black community.

On steel by John Sartain, Phil.ª

Rt. Rev. Richard Allen
1st Bishop of the African M. E. Church

Figure 5.1. Portrait of Richard Allen (1760–1831), clergyman, founder of the African Methodist Episcopal Church [National Portrait Gallery, Smithsonian Institution / Art Resource, New York].

Allen's account of the walkout from St. George's was composed years after the event at a time when he was, by his own account, unable to remember "the exact time of many occurrences." His telescoped account has the perhaps unintentional effect of rooting the separate church movement in a straightforward response to an intensifying pattern of white discrimination within St. George's. In fact, as several scholars have noted, Allen and Jones had begun to move toward racially defined religious fellowship at least five years earlier, when they had joined with six other men to create the Free African Society.[10] The Society had taken the form of a mutual aid organization, but only because, as Jones and Allen explained in the preamble to the Society's constitution, a diversity of "religious sentiments" had prevented members from agreeing on a single "religious society" for the "people of their complexion."[11] Allen was eventually expelled from the group he had cofounded for attempting to "sow division among" the membership, a charge that was never explicitly detailed but probably involved efforts to pressure others to transform the benevolent society into a separate church.[12] The dispute over seating in St. George's Methodist Church may only have provided an issue around which Jones and Allen could rally others to leave the white-controlled church in favor of an "African" congregation. During the decade following the walkout, black Philadelphians built two thriving African churches. Allen and the Methodists engaged in increasingly open battles for autonomy from the white denominational hierarchy, eventually winning legal control of their church through a Pennsylvania Supreme Court decision. Bethel and Jones's St. Thomas set a precedent by which "African" churches became centers of black community organization and of antislavery agitation.

The closing of the Atlantic slave trade constituted the first national triumph for antislavery forces in the United States, and African churches throughout the North, including those founded by Jones and Allen, celebrated the victory. The Founding Fathers had, of course, delayed this triumph by prohibiting Congress from regulating the trade during the first twenty years of the new government's existence. As 1808 approached, however, Congress acted swiftly to outlaw the trade. Not surprisingly, blacks in the North, many of whom lived in states that had only recently passed gradual emancipation laws, hailed the end of the slave trade as a great victory worthy of annual public commemoration. Discussing the closing of the slave trade often pushed black orators at these celebrations to consider the relationship of black Americans to Africa and its residents.

Absalom Jones revealed the strong sense of African identity shared by leaders of Philadelphia's separate church movement in the most powerful of the surviving orations marking the closing of the African slave trade, a speech he gave on January 1, 1808, the day the trade was legally ended.[13] Jones offered his remarks in the form of a "Thanksgiving Sermon" on a text from Exodus: "And the Lord said, I have surely seen the affliction of my people, which are in Egypt, and have heard their cry by reason of their task-masters; for I know their sorrows; and I am come down to deliver them out of the land of the Egyptians. Exodus iii: 7, 8." As Jones explicated this text and explained its relevance to the spiritual and secular lives of his listeners, he portrayed the ties that bound his listeners to one another as, at different times, brethren, countrymen, or nation, and he encoded assertions of chosenness in Old Testament citations. He generally portrayed his people as literal kin who shared a common genealogy, though appeals to blacks' shared history of slavery and oppression balanced and softened the portrayal of Africans as a race that was different from others in essential—what we would call genetic—ways.

Jones began by explaining that the passage from Exodus provided an account of what had preceded God's "deliverance of the children of Israel from their captivity and bondage in Egypt." He described affliction in Egypt, invoking the trials experienced by slaves in the United States, and noting that throughout the original affliction, God had remembered his people and heard their cries. Passages from two psalms underscored God's continuing interest in his chosen people following the exodus, leading Jones to interpret the end of the African slave trade as clear evidence that "the God of heaven and earth is *the same, yesterday, and today, and forever*" (emphasis in original).[14]

In the context of God's constancy, Jones introduced the slippery notions of identity that inform the rest of his sermon. Addressing his "brethren," he referred to the "nations from which most of us have descended"—the different peoples in Africa—as well as the "country in which some of us were born," saying that both had been visited by God's mercy. He then appeared to move to a sense of identity that embraced the nations and the people of the diaspora, when he spoke of the "affliction of our countrymen," which included the wars that whites had "fomented among the different tribes of the Africans," the horrors of the Middle Passage, and the abuses suffered by those held in American slavery. Having tied the suffering of black people in Africa and the Americas together through the trials they had shared, Jones returned to the theme of a chosen people. He celebrated the willingness of "Jehovah" to hear his people and to answer their prayers by coming "*down to deliver* our suffering countrymen from the hands of their oppressors." Because God "*came down*" to the United States in 1788—presumably because the Constitution empowered Congress to close the trade—to Great Britain in 1807, and again to the United States in 1807, the "land of our ancestors" would no longer suffer at British or American hands.[15] It is not completely clear in these passages how Jones conceived the relationship among nation, tribe, countrymen, and brethren, but his story of affliction promises to make of these sufferers a single, unified people.

As Jones moved from the narrative of affliction to the duties that "our nation" owed in return for God's favors, the sermon continued to proceed in the language of chosen-ness. He proposed five ways to offer thanks to God. First, his listeners should give daily thanks for all God's blessings, including both their white allies in the fight against slavery and the privilege "of worshipping God . . . in churches of our own." Thanksgiving, however, was not enough: they should also pray to God to complete "his begun goodness to our brethren in Africa" by convincing the rest of Europe's nations to abolish the trade, and they should also ask him to "dispose the hearts of our legislatures" and of masters to "ameliorate the condition of our brethren who are still in bondage." The building image of African identity hits its climax in the third obligation. Each black American must acknowledge "publickly and privately . . . that an African slave, ready to perish, was our father or our grandfather." Though Jones did not spell out a causal link, this acknowledgment might somehow allow a Joseph to "rise up" among black Americans, as the original Joseph had arisen in biblical times. This black Joseph would "be the instrument of feeding the African nations with the bread of life."[16]

This protonationalist appeal balanced the language of separatism with that of interracial cooperation. Jones followed his call for a second Joseph by asking his listeners to "be grateful" to their mostly white "benefactors" who published and fought "against the trade in our countrymen," a formulation that recognized but downplayed the division between benefactors and countrymen. He then charged his brethren with making January 1 an annual day of thanksgiving through which the black community would pass down "the history of the sufferings of our brethren" to the "remotest generations," creating a story that would presumably take its place beside the chronicles of God's earlier and equally inconsistent favor toward his first chosen people.

Jones closed the sermon with a complicated invocation of the special scriptural history of black people and of the equality of all people. He prayed to the "God of all nations," a God who had "*made of one blood all nations of men.*" If, however, blacks clearly shared the same blood as whites, they remained historically different, and different within sacred as well as secular history. He used scripture to suggest that God had issued a new covenant to black people. A standard invocation of Psalm 68—"May *Ethiopia soon stretch out her hands unto thee*, and lay hold of the gracious promise of thy everlasting covenant"—was followed by passages from Isaiah in which God extended the covenant of David to the nation of Israel (Isa. 11:16; 55:13). God would "dispose . . . to act as becomes *a people* who owe so much to thy goodness" (emphasis added). Jones did not stint on thanking white allies or on asking God to bless "our friends and benefactors in Great Britain, as well as in the United States," and he clearly asserted the common origin and essence of all people. Gratitude for white support and assertions of Christian brotherhood and equality were ultimately sub- servient, however, to a call to blacks to become a people.[17] The foundation on which blacks' status as a people rested was historical rather than racial in any essentialist sense: Jones looked to providential action that would call those bound by shared affliction—by affiliation—into being as a divinely sanctioned chosen people. For Jones, it was not blood kinship but some- thing even stronger—God's choice—that would unite Africans as a people in a way that would transcend secular history.

Parallel struggles were taking place at almost the same time in Baltimore, the second major seedbed for the African Methodist movement.[18] Baltimore was a newer city than Philadelphia with much less deeply entrenched old-line churches, and Methodism proved enormously popular among blacks and whites within the growing port. As the four Methodist chapels that served the city during the 1790s became increasingly crowded, and as the egalitarian antislavery spirit of early Methodism waned, black Methodists began to chafe at their subordination within the church.[19] By the end of the eighteenth century, they were meeting in increasingly racially segregated classes, until finally blacks withdrew into a separate congrega- tion that met at the Sharp Street Chapel. There they also founded a school, but white Methodists insisted that whites serve as teachers at the school, as class leaders, and as ministers at the church. Soon a second black chapel, the Asbury African Church, took shape. Black Methodists' ongoing struggles for greater autonomy soon led them to invite Daniel Coker to Baltimore to become the first black teacher at the African school.

Coker, the light-skinned son of a white servant and an enslaved man, had grown up outside of Baltimore. The close companion of his master's son, Coker had accompanied the boy to school, where he acquired a solid elementary education. As a young man, he fled slavery, running to New York where he furthered his education, and rose to some prominence in the city's free black community.[20] He accepted the invitation to return to Baltimore, becoming the first black man to crack the Baltimore church hierarchy's color line when he was appointed a class leader in 1809. Despite qualifications that easily equaled and often exceeded those of many Methodist ministers, including his friend Richard Allen in Philadelphia, he was not permitted to climb any higher up the ecclesiastical ladder.[21]

Rather than accepting this imposed racial ceiling, blacks in Baltimore developed an alternative religious hierarchy. "By 1810 at least seven black lay ministers preached to the city's African Methodists," and in that year Coker published A Dialogue between a Virginian and an African Minister, a pamphlet that he signed not only as a "descendant of Africa," but, implic- itly flouting white authority to define his position, as the "Minister of the

African Methodist Episcopal Church in Baltimore."[22] In that pamphlet Coker offered a ringing defense of the equality of black people and a stinging attack on the injustices of slavery. The form and specific arguments differed from Jones's thanksgiving sermon, but the vision of a rising African church and people was similar.

The *Dialogue* takes place when a fictional Virginia slaveholder wanders into an "African minister's" office to rebut the supposedly "strange opinion" that the legislature should "enact a law, for the emancipation of our slaves."[23] The fictional minister overcomes the slaveholder's attempts to build defenses of the peculiar institution on natural law, practical reality, and biblical sanction, and forces the Virginian to face the gross inhumanity of both the slave trade and the treatment of slaves within the United States. With remarkable ease the minister convinces the Virginian not only that slavery is wrong in the abstract but also that he should return home and set his fifty-five bondsmen free. The pamphlet is a learned compendium of standard early nineteenth-century arguments against slavery that takes the form of a fantasy in which slaveholders could be convinced to free their chattel through a straightforward appeal to justice and reason.

Though Coker trumpeted his African identity on the title page of the pamphlet, he structured the *Dialogue* itself in a way that initially moved Africa into the background. The African minister tries to obscure the role of indigenous Africans in the Atlantic slave trade when he maintains that masters lack legitimate title to their slaves, because that title reached back "many years" to an unspecified moment when people were "by law converted into property." No legislature, he insists, could ever have the right to effect such a conversion. The argument itself is a standard natural rights attack on slavery, but the form that it takes in the dialogue assumes that this generalized slave is a creole—a man enslaved by the laws of an American polity rather than an African-born man enslaved in the Old World.[24]

The Virginian barges through the door that the African minister has opened, pointing out that it was not "the legislature [that] made them slaves . . . for the Africans enslave one another," and whites only purchase people already "reduced to slavery." Given Coker's personal background—the son of a white mother who grew up in heavily creole Maryland before running off to New York while still young—he had probably had little immediate experience with the power of interethnic and intervillage hostility in Africa, but the African minister's answer suggests that he had studied the trade. The minister insists that Europeans encouraged the wars in which "Africans" enslaved one another, and then rewarded the victors. Ultimately, he does not deign to treat these conflicts as true wars: the Africans were "thieves," not warriors, meaning that slave traders were receivers of stolen goods rather than purchasers of legitimately acquired commodities. This

Figure 5.2. Portrait of Daniel Coker from Daniel Alexander Payne, *History of the African Methodist Episcopal Church* (1891).

rhetorical move destroys slaveholders' title to their chattel while casting a different light on African responsibility for the trade. Who, he asks, is more at fault under these circumstances, the "civilized European or the untutored African?"[25] The hapless Virginian concedes the point. Africa and those who live on the continent are portrayed in this exchange as unsophisticated dupes of crafty and greedy Europeans, but their failures are tied to the stage of development at which they live rather than to any inherent quality.

The *Dialogue* takes an important essentialist turn—a sharper turn than Absalom Jones had taken—toward the end. Having seen each of his arguments demolished by the African minister, the Virginian mounts his final barricade by warning that freeing slaves would "lay a foundation for intermarriages, and an unnatural mixture of blood," thus producing a race of "mulattoes." Given Coker's parentage and the nonessentialist tenor of the dialogue up to this point, one might expect the African minister to respond with a sustained defense of equality. He could have called upon biblical precedent by citing the marriage of Moses or the Song of Songs to argue that scripture sanctioned interracial relationships and that all the nations were, indeed, of one blood.[26] Instead, the African minister agrees that increased miscegenation would be an "alarming circumstance" but informs the Virginian that he is mistaken to believe emancipation would have that effect. In a comment brimming with Oedipal undertones, the minister insists that black men who consort with white women are invariably "of the lowest class" and are "despised by their own people." The minister declares that God has "implanted" in blacks and whites a "natural aversion and disgust" for each other, and that it is the perversion of slavery that leads to miscegenation. In explaining the aversion, the minister notes that God placed "different nations at a great distance from each other," suggesting not only that blacks and whites differ from each other in fundamental ways but also that the physical separation of the races is itself part of God's natural order, a comment that anticipates later events in Coker's life.[27]

Sex between black men and white women made many whites nervous, and one might suspect that Coker flirted with this essentialist and filiative story of racial identity as a strategic move to sidestep what he understood to be a false but dangerous attack on emancipation.[28] That may have been part of Coker's intent, but such a reading becomes less plausible as a complete explanation because of the way Coker brought the text to an end. The conversation concludes with the Virginian declaring that he will return home to manumit his slaves, after which the clerk whom the minister has asked to record the conversation ("Mr. C.") advises the minister to have it published. The *Dialogue* does not, however, end when the dialogue, even this second dialogue, ends. A physical break in the page marks a break between recorded fictional conversations and a short exposition describing "what God is doing for Ethiopia's sons in the United States of America." Coker did not rely on fictional ministers or an omniscient narrative voice to tell this story. He turned instead to the unshakable and direct authority of scripture: "But ye are a chosen generation, a royal priesthood, and an holy nation, a peculiar people; that ye should shew forth the praise of him who hath called you out of darkness into his marvelous light: which in time past were not a people, but are now the people of God: which had not obtained mercy, but now have obtained mercy. 1 Peter, ii. 9, 10." There follow lists of "African Ministers who are in Holy Orders," of "African local preachers of the author's acquaintance," and of "African Churches." Coker reported that there were 31,884 "African Methodists in the United States" and concluded the text with a list of "Descendants of the African Race, who have given proofs of talents."[29]

Coker's invocation of a "chosen generation . . . a holy nation, a peculiar people" who were called "out of darkness into his marvelous light" to become "the people of God" is a fairly transparent and striking call to "Ethiopian" members of "African" churches to ascend to their rightful and distinct position.[30] Placing the passage within its biblical context strengthens that sense. The First Epistle of Peter is written from the church at "Babylon" and addressed to "strangers scattered" throughout Asia Minor. Though biblical scholars disagree, it has often been construed to be addressed to Jewish Christians living among Gentile unbelievers, and it calls on them to endure their suffering in return for the promise of eternal reward. The book is not politically radical, at least in any simple sense—it calls on servants to be "subject to your masters with all fear; not only to the good and gentle, but also to the froward."[31] This, however, makes sense, for Coker was not calling on slaves to rebel or on free blacks to contest unjust laws. He was calling blacks out of their false churches and into "African" ones—in short, calling them to become a people. The lists of separate churches, of "African ministers," and the tally of African Methodist congregants provided, in Coker's text, the index to what God was doing for "Ethiopia's sons." He published here a chapter in the emerging book chronicling the rise of an African nation.

It is probably coincidental that Absalom Jones's St. Thomas Episcopal African Church of Philadelphia had earlier posted a shorter excerpt from the same passage in the First Epistle of Peter—"The People That Walked in Darkness Have Seen a Great Light"—on a side wall, but if so, it is a telling coincidence.[32] Throughout his time in Baltimore, Coker worked in tandem with black Philadelphians like Allen and Jones to call forth an "African" church, and he would later belittle the importance of divisions among denominations. Much of the hard evidence of the cooperation between blacks in Baltimore and Philadelphia has either disappeared or has survived in faint traces, but the tone of familiarity in a surviving letter that Allen wrote to Coker shows that they were in frequent contact.[33] Coker, like Allen in Philadelphia, worked quietly behind the scenes to break free of the white Methodists in Baltimore; like Allen he chose Bethel as the name for the independent church he helped build. The name was of a piece with the rhetoric that Jones and Allen had used in the preamble to the constitution of the Free African Society back in the 1780s, and with both Jones's thanksgiving sermon and Coker's 1810 *Dialogue*, for Bethel was more than the "House of God." At Bethel, Jacob had seen the famous ladder to heaven and God had changed Jacob's name to Israel, promising that from him a great people would arise. Allen, Coker, and Jones sought to found more than separate African churches—they sought to call an African people into existence.[34]

II

When Jones and Coker discussed the nature of the slave trade and, in Jones's case, celebrated its closing, they portrayed the ties binding together Africans as God's chosen people in terms that verged on what might be understood as "blood" or filiative kinship. Others who participated in the separate church movement gave speeches that offered softer versions of African racial kinship within frameworks that emphasized the universal brotherhood of all mankind and the purely historical and affiliative ties binding blacks to one another. Jones's thanksgiving sermon notwithstanding, speakers celebrating the end of the slave trade often took this tack when considering the relationship of black Americans to Africa and to those who lived in Africa.[35]

Such considerations often came at the beginning of speeches, as black orators sought to identify themselves and identify with their audiences in order to establish common understanding. While these talks were often given at self-styled African churches, the speakers sometimes distanced themselves from the continent in subtle ways by, for example, signing as "descendants" of Africa if any personal connection to the continent was asserted on the title page. This process of distancing continued in the body of the talks, as speakers differentiated between "Africans and descendants of Africans." One speaker believed his listeners to be so removed from the continent that he began with a geographical "description of the country of our parents" to set the stage for his discussion of the history of its people.[36]

This subtle estrangement from Africa and its residents came through most clearly when speakers incorporated the history of Africa into the story of the slave trade. With remarkable consistency they portrayed Africans as having been something akin to natural man living in prelapsarian innocence prior to the arrival of European traders on the coast, a vision that historian Wilson Jeremiah Moses has strikingly labeled "Afrotopia." One orator, William Hamilton, described the "country of our forefathers" as a "paradise . . . of ease and pleasure." Another, Peter Williams Jr., presented the "state of our forefathers" as one of "simplicity, innocence, and contentment." For Henry Sipkins, Africa in "its primitive state" had been a land of "innocent inhabitants . . . unacquainted with the concerns of a busy life." George Lawrence portrayed residents of "our mother country" as having been a people whose "employments were innocent, neither did they seek evil, contented in the enjoyments of their native sports; they sued not for the blood of their fellow men; they arose in the morning with cheerfulness before their God, and bowed down their heads at night, fully sensible of his goodness." Early Africa was, in these talks, a true garden of earthly delights.[37]

With the arrival of Europeans, however, "the scene changes."[38] White traders introduced greed to stimulate war. They raised "accursed demagogues" above the people and allowed the "baneful deed of avaricious power" to "pierce the hearts of our ancestors." Not only were countless innocent people dragged across the ocean in slavery, but the land itself was pillaged, leaving a vicious wasteland in its place. The crimes done to Africa and its residents by white slave traders in league with European nations and American buyers were inhuman and their effects heartrending. The end of the Atlantic slave trade presumably promised a new era in which such innocence would return, but these speakers spent little time on any projected transformation of life in Africa that might result from the end of the slave trade.[39] This is especially striking given the attention to exactly that question present in so many contemporary black discussions of Africa and African identity. Equiano and Cugoano, arguing for the abolition of the trade in England, had highlighted the transformative effects that "true" religion and legitimate trade would have on the "dark" continent. Prince Hall and members of Newport's African Union Society made similar arguments. The Nova Scotians devoted their lives to initiating just such a transformation. All had foreseen a linked future for blacks throughout the Atlantic Basin. Paul Cuffe was, at this very time, trying to initiate a program to foster progress throughout the black Atlantic. Celebrants of the legal end of the Atlantic trade, however, largely ignored Africa's possible transformation in their talks.

This inattention to Africa's future does not mean that the speakers were either unaware of or hostile to the project of transformation that others were pursuing. Peter Williams Jr.'s "Oration on the Abolition of the Slave Trade" followed this pattern, but Williams himself participated in Cuffe's efforts to effect just such a transformation.[40] That Africa receded in these texts reflects the way in which the logical push and pull of filiative and affiliative senses of kinship played out within black assertions of African identity. Given the central role of white reformers in ending the slave trade, there was good reason for these black orators to downplay deep senses of racial kinship while highlighting universal equality and interracial cooperation. Affiliative narratives of African identity worked well in this context. Speakers moved quickly from stories of Africa's victimization to the horrors of slavery in the Americas, and then to their real subject: the legislative victory over the forces of greed, oppression, and sin. They projected a future in which the implicitly white public would begin to recognize that the apostles of racial inequality were mistaken, in which prominent white allies like Anthony Benezet, Thomas Clarkson, John Jay, Benjamin Rush, and William Wilberforce would multiply and justice would be achieved. They hoped that the Federalists, whom they thought more open to racial equality, would gain electoral victory, and they asked black listeners to remember and honor the white friends—many of them Friends—who had fought against slavery and racial oppression. They called for racial unity within their own communities—for stronger educational and self-help societies and for the rejection of vices of the flesh and an embrace of middle-class respectability. The resulting sense of unity would be built on culture and affiliation rather than on nature, and it would neither preclude nor trump other senses of identity.

The future they hopefully foretold was an American future. African redemption would not require black American emigration. They called on black people to live upright lives that would earn the continuing support of old allies while winning new ones. The logic of this situation led most speakers, however complicated their personal opinions on the nature of racial identity may have been, to present a relatively simple narrative that situated black Americans less in the land of their ancestors than in that of their birth; in this narrative blacks were linked to one another by shared history rather than shared blood.[41]

One must be careful, however, not to imply that the separate church movement embodied a filiative vision of Africanness, while these more secular celebrants of the end of the slave trade offered an affiliative vision. It is more useful to think of two politically complementary impulses motivating black leaders during the first decade of the eighteenth century, each of which inclined advocates to make strategic moves toward one or the other notion of racial kinship. No evidence of antagonism among those articulating the different perspectives has survived. In fact there is no evidence that there were sides—that anyone engaged in this discussion thought that an important difference of opinion was being expressed, at least prior to 1817. All of these speakers and writers advocated the equality of all men. All recognized that Africa, Africans, and black people had been victimized by Europeans and white Americans. All celebrated the end of the Atlantic slave trade. All worked toward the emancipation of enslaved people in the Americas.

Why, then, point out this difference? The difference matters because the persistence of this tension in black discussions of African identity throughout the first fifteen years of the nineteenth century highlights one of the central hurdles faced by black Americans seeking to become African in the face of Africa's ethnic diversity. The richness and internal contradictions within these discussions came together in the efforts of Paul Cuffe to create a transatlantic African nation.

III

Paul Cuffe, a ship captain and merchant from Massachusetts, was the son of an Akan man named Kofi or Cuffe Slocum and a Wampanoag woman named

Ruth Moses Slocum. He had begun fighting for racial justice by 1780, when the twenty-one-year-old and his brother Joseph joined a group of free black men petitioning the Massachusetts government for exemption from taxation; they argued that because blacks could not vote, they should not be taxed. Not surprisingly, their petition was rejected, and after a brief act of civil disobedience, Cuffe and his brother paid their taxes. Within a few years Cuffe had gone to sea, where he proved remarkably able, working his way up from common mariner to ship captain. He invested his earnings in farmland, in a gristmill, and in bigger and better trading vessels. By the late 1790s he had bought a $3,500 waterfront farm and had built and owned all or part of several ships. Cuffe was a member of the Society of Friends, and, like many Quakers, he committed himself to using his resources to help others, especially fellow people of color. He funded a local school that welcomed black and Indian children as well as whites, and he developed a network of family and friends who supported and benefited from his expansive economic endeavors.[42] Cuffe also developed close friendships and partnerships with other Quakers, including Joseph Rotch and William Rotch Jr., two wealthy neighbors who provided access to extensive transatlantic Quaker business contacts.

By the first decade of the nineteenth century, Cuffe, having ensured his own and his extended family's prosperity, decided to expand the scope of his benevolent activity beyond his local community and immediate network of friends.[43] Given his early determination to fight racial injustice and the long-standing interest in African emigration among blacks in Massachusetts and Rhode Island, he surely knew of the settlement in Sierra Leone during the 1790s. Cuffe's interest in and knowledge of the sea, his contacts with Quaker antislavery figures, and his determination to contribute to the welfare of black people combined to steer him toward the colony at Sierra Leone and the possibilities it offered to black Americans. Like earlier contributors to the black discourse on Africa, Cuffe supported missionary activity among natives of Africa, but over time he became less convinced than others that Christian evangelical work could be the prime foundation for Africa's redemption. Commerce, he believed, would serve an even more important role than the emissaries of Christ in integrating African people into the modern world as equals to Europeans and white Americans. By helping able and industrious black Americans move to Sierra Leone and by fostering a new, more benevolent, triangular trade among "civilized" settlements in Africa, Britain, and black communities in American seaboard cities, Cuffe sought to bring the benefits of secular and religious progress to Africa, while simultaneously creating a robust exchange of goods and people that could anchor black mercantile communities—and ultimately black fortunes—in American cities and on the coast of Africa.

Cuffe first began advocating emigration in language reminiscent of those advocating a Christian errand to the Dark Continent, and an evangelical mission to heathen Africa was always part of his design. Responding to a supportive letter from James Pemberton, a Quaker antislavery advocate from Philadelphia, Cuffe declared his commitment to doing all that he could for his "Brethren the afferican Race," and though he doubted his own capacity—he feared that he was too "Wornout in hard Service" to accomplish much—he hoped that God would make him an "Insterment . . . for that Service." He encouraged Pemberton to write him again on the subject while promising never to lose sight of the "Endeavour" to help his brethren. Pemberton responded by telling Cuffe of the African Institution in London,

Figure 5.3. Captain Paul Cuffee silhouette engraving [© Mystic Seaport Collection, Mystic, Conn., #1999.98.1].

a philanthropic organization seeking to bring its vision of civilization, commerce, and improvement to the continent.[44]

Around 1809 Cuffe began to consider a move to Sierra Leone. His initial plans grew out of previous discussions of black emigration to Africa. He wondered whether the "inhabitants of Africa" could become an "enlightened people," and as one "of the African race," he sought to contribute to such a transformation by taking navigational and agricultural tools and moving there with "several families of good credit." He and his fellow immigrants would become catalysts for the introduction of Christianity and civilization to the natives of the coast. His brother summarized the planned trip as "a religious Visit among the Inhabitance of the Land and our nation," suggesting that evangelical and national visions were intertwined from the beginning.[45] Cuffe called on his Quaker connections to the African Institution in London to ensure that he and his fellow travelers would be accorded both friendship and the temporary privileges of British citizenship once they arrived in Sierra Leone.[46]

He received a cautious welcome from his British sponsors. Warned by Zachary Macaulay, by now back in England, of the wisdom of "seeing and minutely inspecting" the colony before committing to a permanent move, Cuffe organized an exploratory commercial venture to Freetown in order to meet company officials, settlers, and Temne leaders, and to determine how best to pursue his dream for racial uplift.[47] During the winter of 1811, after a year and a half of preparation, Cuffe set off on an eighteen-month trip that would take him to Freetown, then London, and back to Sierra Leone before he finally returned to the United States. Macaulay was right that time in the colony would change Cuffe's view of his project, though he was mistaken if he thought Cuffe would abandon it. Cuffe's first African experience pushed him toward the creation of a diasporic commercial African nation.

Cuffe prepared for his encounter with Africa by reading Thomas Clarkson's work on the abolition of the slave trade, a book that, he wrote, "Batized" him in the standard doctrine that had informed the founding of Sierra Leone.[48] Clarkson summarized the early history of the colony as a commercial failure for investors in the Company but as a beacon of hope for Africa. By introducing "schools, places of worship, agriculture, and the habits of civilized life," by creating a "metropolis, consisting of some hundreds of persons, from which may issue the seeds of reformation to this injured continent," by establishing conditions in which "travelers . . . may be sent [to Africa] . . . who may return to it occasionally as to their homes," in all of these ways Clarkson said that the Company had produced a "medium" of "civilization in Africa" that could fuel "a great intercourse between England and Africa, to the benefit of each other."[49] Cuffe would seek to build a diasporic African nation upon that foundation.

Upon arriving in Freetown he did just what one would have expected of a person baptized in Clarkson's doctrine. He met with Company officials, attended an Anglican service with Governor Edward Columbine, and dined at the governor's table. Cuffe and Columbine discussed the state of the slave trade, and Cuffe heard much about the failures of the colony and, no doubt, of the settlers. During his first days in Freetown he also took care of practical matters, like unloading his cargo and beginning to trade, and he went to a court session to witness a captured Portuguese slaver being condemned at law. He then made initial contact with the Nova Scotian settlers by attending a church service led by the Methodist preacher Henry Warren. Cuffe and his crew turned to Nova Scotian settlers to rent housing in Freetown, and their new landlords surely indulged the captain's desire for "much Conversation" by offering their sense of the colony's history and its shortcomings. Their version of Sierra Leone's history surely differed from the one he had heard when dining with Governor Columbine.[50]

By the time Cuffe arrived in Sierra Leone, Parliament had outlawed the Atlantic slave trade, and Great Britain had ordered Royal Navy ships to patrol the African coast in order to interdict the trade. When Navy ships stopped slavers loaded with their human cargo, the slaves were freed and, instead of being returned home, where they had, after all, been enslaved, they were taken to Sierra Leone. Known as "recaptives," these Africans of various ethnic backgrounds had become the largest nonindigenous group (or groups) of settlers living in the colony, but Cuffe evinced little interest in them. He did note in passing that "12 of the Native Captives" were present when he attended a "Methodist Meeting," and he approved of the way that the recaptives had adopted an "English mode of Cloathing." Cuffe may not have known much about the presence of recaptives before he sailed for Africa and may not have thought of them as a separate group that he would need to integrate into his plan.[51] He did, however, arrive at Freetown with a clearly considered plan for winning over the indigenous peoples of Sierra Leone.

On Cuffe's tenth day in Sierra Leone, King Thomas, a Koya Temne leader, visited him in Freetown, and the following day he received an invitation to visit another local leader, King George. He began his civilizing campaign by giving each man several books, including Bibles and a number of religious pamphlets as well as, in one case, a difficult to identify "Essa on Wars." Two of Cuffe's textual gifts, a *Letter from Elizabeth Webb to Anthony William Boehm with His Answer*, which was the only text he gave to both kings, and Stephen Crisp's *A Short History of a Long Travel from Babylon to Bethel*, offered the Temne kings—and later generations—a version of Cuffe's mission. Webb was an early English Quaker, whose *Letter* described her spiritual journey, including a dream in which her spirit was "carried away into

America."[52] She followed this divine call to travel to the Chesapeake in 1697, where she arrived to find "great numbers of black people, that were in slavery." Thinking them "a strange people," Webb wondered whether "the visitation of God was to their souls." God quickly answered her uncertainty through a dream that confirmed that "the call of the Lord was unto the black people as well as the white." Like Webb, Cuffe was called across an ocean to bring God's word to black people whose spiritual "Buckets were frozen," and he intended, like Webb, to bring fresh flowing water to wash their pagan spirits clean in order to provide "Encouragement of the Nations of Afferica."[53] Cuffe reversed Webb's journey from old world to new but hoped that his trip would initiate the kind of spiritual transformation among black people in Africa that evangelical efforts had achieved among black Americans.

Crisp's *Short History* provides another angle on Cuffe's errand to Africa. The protagonist of the *Short History* leaves his father's house in search of the House of God, only to be misled along the way by false preachers. He finally perceives the light, though he intuits its importance before rationally understanding it, and follows it to God's House where, upon stripping himself of his ragged clothes—the last of his earthly possessions—he is welcomed into the divine home. In the final paragraph of his tale, the protagonist casts his search in terms that must have resonated powerfully with Cuffe:

> Now, if any one has a mind to know my name, let them know I had a name
> in my father's country, but in this long and tedious journey have lost it. But
> since I came hither have a new name, but have no characters to signify it
> by, that I can write or they can read. But if any will come where I am, they
> shall know my name: But for farther satisfaction, I was born in Egypt, spiri-
> tually called; and my father went and lived in Babylon. . . . So I . . . sought a
> city, whose builder is God; and now have found it.[54]

Having left his father's house in the slaveholding Egypt of America, Cuffe came to Africa to find the city built by God. With Crisp's *Short History* and Webb's *Letter*, Cuffe introduced himself to the Temne leaders while inviting them to join his project.

Webb's *Letter* is silent about the reception that her offer found among the enslaved in the seventeenth-century Chesapeake, and Cuffe was equally silent about the Temne response. He did note the presence of Muslims among the native traders in Freetown, but he spent the rest of his short stay seeking information from Governor Columbine and spending time in the churches and homes of different Nova Scotians. He also faced increasing hostility from whites in the colony, though either he or someone else purged evidence of that hostility from his logs.[55] Evidence of his growing allegiance to the Nova Scotians was not, however, removed. As his first visit to Sierra Leone drew to a close, he collaborated with John Kizell on a petition to the governor that spoke in the name of the "inhabitants of Sierra Leone." Twelve people, at least eight of whom were Nova Scotians, signed the petition.[56] The petition asked the governor to welcome "all our Breatheren who may Come from the British Colonies or from america," in hopes that they would help to "Cultivate the Land." Cuffe's personal hand showed in the anticipation that new settlers would, like good New Englanders, establish a "whalefishery."

Some of the signers of the petition elaborated on their hopes in an "Epistle" that Cuffe carried back to England, and this letter shows an even greater Nova Scotian influence. The epistle expressed hope that enslaved "Breatheren who Live in Distant Lands" would be freed to enjoy the liberty that "god has granted unto all his faithfull Saints." The signers hoped to receive all their "African Breatheren" when they were delivered from "the yoke of oppression" as their "Forefathers" had been freed when God had brought them "out of Egyptian Bondage." The signatures of James Reed [Reid], Larzas [Lazarus] Jones, Eli Ackim, and, probably, Moses Wilkinson suggest that this call to a chosen people represented, at least for some, an attempt to reconstitute a movement that reflected the Nova Scotians' earlier project. Cuffe's decision to copy these documents into his log, and to transport and arrange for the publication of the epistle, reflect his growing sympathy for the Nova Scotians.

Sympathy, yes, but not uncritical acceptance. Cuffe thought the settlers too prone to idleness, too fond of liquor, and too inclined toward doctrinal dispute. While he admired their religious devotion, he found the Maroons to be more industrious.[57] Each of these faults helped explain the shortcomings of the colony at Sierra Leone, and each would have to be addressed for Freetown to become the hub of the diasporic African nation that Cuffe was beginning to envision. Nonetheless, when Cuffe projected a relationship between the people of Sierra Leone and London or America, it was the devout Nova Scotians, not the Temne, Maroons, or recaptives, whom he had in mind. They would anchor his rising African nation.

What Cuffe found on his visit to Freetown and the people he met there led him to reconsider his plans for Sierra Leone. Just before sailing to London, he wrote to William Allen, the Quaker leader of London's African Institution, summarizing the situation. He described the settlers' petition to the governor, and he noted that they had organized themselves into three Methodist congregations and one Baptist one. The Nova Scotians' attention to "their Devotions" contrasted sharply with the "Littel of Religion" displayed by the natives—Cuffe called them "the Affricans"—some of whom were "adorers of the New Moon," and others "Professors of Mahomet." He began to give up on reaching these people, for when confronted with "doing Rong," they replied that they were "no White men, and their fathers

taught them thus." He never explicitly abandoned his commitment to converting the indigenous peoples of Africa, but neither did he devote much
energy to proselytizing. He had come to doubt that missionary work could
Christianize the heathen in Africa until commercial transformation prepared the way.

As a result, Cuffe began to elaborate a slightly more secular program.
Rather than more of the spirit, the settlers needed to lessen their reliance
on "Spiritual Liquors," and they needed to break the habit of "haveing a
Number of Servents" if they were ever to develop sufficient "industery on
their farmes." Most interestingly, given Cuffe's past, he thought the settlers
should keep their young men at home rather than allowing them to leave
the colony as "Seamen for other people." Oddly, the way to achieve this
goal would be to introduce "Commerce." By opening a "Small intercourse
between America and Sierra Leone," he hoped to bring wholesome families who could help transform the colony into a bustling and prosperous
seaport. These changes would allow Sierra Leone to progress beyond its
status as a fledgling colony at the margins of the British Empire, and as
Freetown grew and developed, opportunities for settlers would appear.
The final goal would be a colony that would achieve its people's destiny by
becoming part of "a Nation to be Numbered among the historians nations
of the World."[58]

At first glance, Cuffe's prescription for Sierra Leone makes little sense.
How would one bring greater diligence to agriculture, less reliance on other
people's labor, and growing temperance by increasing international trade
with the United States? How would an increase in seaborne commerce discourage young men from going to sea while enhancing the stability and
prosperity of the colony? The answers become clear when viewed in light of
life on the ground in Sierra Leone as well as Cuffe's own past. The servants
with whom the settlers liked to surround themselves were probably
enslaved natives or recaptives, so their presence undercut both the colony's
moral basis and its residents' respect for hard work. The "other peopel" for
whom the colony's young men left to "become Seamen" must have been
slavers or merchants servicing the ongoing illegal slave trade. As Cuffe's life
showed, mariners could make good, and if they did so, the broader benefits
of their success would accrue to their home ports. Cuffe's own investments
in land, education, and industry contributed much to the local economy of
coastal Massachusetts, but the successes of the children of Sierra Leone
would contribute nothing to the colony if those children settled elsewhere.
The elevation of an African nation to equality with the great nations of the
West, a process of world historical significance, could only be achieved
when the local economic activity of industrious black people was put to
work in the interests of a black community.

Only by creating firm commercial ties that remained outside the sphere of the slave trade but were firmly anchored in Sierra Leone could "Africans" rise to become a "historians nation." Only by building an African nation that looked away from the corruption of the slaving coast of Africa could civilization be imported and a transformed "African" people arise. Only with an influx of black Americans who retained their commitment to liberty for all people, and their horror at slavery in all of its forms, could Sierra Leone live up to its promise. When Cuffe set off for London to work toward this new vision, he had not lost his religious conviction. He was troubled enough at the sinful nature of what he had seen in Freetown to note with relief, while in transit, that God provided a "Rainbow at Night . . . as a token that the World Should not be Distroyed With a Deluge or overflow of Waters again."[59] Apparently the chosen people were still redeemable, but just as apparently Cuffe had left the coast of Africa needing a sign to reassure him that such was still the case. If, however, Cuffe now knew that he need not build an ark, he still badly needed to build support among the British philanthropists of the African Institution if his plans were to reach fruition.

Winning their support involved a round of meetings with various wealthy and powerful Britons. Cuffe was at first distracted from his mission when a Royal Navy ship impressed the child of a Sierra Leone settler whom Cuffe had taken on as an apprentice, but he turned this potential setback to his advantage by mobilizing prominent abolitionists like William Wilberforce and Thomas Clarkson to win the boy's release. He then began a round of dinners and visits with philanthropists like William Allen, Cornelius Hanbury, William Rathbone, and William Dillwyn. To learn more of the history of the colony at Sierra Leone, he met once with John Clarkson and several times with Zachary Macaulay. At the African Institution, Cuffe gave the Duke of Gloucester "an African Robe a letter Box and a Dagger," objects whose workmanship and elegance were sure to dispel any misconceptions that "the Africans" were inferior. After making his rounds of London's philanthropists who had interests in Africa, and visiting famous sights, Cuffe returned to Liverpool, where he met with former slave traders.[60]

Throughout his stay he sought "the most advantageous Way" to encourage the "improvement of the Colony of Sierra Leone." While in Freetown Cuffe had decided that development required the opening of a "road . . . from England to America and to Sierra Leone" so that black Americans could travel to Africa to see what Sierra Leone had to offer; some would choose to stay and many who did not would forge permanent ties to Africa during their visits. He had ample grounds for optimism as he departed from England. William Allen declared that Cuffe's visit to Freetown had matched his "most sanguine expectations," convincing both him and Thomas Clarkson that "the present opportunity for promoting the civilization of Africa, through the means of Paul Cuffee [*sic*], should not be lost."[61] They promised any aid they could manage, including a temporary trading exemption for his return trip to Freetown.

Buoyed by this exemption and the generous reception he had received among prominent and well-to-do Englishmen, Cuffe returned to Sierra Leone before heading home. The *Traveller* was more than a month in transit between Liverpool and Freetown, a trip that included gales and a harrowing chase by a French war ship.[62] Upon arrival at Freetown, Cuffe spent his first several weeks supervising the unloading of his cargo, the sale of goods to local residents, and the loading of camwood to take back to the United States. Commerce would, after all, play a central role in the redemption of Africa. At the same time, he attended to the religious beliefs of the settlers and, presumably, to the sacred aspects of his vision by worshipping at the settlers' meeting houses and drawing them out about their religious disputes. He did not simply visit churches. On December 12 he paid a house call on "Moses Wilkson [*sic*] the Lame an belind Man who hath been a Long Standing preacher" to the Nova Scotians.[63] By visiting their meeting houses, paying respect to the Nova Scotians' most prominent religious elder, and hearing out the religious disputants without publicly taking sides, Cuffe established himself as a nonpartisan friend to all settlers, a position from which he could rally the Nova Scotians to overcome past disputes and help build his African nation.

This set the stage for his next step toward institutionalizing his plan. He went to James Reid's house to attend a meeting of the settlers' "Social Society," presumably the same group whose "Epistle" he had previously taken to England, and at this meeting they discussed "a Constitution" for what would become Freetown's "Friendly Society."[64] The members spent a week agreeing on the new society's mission, and the mandate they formulated embodied Cuffe's grand hopes. While the practical activities of the group were to focus on fraternal self-help and encouraging economic development, its goals were more expansive. "Every Matter . . . that apeared to be for the Benificial good of the univarse and to the glory of God" was to come within its purview, and a record was to be made of each meeting to "Stand fair to the Representation of the Word for generations to Come."[65] Sierra Leone's Friendly Society would serve as the catalyst for the development of an African people to be counted among the historians' nations, and it would keep records of its actions to ensure that future historians would be able to reconstruct the story of that nation's rise and progress. Commitment to such record keeping had numerous probable sources, from the importance of the Bible as a record of God's people, to the care with which Quaker meetings kept their monthly and quarterly meeting records, to the contemporary vogue for histories of the American Revolution. It underscores the self-consciously historical nature of Cuffe's nationalist vision, and the characteristic blend of Christianity and Enlightenment thought in his project to create an African people.

Cuffe spent his remaining two months looking after practical details while offering guidance to the Friendly Society. He bought a house at auction to serve as a permanent base in Freetown, and signed over his power of attorney to Dave Edmonds, the Nova Scotian who had become his most trusted friend in the colony, so that his interests could be protected while he was away. He explored the countryside to judge the potential of the land for agriculture or other economic pursuits. He also got a firsthand view of the precarious place of black settlers within the British Empire when the colonial government threatened them with the forfeiture of their "Houses and Loots of Land," if they persisted in their refusal to sign the loyalty oaths to the Crown that settlers feared would oblige them to muster as a militia and become "Subject to the Commanding officer."[66] Rumors that "the Natives Was Coming to Invaid" kept Cuffe awake one night, suggesting that the uncertainty he had taken from his initial meetings with the Temne kings had been intensified by settler stories.[67] He also betrayed anxiety about how the Friendly Society would do in his absence. Frustrated during one meeting, Cuffe complained that there "a peared to be more Debateing then Business Done," and he pointedly sent "8 books to James Reed on the abolishing the Slave trade," perhaps reflecting concern over the settlers' commitment to the cause. Nonetheless, when he used his journal to exhort the settlers in the first person—"if We in Sierra Leone would Rouse our Selves to more industery and Sobriety We Certenly Would . . . make the Better progress"—there could be no doubt about where he had cast his lot.[68] In February 1812 he left Freetown for the United States in order to build the third leg on which his African vision would stand.

Cuffe was no hypocrite. Just as he exhorted the Friendly Society to keep records for "generations to come," so too did he carefully preserve a record of his own efforts to create an African people.[69] This impulse to record the rising nation has resonance with Daniel Coker's contemporaneous effort to record what God was doing for the sons of Ethiopia who were stranded in the Egypt of America, and with the slightly earlier efforts of Prince Hall to preserve and pass on the history of his struggle for self-determination. When Cuffe returned to the United States, he would commit the rest of his life to bringing these and other groups together behind his plan to create an African people and a diasporic African nation.

6

African Churches and an African Nation

*Paul Cuffe, the African Methodist Episcopal Church,
and the American Colonization Society*

Cuffe's attempt to build an African nation hit a major roadblock upon his return to the United States. He arrived home in April 1812 to find that trade with Great Britain had been prohibited, so the goods that he had brought from Sierra Leone could not be unloaded. This hindrance could be dealt with, but within two months Congress declared war, creating what became an insurmountable if temporary barrier to the development of cooperative commercial ventures involving residents of the United States, England, and Sierra Leone. The War of 1812 prevented Cuffe from organizing a quick return to the coast of Africa, but it could not stop him from pursuing his vision. Confined to the United States for three years, he began organizing black Americans who expressed interest in moving to Africa and started to seek and win the support of prominent whites for black emigration. Indeed, Cuffe became a minor American celebrity, using his fame to create an embryonic institutional base in the United States for his projected African nation.

Cuffe benefited from being able to work with and through black institutions like African churches that already existed in most towns and cities throughout the northern United States. During the second decade of the 1800s, as Cuffe won the support of ministers of African churches in Baltimore, Philadelphia, New York, Boston, and other towns, the African Methodist churches of Baltimore and Philadelphia broke their ties with the established Methodist Episcopal Church and founded the African Methodist Episcopal Church (AME). Neither Cuffe nor the leaders of the AME ever resolved the ambivalence toward and about Africa that characterized the expressions of African identity discussed in preceding chapters. That ambivalence, however, was not debilitating. If Africa sometimes appeared as a dark and pagan continent in need of salvation and at others as an earthly Eden victimized by white slave traders, God persistently called on the peoples of its diaspora to participate in its redemption. Whether these peoples were linked to one another through literal kinship and "blood," or through a shared history of oppression at the hands of Europeans, or through the intermediate bond—something more than affiliative, but not exactly filiative—created in sacred or mythic history, they needed to rise up and become *an* African people. By participating in this millennial struggle, "Africans" would achieve individual salvation and collective self-determination.

Believers in this simultaneously sacred and secular mission saw promising signs that God favored their cause and was shepherding it to fruition during the first fifteen years of the new century. The emergence of a robust independent African denomination whose leaders supported Paul Cuffe's nationalist vision pointed toward an African diasporic movement of increasing power and sophistication within African America and perhaps among other peoples of Africa's diaspora. The remarkable economic success of Cuffe in Massachusetts and of James Forten, the Philadelphia sailmaker, heralded a rising black middle class that would share the commitment to racial uplift exhibited by those two worthies. To some black Americans, including Cuffe himself, the foundation of the American Colonization Society (ACS) in 1816 promised the possibility of elite white support for key aspects of this nationalist movement, support that would eliminate concerns about financing black migration to Africa and allow the rapid expansion of what had been a lone ship captain's mission. This optimism would prove to have been mistaken. Although at least one group of black emigrants would move to Africa under the aegis of the ACS in the hope of bending the organization to support Cuffe's vision, that expedition would prove to be anything but inspiring. Black American assertions of African identity had been growing increasingly popular and sophisticated since the 1780s, but the tide of the movement would turn and recede rapidly after 1820.

I

The first challenge that Cuffe faced upon his return to the United States was getting permission to land the goods that he had brought from Sierra Leone. The trials he faced in gaining this permission contributed to his fame and thus, ironically, to what he sought to accomplish. When he discovered that "the imbargo [was] inforce and ... unimportation [was] on," he began seeking an exemption from those regulations. He petitioned the government, called on prominent friends for letters of recommendation, and went to Washington by way of Providence, New York, Philadelphia, and Baltimore. In each city he stayed with friends and began to lay the groundwork for his plans.[1] In Washington he cemented his status as the new nation's most prominent man of color by securing private meetings with President James Madison, Secretary of the Treasury Albert Gallatin, and Secretary of State James Monroe, all of whom received him with kindness. They restored all of his seized cargo "With out Reserve," and promised to do all that the Constitution would allow them to do to "Premote the Good Cause." It was a cause that Jeffersonians, especially from Virginia, could readily support because of their fantasies that blacks might be removed from the state.[2] Cuffe's seeming misfortune in running afoul of American commercial regulations had, notwithstanding the inconvenience of his unplanned trip to Washington, become a tremendous boon, for, in the process of winning the release of his goods, he gained national publicity and the endorsement of the nation's most prominent public officials. He achieved this celebrity among white Americans without doing anything to jeopardize his standing with blacks.

Cuffe and an unidentified supporter capitalized by rushing into print *A Brief Account of the Settlement and Present situation of the Colony of Sierra Leone in Africa*, an opening salvo in his public campaign to build a movement in the United States. This short pamphlet provided a brief overview of the colony's geography and population, reproduced the settlers' 1811 petition asking the governor to welcome black American immigrants, and then summarized the state of education and government in the colony. It closed with an address that Cuffe had written to his "scattered brethren and fellow Country men at Sierra Leone" and with the 1811 "Epistle" that the settlers had asked him to deliver to London.[3] In this way Cuffe marketed his vision of Sierra Leone's promise and his sense of the settlers' eagerness for black American emigration to the American reading public.

The "Address" was the most anomalous and substantive part of the *Brief Account*. The pamphlet offered no reason for including this address to Sierra Leoneans in a pamphlet published in the United States, nor did it provide an introduction to the piece, but readers familiar with the emerging black discourse on Africa probably did not need much introduction. Cuffe's address fell firmly into the tradition that linked Wheatley, Equiano, Absalom Jones, and Prince Hall while presenting the Christian framework within which Cuffe located his secular program for racial uplift. In the opening salutation, he declared kinship with his "fellow countrymen" in the colony, but it was kinship of a specific kind. They were his "scattered kinsmen," and given a later invocation of Psalm 68 in the address, the terminology can hardly have been accidental. In the verse preceding the psalmist's prediction that "princes shall come out of Egypt; Ethiopia shall soon stretch out her hands unto God," the Lord is called upon to "scatter . . . the people *that* delight in war" (Ps. 68:30–31). Wars in Africa had fueled the slave trade and continued to do so in 1812, and it was those very wars that had scattered Cuffe's Africans—a chosen people who had delighted in war had been punished with bondage and exile.[4] With this scriptural warning that the scattering would continue unless the wars stopped, the chosen people's self-appointed prophet of return offered a prayer and exhorted his followers to worship god. He also called on them to meet together each month in pursuit of "mutual good," and, in a slightly altered echo of the advice that he had given to the Friendly Society meeting in Freetown, to "keep a record of your proceedings . . . for the benefit of the young and rising generation," a new book to inspire God's new chosen nation.

How could aspiring Africans bring this nation into being? Should the brethren follow these injunctions, should they pursue God's spirit, then, the prophetic voice promised, they would "increase both [their] temporal and spiritual welfare." This combination of the worldly and the sacred served as a transition to three pieces of more secular "Advice" that were appended to the "Address." Cuffe's followers were to exhibit "sobriety and steadfastness"; they were to encourage the young to be "industrious" while steering them away from "swearing . . . bad company . . . spirituous liquors" and "idleness"; and they were to prepare the minds of their "servants"—recaptives and native apprentices—"for the reception of the good seed, which is promised to all that will seek after it." By being faithful in all things, the brethren could "become a people" and repay the confidence of the patrons who had struggled to liberate them "from a state of slavery." Faith would lay the groundwork for the creation of a nation of the chosen, but it must be accompanied by temperance, industry, and a willingness to respect and proselytize, rather than simply to exploit, native servants. Progress would not come without faith, but neither would it come without practical work in the real world.

As he was putting these views before the public, Cuffe began organizing voluntary societies in port cities to serve as African American—given his plan, the term is not anachronistic—allies of the Friendly Society and as nodes in a mostly black Atlantic commercial system. He traveled overland from Washington to New York, stopping to talk with the "peopel of colour" in each major town about the best "mode to aid Africa." He discussed the project with Daniel Coker in Baltimore, and with Absalom Jones and James Forten in Philadelphia, asking them to form voluntary organizations devoted to his African cause. In New York he called forth "the Africans" to meet at "the African School House," and convinced them that "there Should be a Society imbodied uniting With that of Philadelphia [and] Baltimore" to promote the good of "Africa of which Sierra Leone at present

Semes to be the principel Established colony." By June 1812, he could tell William Allen, his British patron, that the "people of Couller" of each of those cities had decided to form "a Socity to communitycate with Each other and . . . with the African Institution [of London] and with the Friendly Society at Sierra Leone."[5]

Having organized this rudimentary structure, Cuffe would have liked to have begun immediately to deepen the commercial and demographic ties between the United States and Sierra Leone, but the War of 1812 complicated his plan. At first, he sought to work around the war by seeking official permission to trade with the enemy's colony. He pursued the goal through back channels, by approaching a friend of Dolley Madison's, and more directly by petitioning Congress.[6] When his attempt to circumvent the war failed, and he realized that direct commercial ties with Sierra Leone would be difficult or impossible until peace returned, he concentrated instead on strengthening the African Societies that had been founded in the United States, and on deepening the ties among those societies. This work entailed maintaining a steady correspondence with his allies throughout America, writing encouraging letters to the Friendly Society that kept Freetown apprised of his long-term plans to return with new settlers, and writing to William Allen in London to ensure the continuing support of the African Institution's British philanthropists.[7]

One function of the American African Societies that Cuffe helped organize was to screen and recruit people of good character who might want to travel to Sierra Leone, but Cuffe became convinced that he could not rely on the free black populations of northern cities alone for the emigrants needed to stimulate Freetown's development. Plantation crops appeared to offer the most promise in Sierra Leone, so Cuffe turned southward, contacting Christopher McPherson, a prominent free black man from Virginia, and the white Maryland Quaker Elisha Tyson, to offer passage to Freetown for "people of Coular of good caractors" who "understood farming in Rice, tobacco, Cotton [or] Coffee." He sought other skills from other places, turning to Maine in search of a "Schoolmaster" and "a Congregational minister and a professor of the wanted languages." At one point, Prince Saunders, who would later gain prominence for his educational missions to Haiti, expressed a desire to visit and perhaps move to Sierra Leone.[8] A sizeable and diverse group of black Americans showed interest in joining what would be the first expedition allowed to sail to Sierra Leone when peace returned between the United States and England.

Such an expedition would have required greater carrying capacity than Cuffe could offer—the only ship that he could use was his seventy-foot brig the *Traveller*, which was not a passenger ship. Cuffe could not afford to buy a larger ship alone, so he solicited free black northern investors to finance the building of "a Vessell of a bout 200 tons for an African trader" that would keep "open an intercourse between the united States [and] africa" to the "profit and mutual advantage" of investors, settlers, and American merchants. When few expressed willingness to invest in this plan—Prince Saunders explained that such an "enterprise" was too "new to most of the people of colour" to gain support—Cuffe turned to British philanthropists in search of funds for the large expedition that he anticipated launching, but they, too, proved less helpful than he had hoped. If this lack of commitment discouraged Cuffe—and it is hard to believe that it did not—his letters rarely show it. Instead he accepted the constraints within which he had to work and pursued his vision.[9]

When the Treaty of Ghent ended the War of 1812, Cuffe organized a return trip to Sierra Leone on the *Traveller*. A flurry of letters went out to various correspondents in the United States and England, and he began fielding requests from black Northerners who wanted to join the approaching expedition. He got vague assurances of limited financial aid from London but these were conditioned on a relatively small group of emigrants, and his frustration flashed occasionally when various groups failed to deliver the monetary support that they had promised. Nonetheless, Cuffe committed to take several of the passengers "Even if . . . at my own exspence," and advised all emigrants to be able to "stand on their own ground," and to count any aid provided by the African Institution of London as a bonus.[10] In relatively short order he lined up a crew and a group of forty emigrants—thirty-two from Boston, four from Philadelphia, and two each from New York and Newport—and set sail for Freetown at the end of 1815.

They arrived in February 1816, and Cuffe stayed just two months, trading with the merchants and settlers, delivering his passengers to their new homes, and then returning to New York with a cargo of African goods. The families he took to Africa were laborers who sought to farm what they probably expected would be lush tropical land. Most set up around Freetown, taking charge of land owned by the governor or by one of the old settlers, while some cleared their own land. One man, Anthony Servance, had been born in the Congo, sold into St. Domingue before the Revolution, and hoped to return to his homeland from Sierra Leone. He decided instead to take up with a group of recaptured slaves who had been brought to Freetown—in Cuffe's words he went "a little outside of Sierra Leone" in order "to farm with the Congo people as he is one of the nation." By April, satisfied that those he had brought across the Atlantic were settled, Cuffe loaded *Traveller* with African produce and sailed back to New York City.

In the years separating Cuffe's two visits to Sierra Leone, he had developed an increasingly elaborate vision of the rise of an African people. Parts of that vision remain ambiguous because Cuffe never sat down to write a theoretical and consistent blueprint. Instead, his designs for an African nation emerged out of the actions he took in its behalf and the letters he regularly wrote in support of those designs. He was clear on several occasions that he wanted Africans to embark of a project of "National advancement" in order to join "the historian nations," but he used the word *nation* in various ways at different times. Sometimes *nation* could be synonymous with race, as in his insistence to a philanthropist that he sought the "advancement of [his] nation (Viz) the oppresed Africans," or when he told a minister of his gratitude for those selfless people who struggled in the "Cause of [his] nation the African race."[11] At other times *nation* took on a much more specific geographical meaning more in line with conventional meanings of the nation as they developed out of the nineteenth-century West. This connotation became most clear in a letter that he wrote to his friend, Cato Sawyer, in which he described the benefits that would accrue to Africans from settling Sierra Leone. Those who moved there "in order to moralize and fraternize the inhabitance of Africa" would acquire one of the greatest benefits imaginable—these black people would escape the constrained possibilities of America by traveling to the "contry of their origian," and in this new land their children would "become a nation capabul" of having its own national legislature.[12]

This sense of possibility lies beneath Cuffe's nationalist vision and brings together its different strands of thought. His African nation was a process and his goal was to move the process toward an imperfectly understood and thus vaguely defined endpoint. Unlike many participants in the black discourse on Africa, Cuffe's endpoint does not seem to have been defined in explicitly millennial terms. He neither foretold the moment when God would bring justice to the earth, nor warned of divine retribution in the event of failure. He was a Quaker, not a Calvinist Huntingdonian. As a Quaker, he worked to bring an African people into being, so that they could participate in the expansion of liberty through commerce and self-determination. Members of Freetown's Friendly Society must devote themselves to "Commercial per Suites," for commerce would be "the Great out let" through which Sierra Leone would advance "among the historian nations." Such an advance, he told the Friendly Society, would be "the means of improving both your country and nation."[13]

Their "country," or nation-state, was almost surely going to be the Sierra Leone that he foresaw emerging from colonial dependence as an autonomous black polity. It would serve as the crucial base from which blacks would become independent merchants, navigators, and finally legislators, a base from which the next generation of black children would disprove assertions that "people of coulour are not caperable of business," by showing that they could perform "upon a level with our neighbours the white Brother."[14] By "nation," on the other hand, he meant something much grander if less concrete, something that formed the crux of his project to bring his "Brethren the afferican Race" together in a historian's nation.[15]

The scattered brethren would come together as a diasporic nation by forging ties across the Atlantic that would stimulate black enterprise in America and on the coast of Africa. Sierra Leone was a crucial node in this network, for it was the "Country in which this Peopel Might rise to be a Peopel," but only gradually, if ever, would it become the single home of the nation.[16] He was, in fact, comfortable with the prospect of two colonies— ultimately recommending that the one in Sierra Leone be supplemented with one in the southwestern territories of the United States to provide potential homes for freed American slaves who did not want to move to Africa.[17] Two things mattered: a place where freed slaves could live in societies controlled by black people, and the creation of a commercial network "between America and Africa and between England and Africa," which would bring back together people separated by slavery and the history of warfare that had prevented them from rising into the community of nations. It was in light of this goal that one must read his hope that "A mercantile Line of business" could be established from "The United States to Africa."[18] A century before Marcus Garvey sought to build an independent steamship line to transport people, goods, and ideas to and from Africa, Paul Cuffe promoted the commercial development that he thought a necessary precondition before all the "Sons and daughters of the race of Africa" would be able to "Stretch forth their arms to God."[19]

By the time Cuffe had returned from his second trip to Sierra Leone, he had become the most famous black man in America and a powerful spokesperson for colonizing black Americans in Africa. His circle of correspondents included the most prominent leaders among free blacks from Richmond to Boston. The best indicator of his fame may be that a confidence man tried to profit from it. In January 1817 "an African pretending to be the son of the celebrated Paul Cuffee [sic]" showed up in York, Pennsylvania, where he was "entertained by members of the society of friends." The imposter claimed to be "on his way to Congress, for the purpose of soliciting aid" for his colonizing project. "He said he had been seven voyages to Africa, and had been the first man that put a yoke on a pair of oxen in Sierra Leon."[20] The imposter was found out, but the story underscores Cuffe's prominence and the degree to which his celebrity was linked to his "civilizing" voyages to Freetown.

The broad enthusiasm that greeted Cuffe's return from what turned out to be his final voyage to Africa created tremendous momentum behind the early black emigrationist movement. This growing enthusiasm for emigration occurred at a crucial moment in the separate church movement.

Around 1815 Richard Allen in Philadelphia and Daniel Coker in Baltimore allied to bring their struggle against white dominance within the Methodist Church to fruition, by seceding from the parent organization to form a new denomination—the African Methodist Episcopal Church. The AME quickly became a model and inspiration for other African churches seeking ecclesiastical independence.

The separation of what became the AME denomination was the culmination of an ongoing struggle that had begun with the walkouts during the 1790s. Black congregants had always carried the burden of building and supporting their African churches, and they chafed at white Methodists' attempts to exert denominational control, especially as the Methodist order retreated from its early antislavery stands.[21] Members of the two Bethel congregations risked an extraordinary amount of money—more than $10,000 each—to establish or maintain ownership of their church buildings, an indication of how determined they were first to win and then to maintain their independence.[22] Coker and the African Methodists of Baltimore worked secretly to break away from the city's two black Methodist congregations—Sharp Street Church and Asbury African Church—and founded their Bethel Church in 1815. Most of the internal discussions and maneuvering involved in these breaks is unrecoverable, but traces have survived that hint at what Allen and Coker envisioned for the separate denomination they cooperated to found.

The final open break was precipitated when white Methodists in Philadelphia sought to reassert authority over Allen's parishioners by establishing the denomination's ownership of the church building that the congregation had built. Several succeeding presiding elders at St. George's Methodist Church—the church from which Richard Allen and Absalom Jones had walked out in 1792—claimed the right to preach at Bethel without an invitation from the congregation. They convinced a dissident member of Bethel's congregation to join them in a lawsuit asking the state to grant the Methodists ownership of Bethel. In January 1816, the Pennsylvania Supreme Court rejected the last legal assault by the St. George's hierarchy, and Bethel secured its legal independence.[23]

When news of the victory reached Daniel Coker, he delivered a sermon at Baltimore's "African" Bethel Church that hailed his allies' victory in Philadelphia.[24] The brief surviving extract of that sermon indicates that Coker and Allen had already decided on a formal break with the Methodist hierarchy. Coker compared the Methodist conference's control over the Bethel congregations to that of the Babylonians' enslavement of the ancient Jews and charged white Methodists with hypocrisy for claiming to look forward to the day when "Ethiopia might stretch out her hands unto God," but insisting that "the time" had "not yet come" whenever their black parishioners

BETHEL AFRICAN METHODIST EPISCOPAL CHURCH, PHILAD?

Figure 6.1. An 1829 engraving of Mother Bethel Church in Philadelphia, whose congregants' victory in an 1816 Pennsylvania Supreme Court case guaranteed their ownership of the church and helped stimulate the creation of the African Methodist Episcopal Church as an independent denomination (by William L. Breton; original in Library Company of Philadephia).

sought to make the psalm's prophecy come true. Coker underscored the unity of the Baltimore and Philadelphia movements by providing a list of ministers "belonging to the *African Bethel Church*, who have withdrawn from under the charge of the Methodist Bishops and Conference, but are still Methodists." Among these ministers of a single church—"the *African Bethel Church*"—he listed four Philadelphians (Allen, James Champin [usually Champion], Jacob Tapsico, and Jeffrey Bulah) and seven Baltimoreans (himself, Richard Williams, Henry Harden, Abner Coker, Charles Pierce, James Towson, and James Coal). Coker publicly announced the existence of an ecclesiastically independent African Methodist movement before any conference met to institute a new denomination.

Coker almost certainly sent a copy of the sermon to Allen, for less than a month later Allen thanked him for the "kind letter" that included the "hymn that was composed on the victory of Bethel Church."[25] Allen recounted some details leading to the Pennsylvania Supreme Court's validation of his congregation's ownership of its church, made reference to a black Baltimore Methodist who did not join Coker when he seceded from Sharp Street, and authorized the Baltimore minister to "read this letter in your Church as often as you think proper."[26] The hymn that Coker or one of his parishioners composed to celebrate Allen's triumph hailed the "God of Bethel," who had "stopp'd the proud oppressor's frown" and saved that "helpless Church." Just two months later, in April of 1816, Coker and Allen brought their followers together in Philadelphia to formalize the merger between the two Bethel congregations and to create a new denomination.

No minutes were kept at the conference that founded the AME, so accounts of that first meeting rely on inconsistent oral traditions and reminiscences. Richard Allen emerged as the first bishop of the church, though Coker actually won the initial ballot before stepping aside—some suggest that he was pushed—perhaps in response to objections that he was too light-skinned to head an "African connexion."[27] The absence of records from the convention make it impossible to know exactly what these founding fathers of the AME said at the first convention regarding the peoples of Africa or the rise of African people in the United States. Their prior support for Cuffe's emigrationist plans, their roles in the Baltimore and Philadelphia African Societies, and the rhetoric of Daniel Coker's publications all strongly suggest, however, that they perceived their two Bethel congregations, as well as other churches that joined them, to be a part of a single Bethel church, a single church out of which God would raise a chosen people to found a great nation. There seems good reason, in fact, that those who were, at that very time, laying the groundwork for the American Colonization Society, would have welcomed the separation of the AME. An "African" denomination led by prominent supporters of Paul Cuffe might reasonably have been thought to form the ideal organizational base within the black community for a white-supported colony of blacks "returning" to West Africa.

Had the American Colonization Society been willing to accept a role supporting the preexisting black leadership of this diasporic movement, or had it never come into existence, then perhaps the movement Cuffe did so much to create would have had promising prospects in 1816. By linking black Americans' political aspirations to participation in commercial ventures rooted in northern black communities but supported by wealthy British antislavery interests, it offered a path toward activism that would have tied the struggle against Atlantic slavery to the emergence of black mercantile interests in the United States. Because Cuffe's plan envisioned the emergence of African American polities in Africa rather than black participation in American polities, it accorded with many whites' hopes for a whiter nation and thus won broad support from prominent political leaders. Things looked very bright for advocates of African identity and emigration in 1816.

The promising future soon disappeared. In 1816 prominent whites formed the "American Society for Colonizing the Free People of Color in the United States" (later the American Colonization Society, or ACS); it was not an organization inclined to follow the leadership of "African" ministers and activists.[28] The ACS sought to build on black emigrationist movements and to win Paul Cuffe's endorsement in order to convince free black Americans to emigrate from the United States to a planned colony on the coast of Africa. White colonizationists, assuming that the organization's goals complemented those of black emigrationists, thought that everyone could work together to build and people a colony in West Africa. Cuffe and a number of his elite black supporters—Richard Allen, James Forten, Daniel Coker—were initially open to a working relationship with the ACS, but immediate opposition among less elite free blacks would eventually be fortified by growing suspicions that the Colonization Society was a tool of southern slaveholders. These well-founded suspicions would galvanize black opposition to the Society in a way that undercut the political and social utility of assertions of African identity in the eyes of most black Americans.

II

The period between 1816 and 1821 constitutes a crucial turning point in the development of a black discourse on African identity in the United States. Prior to 1815, texts and speeches asserting either a deep, filiative kinship among the peoples of Africa and the diaspora, or an almost equally deep mythic or sacred link, were becoming increasingly common, and the attempt to explain this deep kinship inspired greater intellectual creativity than did the ever-present and equally important but more derivative affil-iative narratives of identity. Paul Cuffe's campaign to build a transatlantic African commercial nation had attracted the most important leaders of independent black churches in the northern and border states. Those lead-ers had then pursued agendas centered on creating (or re-creating) an African people within their churches and local communities, just as they did in their dealings with Cuffe, and as we can assume they did in their lost correspondence with the Friendly Society of Freetown, Sierra Leone. The ACS changed all that.

Just eight months after representatives of African Methodist congrega-tions met in Philadelphia to found the AME, a different group met in the nation's capital. On December 16, 1816, an impressive array of white America's political and cultural leadership came together to found the

ACS.[29] The Colonization Society included many luminaries—Henry Clay, Bushrod Washington, Andrew Jackson, and John Randolph of Roanoke, to mention just a few—but the less famous Robert Finley was one of the driving forces in the movement at its beginning. Finley had written to Paul Cuffe before the inaugural meeting in Washington, seeking advice about Africa and the best place to plant a new colony, and soliciting Cuffe's support. Cuffe encouraged Finley in his "great and laborious task" and wrote enthusiastically to his friend James Forten about the concern being shown "at the seat of Government, for the wellfare of the People of Colour." Cuffe encouraged Finley to work with "the African Instertutions in Philadelphia, New York &c."[30] At first glance, everything seemed to be falling into place for a cooperative effort between white and black Americans to found, people, and support a West African colony of free black people from the United States.

To the surprise of many, broad-based black opposition to the Society arose almost instantaneously. Within a month of the organizational meeting in Washington, free black people in Richmond, Virginia, Georgetown, District of Columbia, and, most famously, Philadelphia had organized meetings that publicly rejected colonization on the coast of Africa. In Philadelphia a huge group—reportedly 3,000 men, or more than a quarter of the total black population of the city—packed Bethel Church, and effectively repudiated their leadership's openness to the Colonization project. Local businessman and community leader James Forten chaired the meeting and signed its resolutions rejecting the "stigma" cast upon free persons of color by the Colonization society and pledging never to forget the "ties of consanguinity, of suffering, and of wrong"—ties of both blood and a shared history of oppression—that connected black Philadelphians to their enslaved brethren in the South. Those in attendance unanimously declined to be "cast into the savage wilds of Africa," seeing emigration neither as a return home nor as an exodus to a promised land, but as "exile . . . from the land of [their] nativity." Scholars have noted that while Forten and Allen were taken by surprise, they accepted the popular will and represented it forcefully.[31]

Black Philadelphians' famous repudiation of colonization became a rallying point for black protest throughout the antebellum years, but blacks in Richmond and Georgetown issued more measured rejections. Neither group wanted, in the words of black Richmonders, to be "exiled to a foreign country," but both claimed to appreciate the benefits of being "colonized"; they sought instead a colony within the limits of the United States.[32] Such a possibility had occurred to Cuffe, who, realizing that many black Americans would be loath to relocate to Africa, had suggested two colonies—one on the west coast of the Old World and one at the western edge of white settlement in the New. Georgetown delegates' portrayal of the historical significance of the colonization process also echoed Cuffe. Henry Adams chaired the meeting and asked Christopher McPherson, the secretary and a correspondent of Cuffe's, to keep a record of all that took place in and as a result of the meeting for the group's archives. Compiling such an archive constituted, Adams asserted, a crucial step in forming the people of color into a "body politic." Speaking from the national capital, these black men sought to create a "universal association throughout the" country with a semiecclesiastical body of officers.[33] If we assume that blacks in Georgetown shared black Philadelphians' fears that the ACS sought to help "the slave holders . . . get rid of" free blacks in order to make slave "property more secure," then their attempt to build a national organization and a black "body politic" may have represented an effort to save the heart of Cuffe's project from the control of the Colonization Society, or, at the very least, from the control of its proslavery members.[34] Doing so entailed turning away from Cuffe's commitment to the continent of Africa and the peoples who lived there, at least in the short run.

White colonizationists tried to convince black leaders that fears of deportation and perceptions of the ACS as a tool of slaveholders were mistaken. They had limited success, in part because whatever the true goals of the Colonization Society—and even more than most large and complex organizations, it included members with divergent visions—the Society's programs did, indeed, work to strengthen slavery in the United States. By the 1830s, black Americans became increasingly unwilling to express a sense of kinship with Africa or Africans, and an insistence on American identity came to dominate much black rhetoric. The commitment to Africa and Africanness that had grown from the time of Phillis Wheatley, however, did not disappear. In 1820 the ACS sent out its first group of black emigrants to Africa, a group that included Daniel Coker, and the troubled course of that expedition suggests that some black Americans continued to envision a future in which an African people would rise on the continent and among the people of the diaspora to assert or reassert its place among the great peoples of the world.

III

Black people's skepticism toward the ACS had come as a surprise to white supporters of the movement, but they believed that they could overcome it by demonstrating the benefits of colonization, and the supposedly benevolent aims of the organization gained some credence because those who devoted their time and energy to the Society were often evangelical Christians who abhorred slavery. They hoped to offer American blacks a haven from white racism while simultaneously creating a beachhead for the Christian conversion of all of Africa. While they never embraced—almost certainly never conceived of—the nationalist aspects of Cuffe's emigrationist program, the goals they pursued were consonant with his. Toward the end of 1817 two such men, Samuel Mills and Ebenezer Burgess, gathered as much information as they could from Cuffe and others in the United States and then set off to scout out the best place to plant a new colony in Africa.[35]

Burgess and Mills stopped in London to talk with the leaders of the African Institution and then sailed on to Sierra Leone where they contacted the Friendly Society that Cuffe had helped found in Freetown. The society's president, John Kizell, had been one of the original Nova Scotians, and a friend and collaborator of Cuffe's, and he became their most trusted advisor about African realities.[36] Kizell was unusually well suited to serve as a cultural broker among the Temne, white Americans, and black American immigrants. A native of the Sherbro region of Sierra Leone, he had been enslaved as a boy and sold into South Carolina on the eve of the Revolutionary War. When the British occupied Charleston, he escaped from slavery and "joined the royal standard." Kizell then decamped to Nova Scotia at the war's end before joining the exodus to Sierra Leone. He did not play a prominent role in the disputes between Company officials and settlers during the 1790s, but he was a Baptist and Macaulay considered him a friend to the Company. He became increasingly prominent during the first decade of the nineteenth century. By 1810, having won the trust of Edward Columbine, then the governor of Sierra Leone, Kizell was sent as emissary to the native peoples living in the region of his birth, near Sherbro Island, about 100 miles south of Freetown, on a mission to win their cooperation with British efforts to interdict the slave trade (see map 4.1). With his knowledge of the region and its peoples, his experience negotiating with indigenous leaders, European slave traders, and powerful Euro-African families like the Caulkers, Taylors, and Clevelands who had become wealthy intermediaries in the Sherbro slave trade, John Kizell offered Mills and Burgess invaluable knowledge.[37]

The two Colonization Society agents, perhaps comforted by Coumbine's assurance that Kizell always "discharged his duty with great integrity," came to think of Kizell as "a second Paul Cuffee," [sic] praising his sense, his "good heart," and his commitment to the "temporal and spiritual welfare of Africans and their descendants." Kizell told Burgess and Mills that the continent would welcome thousands of settlers, for "Africa is the land of black men, and to Africa they must and will come." He predicted that a thriving African colony would benefit everyone, leading to peaceful and gradual emancipation in the United States while allowing America's oppressed black people to "shine as lights in this dark world" by conferring "infinite blessings on this country."[38] Mills died on the expedition, but Burgess survived to bring back an optimistic assessment of the prospects for colonization and a commitment from Kizell to welcome and work with the first settlers when they arrived in Africa. Burgess also brought back the journal that Mills had kept during the expedition, and in that journal, Mills declared from his martyr's grave that "no man in Africa could probably be so useful to" the Colonization Society as John Kizell.

Having explored possibilities in Africa and made contact with Kizell and the Friendly Society, supporters of colonization now had to overcome a number of domestic obstacles to their plans.[39] Among the most daunting of those obstacles was that of convincing a suitable group of black Americans to take a chance on their new settlement. The public repudiation of the Society by blacks in Richmond, Georgetown, and Philadelphia should have tipped off Society officials to the challenge they faced. Little evidence of their initial recruiting efforts survives, but the Colonization Society maintained that most who chose to join the first expedition "had long contemplated a settlement in Africa" and had gone as soon as they were afforded "a favourable opportunity."[40] Daniel Coker, the founder of Baltimore's AME Bethel Church, was among those first settlers.

Scholars of early colonization have generally ignored the claim that Coker had long considered moving to Africa while explaining his decision to emigrate through reference to personal difficulties.[41] After stepping down from the office of bishop in favor of Richard Allen, Coker had remained in the pulpit of Bethel Church in Baltimore, but within two years he suffered the indignity of being excommunicated from the denomination that he had helped to found. Shortly after that, he declared personal bankruptcy. The combined effect of professional and financial failure surely weighed heavily upon Coker and may well have made him more receptive to leaving the country.[42] At least one AME minister later remembered that the Colonization Society had enticed him with assurances that he would be made "President of the Republic of Liberia."[43] Such a promise would have been impossible—Liberia did not yet exist—but the desire for a fresh start and a clean slate may well have played a role in Coker's decision to emigrate.

Nonetheless, Coker left Baltimore for the coast of Africa as a member in good standing with Bethel Church—after serving his one-year expulsion he had been reinstated—and fragmentary but convincing surviving evidence shows that he retained respect among black people in Baltimore and elsewhere.[44] As a settler and missionary in Africa, he pursued strategies consistent with his earlier support for Paul Cuffe, providing the best available indication of how Cuffe's supporters among the African church leadership conceived of their relationship to the continent, and how they would have liked for things to work with the ACS. Coker sought to use the Colonization Society to carve out autonomous space for a black society in Africa, hoping to bring the ACS into harmony with the traditions of black engagement with Africa that had developed over the course of the preceding half century.

Unfortunately for these plans, the expedition itself was a complete disaster. The ship *Elizabeth* cast off from New York with eighty-six black immigrants and three white agents, one representing the U.S. government and two working for the ACS. Everyone was in high spirits as the voyage began, but tensions quickly developed between the ship's crew and the black passengers. After a relatively quick passage the ship arrived in Sierra Leone, and then, following Burgess's advice, the settlers quickly moved on to a site that Kizell had prepared for them at a small village called Campelar that he had built on Sherbro Island, roughly 100 miles south of Freetown. The site was swampy, the water undrinkable, and the prospects less than promising. The white agents, Samuel Bacon, John Bankson, and Samuel Crozer, immediately set about trying to purchase a larger tract of land to serve as a more permanent base for the planned colony, but, unable to make sense of the confusing jurisdictions of different native leaders, the agents distributed gifts at numerous palavers without ever determining which local king had ultimate authority to sell land to the Society. Finally all of the agents and more than a quarter of the black settlers fell victim to "African fever"— probably malaria—and as the last of the agents was dying, he appointed Coker to direct what was left of the settlement.

Coker's supervision over the settlement was not easy. He struggled with some of the other settlers and with John Kizell over the future of the community before finally giving up and leading those who would follow him back to Sierra Leone. There, he settled near Freetown, brought his family over from Baltimore to join him, and became an important religious leader as well as the patriarch of an influential family. His reports helped convince the Society that Sherbro Island was not a suitable site for the permanent colony, and it sent the next expedition with instructions to settle elsewhere. As a result, what came to be Monrovia, Liberia, was founded about 150 miles farther south at Cape Mesurado (see map 4.1).[45]

The Colonization Society needed a scapegoat for this disastrous initial expedition, and Coker served one up to them in the person of John Kizell. In journals that he copied and sent back to the United States, in letters that he wrote to friends and patrons, and especially in verbal reports to U.S. naval officers patrolling the coast of Africa to interdict the slave trade, Coker suggested that Kizell had "employed a secret influence to produce and aggravate the disaffection of the people." In the words of a naval officer who spoke highly of Coker, it was to "Mr. John Kizell . . . alone" that the agents' failure to get land for a permanent settlement "was to be ascribed," and the explanation for Kizell's villainous actions rested on his "motives of self-interest and speculation." Another officer, equally friendly with Coker, called Kizell a "speculator or, deceiver and tyrant," while laying the blame for the expedition's failure squarely at his feet. The standard story told of the first expedition was a tragic morality tale in which the dedicated and well-meaning white agents, joined by Coker, their trusted friend and compatriot, worked conscientiously to settle the immigrants and found a new colony, only to see their noble sacrifices come to naught due to the cupidity of the other settlers and the perfidy of Kizell.[46]

This story served Coker's personal interests as well as the institutional interests of the ACS, but it has also helped obscure the efforts of Coker and Kizell to use the money and influence of the Colonization Society to organize a transformative African Christian colony on Sherbro Island. Kizell was quite open about this goal from the beginning, one reason he may have been susceptible to being scapegoated when things went badly. He had, after all, welcomed Burgess and Mills during their initial visit with the assurance that "Africa is the land of black men," and he had denied that American slaves had "forfeited a right to the inheritance of their fathers, by being carried by force from their country."[47] He offered a simple and straightforward narrative of filiative kinship, tying Africans in America to the land and peoples of their ancestors. This sentiment encouraged leaders of the Colonization Society when they were projecting a successful settlement onto Africa, but the same sentiment could mark Kizell as subversive when a failure had to be explained. His unhappiness with "White Agents" being sent "to govern the Colony," when "'one of their own colour'" should have been appointed "'as ruler,'" helped cement the belief that he was the "chief cause" of the nascent colony's demise.[48] Coker, on the other hand, was officially praised by the board of the Colonization Society, which voted to send him an expensive present in thanks for his efforts on behalf of the failed expedition. His prominence among blacks in the United States, and his status as a noble if unsuccessful black supporter of the ACS, even led the Maryland Auxiliary of the Society to ask where they could find a portrait of Coker to use as the model for a commemorative engraving.[49]

When this story reached Kizell in Africa through the ACS's fourth annual report, he contested it in revealing terms. He sent his old friend Ebenezer Burgess a long and rambling "Apology for For [sic] the Conduct of John Kezell And His associates Occasioned By the Strictures And Denunciations by the Rev. Danel Coker In His Journnall Letters and Informations In the fourth Annual Report," a document in which he systematically and repetitively refuted both the charge that he had acted in a way "betraitorous to [his] Sacred office" and the claim that Coker had behaved as Coker and the naval officers claimed. The misspellings and other mistakes that were rooted in Kizell's informal education reveal one disadvantage that he faced in disputing the account of the well-educated Coker. In fact, the unpolished nature of the pamphlet may explain why Burgess chose to file it rather than publish it as Kizell had hoped.[50]

Neither grammatical mistakes nor creative spelling do anything, however, to conceal Kizell's anger and feelings of betrayal. He denied specific charges, ridiculed the amount of money Coker and the Society had spent on gifts designed to buy land, and accused Coker of favoring his friends and sowing dissension among the settlers. Most interestingly, though, Kizell countered the accusations that he himself had opposed the white agents by insisting that Coker had announced that he "did not Care if Every white man was Dead"; likewise, it was the supposedly loyal Coker who responded to plans to celebrate the Fourth of July on Sherbro by announcing that the "Independence of the United States was Nothing" to him, after which he had openly "Disregarded their flag." In short, Kizell countercharged that Coker was the divisive and racially polarizing figure, and at least two of the three white agents sent out by the ACS with the next group of settlers came to agree that Coker had acted much differently at Sherbro Island than initial reports suggested.[51]

This dispute over who bore most responsibility for the failure of the Society's initial colonizing effort, trivial in itself, has drawn attention away from evidence that both of these supporters of Paul Cuffe had cooperated to build an autonomous "African" settlement at Sherbro Island. During the settlers' initial stopover in Freetown, before decamping for Sherbro, Coker spoke with the "first settlers" of Sierra Leone—the Nova Scotians—and reported their complaints respecting their "landed property" and the "advantages [that had] been taken of them." A few years later Kizell would register these complaints with a parliamentary commission investigating Sierra Leone. Coker took heart from the old settlers' discontent with Crown rule and looked to the "rising generation of Africa," hoping that a settlement at Sherbro would convince "the American people" to leave "the British colony." John Kizell, a Nova Scotian who had weathered the Rebellion of 1800 and then risen to the presidency of Cuffe's Freetown Friendly Society, was a natural ally and potential vanguard figure in this next—and hopefully last—exodus. Together Coker and Kizell could plant the seed for an African nation by creating a black-controlled refuge for people rescued from slave ships and a destination for black Americans seeking to escape from under Pharaoh's hand, whether that hand operated in the form of British paternalism in Sierra Leone or slavery and racism in the United States.

The two did indeed cooperate during their first month or so on the island. They traveled together to negotiate with native leaders, and Kizell translated for Coker when necessary. When dark-skinned settlers questioned whether they should listen to the light-skinned Coker, the African-born Kizell insisted that "'Mr Coker was a descendant of Africa'" who would be obeyed.[52] In two letters written to black friends in Baltimore and published in the appendix to his *Journal*, Coker underscored his commitment to creating an African people. He called on Baptists to come "to establish an African Baptist church," Presbyterians to "support an African Presbyterian church," and Methodists to "support an African Methodist church." This may sound to modern ears like a picture of denominational diversity and religious freedom, but Coker described it as a search for unity rather than the promise of respect for diversity; he hoped new settlers would leave dangerous "divisions . . . in America," so that all could be "sweetly united" in their new home. With such unity he believed Africa would "be a great nation, and a powerful and worthy nation," for "this land only wants industrious, informed, and christian people, to make it one of the greatest nations in the world."[53] He might almost have been calling forth a "historians nation."

At least one black settler reported that Coker and Kizell had conspired to seize control from the white agents following the death of Samuel Crozer (who had been sent out as the agent for the U.S. government). Elijah Johnson, a settler from Baltimore, claimed to have heard Coker preparing for a meeting with Bankson and Bacon, the two surviving agents (of the ACS), by insisting that he would "not submit . . . and bring my brethren into bondage" by going out to negotiate with native headmen for land without the "full power of an agent." "Mr. Kizzell" joined him, pledging that he would "not stir" unless Coker had "the same power Mr. Crozer had." Johnson saw Bacon leave the ensuing meeting "holding up his hands" and exclaiming "*my God. I am ruined.*"[54] Johnson's diary indicates that the split between Coker and Kizell came after Bacon and Bankson died, in which case it may well have been rooted in competing ambitions to serve as the leader of the settlement.

Neither Coker nor Kizell suffered ruin as a result of the failure at Sherbro Island. Kizell lived for at least another seven years and remained prominent enough within Sierra Leone to be one of three original Nova Scotians interviewed by a parliamentary commission sent to investigate the sad state of the colony in 1827.[55] Coker also chose to remain in Sierra Leone. His wife and children joined him there in 1821, and they settled in Hastings, a town founded by the British as a home for slaves liberated during the Royal Navy's battle to repress the slave trade. He maintained ties with friends and supporters in the United States while becoming an important religious leader in Sierra Leone, replicating his efforts in Baltimore by organizing an independent "West African Methodist" Connection in Sierra Leone. Whatever the truth behind reports that some delegates to the founding meeting of the AME had thought him "too white" to be an African bishop in America, he assumed the responsibilities of a bishop in Africa, ordaining at least two new ministers.[56]

No doubt he believed himself to have remained committed to helping "Ethiopia stretch forth her hands unto God" while reconciling himself to the realization that he would not be the agent through whom God would raise an African nation. His inability to play that role did not, however, alter his belief that Africa would rise, and he continued to urge "the people to come," so long as they were "willing to suffer." Casting a positive light on his refusal to join the American colony at Cape Mesurado, he insisted that it was "of small moment where we labour[ed] so it [was] in africa." He continued to "preach the same doctrine (the new Birth)" in Africa that he had preached in Baltimore. "Here," he said, "let me live, here let me die."[57]

The first expedition sent out by the Colonization Society had brought together people with a broad array of goals and reasons for engagement with Africa. The federal government supported the expedition in hopes of founding a settlement that would receive slaves liberated by Navy ships patrolling the Atlantic. The Colonization Society's agents hoped to found missions to bring Christianity to the heathens of Africa, while starting a colony that would offer black Americans a chance to escape the debilitating effects of slavery and American racism. At least some of the black settlers went to fulfill long-standing goals that they had developed as supporters of Paul Cuffe and as participants in the separate church movements. They traveled to Africa in the knowledge that many black Americans had rejected the Colonization Society's overtures, but Daniel Coker and others also knew that prominent friends of Paul Cuffe retained hope that the ACS could become an institution through which Cuffe's emigrationist project might be pursued. Notwithstanding their public opposition to colonization, Richard Allen continued to meet with, listen to, and consult representatives of the ACS into the 1820s.[58]

The failure of the colony at Sherbro Island and the resulting decision by the ACS to acquire land at Cape Mesurado led to important shifts in the nature of the colonization movement. Monrovia, the capital of the American colony of Liberia, did not have the direct ties to the history of black American engagement with Sierra Leone that so influenced black settlers' actions at Sherbro. Those first ninety emigrants sent out by the Colonization Society to settle Sherbro differed radically from those who would come after them. Few if any black American immigrants to Liberia were drawn from free people who had allied themselves with Paul Cuffe before the founding of the ACS. Most were Southerners escaping slavery by accepting emigration as a condition for manumission, or free black Southerners leaving in response to the increasing repression that they faced in the plantation regions where they lived. Nonetheless, many shared with their predecessors a commitment to spread Christianity, and at least some continued to tie the spread of "true" religion to the rise of a new and great African nation, at least for a while.

Those who had followed Paul Cuffe, those who had participated in the black discourse on Africa that stretched back to Phillis Wheatley and Ignatius Sancho, continued to fight against slavery and for racial equality. The increasing prominence of the Colonization Society and of southern figures within the Society pushed expressions of African identity far into the background. Black activists and churchmen, when faced with the fear that powerful whites aimed to deport all free black people, emphasized claims to their native land, insisting that "colored" people were Americans by birth and by right, and that no one could justly question their claims to the lands they had worked or to a place in the American nation that had been built upon their labor. The black discourse on Africanness did not disappear, but it moved underground, and those who claimed African identities were increasingly likely to favor affiliative narratives of racial kinship.

IV

When Paul Cuffe led an emigrationist movement that was seen to be a movement of and for black people, it elicited little overt opposition and won the active support of many prominent African Americans. Daniel Coker of Baltimore, Richard Allen, Absalom Jones, and James Forten of Philadelphia, Peter Williams Jr. of New York, these and other black leaders helped to found local African institutions and expressed their support for Cuffe's emigrationist plan. James Forten explained his belief in the importance of emigrationism by declaring that blacks would "never become a people until they come out from amongst the white people."[59] Those who supported emigrationism and sought to create unity among the peoples of Africa and the diaspora continued to differ over whether that unity was natural—the result of blood kinship—or historical, and, if historical, whether it reached beyond secular history into sacred time. During the first two decades of the nineteenth century, they increasingly agreed, however, that blacks, "Africans," could only lay claim to their status as an autonomous people by escaping from whites culturally, economically, politically, and perhaps physically as well. However far back in time one might trace the ties binding blacks to one another, they could only fulfill their destiny if they united as a properly historical people.

For several decades beginning in the 1820s black Americans would turn away from open declarations of "African" identity, but the momentum that had been generated by a half century of thinking and writing about Africanness did not dissipate overnight. A few black apostles of African identity, believing that the ACS represented an imperfect but acceptable vehicle through which to pursue their dreams, emigrated to Liberia. Others who rejected the organization's efforts to convince them to leave the United States continued to speak of the peoples of Africa as their kin and to believe that Africans of the diaspora had a responsibility to bring the "dark" continent into the light of Christianity and legitimate commerce. Although large numbers of black people in Philadelphia, Richmond, and Georgetown had spoken out in immediate opposition to the ACS, the course of the first expedition sent by the Society to settle in West Africa and the role of the AME's Daniel Coker during that expedition suggest that black public opinion remained more malleable between 1816 and 1820 than is sometimes supposed, in part because prominent leaders of the separate church movement hesitated before rejecting colonization. It would take another decade before black American activists living north of slavery relinquished their last hopes that the American Colonization Society and its settlement at Liberia might yet offer a real opportunity to pursue racial uplift.

7

Becoming American in Liberia and in the United States, 1820–1830

The combination of the northern black public's popular rejection of the American Colonization Society in the United States and the utter failure of the Society's first attempt to plant a colony on the coast of Africa severely undermined a key foundation upon which black discussions of African identity had proceeded over the previous fifty years. Many came to believe that whites labeled blacks "African" in order to strengthen slavery by deporting free blacks and by cementing the association of dark skin with both slavery and savagery. They had ample grounds for this belief. If the substantial number of blacks who had acquired freedom during and after the American Revolution accepted the Colonization Society's offer to send them to Africa, they would, in this view, not only lose their claim on the American lives that they had fought so hard and against such odds to build, they would also abandon blacks left behind, consigning their southern kin—all of whom were metaphorical brethren in affliction, and many of whom were literal brothers, sisters, or cousins—to lives of hopeless, perpetual slavery. Better to remain in the United States fighting racism as free people while battling against the slavery that continued to flourish in the South; many black activists came to believe that they could achieve most for themselves and their race by asserting allegiance to the land of their birth and to the Christian egalitarian values that white Americans professed, however hypocritical blacks believed whites to be when they proclaimed those values.

Just as had been the case during the struggle to build an African identity, the turn away from Africanness proceeded on parallel tracks in America and among black colonists on the coast of Africa. Over the course of the 1820s, Liberia was founded to receive settlers sent out by the Colonization Society;

black colonists in Liberia first struggled with the ACS to control the colony, but once the Society met the settlers' minimal demands for autonomy and self-determination, they gradually moderated their demands. As the Colonization Society offered avenues of social mobility for elite black emigrants, the most vocal residents of the settler society that emerged in Liberia came increasingly to view themselves as blacks building an American society in Africa, and less as "Africans" working to raise a diasporic nation.

At the same time, public opposition to colonization among northern free blacks coalesced into near unanimity, forcing the ACS to turn to the slave states for almost all of its emigrants. Black opponents of the Colonization Society trumpeted their Americanness while pointing out the hypocrisy of colonizationsts' claims that free black people were, on the one hand, too degenerate to remain in the United States without damaging the republic, but, remarkably, that they were perfectly suited to bring Christianity and enlightenment to the benighted residents of Africa. Men like Richard Allen, James Forten, and Absalom Jones had supported emigration to Sierra Leone while asserting their own African identities, but in the wake of these developments, they moved away from such language, and the belief in a shared destiny for all descendants of Africa was displaced by a growing tendency, at least in public expression, to place narrower boundaries on the black community that shared common interests. Free black Northerners intensified their expressions of concern for and kinship with southern slaves, and they expressed increasing interest in Haiti at the same time that they pulled back from Africa.[1] They identified with southern slaves using affiliative language that portrayed racial difference as an accidental product of history rather than an inherent collective essence. The clarity and forcefulness with which they asserted their American identity overshadowed evidence of a persisting concern about Africa among northern blacks that grew directly out of the black discourse on Africa that had flourished prior to the founding of the Colonization Society. Southern free blacks who lived in the dark shadows cast by slavery were more open to moving to Liberia, and fragmentary evidence suggests that some believed the rise of an African people to be crucial to a hopeful shared future.

I

The Colonization Society did not, of course, abandon its goal of establishing a colony on the coast of Africa after the failure at Sherbro. Within a year of the *Elizabeth*'s arrival in Sierra Leone, a second ship called the *Nautilus*, carrying more than thirty emigrants out of Norfolk, Virginia, sailed into

Freetown. This expedition was officially led by two white government agents—Ephraim Bacon and Jonathan B. Winn—and by Joseph Andrus and Christian Wiltberger as agents of the Society, but it became apparent before the ship left Virginia that the dominant figures on the expedition were Lott Cary and Colin Teague. These two black Virginia Baptists traveled to Africa under the auspices of the Colonization Society but as agents of the Baptist Church's Board of Foreign Missions. Cary and Teague had been instrumental in founding an African Mission Society among black Baptists in Richmond during the 1810s, and they sought to take advantage of the opportunity offered by the ACS to travel to Africa in search of souls.[2]

Cary and Teague came to the expedition from backgrounds that differed from those of the apostles of Cuffe who traveled with Coker aboard the *Elizabeth*. Each was born into slavery in Virginia, and grew up in a society committed to slavery. Cary, the dominant figure, was born east of Richmond in 1780, and had been hired into the city to work in one of the tobacco warehouses in Shockoe, the town's waterfront warehouse district. After learning to read and write, he quickly acquired great responsibility at the warehouse, and, with that responsibility, a good wage. By 1813, the newly widowed Cary had saved enough money to buy his freedom, as well as that of his two children, and to purchase a $1,500 house in Richmond. By then both Cary and Teague, a harness maker, had developed reputations for probity and competence among white and black Richmonders. Each credited much of his success to religious awakening within the Baptist Church, and both believed in the transforming power of the gospel. Neither had originally looked to Africa with the primary goal of transforming the residents of the continent into a unified people, but neither were they entirely ignorant of earlier nationalist projects. They had initially hoped to preach the gospel to natives of the continent and serve as agents through whom God would work many individual transformations of the sort they had experienced in Richmond.[3]

The decision to move from raising money in support of an African mission to becoming missionaries on the continent probably reflected some preliminary engagement with a broader vision of African identity. It was, according to a white friend and fellow Baptist in Richmond, the publication of three letters written by residents of Sierra Leone that convinced Cary and Teague to emigrate.[4] The letters, two by settlers who emigrated on Cuffe's 1816 expedition to Sierra Leone and the other by a group from Freetown—probably the Friendly Society—called on black Americans to rally to the cause of an African people. One responded to news that had reached Sierra Leone of black opposition to the Colonization Society by addressing a question to the "Brethren Generally": "When," Samuel Wilson asked, "will you become a nation, if you refuse to come?" Wilson's Cuffe-esque nationalist question was wedded, not surprisingly, to a call to spread the gospel, and given the earlier interest that Cary and Teague had expressed in missionary outreach, they may have been most deeply influenced by Wilson's success in mixing an appeal to secular equality with his dispensationalist reconciliation of God's benevolence with the evils of slavery. God had permitted black Americans' "fathers" to be sold to a "strange land" where they "increase[d] strangers' treasures" in order that those oppressed fathers' children could find true religion and "bring the gospel" to their ancestral and rightful home. Wilson called on black Americans to fulfill their divine destiny in terms that were deeply rooted in black discourse on Africa, and those who refused to answer that call flirted with a return to something akin to slavery, as Wilson's allusion to the gospel of Luke warned: "'He that knows his master's will, and does it not, shall he be beaten with many stripes.'"[5]

The letter from the Friendly Society echoed this message by invoking Isaiah's call to a "people scattered and peeled" to recognize that all that had been suffered was from God and had been allowed by God as part of a plan to "bring the gospel into [their] country." Apparently Cary and Teague were attracted by the claim that "Africa, not America, is your country and your home," and that God had brought their ancestors to a modern Egypt in order for them to return to that home with the gospel.[6] Though they left no evidence of direct involvement with Paul Cuffe, they were called to Africa, at least in part, by his apostles.

Cary, Teague, and the other emigrants probably committed to move to Africa before word of the disaster at Sherbro Island reached the United States. When they arrived in Sierra Leone in the spring of 1821, they discovered that the legacy of the failed first expedition was one they would have to overcome. The government agents quickly decided that the new settlers should not go to the old site at Sherbro, but this left those on the expedition stranded on the coast of Africa without a final destination. For about a year the emigrants were ordered to work as something akin to indentured servants on farms near Freetown in order to support themselves and the expedition, while the ACS played a game of revolving agents that would only end when Eli Ayres arrived in Africa in November 1821.

Lott Cary, frustrated during the months that he was stuck on a farm outside Freetown and denied the right to preach the gospel, led the settlers in an increasingly radical direction. Within a month of landing in Sierra Leone, Teague and Cary asserted their allegiance to the Board of Missions, by declaring that they "would never come under the authority of the Colonization Society." Around the same time, Cary wrote a remarkably scathing letter to the Board of Missions in which he concluded that true Christians who were committed to Africa should not "wait for the Colonization Society, nor for the government, for neither of these are in search of missionary grounds but of colonizing grounds: if it should not suit missionary seeds, you cannot expect to gather in a missionary crop."[7] Cary's religious frustrations became bound up with more secular complaints as discontent grew among the settlers.

With little to offer the colonists except vague assurances of future land, the white agents began to lose control of the expedition. When Ayres arrived in November, he was so shaken by what he considered the settlers' defiance that he issued a proclamation outlawing "sedition, mutiny, insubordination or disobedience." He also acted quickly, if less than ethically, to get the settlers away from Freetown. Ayres and U.S. Navy Lieutenant Robert Stockton traveled down to Cape Mesurado, in present-day Liberia. Having settled on the land they wanted to purchase, they engaged in a series of palavers, or discussions, with King Peter of the Dei people. The negotiations culminated on Dec. 15, 1821, with Stockton putting a pistol to King Peter's head in order to get him to sign a treaty conveying the land for about $300 in goods.[8]

Stockton and Ayres were pleased with their acquisition. Cape Mesurado's beautiful beaches extend out into the Atlantic Ocean beneath a plateau formed by 300-foot-high cliffs. The countryside was heavily forested, and the rain forests stretched along terrain that rose quickly to significant elevations. Like their predecessors at Sierra Leone, these Westerners misinterpreted the lush rain forests and abundant animal life—elephants, leopards, apes, and other exotic beasts abounded—as evidence of potentially lush agricultural land, and believed that the land would support thriving farming communities.[9] The next task was to move the settlers from Sierra Leone to their new home at Cape Mesurado.

The settlers may have appreciated Ayres's unseemly diligence in acquiring land for a permanent settlement, but it did not assure him their loyalty or trust. In December 1821, as Ayres was down at Cape Mesurado stealing land from the Dei, Cary and Teague joined forces with Daniel Coker and Elijah Johnson to form the "American African Union Society" in order to "regulate the conduct of the people." Their immediate grievance involved the disciplining of two settlers who had run afoul of the agents, but members of the Union Society laid claim to a more general right to collective autonomy.[10] Teague, Cary, and perhaps some other colonists who sailed on the *Nautilus*, had come to Africa sharing some of the vision of an African nation that had inspired Cuffe, Kizell, and Coker, and the formation of the American African Union Society suggests that many had been won over to a nationalist vision during their time in Sierra Leone. When they allied themselves with Coker, Johnson, and the veteran settlers, the pattern of conflict that had engulfed Sierra Leone in the 1790s, and recurred on Sherbro Island in 1820, appeared to be repeating.

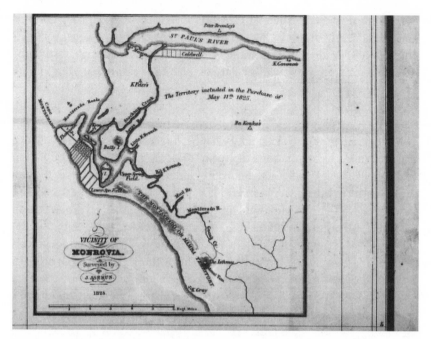

Figure 7.1. Map of Liberia, showing the plans for settlement at Cape Mesurado. Compiled from data on file in the office of the American Colonization Society, under the direction of the Rev. W. McLain, secy., by R. Coyle (original in Library of Congress).

In fact, for the next several years Eli Ayres and Jehudi Ashmun, the two main agents, struggled to win even minimal cooperation from the settlers. Shortly after supervising the move from Sierra Leone to Cape Mesurado, Ayres came to doubt that the housing at the new site could be made ready in time for the rains and suggested a return to the British colony. Lott Cary rallied the settlers to remain at the cape, though they "urged" Ayres to make good on his own plans to leave.[11] By June 1822 all of the white agents had left the small colony of Liberia, and Elijah Johnson, who had emigrated to Africa with Daniel Coker on the *Elizabeth*, but, unlike Coker, had moved to Cape Mesurado with the members of the second expedition, assumed leadership of the colony, a position he retained until Jehudi Ashmun arrived as agent about two months later.[12]

Ashmun originally set out for Liberia as an emissary for a Baltimore mercantile house, and his ascension to the position of colonial agent was accidental. The settlers rallied to his side when neighboring Dei villagers attacked the colony to reclaim the land they understandably believed had been stolen, but Ashmun found it difficult to command respect in the absence of a communal emergency. A series of small confrontations with the settlers culminated when he tried to deny company provisions to twelve men he charged with refusing to contribute their share of time to Monrovia's public works. The following morning those twelve men surrounded the public storehouse and took the provisions to which they believed themselves entitled. None of the other settlers intervened to stop them. This "riot," as the Colonization Society saw fit to call it, and a succession of similarly small-scale acts of unrest, might seem like weak and insignificant sequels to the struggles between the Nova Scotians and the Sierra Leone Company thirty years earlier. As was true in the earlier contest, however, the colonists at Cape Mesurado were staking their claim to more than access to provisions.

In part, the problem was land. As had been true in Freetown, several settlers took up land in Monrovia (the town founded at Cape Mesurado) before Ayres had made an official distribution, and claimed squatters' rights to the lots on which they had been living. Ayres's attempt to reclaim that land for the ACS created arguments that festered for some time. The most fundamental issues, however, involved political rights. Some settlers, perhaps having taken the rhetoric about black rights in Liberia more literally than the Society had intended, insisted that they had gone there "expecting to govern themselves, and had no idea of having white Agents."[13] They had not sailed halfway around the world and taken up the life of pioneers to continue taking orders from white people. As officials with the Colonization Society began to realize, the settlers had developed a "feeling . . . of a union and sympathy of coloured against white people," and unless the agents could allay that feeling, harmony would be difficult to achieve.[14]

Concerns over self-determination may have begun with land, but they extended to issues of governance and commerce, issues that became entangled in the person of Jehudi Ashmun. The mercantile house that had sent him to Liberia—the Baltimore Trading Company—was an association of city merchants who were given a monopoly on the colony's trade in return for an agreement to provide steady passage between Africa and America. The colonists took offense. One can easily imagine that they began to envision a situation in which Liberia would become a perversion of the locus of black freedom that Cuffe and his followers had sought to create. Rather than an African nation with a national legislature and a mercantile community trading with blacks in the United States, it was developing as a colonial endeavor in which a white agent ruled in the interest of his white commercial house in the United States. Lott Cary also had self-interested grounds for taking offense, since he served as the local agent for a group of white Richmond merchants trading with the infant colony.[15] Those settlers who knew of Cuffe's plan for a diasporic mercantile network that would establish the economic foundation for an African nation—and Coker may have told them of that vision when forming the American African Union Society—might understandably have been depressed and discontented. They had been promised the chance to participate in building a society that would contribute to ending slavery in the United States, but they seemed instead to be slipping into bondage in Africa. The colony appeared to be headed toward a persistent violent struggle over control between the Society and the settlers.

That did not happen, but things did continue to go badly in the aftermath of the "riots" of 1823. Ashmun responded by convening the settlers and delivering a scathing account of their behavior in which he berated them for ingratitude and claimed that his life had been threatened. When the colonists continued to reject his leadership, he became despondent and sailed to the Cape Verde Islands in April 1824 planning to return to the United States. While on the islands, a ship carrying Ralph R. Gurley, whom the Colonization Society had appointed temporary agent in Liberia in order to investigate the problems there, stopped at Porto Praya. Gurley met Ashmun, discussed the situation in Liberia, and they returned to the colony together. Once there, they worked within a constitution promulgated by the ACS in 1820 to form a system of civil governance that dispersed some of the power centralized in the agents' hands by incorporating settlers into the process.[16] A committee system was established with justices of the peace, constables, and committees of agriculture, public works, and the colonial militia, as well as various other offices, all of which integrated the colonists into the government. The constitution of 1820 conferred final authority on the Society's official agent, but, if taken seriously, the committees promised to answer the colonists' fear that they faced a new form of slavery in Liberia, and by doing so the new system won their cooperation.

Ashmun himself distrusted the colonists' initial expressions of loyalty, finding their "unanimity . . . painful," because he felt certain that it masked either miscomprehension or secret opposition. Convinced that the settlers' initial opposition stemmed from bad faith, he doubted that the modest political reforms that had been instituted could have brought about real change. By the end of 1824, however, he reported that his fears had been "unfounded," and that there was "an enlightened and growing attachment rooted in the bosoms of the great body of the people, to their laws, their officers, and the authority of the Society." The governmental responsibility that had been granted to black officers had created a "modesty of deportment and opinion" that the settlers had "never manifested before," and it had secured "to the government the united support of the people." Ashmun then noted the real key to this new system: "the agent has adopted the rule never to interpose his authority, where that of the proper officer, however inferior, is adequate to the emergency."[17] With this decision he transferred most day-to-day governing decisions from white company or government agents to black settlers.

One need not accept the terms that Ashmun used to explain the change—enlightenment and loyalty—to recognize that the new plan of government satisfied some of the colonists' minimal demands for self-determination, and though the history of Liberia after 1824 would often be characterized by strife, it would be one in which a substantial group of Americo-Liberians understood their interests to be served by allegiance to the Colonization Society. Lott Cary led and exemplified this turn of events. He had been Ashmun's chief antagonist before 1823, but financial incentives and political concessions convinced him that struggles over control of the colony would detract from Liberia's mission. He gained political and economic power through his alliance with Jehudi Ashmun, which he tried to use to further his missionary work and to battle the slave trade.[18] Cary came to see the society that black Americans would build in Liberia as a cultural colony of the United States that offered settlers a chance to achieve economic and social status, while establishing an outpost of civilization on a savage and pagan continent.[19] He died in an accidental explosion while preparing ammunition for a battle against the colony's indigenous neighbors. Before that emblematic death, however, he helped lead the black American settlers of Liberia toward a compromise in which they received a more substantial stake in the colony that the ACS was building; in return, the colonists turned away from the nationalist project that they had begun to pursue. While some would continue to travel to Liberia in the hopes of pursuing something like Paul Cuffe's dream of creating an African people, dominant groups among the settlers pursued local agendas tied more to personal advancement than to a nationalist vision.

II

During the 1820s, while settlers in Liberia began to focus on building an American society in Africa, black opponents of the Colonization Society who remained in the United States developed an alternative language to express racial solidarity, choosing to call themselves "Colored Americans" rather than Africans. The straightforward response to the Colonization Society's efforts to win support among politicians, financial backers, and potential emigrants entailed an unacknowledged rejection of discussions reaching back several decades, discussions in which black people from different backgrounds and statuses had tried to understand the place of Africa in the sense of racial identity that had emerged out of two centuries of slavery in Anglophone America. That the founding of a single institution could so quickly deflect the trajectory of this discourse on Africa is an indication of the power of early nineteenth-century white culture to affect the terms that black Americans, whether enslaved or free, could use when publicly discussing their collective situation and the world in which they lived. The efforts of black orators and activists to preserve and adapt some aspects of the black discourse on Africa, while responding to the conditions created by the growing influence of the ACS, provide an interesting case study in subversive political action while underscoring the vitality of a tradition in which black Americans saw themselves as the foundation of a people whose history and future involved, but was not limited to, the United States.

The broad contours of the story are familiar. Throughout the 1820s black people throughout the North rallied to reject both the Colonization Society and any expression of interest in black emigration to Africa. The 1817 Philadelphia meeting discussed in the previous chapter became a touchstone for black antislavery thought and activism, in part because it set the tone for a series of similar meetings in other northern cities. Speakers developed something close to a formula in which they combined varying elements to attack the Colonization Society and its program. Blacks, they pointed out, had been born in the United States and had fought beside whites for the new nation's independence in 1776 and in 1812. Black labor had made the United States prosperous. Then, these orators pointed out, when more and more black people were winning their freedom and demanding the equal treatment to which they were entitled, the Colonization Society was founded as a stalking horse for the interests of the slave South. White colonizationists hid behind a false veil of benevolence by claiming to be interested in the welfare of Africa and of black victims of American racism, but, in truth, they sought to remove free black people, in order to shackle the enslaved more securely. The black rejection of the Colonization Society became a stepping-stone toward embracing what came to be known as Garrisonian immediate abolitionism.[20] This position was summarized in resolutions passed at a meeting of "People of Color" in New York City in 1831: "Resolved, That we claim *this country, the place of our birth, and not Africa,* as our mother country, and all attempts to send us to Africa, we consider as gratuitous and uncalled for."[21]

There was much going on below the surface, however, that reflects the persistence of a commitment to Africa and an African identity among many black people, especially from Philadelphia southward. Within Philadelphia itself, black expressions of sympathy for the Colonization Society became largely taboo, but those who had previously argued that the fate of black Americans was entwined with that of the continent of Africa did not change their minds overnight. Richard Allen held a worship service for emigrants leaving for Liberia in 1822, and, as late as 1827, a decade after the Colonization Society was founded, he still had to respond to rumors that he was a closet colonizationist. He acknowledged the basis of the rumors, not-ing that he had spent several years "striving to reconcile" himself to "the col-onization of Africans in Liberia," before concluding that there were no defensible grounds for colonization, and that the "land which we have watered with our tears and our blood, is now our mother country."[22] James Forten made no public confession of his doubts, but the harsh terms he used to reject Africa itself, as well as colonization, suggest that he sought to dis-tance himself from his former support for Cuffe's emigrationism. He report-edly referred to Africa as "a land of destruction where the Sword will cut off the few wretched beings whom the climate spares," and elsewhere he called it a "Land, inhabited . . . by those who have little to designate that they belong to the human species."[23] Surely one explanation for Forten's journey from Cuffe's hopeful projection of a shared African future to this remark-ably negative and distressingly racist description of Africa in 1817 is his need to establish his reliability as an opponent of the ACS.

Because they lived in a slave state, free black residents of Baltimore, though skeptical of the Colonization Society, were much less unanimous in their repudiation of colonization itself. While few black Baltimoreans fol-lowed Coker to Africa, a number corresponded with the Colonization Society, or met with representatives of its Maryland auxiliary while con-templating emigration. Charles C. Harper and John H. B. Latrobe, the two most prominent white members of the Maryland auxiliary in Baltimore, reported meetings at black churches, and they organized a committee of "three coloured men to receive the applications" of potential emigrants. Most interestingly, Hezekiah Grice led a group centered in Baltimore, but including blacks from cities farther to the north, that sought to found a "commercial company to trade with Liberia." By creating a "regular inter-course" between the colony and America—a clear echo of Cuffe's lan-guage—Grice and his friends hoped to make money while gaining reliable information about the "situation of the Colony and the advantages" that it might "offer emigrants."[24] Grice sought to revive a central aspect of Cuffe's plan by competing directly with the white Baltimore merchants who had sent Ashmun out as their commercial agent in Liberia. His expectation that a black mercantile line might, by creating a reliable conduit for information about Liberia, overcome black suspicion that the Society controlled the information coming out of the colony suggests that many blacks continued to hope that, despite their skepticism about its goals and leadership, the ACS could be used to pursue something akin to Cuffe's vision. The trading company never got off the ground, and popular skepticism continued to plague supporters of colonization, as indicated by the "sensation" in favor of the "cause among the blacks" when an emigrant returned with positive reports about the colony.[25] Skepticism is not, however, outright rejection, and that sensation indicates that many blacks in Baltimore continued to feel the pull of Paul Cuffe's dream while wondering if the American Colonization Society might offer a way to pursue that dream.

Free black people living south of Maryland proved even more torn between their hopes for an African colony and their distrust of the Colonization Society. Black Virginians and North Carolinians proved especially ambivalent in response to the Society's efforts. In both states, free black people lived under the perpetual threat of kidnapping, and experienced daily indignities rooted in both legal inequality and the pernicious effects of white racism. As a result, emigration out of the state appealed to many and the efforts of ACS agents guaranteed that potential emigrants would consider Liberia. Some of the black Americans who considered moving to Liberia also continued to link the development of a "civilized" African society to a broad vision of racial uplift.

Others retained a belief in communal emigration as part of a project of uplift but sought other places to settle. The Haitian governments of Henri Christophe and then of Jean-Pierre Boyer sought to attract free black settlers from the United States, and blacks in Virginia and North Carolina discussed this option.[26] Others argued that black settlements in Ohio or Canada offered the safest escape from white racism. Southern advocates for the colony in Liberia thus faced a different challenge than did those in Baltimore and northern towns, for southern blacks constituted a ready audience for the claim that the future might look brighter elsewhere. Colonizationists' first task was to increase that audience and the second was to convince as many as they could that Liberia offered not only something that would be measurably better than life in Virginia or North Carolina but also better than life in Canada, Haiti, Philadelphia, or Ohio.

Authentic black voices willing to speak from personal experience in favor of Liberia offered what appeared to be the surest answer to the doubts of free people of color. When the settler William Draper made a return visit to the United States, he spent a day speaking to potential emigrants in Fredericksburg, and William Blackford, a local white colonizationist, had "no doubt" that Draper had "incline[d] many to immigrate." The boom in interest either did not last long, or else it did not extend south to Petersburg, for within a few years the free people of that town displayed a "great unwillingness . . . to go to Africa," preferring Philadelphia, Ohio, or Canada as potential destinations. George Edwards, a black minister in the town who was interested in Liberia, offered to make a reconnaissance trip and then return to Petersburg with reliable intelligence to counter the bad reports about life in Monrovia that had spread through the town.[27]

Things were much the same in North Carolina, though with a peculiar twist rooted in different state laws. Unlike Virginia, North Carolina did not liberalize manumission laws in the wake of the American Revolution. A substantial number of Quakers lived in the state and concurred with the denomination's condemnation of slavery, but they were legally prohibited from following their consciences and freeing their bondspeople. Instead they deeded their slaves to their Meetings (or congregations), creating a community of quasi-free black people who were legally owned by Quaker Meetings. These people sometimes flirted with the Colonization Society's offer of transportation to Africa, but they were unwilling to make such an irrevocable change without knowledge of Liberia that came to them through avenues uncontrolled by the ACS. White agents advised the Colonization Society to send over a trusted local man who could return and provide an account of Liberia that his neighbors might believe, but these requests went unheeded and unanswered, and North Carolina's almost free people turned increasingly toward Ohio or Canada rather than Liberia.[28]

Some grassroots black support for colonization did develop, though this generally happened either without or despite encouragement—or interference—from the Society. For example, John Hepburn, a prominent free black colonizationist from Alexandria, Virginia, tried without success to convince the ACS to hire black recruiting agents so that free people of color might believe that they were to be trusted to govern themselves in the new colony. Free blacks in Nashville, Tennessee founded their own auxiliary to the Colonization Society—the only one in the city. Most curiously, a group of blacks enslaved in Cherokee country formed the "Wills valley *African Benevolent Society*" to support the cause and do "good of their coulered brethren."[29] Over the years, immigrants to Liberia were increasingly drawn from slaves who were manumitted on the condition that they leave the United States,[30] but at least through the 1820s, some free black Southerners remained interested enough in the settlement to follow events by subscribing to the ACS's *African Repository* and to work in support of the Society.

It is more difficult to say precisely what southern black supporters of colonization envisioned as the end result of emigration. Black Southerners had fewer opportunities to organize and express their beliefs than did their northern counterparts, and surviving evidence suggests that colonization offered a rare outlet through which free black people in the South could express their opposition to slavery. The nearly hopeless conditions in which black Southerners found themselves stimulated some to rest their hopes on a trajectory of racial uplift that linked the fates of black Americans to Haitians and to blacks living in Africa. Some black Southerners, then, claimed an "African" identity for at least a decade after the appearance of the Colonization Society had muted such claims in the North.

This vision found what may be its clearest surviving expression on July 4, 1829, when the "Free Coloured People of Richmond" held a dinner to commemorate "the abolition of Slavery in the State of New York." The speaker at the dinner was Francis Taylor, a light-skinned free man who had been born in Richmond, before gaining a practical commercial education and working in mercantile houses in Richmond and Liverpool, England. The substance of Taylor's oration has not survived, but a series of remarkable after-dinner toasts was recorded. Amid tributes to George Washington, Benjamin Franklin, Lott Cary, and Jehudi Ashmun, the diners also toasted the American Colonization Society's efforts to emancipate "our suffering countrymen," and called for the "Universal Emancipation" of the "decendants of Africa" under the "Wing of Liberty." Toasts were offered to "Virginia the land of our birth," to the "prosperity of Liberia," and to "Africa home for the brave and freedom for the slave." Perhaps most amazingly, Taylor offered a toast to "George the IV and the British Parliament" for emancipation in the West Indies, and expressed hope that this admirable act would be "emulated by the Government of Virginia," while William Bowler called on the Almighty to deliver the "decendents of Africa" from bondage, by sending a "Moses to guide them to the promised land." Unlike black Northerners, those attending this dinner in Richmond continued to discuss the prospects for black progress in explicitly diasporic terms, tying their hopes for emancipation in Virginia to the progress of black people in Liberia, in the northern United States, and in the British colonial world. Francis Taylor ultimately chose to emigrate to Liberia, and the toasts that followed his speech suggest that going there remained intimately connected to a vision of racial improvement with strong echoes of the discussions of African identity that had been so prominent a few years earlier.[31]

It is less startling that black Richmonders had developed this vision than that a document recording it has survived. Even before the white reaction to Nat Turner's rebellion raised formidable barriers to antislavery expression in the South, it is surprising that black people were permitted to hold public dinners celebrating abolition in New York while they called for universal emancipation and the extension of the "patrimony of liberty" to the "degenerate Sons of Africa."[32] Free Blacks in Charleston who met to discuss "emigrating to Liberia" did so in much more moderate terms. They declared their interest in leaving the "land that gave us birth" in order to "emigrate to Liberia, in Africa, the land of our ancestors," where they would be able to live in "union and brotherly love," but they simultaneously assured any whites who might be worried about the "purity of [their] intentions," that they were determined not to "encourage any designs that may tend to . . . alienate the affections of our brethren who are held as property."[33] They expressed affection for, and kinship with, the peoples of Africa, but they divorced this assertion from any taint of antislavery sentiment. Thomas C. Brown, a black Charlestonian who returned from

Liberia, painted a picture of life in the colony that differed from the hopeful projections. He claimed always to have considered himself "an American," and said that he had gone to Africa to better his condition rather than to return home. He found few economic opportunities in Liberia. More disturbing, the settlers were inclined to buy slaves and remained so separate from indigenous residents that "the natives call the colonists white men, as a term of distinction."[34] Brown's Monrovia replicated the very aspects of the United States that had blocked his advance at home.

Thomas Brown returned to the United States when Liberia did not offer what he sought, and his story presumably found its way into print precisely because it undercut the arguments that the Colonization Society and its supporters were making for immigrating to Africa. The text took the form of an interview with Brown, and most questions focused on the practical realities of life in Monrovia—whether property held its value, if settlers were licentious, what the size of merchants' ships was—rather than on the place of Liberia in a projected history of the race. In this sense, Brown's interview represents more than his individual experience of Monrovia, for it centered on the quality of life issues that had replaced African nationalism at the center of black discussions of emigration during the preceding decade.

Nonetheless, elements of earlier protonationalist thought persisted even in the most pragmatic arguments for settling in Liberia. A three-sided 1827 exchange among pro- and anticolonizationist black Baltimoreans, and Lott Cary illustrates the persistence of filiative assertions of African kinship in a debate that increasingly turned on arguments about whether Liberia or the United States offered blacks the better chance to surmount the obstacles to individual betterment created by the history of oppression that they shared. The exchange began with the publication of a "Memorial of the Free People of Colour" of Baltimore. Meetings held in the two black churches where Daniel Coker had once preached—the Sharp Street Methodist Church and the Bethel AME Church—had passed resolutions regarding colonization. The memorialists were convinced that white racism and the degrading effects of slavery had the inevitable "effect of crushing, not developing, the capacities that God" had given blacks, and that this would continue to be the case so long as black people remained in America. Only in Africa could blacks "be freemen," and as freemen, the memorialists assured white Baltimoreans, they would implant "your language, your customs, your opinions and Christianity" on that "distant shore." The main thrust of the memorial emphasized the fundamental similarities among black and white people, and argued that blacks should move to Liberia because Africa provided them the best hope for the opportunities that history (rather than nature) had denied them in the United States. When, however, the memorial referred to those who would lead the migration to Liberia as "pioneers in *African restoration*" (my emphasis), it suggested that Africa was the natural home for all blacks of the diaspora.[35]

Predictably, black opponents of colonization quickly answered the memorial, and just as predictably some either failed to notice or else ignored the reference to "African restoration," choosing to concentrate on refuting the memorialists' arguments about blacks' poor prospects in the United States and the brighter future offered in Liberia. "Africanus" denied that the memorialists spoke for most free people of color in Baltimore. He questioned the antislavery motives that the memorialists' attributed to the ACS, and he asserted that, having been "born in the United States," it would have been "very unnatural" for him "to have no love for [his] country." After all, the "American Republic" had shaped his "taste, manners, habits, customs, and opinions," and he was "perfectly contented" to remain in the United States enjoying "the blessings that flow[ed] from . . . its free principles." "A Colored Baltimorean" echoed Africanus's insistence that the memorialists did not speak for the town's entire free black population. He assured his "colored brethren of Philadelphia and New York" that their "well known opinions" were shared by most blacks in Baltimore, as illustrated by the paucity of emigrants from the town on the Colonization Society's latest expedition to Liberia. The Colored Baltimorean refuted the memorialists point by point, offering the lone public response to the implied essentialism of the memorial: "That instrument [the memorial] holds out the idea that Africa is the *only* country to which" blacks "can go, and enjoy those privileges for which they leave their native land." But blacks were found in all "habitable [parts of the] globe," so why could they not pursue their dreams wherever they lived?[36] Neither Africanus nor the Colored Baltimorean believed that blacks born in the United States need seek their futures elsewhere.

When news of this dispute reached Liberia, Lott Cary tried to weigh in with a pamphlet supporting the Baltimore Memorialists and answering the doubts of the many black Americans who despised the ACS and rejected colonization. The bulk of the unpublished pamphlet echoed his Baltimore allies' insistence that white racism would always block blacks' path to equality in the United States, a situation he contrasted with his experience of having "almost forgotten" that race prejudice existed after living several years in Liberia. Cary took for granted that all black Americans longed to conduct "the affairs of [their] own Government," but found it so inconceivable that whites would ever allow that to happen in America that he declared blacks who spoke of liberty in the United States to be "like our Parrots are to us—using words without regard to the person or character to whom they are applied." Blacks' only real opportunity to become good men and citizens— good Americans—was in Africa.[37]

If, however, Cary's primary reasons that blacks should move to Liberia involved practical matters that were rooted in the history of race and slavery in America, he flirted with racial essentialism when discussing why blacks were less well suited for the New World than the Old. While acknowledging that a few blacks prospered in Philadelphia—"the Revd Richard Allen or Fortune [James Forten] or [John] Gloucester"—he described most blacks living in "the Frigid Zone" as hopelessly dependent on white charity. Blacks simply were not meant to live outside of tropical climates, and should reassert their ancestral and natural claim to an African home: "as long as Africa remains unpeopled by any other nation.—You may know that she is waiting for her rightful Sons, and here you or your children must and shall come." Should black Americans "refuse to be restored" to Africa, they would hurt emancipation's chances in the South and strengthen racism throughout America.[38] This late and relatively brief turn toward the language of an African nation, and toward a claim that blacks had a natural affinity for Africa, does not reveal that Cary's true beliefs ran toward filiative notions of black kinship, but it does underscore the persistence of the language of African identity even during the ascendancy of the Colonization Society.

When black Nova Scotians had contemplated their exodus to Sierra Leone, many had explicitly acknowledged that the hardships and growing pains associated with starting a new colony would be the price to pay to be members of a glory-seeking charter generation of pioneers founding a new nation. By the end of the 1820s black Americans contemplating emigration saw things differently. Both advocates and opponents of emigration focused on where blacks could find the greatest individual opportunity—where they could best fulfill their dreams of living American lives. This turn toward a more pragmatic approach to the prospects of living in Africa did not, however, completely subsume the earlier discussions of African identity.

III

The case of John B. Russwurm brought these issues to a head. Russwurm was the son of a white Virginia merchant who was living in Jamaica and a Jamaican woman of African descent. When his father returned to the United States in 1807, he sent his eight-year-old mixed-race son to Quebec, presumably because he would face less stigma there than in the U.S. South.[39] Russwurm attended secondary school in Quebec and then went to Bowdoin College, becoming one of the first African Americans to earn a college degree, and delivering an address at his graduation on "The Condition and

Prospects of Hayti."[40] After college he moved to New York City where, in 1827, he signed on as junior editor to Samuel E. Cornish on *Freedom's Journal*, the first black newspaper published in the United States. In the absence of a reference to Africa in its title as well as in much of its editorial content, *Freedom's Journal* embodied the decline in public black discussions of African identity during the 1820s. It began as an explicitly anticolonization newspaper, and the editors invoked a particularly powerful icon of freedom in nineteenth-century black American culture when they proudly declared that the Constitution of the United States would be their "polar star" as they sought to give voice to "FIVE HUNDRED THOUSAND FREE PEOPLE OF COLOUR."[41] The paper voiced free black Americans' determination to find a place as equal citizens in the United States.

The editors pledged to keep their "columns . . . open to a temperate discussion" of a wide range of topics and lived up to that promise by publishing articles on history and science as well as critiques of some black Americans' dandyism on the one hand, and others' crudity, on the other. They published articles by supporters of the Colonization Society as well as its critics.[42] The paper's columns reflected the editors' interests in events affecting black people throughout the world, with news from Europe and extended travel accounts from western explorers of Africa. In fact, though the editors did not claim to be "Africans," they showed particular interest in Africa, including regular updates on events in Sierra Leone and Liberia. Russwurm continued to display an interest in news from Haiti and *Freedom's Journal* published a serialized short story that was set on the island republic. The paper reported on slavery in the southern United States and on the activities of free black people in free and slave states. Each issue listed "Authorised Agents" in different states reaching from North Carolina to Maine, and international agents in Liverpool and Port-au-Prince,[43] and the editors published correspondence sent from throughout the United States. *Freedom's Journal* published extensively on Africa and on colonization, but the visions of colonization that were debated in its columns were just that—visions of colonization, rather than discussions of the emigrationist projects that were so prevalent among black Americans prior to 1817.

Freedom's Journal ceased when Russwurm stepped down as editor after two years, and just before doing so he announced a change of heart regarding the Colonization Society and Liberia. After regretfully reporting the sad news of Lott Cary's recent death in Monrovia, he announced that his "views [were] materially altered," and he offered an extended explanation of his new position that stretched across three issues.[44] Many former allies felt betrayed by his decision and attacked him as a traitor, reportedly burning him in effigy at one meeting. Though they did not yet know that Russwurm had been seeking a position with the ACS, his critics maintained that he was nothing more than an opportunist, switching sides upon discovering that editing an anti-colonization newspaper offered such meager material rewards.[45]

One need not look for questionable motives, however, to explain Russwurm's interest in emigration; in his graduation speech just three years earlier he had hailed the "pleasing hope" that Haiti was laying "the foundation of an Empire that will rank with the nations of the Earth," and he was reported at the time to be preparing "to settle in Hayti."[46] It seems more reasonable to accept his own explanation that he had come to think that "citizenship in this country" was a chimera and to believe that the widespread suspicions of the Colonization Society among black Americans were based on prejudice. In that light he had determined that Liberia offered black Americans their best hope of a place to "enjoy all the rights of freemen."[47] The popular refusal to take Russwurm at his word, the conviction that he was, instead, duplicitous and a traitor to the cause, reflects how much some opponents of the Colonization Society believed was at stake.

To be sure, not everyone reacted this way. His former coeditor, Samuel Cornish, and Peter Williams Jr. both rejected Russwurm's arguments in favor of the ACS and of colonization as the answer to America's racial problems, but they supported his personal decision to emigrate to Liberia by responding to inquiries from the Colonization Society with testimonials to his good character.[48] Williams later elaborated on his position in a speech to black New Yorkers in which he rejected Russwurm's logic, insisting that he retained faith that the "principles of the Declaration of Independence and of the Gospel of Christ" could raise black people to citizenship in the United States. Nonetheless, he had never opposed "any man of color" who had "carefully considered the subject" and decided it was "best to emigrate to Africa," and he was proud to have "helped John B. Russwurm to go to Liberia." The thermometer that Russwurm had given Williams "as a token of gratitude" was on proud display in the New Yorker's house.[49] Williams's position reveals the terms in which colonization was debated when assertions of African identity receded. He disagreed with Russwurm about where black people could most reasonably achieve the rights that all Americans—all people—should enjoy, but he respected those who exercised their free choice by deciding that emigration to Liberia offered the best chance to achieve those rights. The best interests of black Americans were very much at issue and open to debate, but, even for a former colleague of Cuffe, questions about the fate of an "African people" or nation simply did not arise.

The same thing could almost be said of the other side of the debate, but not quite. Russwurm argued, both explicitly and implicitly, that Liberia and colonization offered black people the broadest scope for individual advancement and the greatest opportunity to claim their basic human rights—that, in a very real sense, Liberia offered blacks their best chance to live as Americans. In answering concerns about the difficulty of moving to a new colony, he provided an extended comparison of the challenges facing the first English settlers of Virginia and those moving to the "flourishing, but infant colony" of Liberia. Like promoters of early English colonization, he offered a brief bow to the importance of serving as "pioneers of civilization and Heralds of the Cross" to an "unexplored quarter of our globe," but the weight of his argument rested on the claim that blacks faced a brighter prospect in Liberia than in the United States.

There is, however, reason to suspect that he may have hoped for something grander. His graduation speech had, after all, invoked the future greatness of the Haitian nation. More to the immediate point, as he prepared to leave for Monrovia, he visited Baltimore, where he stayed with Hezekiah Grice, the earlier proponent of a black Baltimore trading company. He and Grice met with supporters of colonization to revive discussions of the trading "Company which the C[olored]. Peo[ple]. of B[altimore]" hoped would establish regular commercial and human exchanges between Liberia and blacks in the United States.[50] Whether this represents crass commercial interest, a private commitment on Russwurm's part to a nationalist program, or the lingering influence of Cuffe's nationalist vision remains obscure and perhaps unimportant. By 1829, the best way to argue for black emigration was to emphasize the chances for personal advancement and the possibility of building a society in which black people would be able to enjoy the rights and privileges that should have been theirs in the United States.

Russwurm's career in Liberia stood as an emblem of such a belief. Even before emigrating, he openly pursued careerist goals, corresponding with the ACS to ensure that the Society would appoint him to a position suitable to his education and ability. He sailed for Monrovia in the fall of 1829 to take up his charge as superintendent of schools for the colony, and in remarkably short order he also assumed the position of colonial secretary, purchased a boat, and became one of the colony's leading merchants. He also founded and edited the *Liberia Herald*. By 1836, having reached the Colonization Society's glass ceiling for black people, Russwurm accepted an invitation to move to the Maryland Colonization Society's new allied but autonomous Liberian colony at Cape Palmas, where he was appointed governor, a position he held until his death in 1851.[51]

As governor of Maryland in Africa, a name that perfectly embodied the idea of creating an American society in Liberia, Russwurm became the most prominent Americo-Liberian of his generation. He assumed leadership of a colony that, unlike the one centered on Monrovia, had a constitution and bill of rights, and one that officially discouraged trade with neighboring peoples in what seems to have been an effort to insulate the settlers from the corrupting influences of Africa.[52] During his long tenure as governor, he sought to encourage the agricultural independence of the settlement and to foster peaceful and regulated commercial and diplomatic relations with neighboring peoples, all in an effort to build an American society on the coast of Africa.[53] Had the discourse on African identity continued to develop after the foundation of the ACS, then Maryland in Liberia with John Russwurm as its governor might have stood as a prototype of the black polity on the coast of Africa that Paul Cuffe had considered necessary to the development of a commercial African diasporic nation. Instead, the cosmopolitan Russwurm who had lived in Jamaica, Quebec, the United States, and Liberia, where he had worked as a writer, editor, merchant, politician, and racial activist, sought to create a black American state as an enclave on the coast of Africa, a place where black settlers from the United States could become more fully American.

IV

The commitment to emigrationism and the vision of an African nation that lay behind it were deep, and it took the better part of a decade for many to give up that vision. Some black activists who eschewed colonization continued, in fact, to offer narratives of African identity that fall squarely within the boundaries of the earlier tradition.[54] Others offered idiosyncratic portrayals of a deep and ongoing connection between black people in Africa and America.[55] Many more straddled the traditional assertion of kinship with blacks in Africa, and the increasingly dominant emphasis on Americanness.[56] But the existence of a variety of responses should not obscure the larger truth, that the general movement among black activists from the 1820s through the 1840s was away from assertions of African identity, precisely because the assertion of such an identity or the expression of interest in emigrating to Africa effectively allied one with a movement that many believed was devoted to eliminating the nation's free black population in order to fasten slavery's chains ever more securely on those who remained behind.

Black activists in the United States spoke increasingly of their commitment to the land of their birth, rather than to that of their fathers, and they insisted on their basic Americanness. The great black protest movement of the 1830s was, revealingly, the "Colored Convention" movement. The shift from "African" institutions to "Colored" ones was not simply a matter of fashion, as Russwurm's former colleague Samuel Cornish made clear when he issued this call: "Let us and our friends unite, in baptizing the term 'Colored American,' and henceforth let us be written of, preached of, and prayed for as such. It is the true term, and one which is above reproach." And why was it above reproach? In part because it lacked the negative connotations of other terms (*"Negroes, Africans,* and *blacks"*), but also, presumably, because it embodied the belief that Cornish had long held: that blacks "should some day possess in" their "native-land, *a perfect equality, in all respects,* with" their "white brethren."[57]

A generation of scholarship has shown that black activists working within this vein played a crucial role in the fight against slavery by insisting that slaves enjoyed equality before God and that they had legitimate claim to full human rights, a claim that slavery mocked and only immediate abolition could make good. It might be useful, though, to look at this shift in language from the perspective of the original founding insights of historian David Roediger's work on whiteness. Roediger argued that white racial identity was different from other forms because it was essentially a negative identity—being "white" meant nothing beyond being not black and not enslaved.[58] The content of "colored American" was not quite the same: it was less a negative identity than a claim to essential sameness, an insistence that racial difference was superficial rather than fundamental—in modern terms, that it involved the color of one's skin, but told nothing about character or essence. However much one agrees with that perspective, this linguistic turn exacted a cost. It shifted the emphasis in racial activism away from the shared history of oppression experienced by the peoples of Africa's diaspora and toward more formalist claims for equality. Such claims could and did undercut arguments for the perpetuation of legal inequality and thus helped in the struggle against slavery, though the nationalist claims of activists like Paul Cuffe could have been equally effective in that struggle.

The language of formal equality was not, however, an equally effective rhetorical weapon in the struggle for socioeconomic equality. It explained why slavery should be abolished, but it provided a less powerful rationale for collective action to "uplift the race." When, in the wake of the Fugitive Slave Act of 1850, and then emancipation, black Americans recognized the poverty of the language of formal equality in the struggle for social justice, they had to develop new arguments for collective economic action or reactivate the legacy of the kinds of protonationalist programs that Cuffe had pioneered and that followers like Daniel Coker had sought to perpetuate. The early black discourse on African identity laid claim to the rhetorical power of nationalism while avoiding much of the chauvinism that nationalism usually brings in its wake, and it did so without rejecting sociocultural engagement with white American society. The forces arrayed against this incipient African national movement were enormous and I am not suggesting that the unfortunate appearance of the American Colonization Society blocked what would otherwise have been an answer to the problem of racial injustice. The struggle against racial inequality was, however, weakened when the movement was driven underground.

Epilogue

The Fugitive Slave Law of 1850 and Renewed Assertions of African Identity

Much of the interest in an early black discourse on African identity rests on the persistent appeal of black nationalist programs and rhetoric throughout the twentieth and into the twenty-first centuries. As the preceding analysis shows, early black discussions of African identity lacked most of the racial essentialism present, either implicitly or explicitly, in many later assertions of black nationalism within the Anglophone Atlantic. Explaining the contours of postbellum nationalist thought would require a different book, but an abbreviated examination of the resurgence of black interest in Africa in the wake of the Fugitive Slave Law of 1850 can point to a few key aspects of the story in order to highlight much that was lost when the rise of the Colonization Society forced black Americans to abandon Cuffe's vision.

It was not lost all at once. In 1829 and 1830 David Walker published his *Appeal to the Coloured Citizens of the World*, revealing in its title the rise of the language of colored Americanism, while showing in its content that such language need not reflect a rejection of the substance behind assertions of African identity. Walker's *Appeal*, justly famous as one of the most radical early black nationalist texts, ranges widely, using examples stretching from scripture, to classical history, to the contemporary world to show that blacks suffered more grievously under American slavery than had any other oppressed group. When making that argument, Walker most often referred to "coloured people," but that did not represent a rejection of ties to Africa. He forthrightly proclaimed himself "one of the oppressed, degraded and wretched sons of Africa," and on several occasions he discussed African history. Sometimes this was done in ways that drew analogies to black American history—the great African general Hannibal might have defeated

Rome had his people not been "disunited, as the coloured people are now, in the United States of America." At other times, he confronted whites with their crimes in Africa in language that tied black Americans directly to the continent of their forebears: "have you not . . . entered *among us*, and *learnt us* the art of throat-cutting" (emphasis added) so that we would "make slaves for you and your children?" At still other times, he called forth racial pride, discussing the "sons of Africa or of Ham, among whom learning originated." Notwithstanding Walker's engagement with the same kinds of classical and historical sources that had informed Prince Hall's construction of the history of African Freemasons, one of the main thrusts of his *Appeal* is a refutation of the claims and program of the American Colonization Society. As the historian Peter Hinks has shown, David Walker wielded his radical pen to demand that whites cease denying "coloured Americans" the American rights that were properly theirs. Walker sought to rally blacks to claim the United States as their home, not to organize emigrants to travel to Freetown or Monrovia in order to build a diasporic nation.[1]

White political action during the 1850s would create conditions, however, in which emigrationism and appeals to African identity would resurface and gain new purchase within black liberation movements. During the 1830s and 1840s most black and many white antislavery activists continued to reject the Colonization Society and insist that once abolition was won, the freedmen would take their proper places within the republic as "colored Americans." Free black Northerners were among the most ardent advocates of immediate abolition, and they also sought to overturn racially discriminatory laws in the free states as part of their struggle for justice and equality.[2] The 1830s and 1840s were, however, difficult years for Americans opposed to slavery. Antiabolition riots often morphed seamlessly into mob attacks on northern black communities; northern state legislatures passed increasingly discriminatory legislation targeting African Americans; all the while, from gag rules governing debate in Congress to the formation of foreign policy, the federal government worked to protect and expand the domain of slavery.[3] Shortly after the United States acquired California in the Mexican War, the gold rush began, precipitating a sequence of events that pushed many black Americans past their tolerance for American racism and toward a reengagement with Africa and emigrationism.

The gold strike at Sutter's Mill brought a wave of prospectors who quickly pushed California's population over the threshold required for statehood. The lawlessness associated with the young, unattached male adventurers who moved west to seek their fortunes stimulated leading settlers to organize rapidly, and by 1850 California had submitted a constitution to Congress and requested admission into the union. That constitution prohibited slavery in the new state. California's entry into the union as a free state threatened to tip the carefully maintained balance between free and slave states in the Senate, so southern representatives stalled the measure.

The stalemate ended with the Compromise of 1850, which granted statehood to California in return for, among other things, passage of the draconian Fugitive Slave Act of 1850. The new law empowered southern slave catchers to command Northerners to help capture alleged runaways, and it created a presumption that any black person claimed by a slave owner was, in fact, enslaved. It created special courts with magistrates appointed solely to adjudicate fugitive slave cases. Judges were paid for each case that they heard, and they were paid more if they decided that the alleged runaway was a slave than if they determined that she was entitled to freedom. In the words of the black abolitionist Martin R. Delany, the Fugitive Slave Law made "the colored people of the United States . . . liable at any time in any place, and under all circumstances, to be arrested—and upon the claim of any white person, without the privilege, even of making a defense, sent into endless bondage." He concluded that "a people capable of originating and sustaining such a law . . . are not the people to whom we are willing to entrust our liberty."[4] Delany began to advocate emigration.

Delany, the son of a free black woman and an enslaved man, had moved from his birthplace in Charles Town, Virginia (now Charleston, West Virginia), to Chambersburg, Pennsylvania, as a boy. As a young man, he moved to Pittsburgh where he acquired an education and apprenticed with a white doctor before setting up as a cupper, bleeder, and leecher.[5] He soon founded a small newspaper in Pittsburgh called the *Mystery*, eventually attracting the attention of Frederick Douglass and William Lloyd Garrison and earning an invitation from Douglass to serve as coeditor of the *North Star*, the newspaper that Douglass founded in Rochester, New York. Delany spent most of his time as coeditor (1847–49) traveling through the western half of the United States drumming up subscribers, and writing dispatches on black life in the West. Throughout the 1840s he joined with Douglass, Garrison, and other immediate abolitionists in condemning the American Colonization Society and colonization more generally. One of the major essays that he published during his tenure with the *North Star* was, in fact, a polemic attacking the newly independent republic of Liberia as a land of false promise.[6]

Disgusted and depressed by the passage of the Fugitive Slave Act, Delany broke with Douglass and embarked upon what became a more complicated and contradictory career than his reputation as the "father of African nationalism" might suggest. In a world that offered no clear paths to black advancement, Delany's pursuit of racial uplift led him down one dead end after another. He was a doctor, a journalist, a novelist, an activist, an explorer, a politician, and a scholar. At different times, he supported emigration to

Canada, to Latin America, to East Africa, and to West Africa. With the onset of the Civil War, he regained hope for a better future in the United States and served the Union valiantly. In Reconstruction he fought for Freedmen's rights and ran for Lieutenant Governor of South Carolina before becoming so unhappy with what he thought were the false promises of the Republican Party that he endorsed Wade Hampton, the ex-Confederate "Redeemer" Democrat, for governor in 1876. Toward the end of his life, he returned to his interest in Africa, publishing *Principia of Ethnology*, a celebration of ancient African civilizations and of the inherent superiority of African people. If, however, his positions on the proper path to racial uplift changed in response to events, his commitment to the cause was constant. Exploring the ways that he revitalized claims to African identity and the project of emigration in the wake of the Fugitive Slave Act of 1850 reveals some important changes in the conditions shaping black activism between the first decade of the nineteenth century and the 1850s, changes whose influence reached deep into the twentieth century.

Delany, like Cuffe before him, believed that African peoples could only achieve their destiny by becoming a people and building their own nation. He explained his position in what was probably his single most important speech, his keynote address to the 1854 National Emigration Convention of Colored Men in Cleveland, Ohio: "Political Destiny of the Colored Race on the American Continent."[7] He rejected the common "false impression" that extending "the privilege of *voting*" to black Americans would confer on them the "*rights of citizenship*" (emphases in original). Those who placed so much faith in the ballot ignored the "great principle of political economy" that "no people can be free who themselves do not constitute an essential part of the *ruling element* of the country in which they live." Only when black people controlled their own destinies, only when they constituted a majority of the population of a nation and thus could defend their economic and political autonomy, could they truly possess sovereignty as a people. This would never happen in the United States, so Delany proposed emigration as the only "remedy" for the "disease" afflicting his people. Where, though, should black Americans go?[8]

Delany's answer to this question distanced him from Cuffe's legacy. To begin with, he placed far greater importance on the projected locale of an African nation. Cuffe had focused his nationalist activism on Sierra Leone but had recognized that many black Americans did not want to move to Africa, so he had considered alternative possible locations for a black polity. It might seem that Delany's consideration of multiple locales simply replicated Cuffe's, but that seeming similarity conceals the different stakes that each thinker saw in the question. Cuffe had raised the possibility of different locales for a black colony in a catholic spirit that rested less on the inherently proper place for such a nation than on the practical question of where black American emigrants might choose to go. If black Americans did not want to go to Sierra Leone, then a colony in the western portions of the United States might help serve the same purposes. The diasporic black nation that he sought to create was not going to rise in conflict against European nations— instead it would assume a peaceful role in the commercial system of the Atlantic world—and Cuffe never wrote as if the rising people would need to consolidate their hold on the new nation against internal or external enemies.

Delany, writing in the wake of a quarter-century of hardening racial science, a period in which he and other antislavery activists had seen the Slave Power cement its dominance of the United States, was less inclined to envision international cooperation. Noting that even seemingly progressive white Americans sought "*universal Anglo-Saxon predominance*" (emphasis in original), Delany anticipated W. E. B. DuBois by insisting that "the great issue, sooner or later, upon which must be disputed the world's destiny, will be a question of black and white, and every individual will be called upon" to identify "with one or the other." Black Americans needed to settle in a place where the vast majority of residents would come down on the black side of that divide; otherwise anything they accomplished would contribute to their enemy in the looming contest. This led Delany to propose an alliance of "blacks and colored races," and thus to see the "West Indies, Central and South America" as the "countries of our choice" for an African nation, when he surveyed the possibilities in 1854. Later he would travel to West Africa scouting possible sites in the Old World for the nation he sought to help found, even going so far as to reconsider his hostility toward Liberia and its formerly American leaders. If, however, he wavered with regard to the best site on which to begin building this new nation, his ultimate goal remained the same during the entire period he advocated emigration: to found a locus of resistance to Anglo-Saxon domination of the colored races.[9]

His focus on the struggle between the races reflected Delany's engagement with nineteenth-century science as well as his reaction to American politics. Delany had a more purely filiative notion of racial difference than had Paul Cuffe. While both looked to history to describe what separated white and black people, Delany, well versed in nineteenth-century racial science, saw in historical patterns more fundamental inherent differences. "The truth," he announced to the 1854 Convention in Cleveland, "is, that we are not identical with the Anglo-Saxon or any other race of the Caucasian or pure white Type of the human family." He believed that there were "inherent traits, attributes—so to speak—and native characteristics, peculiar to our race," and that the purpose of a black nation would be to "cultivate these and develop them in their purity, to make them desirable and emulated by the rest of the world." Only by acknowledging and pursuing the natural gifts of their race could blacks achieve their place in world history. The black nation that would arise—whether it did so in Africa or Latin America—would express the essential characteristics of the African race, and it would uphold those characteristics in opposition to the racial qualities that found expression in white nation-states like the United States.

The "colored races" were "civil, peaceable and religious to a fault," and though they had less aptitude for "mathematics, sculpture and architecture" as well as "commerce and internal improvements," they were preeminent in "languages, oratory, poetry, music, and painting" as well as "ethics, metaphysics, theology, and legal jurisprudence." A separate nation would permit "the black race" to show its superiority in "the true principles of morals, correctness of thought, religion, and law or civil government."[10] Cuffe had also clearly envisioned a black nation arising to take its place among the nations of the Western world—among what he had called the "historians' nations"— but the nation he foresaw would assume its place harmoniously and cooperatively. It would allow blacks to enjoy and express universal human qualities and aspirations. The nation that Delany hoped would emerge from the emigration of black Americans to a new land would assume its place in a more contentious world of nation-states, a world in which it would struggle for, and ultimately win, dominance.

The most significant difference between Delany's nationalist vision and that of Cuffe involves the way their ideas were received. Just as Cuffe projected a nation that would exist harmoniously in a world of nation-states, so too did he pursue his plan without facing serious black opposition. The vast majority of black Americans preferred to stay in the United States rather than emigrate to Sierra Leone, but none left evidence of having found Cuffe's advocacy of emigration dangerous or troubling. Cuffe was a unifying figure.

Delany was quite the opposite. His support for emigration necessitated a split with his former friend and colleague Frederick Douglass, and that very public split initiated a struggle between the two for leadership of the black antislavery movement, a struggle that set a pattern that persisted through much of the twentieth century.[11] Activists advocating emigration in the wake of the ACS had to establish a clear distance from the policies of the Society, and this need, as well as other political developments, pushed them toward a more determined separatist position. This became evident in the split between Frederick Douglass, the voice of integration and cooperation, and Martin Delany, speaking for separatism and emigration. Similar recurring tensions would come to characterize the black struggle for equality, running from these antebellum figures to the competitions for racial leadership between Booker T. Washington and W. E. B. DuBois, between

DuBois and Marcus Garvey, and between Martin Luther King Jr. and Malcolm X. It might seem that this persistent antagonism echoed the tension between filiative and affiliative notions of African identity that had emerged out of the eighteenth century and the first wave of black discussions of African identity, and it is certainly true that, just as was true of eighteenth-century thinkers, one can find elements of separatism in the thought of any integrationist leader (and vice versa).

Notwithstanding the real parallels between these two oppositions, much more had changed than remained the same. Participants in the early black discussions of African identity never insisted that followers choose between filiative and affiliative narratives of identity. Cuffe's vision could and did encompass a broad spectrum of belief, in part because the world of nation-states into which he hoped to propel the African people was, in his mind, a world of benevolent commerce in which different nations could travel a path toward progress simultaneously. It was one in which African nationalism could link black communities in Philadelphia, New York, Boston, Baltimore, London, and Freetown without clashing with British or U.S. national traditions and identities.

Delany's nationalism, the black nationalism that informed late nineteenth- and twentieth-century nationalist movements, reflected the harsh and incipiently Darwinist context out of which it emerged. Nations and the races that found their expression in nationalism were engaged in a struggle for mastery. Winning that struggle meant that others would lose. Periodic hopeful bouts with universalism aside, the black nationalist Delany saw world history in terms of this battle for racial dominance. Blacks who failed to join the battle strengthened the enemy race, and white professed allies could only be trusted hesitantly. If black nationalism has struggled with this polarizing legacy of Delany's thought—and it has—that struggle has been part of a more global failure to escape the racial chauvinism central to nineteenth-century nationalism.

It is tempting to believe that this struggle might have been easier to win had the visions of African identity that culminated in Paul Cuffe's program remained vibrant within black thought. Perhaps a black abolitionist movement in which figures like James Forten, Richard Allen, and Daniel Coker had continued to spearhead attacks on the Peculiar Institution while tying racial uplift to a progressive movement linking the progress of all African peoples could have mediated the splits between integrationist and separatist advocates of black rights. For this to have happened, however, black nationalists would have had to stand aloof from the main currents of nationalist thought throughout the world. As much as one might want to believe that might have happened, doing so requires more faith in the power of benevolent ideas than most can muster.

The importance of the early conversations about African identity that have been analyzed in *Becoming African in America* speaks both to our understanding of the era of the early republic and to the broader discourse of African identity that these discussions helped create. In many ways, the efforts of Prince Hall, Paul Cuffe, Daniel Coker, and others to forge a consensual nation upon assertions of the mythic unity of the people parallel the rhetorical constructions of the nation in Anglo-American political thought. The turn to the trope of a chosen people also had parallels in the nationalism of the United States and Great Britain. The creative variant of this thought that informed blacks' claims to an African identity and their project of African nationalism underscores the power of the vision of a consensual nation that emerged during this period, though the common reliance on the claim to chosen-ness simultaneously suggests the fear that consent provided too fragile a prop to secure the people's allegiance. The early discourse on African identity also casts interesting light on some later expressions of black nationalism, by reminding us that claims to the timeless unity of all African people—like claims to the timeless unity of other peoples— are, themselves, anything but timeless.

Notes

1. *Memoir and Theatrical Career of Ira Aldridge, The African Roscius*, 8–9 (story of African origins). My discussion of Aldridge draws heavily on Herbert Marshall and Mildred Stock, *Ira* and Shane White, *Stories of Freedom in Black New York*. For the authorship of *Memoir*, see White, 96, 239n49. My quotations from *Memoir* will be from the copy at the Harvard Theatre Collection, Harvard University Libraries, a copy in which the original pages have been cut out and pasted into a notebook with illustrations, stage bills, obituaries, and other material interspersed.

2. White, *Stories of Freedom*, chap. 2. For a wonderful collection of documents, see George A. Thompson Jr., ed., *A Documentary History of the African Theatre*.

3. Dick Russell, *Black Genius and the American Experience*, chap. 8; also see the Ira Aldridge Clippings File, Harvard Theatre Collection, Harvard University Libraries.

4. Quoted in Marshall and Stock, *Ira Aldridge*, 10. Roscius was a Greek slave who became a celebrated actor on the ancient Roman stage. Aldridge apparently told other origin tales, sometimes claiming to have been from Maryland. At least one newspaper reported that he had been born in Bel Air, Maryland, that his real name was Hewlett—presumably a reference to James Hewlett, the star of New York's African Theatre, and that he had "apprenticed to a ship-carpenter and learned his trade in the same yard with Molyneux, the celebrated negro pugilist." Ira Aldridge Clippings File, Harvard Theatre Collection.

5. *Memoir*, 9.

6. Philip Curtin, *The Image of Africa*; Winthrop D. Jordan, *White over Black*, esp. chaps. 1 and 6; Kwame Anthony Appiah, *In My Father's House*; Kathleen M. Brown, *Good Wives, Nasty Wenches and Anxious Patriarchs*, chap. 1 are important works in

the voluminous literature on early understandings of racial difference. Essays by David Brion Davis, Emily C. Bartels, Alden T. Vaughan and Virginia Mason Vaughan, and Benjamin Braude in a special issue on race of *The William and Mary Quarterly*, 3rd ser., 54 (January 1997) testify to the complexity of medieval and early modern western understandings of Africa and race. See Colin Kidd, *The Forging of Races*, esp. chap. 4 for race, Christianity, and the Enlightenment. Tunde Adeleke, *Unafrican Americans*, Introduction and chap. 1 provide a concise review of much secondary literature. Emmanuel Chukwudy Eze, ed., *Race and the Enlightenment: A Reader* includes a useful selection of edited primary texts on "racial" thought from Linnaeus to Hegel; and see Ivan Hannaford, *Race*, chaps. 6–8 for an overview.

7. The literature on early black writing is large and growing. For an introduction to it, see Paul Edwards, "Three West African Writers of the 1780s," 175–98; William L. Andrews, *To Tell a Free Story*, chaps. 1 and 2; Henry Louis Gates Jr., *The Signifying Monkey*; Dickson D. Bruce, Jr., *The Origins of African American Literature*. This book is deeply indebted to Vincent Carretta's important interpretive and editorial work, as will be obvious from my frequent citations of his editions of, and commentary on, these texts. See especially, Olaudah Equiano, *The Interesting Narrative and Other Writings*; Quobna Ottobah Cugoano, *Thoughts and Sentiments on the Evil of Slavery*; Ignatius Sancho, *Letters of the Late Ignatius Sancho, an African*; and Carretta, ed., *Unchained Voices*. Carretta brings together many themes that grow out of his work on these texts in *Equiano the African*.

8. Throughout this essay I will refer to "race" and "racial thinking," even though it is becoming increasingly clear that classic "racial thinking"—thinking based on the assumption that people of different "races" inherited qualities that made them inherently different from people of other "races"—did not develop until the nineteenth century (see Hannaford, *Race*). During the second half of the eighteenth century many western thinkers were debating whether to explain the differences among human races through recourse to environmental or genetic factors. While these distinctions are important for a history of the idea of race or a history of racism, they are more peripheral for a history of oppositional constructions of racial difference by black authors. See the works cited in n. 1 for the move from environmental and historical to biological and genetic explanations for perceived differences between Europeans and other peoples.

9. Helena Woodard, *African-British Writings in the Eighteenth Century*, chap. 4 explores this issue in a reading of Equiano/Vassa. One can imagine ways an African identity could have been constructed in which this would not have been required, but only if it was constructed outside of the cultural traditions of the West. For an important illustration of the possibility of such a counter-tradition, as well as the difficulty of working with it, see Ronald A. Judy, *(Dis)Forming the American Canon*. For explorations of the social history of enslaved African Muslims—the subjects of Judy's literary analysis—see Michael A. Gomez, *Exchanging Our Country Marks*, chap. 4, and Sylviane A. Diouf, *Servants of Allah*.

10. This language comes from Werner Sollors, *Beyond Ethnicity*.

11. *Barbaric Traffic*; Christopher Leslie Brown, *Moral Capital*; James T. Campbell, *Middle Passages*, chap. 1.

12. Simon Schama, *Rough Crossings*, part 1.

13. Recent books by three prominent historians emphasize the importance of the Nova Scotians: Campbell, *Middle Passage*; Schama, *Rough Crossings*; Cassandra Pybus, *Epic Journeys of Freedom*. Two important older books discuss the Black Loyalists: Ellen Gibson Wilson, *The Loyal Blacks*, and the excellent James W. St. G. Walker, *The Black Loyalists*.

14. For an introduction to this enormous, sophisticated, and contentious body of scholarship, see Melville J. Herskovits, *Life in a Haitian Valley*; E. Franklin Frazier, *The Free Negro Family*; Sidney W. Mintz and Richard Price, *The Birth of African-American Culture*; Robert Farris Thompson, *Flash of the Spirit*; Gomez, *Exchanging Our Country Marks*; Gwendolyn Midlo Hall, *Slavery and African Ethnicities in the Americas*; Douglas B. Chambers, *Murder at Montpelier*; Philip D. Morgan, "The Cultural Implications of the Atlantic Slave Trade: African Regional Origins, American Destinations and New World Developments," 122–45; John Thornton, *Africa and Africans in the Making of the Atlantic World*; Toyin Falola and Matt Childs, ed. *The Yoruba Diaspora in the Atlantic World*.

15. Sterling Stuckey, *Slave Culture*; James Oliver Horton and Lois E. Horton, *In Hope of Liberty*; Ira Berlin, *Generations of Captivity*, 86–87; cf. Wilson Jeremiah Moses, *Afrotopia*. This and other works of Moses have influenced my approach to this question.

CHAPTER 1

1. Virginia Mason Vaughan, *Performing Blackness on English Stages, 1500–1800*; Roxann Wheeler, *Complexion of Race*; Srinivas Aravamudan, *Tropicopolitans*; George Eleftherios Boulukos, "The Grateful Slave"; Thomas W. Krise, ed., *Caribbeana*; Catherine Molineux, "The Peripheries Within"; Catherine Molineux, "Hogarth's Fashionable Slaves: Moral Corruption in Eighteenth-Century London."

2. David Eltis, *The Rise of African Slavery in the Americas*, chaps. 8, 9; Christopher Leslie Brown, *Moral Capital*; Molineux, "Peripheries Within"; Aravamudan, *Tropicopolitans*, chaps. 1 and 6. Vincent Carretta and Philip Gould, ed., *Genius in Bondage* is an anthology of essays exploring different eighteenth-century black authors.

3. Ignatius Sancho, *Letters of the Late Ignatius Sancho, an African* (hereafter *Letters of Sancho*); Phillis Wheatley, *Complete Writings*.

4. The distinction between origins and beginnings is central to what has been awkwardly labeled "postmodern theory." For a concise discussion, see Edward W. Said, *Beginnings*, chap. 1. The distinction has been famously crucial for the work of Michel Foucault (and other "postmodern" philosophers and critics responding to Nietzsche's notion of genealogy). My interpretation of the importance of the works of Sancho and Wheatley as "beginnings" for an anglophone black discourse on Africa is indebted to

these works, but it is worth noting that historian Marc Bloch, horrified by his experiences living through the rise of European fascism, inveighed against the false god of origins half a century before the "postmodern moment" (see his *The Historian's Craft*).

5. Wheatley, *Complete Writings*, 7 (J. Wheatley's letter), 5 (P. Wheatley's preface). Her letters also contain evidence that suggests this is how she understood her life: in a letter to her friend Obour Tanner, a black woman from Newport, Rhode Island, Wheatley referred to herself as "a poor little outcast and a stranger when" Susannah Wheatley "took [her] in" (*Complete Writings*, 153). Wheatley's "true" feelings are less important to my argument, however, than her literary persona.

6. While this might call into question whether he intended to be published as an "African," he did, in fact, publish music that he composed under that title. See Josephine R. B. Wright, *Ignatius Sancho (1720–1780): An Early African Composer in England*, xxv. And, again, his intent, while relevant to my argument, is less important than the text that was published. *Letters of Sancho*, xiv–xv, xxiv–xxvi (Carretta on publication).

7. *Letters of Sancho*, 5.

8. Ibid., 73. Brycchan Carey, "'The Extraordinary Negro'" for the problems with the reliability of Joseph Jekyll's biographical sketch of Sancho.

9. Wheatley, *Complete Writings*, 169 (sacred fire), 7 (J. Wheatley's letter); *Letters of Sancho*, 73 (application), 112 (Heaven).

10. Wheatley, ibid., 10 (sable race), 5 (learning).

11. *Letters of Sancho*, 82 ("our" rather than "we"), 109, 113 (claims to be "actuated by zeal to my prince"), 214–15, 216. There were important occasions when he seemed to deny British citizenship (your country's conduct, 130; I am only a lodger, 177), but they took their meaning from his assumed status as unusual insider. I discuss them below. Wheatley, *Complete Works*, 40, 92–93. Poetic language is, of course, often ambiguous, and Wheatley's "we" is at least partly ironic. Nonetheless, it seems clear that Wheatley asserted a New England self. See David Grimsted, "Anglo-American Racism and Phillis Wheatley's 'Sable Veil,' 'Length'ned Chain,' and 'Knitted Hearth',", 348–52 for her support for the Revolution. Frank Shuffleton, "On Her Own Footing," 186–87 for Wheatley's "patriotic 'we.'" Betsy Erkkila, *Mixed Bloods and Other Crosses*, 77–88 argues that Wheatley used an in-between voice in order to "hybridize, reaccent, and revolutionize . . . terms" (80).

12. Grimsted, ibid., 371–94 (esp. 392–93) argues that Susannah Wheatley's circle of evangelical female friends included Phillis Wheatley and provided her crucial emotional support.

13. Wheatley, *Complete Works*, 72, 75. Sondra O'Neale, "A Slave's Subtle War," 153 (Ethiopianism).

14. Wheatley, *Complete Works*, 16 (Saviour), 13 (angelic train). See also Katherine Clay Bassard, *Spiritual Interrogations*, 38–39 (for an insightful reading of angelic train).

15. *Letters of Sancho*, 93.

16. See his letter to Laurence Sterne dated July 1776, *Letters of Sancho*, 73–74 for the most famous example. See 111, 112 (regarding Wheatley), 130–31 for others. As S. S. Sandhu, "Ignatius Sancho and Laurence Sterne" makes clear, however, a theologically

moderate but deeply held sense of Christian faith was important for both Sterne and Sancho.

17. Gretchen Gerzina, *Black London*; Molineux, "The Peripheries Within"; Vincent Carretta, "Soubise, Julius (C. 1754–1798)"; Vincent Carretta, ed., *Unchained Voices*, 103n3; Aravamudan, *Tropicopolitans*, chap. 1.

18. *Letters of Sancho*, 63 (books), 111 (heaven).

19. *Letters of Sancho*, 74, 118, 150, 180 (Sancho as blackamoor). For the man of feeling in eighteenth-century Anglo-American culture, see Julie Ellison, *Cato's Tears*. Ellison reads Wheatley as a poet of sentiment (114–21). The *Oxford English Dictionary* defines "blackamoor" as "a black-skinned African, an Ethiopian, a Negro," underscoring the way the word had emerged out of vague literary invocations of Africa.

20. Wheatley, *Complete Writings*, 139 (letter to Huntingdon), xiv–xix (path to publication).

21. Markman Ellis, "Ignatius Sancho's Letters," 200–202.

22. Gates, *Figures in Black*, 25.

23. Ellis, "Ignatius Sancho's Letters," 200 and 212n8. For Wheatley, see Rafia Zafar, *We Wear the Mask*, 15–24; Grimsted, "Anglo-American Racism," 338–444; O'Neale, "A Slave's Subtle War," 144–65; William H. Robinson, *Phillis Wheatley and Her Writings*, introduction; John C. Shields, "Phillis Wheatley's Struggle for Freedom in Her Poetry and Prose," 229–70; Betsy Erkkila, "Phillis Wheatley and the Black American Revolution," 225–40; Erkkila, *Mixed Bloods and Other Crosses*, 77–88; Shuffleton, "On Her Own Footing," 175–89.

24. The best introduction to early black anglophone writing is Carretta, ed., *Unchained Voices*. This anthology looks like a tool for teaching and serves that purpose, but Carretta's factual and interpretive notes to each text make it a significant work of scholarship whose importance extends beyond the classroom.

25. The concept of Africa goes far back into classical Western culture, and inquiries into the emergence of a concept of the "African" in anglophone and other European cultures have reasonably chosen many alternative starting points from Herodotus to the Romans to medieval religious scholars to Shakespeare and other Renaissance playwrights. For a sampling of such work, see Martin Bernal, *Black Athena*, the essays in *The William and Mary Quarterly*, 3rd ser., 54 (1997), especially David Brion Davis, "Constructing Race," 7–18; Emily C. Bartels, "Othello and Africa: Postcolonialism Reconsidered," 45–64; Benjamin Braude, "The Sons of Noah and the Construction of Ethnic and Geographical Identities in the Medieval and Early Modern Periods," 103–42. Also see Winthrop Jordan's classic *White over Black*; Ivan Hannaford, *Race*; Joyce Chaplin, "Race," 154–72.

26. Sandhu, "Ignatius Sancho and Laurence Sterne"; Carretta, "Introduction," *Letters of Sancho*, xii–xiv; *Letters of Sancho*, 10–24 (for the original subscription list, which includes John Meheux, the Duke and Duchess of Montagu, two Wingraves, two Irelands, and various other names from among Sancho's correspondents). For concise analyses of subscription and copyright in eighteenth-century British publishing, see

James Green, "The Publishing History of Olaudah Equiano's Interesting Narrative," 364–65; Vincent Carretta, "'Property of the Author': Olaudah Equiano's Place in the History of the Book," 130–50.

27. Bruce, *Origins*, 42–46 ; Carretta, "'Property of the Author,'" 136–37.

28. *Letters of Sancho*, 111–12, xxxi (for Carretta's discussion).

29. Said, *Beginnings*, xiii. Said argues that "modernism was an aesthetic and ideological phenomenon that was a response to the crisis of what could be called *filiation*—linear, biologically grounded process, that which ties children to their parents—which produced the counter-crisis within modernism of affiliation, that is, those creeds, philosophies, and visions re-assembling the world in non-familial ways." The black discourse on Africa did not emerge as a uni-directional movement from affiliation to filiation; the persistent tension between the two is central to the discourse.

30. Grimsted, "Anglo-American Racism," 338–444; O'Neale, "A Slave's Subtle War," 144–65; Robinson, *Phillis Wheatley and Her Writings*, "Introduction"; Shields, "Phillis Wheatley's Struggle for Freedom in Her Poetry and Prose," 229–70; William H. Robinson, *Black New England Letters*, chap. 2. Sandhu, "Ignatius Sancho and Laurence Sterne."

31. Margaretta Matilda Odell, *Memoir and Poems of Phillis Wheatley, a Native African and a Slave*, 10 (emphasis in original). Odell descended from the Wheatleys and wrote the "memoir" that preceded an edition of Wheatley's poems. Grimsted, "Anglo-American Racism," 364 suggests that the prominence of solar imagery in Wheatley's poetry can be read as a coded reference to this memory of her mother.

32. *Letters of Sancho*, 131; Wheatley, *Complete Works*, 87; Bruce, *Origins*, 58–59; Shuffleton, "On Her Own Footing," 84–85; Anthony J. Barker, *The African Link*, chap. 1 (British cultural sources).

33. *Letters of Sancho*, 131; Wheatley, *Complete Works*, 13. There are various readings of this poem. See, for example, Katherine Clay Bassard, *Spiritual Interrogations*, 38–39; Erkkila, "Phillis Wheatley," 233–34; Philip Gould, *Barbaric Traffic*, 64–66.

34. Wheatley, *Complete Works*, 40; *Letters of Sancho*, 60 (Guiney-born), 200–201 (was he an African—but it's no matter, he can't help the place of his nativity). Wheatley did, however, show interest in missionary work in Africa and an appreciation of the role of cultural difference within West Africa in some private letters that will be discussed below (*Complete Works*, 151–52, 154–56).

35. *Letters of Sancho*, 86 (Negroe), 113 and 214–15 (Africanus), 216 (son of Afric).

36. Wheatley, *Complete Works*, 61 (Afric muse), 72 (Ethiopians must be employ'd), 75 (Ethiopians speak).

37. Except, of course, that Wheatley, like other evangelical Protestants at the time, believed herself to be a sinner and thus fundamentally unworthy in God's eyes.

38. *Letters of Sancho*, 74 (Sterne), 111 (diabolical), 112 (Wheatley); Wheatley, *Complete Works*, 92–93. Sancho could not, of course, have known that the white Wheatleys would later manumit Phillis.

39. Wheatley, *Complete Works*, 152, 159.

40. For an example of the way such news found its way to London and thus would have reached Sancho, see Eltis, *The Rise of African Slavery in the Americas*, 233n35. For revolts in the British Caribbean, see Michael Craton, *Testing the Chains*. For contemporary discussions of slavery in British culture that were framed by Caribbean resistance, see Krise, ed. *Caribbeana*, 101–40.

41. Wheatley, *Complete Works*, 142.

42. Ibid., 116 (emphasis in original); Zafar, *We Wear the Mask*, 18.

43. Wheatley, *Complete Works*, 152–53 (Thornton: "disdain not to be called the Father of Humble Africans and Indians"), 150 (Occom). For Occom's struggle with putatively benevolent racism, see James Axtell, *The Invasion Within*, 210–11.

44. There were Muslim slaves in North America (see Michael A. Gomez, *Exchanging Our Country Marks*; and Sylviane A. Diouf, *Servants of Allah*), but Sancho cannot be understood to have been referring to them.

45. *Letters of Sancho*, 180.

46. Ibid., 67 (command), 216 (lipped).

47. Carretta, "Soubise, Julius"; Gerzina, *Black London*, 54–59; see Ellis, "Ignatius Sancho's Letters," 209–12 for Soubise and libertinism in Sancho's letters. For Carretta's sketch of Wingave, see *Letters of Sancho*, 253–54n1.

48. For a similar injunction from the Queensberry family, see Charles, Third Duke of Queensberry to Julius Soubise, Ambresbury, Nov. 8, 1772, box 7, Soubise Folder, Miscellaneous American Letters and Papers, The Schomburg Center for Research in Black Culture, The New York Public Library, New York City.

49. *Letters of Sancho*, 46. To this catalogue, he added "the ill-bred and heart-racking abuse of the foolish vulgar."

50. Ibid., 129–33, 204–7.

51. Gould, *Barbaric Traffic*; and Brown, *Moral Capital*, esp. chaps. 1–2, analyzes the critique of British involvement in the slave trade that forms the context for Sancho's comment.

52. J. G. A. Pocock, *Barbarism and Religion: Barbarians, Savages and Empires* traces the complicated and very different meanings that eighteenth-century British historiography developed for the terms *savage* and *barbarian*, meanings intimately tied to Enlightenment conceptions of New World history. Sancho and Wheatley may have known of these discussions—sometimes they seem to have—but their uses of the terms are too occasional and brief to be sure.

53. See Carretta, "Soubise, Julius," for Soubise's life in India.

54. Sancho did not offer the transformation he had undergone as a "group" solution. Obviously only a small number of relatively privileged black Britons, like Soubise, would be able to follow Sancho's path. And Soubise would only be able to do so to the extent to which he could control the passions that his engagement with British culture had unleashed. That Soubise, like Caliban, was accused of assaulting a woman from his "teacher's" household makes the analogy almost uncomfortably apt.

55. See Molineux, "The Peripheries Within" for the meanings of Africans for British culture during the seventeenth and eighteenth centuries. Compare Barker, *The African Link*, chaps. 1, 2.

CHAPTER 2

1. A starting point into the enormous scholarly literature on this includes: Dickson D. Bruce Jr., *The Origins of African American Literature, 1680–1865*; William L. Andrews, *To Tell a Free Story*; Charles T. Davis and Henry Louis Gates Jr., eds., *The Slave's Narrative*; Henry Louis Gates Jr., *The Signifying Monkey*. Gronniosaw was a contemporary of Wheatley and Sancho; the other authors discussed in this chapter were near contemporaries who pushed discussions of African identity in new directions.

2. Vincent Carretta has cast doubt on whether Equiano was born in Africa, but where Equiano the boy was born is less significant for black discourse on Africa than where the figure in the text was born. I will write as if Equiano was born in Igboland, because the Equiano I am analyzing—the figure in the *Interesting Narrative*—was born there. This is not a rejection of Carretta's important discoveries and interpretations. See Carretta, "Olaudah Equiano or Gustavus Vassa? New Light on an Eighteenth-Century Question of Identity," 96–105; and Carretta, *Equiano the African*, where he, too, discusses Equiano's childhood as if it had taken place in Africa (chap. 1).

3. Philip Gould, *Barbaric Traffic*.

4. For black authors whom I will not deal with (Briton Hammon, Jupiter Hammon, Francis Williams), see Vincent Carretta, ed., *Unchained Voices*, 20–31, 72–76; Carretta, "Who Was Francis Williams?" 213–37; Robert Desrochers Jr., "'Surprizing Deliverance'?: Slavery and Freedom, Language and Identity in the *Narrative* of Briton Hammon"; Rosemary Fithian Guruswamy, "'Thou Hast the Holy Word': Jupiter Hammon's 'Regards' to Phillis Wheatley" both in Carretta and Gould, eds., *Genius in Bondage*; Bruce, *Origins*, chap. 2. For the black Atlantic tradition more generally, see Gates, *The Signifying Monkey*, chap. 4; Paul Gilroy, *The Black Atlantic,* chaps. 1–2; Carretta, *Equiano the African*, 299–300.

5. For discussions of conventionally racist assumptions about blacks as writers, see Carretta, "Who Was Francis Williams?"; and Gates, "Editor's Introduction: Writing 'Race' and the Difference It Makes," in *"Race," Writing, and Difference*, 1–20, and the preceding chapter of this book.

6. As will become clear later, Quobna Ottobah Cugoano's text, though it has elements of spiritual narrative, is less autobiographical than the others; Carretta argues convincingly that it is best seen in the tradition of the jeremiad. See Carretta, "Introduction," Quobna Ottobah Cugoano, *Thoughts and Sentiments on the Evil of Slavery*, xxi–xxiii.

7. John Marrant, *A Narrative of the Lord's Wonderful Dealings with John Marrant, a black (now going to preach the gospel in Nova Scotia) born in New-York, in North-America* in Carretta, ed., *Unchained Voices*, 110–33 [first published 1785]. The text was actually written by William Aldridge, who claimed to have "preserved Mr. *Marrant's* ideas, tho' I could not his language" (111). See chaps. 3 and 4 below for Marrant in Nova Scotia and Boston.

8. Ibid., 113.

9. John Marrant, *A Sermon Preached on the 24th Day of June 1789 Being the Festival of St. John the Baptist, at the Request of the Right Worshipful The Grand Master Prince Hall, and the rest of the Brethren of the African Lodge of the Honorable Society of Free and Accepted Masons in Boston* in Joanna Brooks and John Saillant, eds., *"Face Zion Forward,"* 92. Prince Hall probably revised the sermon for publication (see Vincent Carretta, "Review of 'Face Zion Forward': First Writers of the Black Atlantic," 175–77), but there is no reason to suspect that Hall altered the substance of the sermon. The sermon is discussed more fully in chap. 4 below.

10. James Albert Ukawsaw Gronniosaw, *A Narrative of the Most Remarkable Particulars in the Life of James Albert Ukawsaw Gronniosaw, An African Prince, As Related by Himself* in Carretta, ed., *Unchained Voices*, 32–58 [first published 1772]. Like Marrant's, Gronniosaw's text was written down by an amanuensis. Also see Folarin Shyllon, *Black People in Britain, 1555–1833*, 169–71.

11. Carretta, ed., ibid., 34 (birth), 53 (pilgrims).

12. Ibid., 34–38.

13. Given More's role in the production of the book, however, it would be a mistake to place great analytical weight on the presence or absence of any single term. See Christopher Leslie Brown, *Moral Capital*, chap. 6 for a discussion of Hannah More's antislavery activity; also William Roberts, *Memoirs of the Life and Correspondence of Mrs. Hannah More.*

14. Marrant then left America and returned to England in 1790 (*Unchained Voices*, 132–33n61).

15. The allusion is to Romans 9:2–3: "That I have great heaviness and continual sorrow in my heart. For I could wish that myself were accursed from Christ for my brethren, my kinsmen according to the flesh," *Unchained Voices*, 127, 131n56.

16. Joanna Brooks and John Saillant, ed., *"Face Zion Forward,"* 93–176.

17. For influence, see Cugoano's explicit reference to Gronniosaw (spelled "Groniosaw") and Marrant (A. Morrant) in *Thoughts and Sentiments*, 23–24; and Carretta, *Equiano the African*, 299–300.

18. For the early antislavery movement see Christopher Leslie Brown, "The Empire without Slaves: British Concepts of Emancipation in the Age of the American Revolution," 273–306; Brown, *Moral Capital*, esp. chaps. 3, 4, 5; Carretta, *Equiano the African*, chaps. 11, 12; David Brion Davis, *The Problem of Slavery in the Age of Revolution, 1770–1823*, esp. chaps. 1, 2, 5, 8; Seymour Drescher, *Capitalism and Antislavery*, chaps. 1–4.

19. Shyllon, *Black People*, 173; Adam Potkay and Sandra Burr, ed., *Black Atlantic Writers of the Eighteenth Century*, 128 (Equiano's editorial help).

20. Olaudah Equiano, *The Interesting Narrative and Other Writings* (hereafter *Interesting Narrative*). See Carretta, *Equiano the African*, 230–31, 256–57, 260, for examples of collaboration between Equiano and Cugoano.

21. Cugoano, *Thoughts and Sentiments*, 7.

22. Carretta, "Introduction," *Thoughts and Sentiments*, xxii.

23. Karin Michele Thomas, "Traveling Eyes: African American Travelers Create a World, 1789–1930," chap. 1 (esp. 32–37).

24. See Alexander X. Byrd, "Eboe, Country, Nation and Gustavus Vassa's *Interesting Narrative*" for a penetrating analysis of Equiano's invocations of Eboe (Igbo in this essay) identity, although Byrd has less interest in his invocations of African identity.

25. Carretta, "Introduction," *Thoughts and Sentiments*, xxv (Cugoano writes to his readers directly in the voice of the African). As should be clear by now, I do not, by "African" voice, mean a voice that reflects an upbringing in Africa; rather I mean a voice self-consciously rooted in the shared history of African-descended people in the age of the slave trade. My usage is consistent with, though not the same as, Carretta's.

26. I follow current usage in referring to Equiano rather than Vassa, though as historian Paul Lovejoy points out, the author himself almost always signed as "Gustavus Vassa." As should be clear from my analysis, I think that the identity claimed in the *Interesting Narrative* encompassed both names, but it is unwieldy and almost unreadable to refer constantly to "Olaudah Equiano, or Gustavus Vassa, the African." See Paul Lovejoy, "Autobiography and Memory: Gustavus Vassa, Alias Olaudah Equiano, the African"; Carretta, *Equiano, the African*; and Byrd, "Eboe, Country, Nation, and Gustavus Vassa's *Interesting Narrative*" who alternate Vassa and Equiano in their texts.

27. *Thoughts and Sentiments*, 7 (African name), 110 (ancestors). Cugoano reinforced his position on the politics of naming when he referred to the narrative of "Ukawsaw Groniosaw, an African prince, who lived in England" (23); note that Cugoano deleted "James Albert."

28. See note 2 above for the issue of Equiano's place of birth.

29. Adam Potkay, "Introduction," in Potkay and Burr, ed., *Black Atlantic Writers of the Eighteenth Century*, 12–13, for an analysis of Equiano's names. Carretta, *Equiano the African*, chap. 14, offers a different but compatible reading of Equiano's African identity.

30. For the picaresque in Equiano, see Angelo Constanzo, *Surprising Narrative*, 46; for picaresque in slave narrative more broadly, but without a discussion of Equiano, see Charles H. Nichols, "The Slave Narrators and the Picaresque Mode," in *The Slave's Narrative*, 283–98.

31. Wilson Jeremiah Moses, *Afrotopia*, chaps. 2 and 3, discusses these issues as part of an analysis of the historical roots of modern Afrocentrism.

32. Sidney W. Mintz and Richard Price, *The Birth of African-American Culture*.

33. *Interesting Narrative*, 51 (understood). Equiano's experience as a victim of the slave trade prevented him from mistaking shared linguistic traditions for shared interests—he described some of these very people as "sable destroyers of human rights" (51).

34. *Interesting Narrative*, 56 (friendly), 60 (prisoners). The standard black nationalist interpretation of the emergence of a diasporic identity during the Middle Passage is from Sterling Stuckey, *Slave Culture*, chap. 1. Stuckey portrays as more "natural" and unproblematic the process that I present as partial and historically contingent. Compare Appiah, *In My Father's House*; and Mintz and Price, *The Birth of African-American Culture*. Gomez, *Exchanging Our Country Marks*, attempts to isolate the contributions of specific ethnic groups to a diasporic African American culture.

35. *Interesting Narrative*, 220 (complexion), 37 (distance), 224 (brethren), 226 (Africa).

36. Ibid., 41 (circumcision and purifications), 44 (primitive state). Being identified with Jews was no unalloyed good in eighteenth-century Europe, but identifying with ancient Israel was different, and its advantages were greatest among dissenting communities, many of which were inclined to see themselves as the "new Israel." See Frank E. Manuel, "Israel in the Christian Enlightenment," in *The Changing of the Gods*, 107–10, 119, 122; and Manuel, *The Broken Staff*, 168–69, 179. For a dissenter illustrating extreme identification with ancient Israel, see E. P. Thompson, *Witness against the Beast*, 29. For more conventional notions of England as the "new Israel" or the "Elect Nation," see Linda Colley, *Britons*, chap. 1 (esp. 29–32) and throughout; and Jack P. Greene, "Empire and Identity from the Glorious Revolution to the American Revolution," 208–30.

37. *Interesting Narrative*, 44. Cugoano makes a similar though more contingent claim: "and some think that Africa got its name from the King of Lybia marrying a daughter of Aphra, one of the descendants of Abraham, by Keturah" (*Thoughts and Sentiments*, 33). Carretta, *Equiano the African*, 315–19, discusses Equiano's invocation of Judaism and notes that earlier travel writers had compared native African and Old Testament practices, though to different ends.

38. Equiano also explicitly equated the Igbo with the Greeks, the secular "fathers" of "civilized" European society (167–68, 242n44).

39. *Interesting Narrative*, 32 (language), 33 (marriage). Equiano altered paragraph breaks in different editions. Carretta's endnotes record the changes by edition.

40. For example, he went from "Our tillage" to "their . . . [agricultural] instruments," before noting that "we are visited by locusts" in the course of three sentences describing agriculture in the village of his birth (Ibid., 38).

41. See Byrd, "Eboe, Country, Nation and Gustavus Vassa's *Interesting Narrative*," for Equiano's uses of "country" and "countrymen."

42. *Interesting Narrative*, 205, 211 (for restricting uses); 231 (African countrymen); 85 (for unclear use); 172 (Kingston).

43. Ibid., 172 (fame), 178 (eternal), 190 (unsealed book), 191 (hope).

44. Adam Potkay, "Olaudah Equiano and the Art of Spiritual Autobiography," 677–92. Also see Potkay, "Introduction," *Black Atlantic Writers*, 12–14, for the spiritual narrative traced in the progression of Equiano's names.

45. *Interesting Narrative*, 194–97.

46. Moses, *Afrotopia*, 22–23, 26, 50–51 for Ethiopianism. Cugoano invoked Ethiopia (e.g., *Thoughts and Sentiments*, 33, 39, 41). Equiano and Cugoano used the language of Ethiopianism to assert kinship rather than as part of a claim that Ethiopia was the literal place of origin of all black people (as did some analyzed by Moses).

47. *Interesting Narrative*, 200 (priest), 202 (Irving and Christ). Equiano had been Irving's personal servant during different stints in London, and it was with Irving that Equiano had embarked on an Arctic expedition. Carretta, *Equiano the African*, chap. 9 (esp. 180–90) for the Mosquito Coast.

48. *Interesting Narrative*, 205 (countrymen), 204 (white men), 209 (sable people), 210 (heathenish form and complexions), 211 (affection). George Boulukos, "The Grateful Slave," recovers and analyzes the literary convention of the "grateful slave" in eighteenth-century British fiction, a convention that informs Equiano's description of the slaves' gratitude.

49. *Interesting Narrative*, 211 (creatures), 217–18 (drowned). Gomez, *Exchanging Our Country Marks*, chap. 6, argues that Igbos were prone to suicide, often by drowning in acts that they understood as part of a spiritual return to Africa. If one reads this incident from Equiano's *Narrative* this way, then the "accident" becomes even more analogous to a "baptism," especially as Gomez portrays the meaning of baptism.

50. *Interesting Narrative*, 205 (Lybia), 292n569 (Purver's Bible). This was not as obscure a reference as it now seems. James Grainger used "Libians" to refer to all blacks in his poem "The Sugar Cane" (Krise, ed., *Caribbeana*, 242).

51. See Brown, *Moral Capital*, 274–82, for the British colony at Senegambia, including a brief discussion of Matthias Macnamara, the governor for whom Equiano worked.

52. Carretta, *Equiano the African*, chap. 9, uses creative detective work to reconstruct Equiano's life during this period.

53. *Interesting Narrative*, 221 (country), 224 (brethren).

54. Ibid., 226. Stephen J. Braidwood, *Black Poor and White Philanthropists*; Richard West, *Back to Africa*, 25–33; Cassandra Pybus, *Epic Journeys of Freedom*, chap. 7 and 139–44 for the basic story of the "Black Poor" and Sharp's Province of Freedom.

55. See Carretta, *Equiano the African*, 223–32, for Equiano's role. Of the more than 400 black poor who sailed from London in 1789, only about 60 remained alive and present in Sierra Leone three years later when the next expedition was sent. See chap. 3 below.

56. *Interesting Narrative*, 233.

57. See Brown, *Moral Capital*, esp. chap. 5; and Philip Gould, *Barbaric Traffic*, for antislavery thinkers' commercial vision for Africa. In addition to borrowing ideas from thinkers discussed by Brown and Gould, Equiano's program anticipated aspects of both antebellum black nationalism and justifications of nineteenth-century

imperialism; see Wilson Jeremiah Moses, *The Golden Age of Black Nationalism,
1850–1925*, 11 and throughout; Tunde Adeleke, *Unafrican Americans*.

58. *Interesting Narrative*, 220.

59. Such connections between sacred truth and secular history were conventional
in eighteenth-century Anglo-American thought. See, for example, David Brion Davis,
Slavery and Human Progress; Susan Juster, *Doomsayers*; Sacvan Bercovitch, "The
Typology of America's Mission," 135–55 (esp. 146–47); Ernest Lee Tuveson, *Millennium
and Utopia*; Anthony J. Barker, *The African Link*, 95–96; Ronald L. Meek, *Social
Science and the Ignoble Savage*.

60. They wrote as the slave trade was increasingly coming to be seen as an
illegitimate form of commerce in "enlightened" Anglo-American thought. See Philip
Gould, *Barbaric Traffic*; Thomas Bender, ed., *The Antislavery Debate*; Brown, "The
Empire without Slaves"; Brown, *Moral Capital*; David Brion Davis, *The Problem of
Slavery in the Age of Revolution*, esp. chaps. 1, 2, 5, 8; Drescher, *Capitalism and
Antislavery*, chaps. 1–4. The experience of having been sold also served as the base from
which Equiano entered the literary marketplace to resell his life, this time as text (see
James Sidbury, "Early Slave Narratives and the Culture of the Atlantic Market," 260–74).

61. *Interesting Narrative*, 37 (suffered to pass), 40 (community). Cugoano states
that "some of the Africans in my country keep slaves, . . . but those which they keep
are well fed, and good care taken of them" (*Thoughts and Sentiments*, 150). Many
historians concur regarding the influence of the Atlantic trade on African slavery.
See, for example, Patrick Manning, *Slavery and African Life*. John Thornton, *Africa
and Africans in the Making of the Atlantic World*, chaps. 2 and 3, offers an alternate
interpretation with a historiographical discussion.

62. *A Narrative of the Life and Adventures of Venture, A Native of Africa: But
resident above sixty years in the United States of America* (1798) in Carretta, ed.,
Unchained Voices, 373. Smith's story fits Walter Rodney's "gun-slave cycle" interpretation
of the slave trade (Thornton, *Africa and Africans*, 113–16 critiques Rodney).

63. *Interesting Narrative*, 48.

64. The texts borrow the term *nation* from the King James Version of the Bible,
which maintains that God "made of one blood all the nations of men for to dwell on
the face of the earth" (Acts 17:26). Equiano explicitly cites this (45) as do other black
authors from the nineteenth century. Equiano and Cugoano did not offer a vision of a
black nation-state as the home of the African nation, but they contributed to discussions
that produced Paul Cuffe's innovative nationalist project (see chap. 6 below).

65. *Interesting Narrative*, 51.

66. *Thoughts and Sentiments*, 12 (matter[ed] not), 16 (complexion).

67. *Interesting Narrative*, 117–18.

68. *Unchained Voices*, 379. Gronniosaw also told stories of being cheated by
Britons because he was black.

69. For other examples see *Interesting Narrative*, 139, 157, 172, 218. Sidbury, "Early
Slave Narratives and the Culture of the Atlantic Market," expands on this analysis.

70. This was not true in all North American slave societies. See Thomas N. Ingersoll, "Free Blacks in a Slave Society: New Orleans, 1718–1812," 173–200; Kimberly Hanger, *Bounded Lives, Bounded Places*; Kenneth Aslakson, "Making Race," chap. 3 for discussions of the Spanish law of *coartación*.

71. Sidbury, "Early Slave Narratives and the Culture of the Atlantic Market."

72. Geraldine Murphy, "Olaudah Equiano, Accidental Tourist," 551–68, winces with "postcolonial hindsight" at Equiano's faith in free trade, though she adds helpfully that "Equiano did not have classic underdevelopment in mind for his homeland" (561). For a more historicized reading of Equiano as traveler, see Thomas, "Traveling Eyes," chap. 1 (esp. 37–41).

73. Colley, *Britons*, chap. 1 (esp. 29–32, 37–38) and throughout; David Armitage, *The Ideological Origins of the British Empire*; Elijah H. Gould, *The Persistence of Empire*; Kathleen Wilson, *The Sense of the People*; Greene, "Empire and Identity," 208–30 (esp. 213–16).

74. Richard Bushman, *From Puritan to Yankee*. This issue reaches back to Max Weber and through Perry Miller. For an excellent introduction to the controversies and an important contribution to the debate, see Stephen Innes, *Creating the Commonwealth*, 25–38 (historiography and theory) and throughout.

75. *Interesting Narrative*, 233 (Africa), 234 (Great Britain), 235 (manufactures).

76. Brown, *Moral Capital*, esp. chap. 5.

77. *Thoughts and Sentiments*, 172 (Africa), 172–73 (Great-Britain).

78. Meek, *Social Science and the Ignoble Savage*; Gould, *Barbaric Traffic* for this critique in eighteenth-century Anglo-American culture more generally. J. G. A. Pocock, *Barbarism and Religion*, vol. 4, *Barbarians, Savages and Empires*, discusses these issues in the context of eighteenth-century history writers.

79. *Thoughts and Sentiments*, 111.

80. Ibid., 10.

81. Ibid., 17. For a discussion of the alternately radical and complacent implications of Protestant visions of England as Elect Nation—one of the traditions out of which these assertions of Cugoano's grow—see Colley, *Britons*, 29–32; and Greene, "Empire and Identity," 213–16.

82. *Thoughts and Sentiments*, 43 ("And, therefore, any thing which had a seeming appearance in favour of slavery, so far as it was admitted into the law [of ancient Israel], was to shew that it was not natural and innocent, like that of different colours among men, but as necessary to be made an emblem of what was intended by it, and consequently, as it stands enjoined among other typical representations, was to shew that every thing of any evil appearance of it was to be removed, and to end with the other typical and ceremonial injunctions, when the time of that dispensation was over.") Also ibid., 40 ("and that all men are like Ethiopians [even God's elect] in a state of nature and unregeneracy, they are black with original sin, and spotted with actual transgression, which they cannot reverse").

83. Ibid., 28.

84. Ibid., 68–70; Brown, *Moral Capital*, part 4 and throughout.

85. *Thoughts and Sentiments*, 78 (seize), 92 (labour of slaves), 109 (philosophers); he specified David Hume and James Tobin.

86. This plan was not offered in opposition to the Sierra Leone settlement. Cugoano expressed explicit if critical support for the planned colony and may even have considered immigrating there (ibid., 104–6; Carretta, "Introduction,"; ibid., xx).

87. *Thoughts and Sentiments*, 99. Cugoano made clear that this should not be a deportation scheme: "The rest [that is, freed slaves who did not return to their former homes] would become useful residents in the colonies."

88. Ibid., 101.

Chapter 3

1. For other "African" institutions, see Sterling Stuckey, *Slave Culture*, chap. 4; Horton and Horton, *In Hope of Liberty*, chap. 8; Elizabeth Rauh Bethel, *The Roots of African-American Identity*. Though these books differ, all see references to "Africa" in the names of these organizations as invocations of communal memories of life in Africa.

2. Joanna Brooks, *American Lazarus*, chap. 3; Joanna Brooks and John Saillant, ed. *"Face Zion Forward,"* Introduction; John Marrant, *A Narrative of the Lord's Wonderful Dealings with John Marrant, a Black* (1785) in Carretta, ed. *Unchained Voices*, 110–33.

3. Alan Gallay, "Planters and Slaves in the Great Awakening," 19–36; Sylvia Frey, *Water from the Rock*; and Frey and Betty Wood, *Come Shouting to Zion* (which has strongly influenced this portion of this chapter). Also see Peter H. Wood, "'Liberty Is Sweet': African-American Freedom Struggles in the Years before White Independence."

4. Frey and Wood, *Come Shouting to Zion*, 112–14; and Winthrop D. Jordan, *White over Black*, 209–10, for Margate.

5. Margate quoted in James Habersham to Robert Keen, Savannah, May 11, 1775, *Collections of the Georgia Historical Society*, vol. 6, 244; Piercy quoted in Frey and Wood, *Come Shouting to Zion*, 113.

6. Habersham to Keen, Savannah, May 11, 1775, *Collections of the Georgia Historical Society*, vol. 6, 243.

7. Mechal Sobel, *Trabelin' On*, 188–90; Thomas J. Little, "George Liele and the Rise of Independent Black Baptist Churches in the Lower South and Jamaica," 188–204. See Frey, *Water from the Rock*, chap. 3 and throughout for the Revolutionary War in the Deep South.

8. Henry Sharpe had died, and his heirs sought to reenslave Liele, so he ran to the British for freedom even though he was free (Little, "George Liele," 192).

9. Emanuel King Love, *History of the First African Baptist Church*, 38–40; Little, "George Liele," 192–93, 198; Sydney Kaplan and Emma Nogrady Kaplan, *The Black*

Presence in the Age of Revolution, 92–96. During the antebellum years the First Church split into the Bryan Baptist Church and the African Baptist Church.

10. John Rippon, *The Baptist Annual Register*, 4 vols. (London: n.p., 1793–1802). The relevant letters have been edited, annotated, and published in Carretta, ed. *Unchained Voices*, 325–68.

11. Brooks, *American Lazarus*, 46 (for transforming moment of conversion) and throughout (for centrality of the trope of regeneration in African American culture).

12. Carretta, ed., *Unchained Voices*, 326. Also David George chose to leave Halifax for Shelburne because there was "no way open" to him in Halifax "to preach to my own colour" (*Unchained Voices*, 337). For willingness to preach to white worshippers, see *Unchained Voices*, 327 (Liele), 337 (George).

13. Mechal Sobel, *The World They Made Together*, chap. 15; Sobel, *Trabelin' On*, chap. 7.

14. Carretta, ed., *Unchained Voices*, 343 (home). See chap. 4 of this book for George and the Baptists in Sierra Leone.

15. Brooks, *American Lazarus*, chap. 4.

16. Sean Wilentz, *The Rise of American Democracy*, 272–80.

17. Steven C. Bullock, *Revolutionary Brotherhood*, esp. chaps. 2–9 (158–60 for Prince Hall and African Masonry); Bethel, *The Roots of African American Identity*, 64–68; Brooks, *American Lazarus*, chap. 4. For the British background, see Margaret C. Jacob, *Living the Enlightenment*.

18. Bullock, *Revolutionary Brotherhood*, 158–60; Charles H. Wesley, *Prince Hall: Life and Legacy*, chaps. 1–3; Kaplan and Kaplan, *The Black Presence in the Era of the American Revolution*, 202–9; Bethel, *The Roots of African-American Identity*, 64–67. Hall's early life is shrouded in myth, but it is not particularly important for my argument.

19. Harry E. Davis, "Documents Relating to Negro Masonry in America," 411–32; Brooks, *American Lazarus*, 122–23. Brooks points out that this allied African Freemasonry with the Ancient lodges (124–26).

20. William Bentley (a prominent minister from Salem, Mass.) quoted in Bullock, *Revolutionary Brotherhood*, 159.

21. Brooks, *American Lazarus*, 136–38 shows that Hall's offer to fight the Shaysites was tied to questions about the radicalism of Freemasonry. See also Kaplan and Kaplan, *The Black Presence*, 206.

22. Prince Hall, *A Charge Delivered to the Brethren of the African Lodge on the 25th of June, 1792, At the Hall of Brother William Smith in Charlestown. By the Right Worshipful Master Prince Hall* (Boston, 1792). This Charge can be found in Dorothy Porter, ed. *Early Negro Writing*, 63–69, and in Wesley, *Prince Hall*, 55–61, and in Brooks and Saillant, ed., *"Face Zion Forward,"* 191–208. Quote taken from Wesley, *Prince Hall*, 55.

23. For the general context of slavery and race in New England during and after the American Revolution, see William D. Piersen, *Black Yankees*; James Oliver Horton, *Free People of Color*, chaps. 2 and 7; Horton and Horton, *In Hope of Liberty*, esp. chaps. 2–8; Joanne Pope Melish, *Disowning Slavery*; John Wood Sweet, *Bodies Politic*.

24. January 4, 1787 Petition to the Massachusetts General Court, quoted in Kaplan and Kaplan, 207. See also Floyd J. Miller, *The Search for a Black Nationality*, 3–5 (and throughout for the early emigration movement).

25. The petition is in Kaplan and Kaplan, *The Black Presence*, 206–9; and in Wesley, *Prince Hall*, 67–68.

26. See chap. 2 above; Gould, *Barbaric Traffic*; and Brown, *Moral Capital* for the intellectual context for this vision.

27. More generally the voluntary organizations founded by free black people during this period with their formal constitutions or bylaws and their reformist agendas participated in cultural trends that were equally important among white Americans. See Shane White, "'It Was a Proud Day,'" 13–50; Horton and Horton, *In Hope of Liberty*; Robert H. Abzug, *Cosmos Crumbling*; and Ronald G. Walters, *American Reformers*.

28. See Horton and Horton, *In Hope of Liberty*, 127; and Horton, *Free People of Color*, 153–56 for a survey of such organizations. The key source for the Newport African Union Society is William H. Robinson, ed., *The Proceedings of the Free African Union Society and African Benevolent Society, Newport, Rhode Island, 1780–1824*, which includes the contents of three manuscript volumes: "The Correspondence of the African Union Society, 1772–1824 [1787–1797]," (1–50 of Robinson vol.; hereafter *Proceedings*); "The Proceedings of the African Union Society, 1790–1796 [1807–1824]," (51–151); and "The Proceedings of the African Benevolent Society" (152–conclusion). John Wood Sweet kindly loaned me photocopies of the originals. Also see Sweet, *Bodies Politic*, 328–36; Kaplan and Kaplan, *The Black Presence*, 209; Miller, *Search*, 6–15.

29. Rachel Chernos Lin, "The Rhode Island Slave-Traders," 21–38; Sweet, *Bodies Politic*, 60–62.

30. Pierson, *Black Yankees*, 15; Horton and Horton, *In Hope of Liberty*, 4–5; Elaine Forman Crane, *A Dependent People*; Melish, *Disowning Slavery*, 11–16, 41–45; Lin, "The Rhode Island Slave-Traders"; Sweet, *Bodies Politic*, chaps. 2, 6.

31. Horton and Horton, *In Hope of Liberty*, 57; Sweet, *Bodies Politic*, 114–16; Catherine A. Brekus, *Strangers and Pilgrims*, 74–75.

32. Miller, *Search*, 6–8; Kaplan and Kaplan, *The Black Presence*, 209; Horton and Horton, *In Hope of Liberty*, 57; Sweet, *Bodies Politic*, 331. This was in keeping with Hopkins's dispensationalist theology; for brief, clear explanations, see John Saillant, *Black Puritan*, chap. 3; and Brooks, *American Lazarus*, 89. See also Edmund S. Morgan, *The Gentle Puritan*, for Ezra Stiles (451 for turn away from emigrationism).

33. Anthony Taylor in the Name of the Society to [Boston blacks], Newport, R.I., Jan. 24, 1787 in *Proceedings*, 16. Also see Sweet, *Bodies Politic*, 331–35.

34. Robinson, ed., *Proceedings*, 16–22, 24–29. "Brethren in affliction" appears often.

35. Ibid., 31–34, 36–37 for letters that Thornton wrote to various international figures and copied to the Society. See 43 for a letter that expresses the Society's concern about falling under the sway of white philanthropists. For Thornton see Horton and Horton, *In Hope of Liberty*, 179–80; Miller, *Search*, 9–15. Thornton was building on the

ideas of Malachy Postlethwayt and Henry Smeathman; see Brown, *Moral Capital*, chap. 5; Deirdre Coleman, *Romantic Colonization and British Anti-Slavery*, chap. 1.

36. *Proceedings*, 19–21; they wrote a similar letter to the "Free African Society at Philadelphia" (24–25). See also Miller, *The Search for a Black Nationality*, 6–15; Bethel, *The Roots of African-American Identity*, 74–75.

37. African Union Society to Prince Hall, Newport, n.d., in *Proceedings*, 29; also see the minutes of meetings held on Jan. 6, 1791 (73); Sept. 8, 1791 (86–87); Feb. 2, 1792 (91–92).

38. Ira Berlin, *Many Thousands Gone*. Philip D. Morgan, "British Encounters with Africans and African-Americans," 157–219, remains the best general synthesis. See David Eltis, *The Rise of African Slavery in the Americas* for the slave trade.

39. Frey and Wood, *Come Shouting to Zion* traces this diaspora into the Caribbean. Cassandra Pybus, "Jefferson's Faulty Math"; and Pybus, *Epic Journeys*, 71 (9,000), chap. 5 (presence in London). See Gerzina, *Black London*, chap. 5; and James Walvin, *England, Slaves and Freedom, 1776–1838*, part 1 for London.

40. See James Sidbury, *Ploughshares into Swords*, chap. 1; Frey, *Water from the Rock*; Rhys Isaac, *Landon Carter's Uneasy Kingdom*.

41. Isaac, ibid.; Frey, ibid., chap. 4 for the Philipsburg Proclamation (promise issued by British general Sir Henry Clinton to slaves who deserted Whig masters). Also see Benjamin Quarles, *The Negro in the American Revolution*; Walker, *The Black Loyalists*, chap. 1; and Wilson, *The Loyal Blacks*, chaps. 1–3. Cassandra Pybus' ongoing work on Moses Wilkinson's Methodist community from eastern Virginia and its exodus during the Revolution promises to provide a much fuller portrait of a community escaping from slavery during the Revolutionary War than has previously been available.

42. Frey, *Water from the Rock* is the best account. Also see Mary Beth Norton, "The Fate of Some Black Loyalists of the American Revolution," 402–26.

43. Elizabeth A. Fenn, *Pox Americana*, chaps. 3–4.

44. Pybus, *Epic Journeys*, 50–55; Schama, *Rough Crossings*, 123. See also Pybus, "Jefferson's Faulty Math," for a concise account of the fates of those who fled to the British.

45. Schama, ibid., 146–49; Pybus, ibid., 66–71; Gary Nash, *The Forgotten Fifth*, 45–48; Graham Hodges, ed., *The Black Loyalist Directory*, introduction. Also Walker, *The Black Loyalists*, chap. 1; Ellen Gibson Wilson, *The Loyal Blacks*, chap. 4.

46. Christopher Fyfe, *A History of Sierra Leone*, chap. 1; Walker, ibid., chap. 5; Wilson, ibid., chap. 9; John Peterson, *A Province of Freedom: A History of Sierra Leone 1787–1870*, chap. 1; Stephen J. Braidwood, *Black Poor and White Philanthropists*; Pybus, ibid., 117–19 (Griffith quotation at 119); Schama, ibid., chap. 7; John Matthews, *A Voyage to the River Sierra Leone on the Coast of Africa*, 29–30.

47. Matthews, ibid., 20–21; Fyfe, ibid., 7; David Hancock, *Citizens of the World*, chap. 6.

48. Pybus, *Epic Journeys*, 139–42; Schama, *Rough Crossings*, 212–14.

49. Pybus, ibid., 139–45; Schama, ibid., 210–14.

50. See Brown, *Moral Capital*, 377–89 for an important reevaluation of the role of Clapham "Saints" in early antislavery movements; Standish Meacham, *Henry Thornton of Clapham, 1760–1815*; and Schama, ibid., chap. 9.

51. Laird Niven and Stephen A. Davis, "Birchtown: The History and Material Culture of an Expatriate African American Community," 59–83 (esp. 64–67).

52. Clarkson Papers, vol. 2, n.p. add. ms. 41, 262B, British Library (hereafter BL). This is John Clarkson's memo book that he carried while recruiting settlers to go to Sierra Leone. The quotes are taken from his notes on why black Nova Scotians said they wanted to leave.

53. Walker, chap. 3 (for general hardships faced by blacks in Nova Scotia), esp. 55–56 (for legal discrimination); Pybus, *Epic Journeys*, 145–49; Schama, *Rough Crossings*, chap. 8.

54. For many stories of such communal aid, see John Marrant, *A Journal of the Rev. John Marrant, from August the 18th, 1785, to the 16th of March, 1790* in Brooks and Saillant, ed. *"Face Zion Forward,"* 97–160 (hereafter *Journal of Marrant*).

55. See Brooks, *American Lazarus*, chap. 1 for an unusually clear discussion of different evangelical groups' theologies and their efforts to proselytize among blacks.

56. Brooks and Saillant, eds., *"Face Zion Forward,"* 218, 222. King reported having begun to "commiserate" in 1787.

57. Pybus, *Epic Journeys*, 31. Pybus will further document this claim in forthcoming work.

58. See *Journal of Marrant*; Brooks, *American Lazarus*, chap. 3 for analysis. Also see John Saillant, "'Wipe Away All Tears from Their Eyes.'"

59. *Journal of Marrant*, 97–105 (diverse audiences).

60. Brooks, *American Lazarus*, 106.

61. See *Journal of Marrant*, 124–26, 130, 136, 143 for characterizations of Wilkinson and the Wesleyans.

62. Pybus, *Epic Journeys*, 147–48 (quotation at 147).

63. Gary B. Nash, "Thomas Peters: Millwright and Deliverer," 69–85 (reprinted in Nash, *Race, Class, and Politics*, chap. 10). Walker, *The Black Loyalists*, chap. 5; and Ellen Gibson Wilson, *The Loyal Blacks*, chap. 10 narrate Peters's mission to London. See Pybus, ibid., 215–16 for a brief biography.

64. "Thomas Peters's Petition" in Christopher Fyfe, ed. *Sierra Leone Inheritance*, 118–19.

65. Fyfe, *A History*, chap. 1; Walker, *The Black Loyalists*, chap. 5; Ellen Gibson Wilson, *The Loyal Blacks*, chap. 9; Peterson, *A Province of Freedom*, chap. 1; Braidwood, *Black Poor and White Philanthropists*; Pybus, *Epic Journeys*, 139–42; Schama, *Rough Crossings*, chap. 7.

66. Meacham, *Henry Thornton*. See Lamin Sanneh, *Abolitionists Abroad*, esp. chap. 2.

67. Ellen Gibson Wilson, *The Loyal Blacks*; Ellen Gibson Wilson, *John Clarkson and the African Adventure*; and Schama, *Rough Crossings*, part 2 are the best accounts of Clarkson and his relationships with the Nova Scotians. Also see Clarkson Papers, vols. 1–3, BL; John Clarkson, *Clarkson's Mission to America 1791–1792* (hereafter *Clarkson's Mission*); and "Diary of Lieutenant Clarkson, R.N.," 1–114 (hereafter "Diary of Lieutenant Clarkson").

68. See Julius Sherrard Scott III, "A Common Wind"; Peter W. Hinks, *"To Awaken My Afflicted Brethren"*; and, esp., W. Jeffrey Bolster, *Black Jacks*. Peter Linebaugh and Marcus Rediker, *The Many-headed Hydra*, argue for a precociously progressive and multiracial eighteenth-century seaborne proletariat.

69. Hall emphasized the significance of Marrant's sermon in the introduction to the first of his Charges (1792) by noting that it was requisite that the Lodge "give some reason as a foundation" for meeting together at the Festival of St. John the Baptist, but noted that this had "already been done, in a discourse delivered in substance by our late Reverend Brother *John Marrant.*" Hall had merely to "raise part of the superstructure" (Wesley, *Prince Hall*, 55). Hall again said that he was building a "superstructure" in his 1797 Charge (Wesley, 111). Hall probably helped compose Marrant's sermon (Brooks, *American Lazarus*, 128).

70. John Marrant, *A Sermon Preached on the 24th Day of June 1789 Being the Festival of St. John the Baptist, At the Request of the Right Worshipful The Grand Master Prince Hall, and the rest of the Brethren of the African Lodge of the Honorable Society of Free and Accepted Masons in Boston* (Boston, 1789), 5.

71. See Brooks, *American Lazarus*, 126–30 for a wonderful reading of Marrant's use of Cain.

72. Marrant, *Sermon*, 8 (for proposition), 9–17 (for narrative from Cain to Temple).

73. Marrant, ibid., 19–20.

74. "The name of the second river [emerging out of the Garden of Eden] is Gihon, the same is it which compasseth the whole land of Ethiopia (or Cush as it is in the original) there is reason to believe that this Gihon is the river of Nile, as the forenamed Josephus and most of the ancient writers of the church hold" (Marrant, *Sermon*, 8).

Chapter 4

1. Charles Bruce Fergusson, ed. *Clarkson's Mission to America 1791–1792*, Oct. 1, 1791 (38); Nov. 2, 1791 (60). Hereafter *Clarkson's Mission*.

2. Joanna Brooks and John Saillant, ed., *"Face Zion Forward,"* "Introduction"; and Joanna Brooks, *American Lazarus*, chap. 3 for readings of Marrant's *Journal* that document the New Divinity dispensationalist theology behind Nova Scotian Huntingdonians' belief.

3. Clarkson spoke to potential emigrants, ostensibly to recruit settlers, but his listeners had almost certainly decided to emigrate before going to hear him, for he reported encountering unanimously receptive audiences despite the fact that a significant number of blacks chose to remain in Nova Scotia. See James W. St. G. Walker, *The Black Loyalists*, esp. chaps. 2 and 6; and Cassandra Pybus, *Epic Journeys of Freedom*, 145–48 (denominational conflicts).

4. *Clarkson's Mission*, Oct. 28, 1791 (56) for importance of children's future; Oct. 31, 1791 (59).

5. Ibid., Oct. 25, 1791 (51) for personal danger; Nov. 2, 1791 (60) for one example of insistence on hardships; Clarkson to Henry Thornton, Nov. 28, 1791 (81) for one of many examples of his care in outfitting the voyage; Oct. 31, 1791 (59) for help saving child.

6. See, for example, Boston King's discussion of his rising material standard of life before migrating to Sierra Leone (*"Face Zion Forward,"* 228).

7. *Clarkson's Mission*, 63. See Pybus, *Epic Journeys*, 150–51 for emigrants who lost property by moving.

8. Clarkson to Henry Thornton, Oct. 19, 1791, *Clarkson's Mission*, 46. Pybus, *Epic Journeys*, 148 estimates that all of the black refugees "received their land by 1788," but notes that they received less than whites; Simon Schama, *Rough Crossings*, 223 says most never received land, perhaps a minor misinterpretation of Clarkson's claim that most never got more than a couple of acres.

9. Sidney W. Mintz, *Caribbean Transformations*; Melvin Patrick Ely, *Israel on the Appomattox*, esp. 360–65; Thomas C. Holt, *The Problem of Freedom*, esp. chap. 5; Steven Hahn, *A Nation under Our Feet*.

10. Clarkson to Thornton, Nov. 28, 1791, *Clarkson's Mission*, 82.

11. He "particularly mentioned" that he would "not stay with them in Africa" (*Clarkson's Mission*, 180).

12. Ibid., Oct. 26, 1791 (55–56).

13. Walker, *Black Loyalists*, chap. 6; Schama, *Rough Crossings*, 285–88.

14. Pybus, *Epic Journeys*, 169; in 1796, Zachary Macaulay, by then the governor of Sierra Leone, estimated that there were approximately 270 Wesleyan Methodists, 70 Huntingdonians, and 60 Baptists among the black settlers in the colony. It's not clear but seems likely that his count is of household heads. Zachary Macaulay, Journal, Apr. 9, 1796, Zachary Macaulay Papers, microfilm, reel 7, Abolition and Emancipation, Part 1, Adam Matthews microfilm collection, Huntington Library, San Marino, California.

15. David George to John Rippon, Free Town, Sierra Leone, Oct. 13, 1793, in Vincent Carretta, ed., *Unchained Voices*, 343, 350n68. Rippon explained George's use of "home" in a footnote. It may be significant that the Baptist Church founded in Jamaica by George Liele, a fellow congregant of George's in Savannah prior to the American Revolution, ministered to both blacks and whites, and ultimately proved to be too racially inclusive and politically conservative for the "Native Baptists" who organized the "Baptist War" in 1831 (Sylvia Frey and Betty Wood, *Come Shouting to Zion*, 130–32).

16. Pybus, *Epic Journeys*, chap. 9; Nathan Bangs, *The Life of the Rev. Freeborn Garrettson*, 152–61.

17. *Clarkson's Mission*, Nov. 2, 1791 (60). Other examples are discussed below. Schama, *Rough Crossings*, 295 reports that "fifty . . . had been born in Africa" but provides no documentation.

18. Walker, *Black Loyalists*, 123 (congregations deciding together); *Clarkson's Mission*, 114 ("Petition of the inhabitants of Birch Town to the Honourable Mr. Clarkson, Agent of the Sierra Leone Society," Dec. 20, 1791, which is the source of the quote), 117 (similar petition from the people of Preston), 105 ("I this evening, appointed Thomas Peters, David George, and John Ball to superintend the whole and to communicate to me their wants and complains, desiring them to inform the people at the different Barracks not to come to me with their particular complaints, but to inform me through them").

19. Thomas Peters and David Edmons to John Clarkson, Halifax, Dec. 23, 1791; Henry Thornton to John Clarkson, London, Dec. 28, 1791, Clarkson Papers, vol. 1, BL.

20. Ellen Gibson Wilson, *The Loyal Blacks*, 233; Schama, *Rough Crossings*, 313. "Governor Clarkson's Diary," in the Right Rev. E. G. Ingham, ed., *Sierra Leone after a Hundred Years*, 36 (hereafter Ingham, ed., "Governor Clarkson's Diary").

21. Ingham, ed., ibid., 18, 23; Sierra Leone Company, *Substance of the Report of the court of directors of the Sierra Leone Company, Delivered to the General Court of Proprietors, on Thursday, the 26th Day of February, 1795*, frontispiece map. The company claimed land farther to the east, but it would not settle any of it during the eighteenth century.

22. Ingham, ed., ibid., 24 (quotation); Christopher Fyfe, *A History of Sierra Leone*, 30 (Naimbana's sons). See John Matthews, *A Voyage to the River Sierra Leone on the Coast of Africa*, 170–71n (for area headmen seeking European educations for their sons). For cosmopolitanism, see Ira Berlin, *Many Thousands Gone*, part 1; and Randy Sparks, *The Two Princes of Calabar*.

23. See Walker, *Black Loyalists*, chaps. 7–10 for the full narrative.

24. Henry Thornton to John Clarkson, Dec. 30, 1791, Clarkson Papers, vol. 1, BL; Sierra Leone Company, *Substance of the Report . . . 1795*, 61.

25. Henry Thornton to John Clarkson, Dec. 30, 1791, Clarkson Papers, vol. 1, BL.

26. For the early inclination to opposition, see Anna Maria Falconbridge, *Narrative of Two Voyages to the River Sierra Leone during the Years 1791-1792-1793*, ed. Christopher Fyfe, 78 ("The Blacks are so displeased that they have not their promised lands; and so little do they relish the obnoxious arrogance of their rulers, that I really believe, was it not for the influence of Mr. Clarkson, they would be apt to drive some of them into the sea").

27. "Diary of Lieutenant Clarkson," entries for Sept. 1, 1792 (Snowball); Sept. 2, 1793 (confidence), 35.

28. Braidwood, *Black Poor and White Philanthropists*, 88–89; "Diary of Lieutenant Clarkson," entries for Aug. 13, 1792; Aug. 14, 1792, 9, 10; John Clarkson to Henry Thornton, Apr. 18, 1792, Clarkson Papers, vol. 1, BL; "Diary of Lieutenant Clarkson," Aug. 9, 1792, 6. Further complaints about sailors in Freetown can be found on 7, 12, 13, 14, 41, 45, 47, 54, 57, 67, and 88 (incident reflecting anxious relationships with natives). Clarkson to Dawes, Oct. 5, 1792, ibid. 74–84, shows his genuine but condescending concern. CO 270/2, Feb. 17, 1792 (hearing for old settler accused of slaving); Apr. 30, 1792 (Old Settlers' letter defending themselves).

29. Ingham, ed., "Governor Clarkson's Diary," 39. For accounts of Peters's challenge to Clarkson see Ellen Gibson Wilson, *The Loyal Blacks*, chap. 13; Walker, *Black Loyalists*, chap. 7; Schama, *Rough Crossings*, chap. 11; and Pybus, *Epic Journeys*, chap. 9.

30. John Clarkson to Lawrence Hartshorne, Wisbeach, Cambridgeshire, Aug. 9, 1793, Clarkson Papers, vol. 3, add. ms. 41, 263, BL; Mr. James Strand's Journal of Occurences [*sic*] fr. April 21st to Sept. 10th, 1792, 11–12, Papers Relating to Sierra Leone, British Museum, add. mss. 12, 131 BL. Strand was one of several Swedenborgians who traveled to Sierra Leone in hopes of finding a utopian community prophesied by Immanuel Swedenborg. Strand did not normally speak highly of Peters ("This Peters not content, but constantly in concert with a preacher and another person worked on the naturally suspicious temper of the Blacks").

31. Ellen Gibson Wilson, *The Loyal Blacks*, 250 (George signing petition); Clarkson to Hartshorne, Wisbeach, Cambridgshire, Sept. 1793, Clarkson Papers, vol. 3 (assassination); Ingham, ed., "Governor Clarkson's Diary," 43 (Anabaptists).

32. Clarkson to Hartshorne, Wisbeach, Cambridgeshire, Aug. 9, 1793. Clarkson surely overstated his victory, and retained enough respect for Peters's popularity to authorize special funeral arrangements.

33. For Sierra Leone during Clarkson's governorship, see Ellen Gibson Wilson, *The Loyal Blacks*, chaps. 13–14; and Walker, *Black Loyalists*, chap. 7. For Clarkson's methods, see "Diary of Lieutenant Clarkson," 33–37, 45–46 (quotes), 61–62.

34. "Diary of Lieutenant Clarkson," 51.

35. Schama, *Rough Crossings*, 342.

36. Walker, *Black Loyalists*, chap. 8; Ellen Gibson Wilson, *The Loyal Blacks*, chap. 15; Falconbridge, *Voyages*, 112–14; Isaac DuBois Journal, Feb. 7, 1793, Clarkson Papers, vol. 3, BL. DuBois, a Wilmington, N.C. planter and Loyalist, left the United States after independence. He was a friend and confidant of Clarkson's in Sierra Leone, a supporter of the settlers against Clarkson's successors. See Fyfe's biographical sketch of DuBois—he ultimately married Anna Maria Falconbridge, which is why he includes the bio in that volume (Falconbridge, *Voyages*, 83n74).

37. John Gray to Clarkson, Freetown, Sierra Leone, Feb. 15, 1794, Clarkson Papers, vol. 3, BL.

38. Pybus, *Epic Journeys*, 132–33, 160–62 (Dawes); Schama, *Rough Crossings*, 354–57 (Macaulay). Viscountess Knutsford, *Life and Letters of Zachary Macaulay* provides a biographical account of Macaulay along with heavily edited excerpts from his journals and letters. I cite this book when possible, because of its availability. Macaulay's papers have been microfilmed in the Abolition and Emancipation series by Adam Mathews Publishers. I cite these for material that is not included in Knutsford, as Macaulay, "Journal" or "Letters," with the date and microfilm reel number.

39. Braidwood, *Black Poor and White Philanthropists*, chap. 2; CO 270/2, Dec. 12, 1792 (Clarkson's proposal), Dec. 31, 1792 (Dawes and Macaulay and quote). Though this plan was based upon Sharp's original plan, it did not offer settlers the political control over the colony that Sharp had intended.

40. CO 270/2, May 27, 1793 ("according to a law [for penning livestock] proposed by the Hundredors and Tythingmen of this town"). Three months later, they proposed that the Company raise their wages (CO 270/2, Aug. 21, 1793).

41. Cato Perkins and Isaac Anderson to John Clarkson, London, Oct. 26, 1793, Clarkson Papers, vol. 3, BL. Perkins and Anderson sent a copy of the petition to Clarkson after arriving in London.

42. DuBois gave Clarkson's address to Anderson and Perkins, but the directors rebuffed the petitioners' request for further discussion even after Clarkson agreed to travel from Cambridgeshire to London to meet with the directors and the settlers' representatives (Ellen Gibson Wilson, *The Loyal Blacks*, 294–99; Ellen Gibson Wilson, *John Clarkson and the African Adventure*, 138–40).

43. Perkins and Anderson to John Clarkson, London, Nov. 9, 1793, Clarkson Papers, vol. 3, BL.

44. Macaulay Journal, Sept. 15, 1793, reel 6; Mechal Sobel, *Teach Me Dreams*, chap. 3 for dreams in African American Christianity.

45. Knutson, 181–82; Macaulay Journal, Oct. 3, 1793, reel 6. Later Macaulay dismissed Beverhout as schoolmaster for taking "unwarrantable Freedom[s]" with girls in his school (CO 270/2, June 14, 1794).

46. CO 270/2, Nov. 4, 1793; Nov. 8, 1793. The two boys were declared free and named Samuel Garwin and Isaac Watts.

47. CO 270/2, Nov. 11, 1793.

48. Ingham, ed., "Governor Clarkson's Diary," 158–59 (quote at 158); CO 270/2, Nov. 11, 1793.

49. Grierson made at least five slaving voyages before 1794 and at least three afterward, selling slaves in Bermuda, Grenada, Barbados, Jamaica, and St. Kitts. David Eltis, Stephen D. Behrendt, David Richardson, and Herbert S. Klein, *The Trans-Atlantic Slave Trade*, voyage identity numbers 82288, 81390, 81755, 81730, 81756, 83152 (1794 voyage), 82641, 80446, 82989.

50. CO 270/2, June 16, 1794 (initial account of fight and quote); Walker, *Black Loyalists*, 178–81.

51. CO 270/2, June 16, 1794–June 30, 1794 (for this paragraph and the previous one; several "rioters" were sent back to London to be tried). Emphasis in quotes in the original.

52. Knutsford, *Life and Letters of Zachary Macaulay*, 60 (July 23, 1794, entry). Stephen Peters, who accompanied Wilkinson, had been denied employment with the Company for his support of the riot. Macaulay refused to reinstate him.

53. Knutsford, ibid., 60–61; Macaulay, Journal, July 23, 1794, reel 7. Clarke admired at least one settler ("Singular Piety in a Female African," *Evangelical Magazine* 4 [1796], 460–63).

54. For the attack, see Walker, *Black Loyalists*, 181–84; and Ellen Gibson Wilson, *The Loyal Blacks*, 317–23. Also see Christopher Fyfe, ed., *Sierra Leone Inheritance*, 122–24.

55. Knutson, 71–77 (entries for Sept. 30, 1794; Oct. 6, 1794; Oct. 13, 1794). Also see the entry for Nov. 26, 1794 (83) in which Macaulay summarizes the invasion. B. Mitchell to a Gentleman in London, Free-Town, July 13, 1795, *Evangelical Magazine* 4 (1796), 18 (shared living circumstances).

56. Knutson, 77–78 (entries for Oct. 13, 1794; and Oct. 14, 1794).

57. Macaulay, Journal, Nov. 26, 1794, reel 7.

58. "Luke Jordan, John Jordan, Rubin Simmons, Amarica [*sic*] Tolbert, Moses Wilkinson, preacher, Isaac Anderson, Stephen Peters, James Hutcherson, A Great many More tho paper wont aford to John Clarkson, Sierra Leone, 19 November 1794," Clarkson Papers, vol. 3, BL; Ellen Gibson Wilson, *The Loyal Blacks*, 320–25; Walker, *Black Loyalists*, 182–84.

59. Macaulay, Journal, Mar. 19, 1796; Mar. 23, 1796, reel 7.

60. James Liaster to John Clarkson, Free Town, Sierra Leone, Mar. 30, 1796, in *"Our Children Free and Happy,"* ed. Christopher Fyfe with a contribution by Charles

Jones, 49–50; Nathaniel Snowball and James Hutcherson to Clarkson, Free Town, May 24, 1796, Clarkson Papers, vol. 3, BL.

61. Quote from Liaster to Clarkson, Mar. 30, 1796, in Fyfe, ed. *"Our Children Free and Happy,"* 49–50. Similar language is used in James Hutcherson and Mosis Murry to Clarkson, Freetown, May 24, 1796, Clarkson Papers, vol. 3, BL.

62. Macaulay, Journal, Apr. 9, 1796, reel 7. Macaulay reported that the "people here who call themselves religious . . . may amount to about 400" and then totaled the different congregations. He may have been counting total congregants, adult congregants, or adult male congregants; adults seems most likely.

63. CO 270/3, Nov. 5, 1795 (settler boat); CO 268/5, Dawes to court of directors, Apr. 11, 1795 ("settlers have opened a Trade with the Neighboring Rivers for Stock Rice etc.").

64. CO 270/3, Dec. 11, 1794 (Rio Nunez), Feb. 21, 1795 (ordeal by fire), Mar. 21, 1795 (adultery); CO 270/4, June 9, 1799; June 24, 1799 (cattle). Thomas Winterbottom, *An Account of the Native Africans in the Neighborhood of Sierra Leone*, 1:128 (use of hot iron in ordeal; Winterbottom reported that sometimes the ordeal involved putting an "arm into a vessel full of boiling palm oil" instead).

65. Macaulay to Thomas Babington, Freetown, Sept. 28, 1796, in Knutsford, *Life and Letters of Zachary Macaulay*, 154.

66. Entry for Nov. 19, 1796, in Knutsford, *Life and Letters of Zachary Macaulay*, 156; Macaulay, Journal, Nov. 19, 1796, reel 7; Macaulay, Journal, May 10, 1796, reel 7; Knutsford, *Life and Letters of Zachary Macaulay*, Dec. 15, 1796, 158 (election).

67. Some have seen this as a missed chance to stop the escalating confrontations (e.g., Walker, *Black Loyalists*, chap. 10, esp. 224–25).

68. Knutsford, *Life and Letters of Zachary Macaulay*, entry for Dec. 10, 1796, 157; Macaulay, Journal, Dec. 10, 1796, reel 7; Macaulay, Journal, Dec. 21, 1796, reel 7.

69. Macaulay insultingly told the settlers to "go home and mind their business" (Macaulay, Journal, Dec. 19, 1796, reel 7). At least one Hundredor braved Macaulay's ridicule to broach the matter privately (Journal, Aug. 23, 1797, reel 7).

70. Isaac Streeter, Chairman of the Tything. And George Carrol, Chairman of the Hundredors to Macaulay, Aug. 5, 1795, CO 270/4, Aug. 17, 1797 (Aug. 5 letter copied into minutes of Aug. 17 meeting).

71. Knutsford, *Life and Letters of Zachary Macaulay*, 143–47; Macaulay, Journal, entries for July 7, 1796; July 8, 1796; July 10, 1796, reel 7. CO 270/4, July 11, 1796. This became tied to Macaulay's attempt to expel John Garvin, a white Methodist preacher (CO 270/4, July 18, 1796 for Garvin trial). Schama, *Rough Crossings*, 373–74; Walker, *Black Loyalists*, 207–9.

72. Knutsford, *Life and Letters of Zachary Macaulay*, July 11, 1796 entry, 146; CO 270/4, July 11, 1796. The Baptists, Huntingdonians, and Wesleyans attended one another's services ("A Letter from Africa," Free-Town, Apr. 22, 1796, *Evangelical Magazine* 4 [1796], 419–20).

73. Macaulay, Journal, Apr. 25, 1797, reel 7. George relented at the end of a twelve-hour discussion, but even Macaulay wondered if he did so "from art or conviction." Macaulay's practice of intimidating settlers into pretending to accede to his arguments is reflected in the way he "silenced" George "with a very striking passage, quite in point from your

Archbishop of Leighton. . . . 'Such reasoning' says he 'is the corrupt [ ] of the flesh, its base sophistry.'" It is easy to imagine George deciding to let the discussion die in response.

74. Macaulay, Journal, Sept. 15, 1796, reel 7.

75. Macaulay, Journal, Aug. 23, 1797, reel 7.

76. J. R. Pole, *Political Representation in England and the Origins of the American Republic.*

77. I have not located the document. See Knutsford, *Life and Letters of Zachary Macaulay*, 175–76 (heavily edited); and Macaulay, Journal, Sept. 30 (quote); Oct. 2, 1797, reel 7.

78. Macaulay, Journal, Oct. 2, 1797, reel 7.

79. Ibid., Dec. 20, 1797, [ ] Jan. 1798, reel 7. Only Ishmael York, among sitting Hundredors, won reelection. Fourteen Tythingmen were reelected (thirty Tythingmen were elected in 1797 and twenty-three or twenty-five in 1798—Macaulay listed twenty-five slots but recorded only twenty-three victors), and six of the fourteen were men Macaulay had approved in 1797. Macaulay labeled only seven of the twenty-three winners in 1798 "bad." The smaller number of men elected (five rather than six Hundredors, twenty-three to twenty-five rather then thirty Tythingmen) probably represents the secession of Pirate's Bay settlers (see below).

80. Knutsford, *Life and Letters of Zachary Macaulay*, entry for Jan. 29, 1798, 187.

81. Ishmael York, Stephen Peters, Isaac H. Anderson, Hundredors to the Honorable Captain Ball, Freetown, Jan. 15, 1798, in Fyfe, ed., *"Our Children Free and Happy,"* 57–58 ("we are not used here as free settlers").

82. Macaulay, Journal, Feb. 4, 1798 (Prostitution on ship; Knutsford edited this out, 188), and Oct. 8, 1798 ("ministering to their wants"), reel 6. Macaulay was shocked that married women going out to the ships met no "particular discouragement from their Husbands," though the "conduct of unmarried women was still less restrained by moral or prudential considerations."

83. Macaulay, Journal, Apr. 25, 1797, reel 7.

84. Winterbottom, *An Account of the Native Africans*, 1:276.

85. Brooks, *American Lazarus*, chap. 4 sees a transformation in Hall's politics during the five years separating the petition discussed above and Hall's first Charge. I'm not fully convinced that the change was as fundamental as she contends, but the continuities that I see in the approaches to African identity can be consistent with Brooks's reading. For the "Charges" themselves, see Charles H. Wesley, *Prince Hall*, 55–61, 110–19; or Brooks and Saillant, ed., *"Face Zion Forward,"* 177-98.

86. Wesley, ibid., 55–56.

87. The second charge is in ibid., 110–19.

88. See C. F. Volney, *The Ruins, or, Meditation on the Revolutions of Empires: And the Law of Nature* for a French contemporary using African history to make a similar argument.

89. Wesley, *Prince Hall*, 115. Hall combined this support for revolution with loyalty to established order: "My brethren, let us pay all due respect to all whom God hath put in places of honor over us: do justly and be faithful to them that hire you, and treat

them with that respect they may deserve; but worship no man. Worship God, this much is your duty as christians and as masons" (117).

90. For Hall's notes on important Africans from classical history, see Letters and Sermons by Prince Hall, 1787–1802, Prince Hall Records by H. V. B. Voorhis, 1950, made from negative film at Boston Grand Lodge, Boston Grand Masonic Lodge Library. Much of the film is illegible because of apparent water damage to the originals.

91. Bonner Brown (Pres.) and London Spears (Vice P.) to the Governor and Company of Sierra Leone, Providence, Nov. 26, 1794, and Resolutions, Feb. 21, 1795, Council Minutes, CO 270/3; Zachary Macaulay to Samuel Hopkins, Freetown, March 19, 1795, Governor's Letter Book 1794–98, CO 268/5; Floyd J. Miller, *The Search for a Black Nationality*, 14–20; Elizabeth Rauh Bethel, *The Roots of African-American Identity*, 75.

92. *Proceedings*, 44–45. Zachary Macaulay to Henry Thornton, Freetown, Jan. 31, 1795, CO 268/5.

93. Ibid., 91–92.

94. Macaulay, Journal, Jan. 5, 1799, reel 6. For contemporary rural New Englanders' treasure dreams see Alan Taylor, "The Early Republic's Supernatural Economy: Treasure Seeking in the American Northeast, 1780–1830," 6–34; and John L. Brooke, *The Refiner's Fire*.

95. Macaulay, Feb. 25, 1799, reel 6. See F. B. Spilsbury, *Account of a Voyage to the Western Coast of Africa*, 21 for more settler-native tension. A white resident described Temne life and highlighted their perceived differences from settlers in "A Letter from Africa," Free-Town, Apr. 22, 1796, *Evangelical Magazine* 4 (1796), 421–22. David George postponed evangelizing among the natives because they were "at war with one another though they are at peace with us" (Carretta, ed., *Unchained Voices*, 345).

96. Council Records, Nov. 17, 1801 Meeting, CO 270/6. The quote is from a letter Ludlam included in the records of the meeting when asking the directors to halve the quitrent.

97. "Grievances presented by the Hundredors and Tythingmen to the Governor and Council," Feb. 13, 1800 Council Records; Mar. 4, 1800 Meeting ("get justice"); Nathaniel Wansey and Cato Lynus to the Governor and Council, n.d., Appendix to the Minutes for the Year 1800 ("sit in judgment"), CO 270/5.

98. Ludlam to Wansey and the Tythingmen, n.d. Appendix to the Minutes for the Year 1800, CO 270/5. Emphasis in original.

99. Ibid., CO 270/5. The laws are in Fyfe, ed., *Sierra Leone Inheritance*, 124–26. They were offered in the name of "the Hundredors and Tythingmen and Chairman," and signed by "James Roberson, Hundr. Ansel Zizer, Hundr. Isaac Anderson, Hundr. And Nath. Wansey, Chairman."

100. T. Ludlam for the Council to James Robinson, Thornton-Hill in Freetown, Sept. 14, 1799, CO 270/5. This letter is reproduced as an appendix to Ludlam's "Narrative" cited below.

101. Ludlam, "A Narrative of the Rebellion which broke out in this Colony on the 25th of Septr. 1800," Appendix to the Minutes for the Year 1800, CO 270/5. This report slants toward the Company. For insightful analyses of the Rebellion of 1800, see

Walker, *Black Loyalists*, chaps. 10, 11; and Ellen Gibson Wilson, *The Loyal Blacks*, chap. 19. Both see the Rebellion as the beginning of the end of the Nova Scotians' dominance of settler society in Sierra Leone.

102. Ludlam blamed the rebels for initiating violence, reporting that Robinson responded to Crankapone's order that he surrender by striking "a severe blow . . . with a stick," but John Kizell, a Nova Scotian, whom Macaulay considered a reliable supporter of the Company in 1797, was interviewed in 1827 and recalled things differently: the governor, having learned "where the people mett . . . send down some men, under arms" even though the rebels "had no arms whatsoever." Upon being fired upon while meeting, Kizell said, the rebels "took fence sticks and began to knock the Governor's people down." Sierra Leone Commissioners of Enquiry 1827, vol. 2, appendix B, item 5, CO 267/92.

103. Pybus, *Epic Journeys*, 197–202 (account of uprising), 215 (biographical sketch of Perkins); Council Records, Nov. 17, 1801 Meeting, CO 270/6.

104. After losing the Second Maroon War in Jamaica in 1795–96, the Maroons were double-crossed and deported from the island. They arrived in Nova Scotia in 1796, but complained that they could not "thrive where the Pine Apple does not," and asked to be moved ("Petition of Captains John Jarret, Andrew Smith, James Barrel, James Lawrence, Thomas Johnstone, and Charles Shaw . . . and . . . the Maroons now . . . in the Province of Nova Scotia," Samuel Thornton to Duke of Portland, London, Jan. 4, 1799, CO 217/70). Despite Company discomfort, they were sent to Sierra Leone. Mavis Christine Campbell, ed., *Back to Africa*. Also see Mavis C. Campbell, *The Maroons of Jamaica, 1655–1796*.

105. Walker, *Black Loyalists*, chap. 11 (243–44 for Temne attacks); Ellen Gibson Wilson, *The Loyal Blacks*, chap. 19.

106. Spilsbury, *Account of a Voyage to the Western Coast of Africa*, 38.

107. CO 270/11, Oct. 8, 1808, and Nov. 11, 1808, for slavery and apprenticeship. The Nova Scotians were not, of course, the main group responsible for F. B. Spilsbury's 1807 claim that "the Sierra Leone colony, though expressly established for the abolition of the slave trade, has produced more slave-factors than any other settlement (*Account of a Voyage to the Western Coast of Africa*, 27n). Depositions of Kizell, Aikin, and Jones are in the Sierra Leone Commissioners of Enquiry, 1827, vol. 2, appendix B and C, item 5, PRO 267/92. Quotation from Jones.

CHAPTER 5

1. See Gary B. Nash, *The Forgotten Fifth* for a recent brief in favor of the emancipatory potential of the Revolution; and George M. Frederickson, "Redcoat Liberation," 51–53 for a concise statement of the less hopeful case.

2. See Arthur Zilversmit, *The First Emancipation* for legal emancipation in the North; Gary B. Nash and Jean R. Soderlund, *Freedom by Degrees*; Shane White, *Somewhat More Independent*; Graham Russell Hodges, *Root and Branch*, esp. chaps. 6

and 7; Joanne Pope Melish, *Disowning Slavery* for the social and cultural processes of emancipation in the North.

3. Laurent Dubois, *Avengers of the New World*; Robin Blackburn, *The Overthrow of Colonial Slavery, 1776–1848*; David Patrick Geggus, *Slavery, War, and Revolution*; David Patrick Geggus, *Haitian Revolutionary Studies*, esp. parts 1 and 5; David Brion Davis, *Inhuman Bondage*, chap. 8; and James Sidbury, "Saint Domingue in Virginia."

4. Blackburn, *Overthrow*; David Eltis, *The Rise of African Slavery in the Americas*; David Brion Davis, *The Problem of Slavery in the Age of Revolution, 1770–1823*; David Brion Davis, *Inhuman Bondage,* chaps. 8, 12, 13; William W. Freehling, *The Reintegration of American History*, 26–29.

5. Modern scholarly accounts begin with W. E. Burghardt DuBois, *The Philadelphia Negro*, chap. 9; Carter G. Woodson, *The History of the Negro Church*, esp. chaps. 4–6; Charles H. Wesley, *Richard Allen*. More recent accounts include Gary B. Nash, *Forging Freedom*, esp. chap. 4; Albert J. Raboteau, *A Fire in the Bones*, chaps. 2 and 4; Milton C. Sernett, *Black Religion and American Evangelicalism*, chap. 5; Carol V. R. George, *Segregated Sabbaths*. See also Lewis V. Baldwin, *"Invisible" Strands in African Methodism* for Delaware; and Christopher Phillips, *Freedom's Port*, esp. chap. 5 for Baltimore. James T. Campbell, *Songs of Zion*, chaps. 1–3 has influenced this project from its inception.

6. See James Oliver Horton and Lois E. Horton, *In Hope of Liberty*; Elizabeth Rauh Bethel, *The Roots of African-American Identity* for the context within which the separate church movement in Philadelphia developed.

7. See Wesley, *Richard Allen*; and George, *Segregated Sabbaths* for Allen's life.

8. Richard Allen, *The Life Experience and Gospel Labors of the Rt. Rev. Richard Allen*, 25. A contemporary white Methodist confirmed much of the story: Lorenzo Dow, *Quintessence of Lorenzo's Works*, 558–62.

9. George F. Bragg, *Heroes of the Eastern Shore*, 4 (Black Bishop); Dorothy Ripley, *The Extraordinary Conversion and Religious Experience*, 132 (Absalom Jones, the Black Bishop).

10. Allen, *Life Experience*, 13; Benjamin T. Tanner, *Outline of Our History and Government for African Methodist Churchmen, Ministerial and Lay*, 16–17; Sernett, *Black Religion*, 117, 218–20nn24, 25 (dates walkout); Raboteau, *A Fire in the Bones*, 83–87; Nash, *Forging Freedom*, 109–33.

11. Herbert Aptheker, ed., *A Documentary History of the Negro People in the United States*, 17–18.

12. William Douglass, *Annals of the First African Church, in the United States of America, Now Styled the African Episcopal Church of St. Thomas, Philadelphia*, 24; Raboteau, *A Fire in the Bones*, 85.

13. Absalom Jones, "A Thanksgiving Sermon, Preached January 1, 1808, in St. Thomas's, or the African Episcopal, Church, Philadelphia: On Account of the Abolition of the African Slave Trade," *Early Negro Writing*, 335–42.

14. Jones includes Ps. 97:2; 98:1, 3. Both insist that God favors friends of justice on earth and both invoke Isaiah. Jones skipped Ps. 98:2, perhaps because it focuses on "heathen" in a way that would have redirected attention away from false Christian evildoers ("The Lord

hath made known his salvation: his righteousness hath he openly shewed in the sight of the heathen"). See chap. 3 above and Glaude, *Exodus!* for other uses of the trope of exodus.

15. Jones, "Sermon," 338. Jones claimed inaccurately that the Constitution stopped "the trade in our African fellowmen" in 1808.

16. William Miller, *A Sermon on the Abolition of the Slave Trade*, 13–14 similarly predicted that God would raise "thousands of witnesses" among black Americans to "visit the land of their forefathers" and proselytize their "African kinsmen." See Phillip Richards, "The 'Joseph Story' as Slave Narrative: On Genesis and Exodus as Prototypes for Early Black Anglophone Writing," 221–35; and John Saillant, *Black Puritan, Black Republican*, 87 for Joseph in black antislavery writing.

17. See Saillant, *Black Puritan*, chap. 3 for Lemuel Haynes on covenant theology and race.

18. Material on Methodists in Baltimore is drawn from Phillips, *Freedom's Port*, chap. 5, unless otherwise noted.

19. Cynthia Lyn Lyerly, *Methodism and the Southern Mind, 1770–1810*, chap. 6; Donald G. Mathews, *Slavery and Methodism*; David Hempton, *Methodism*, 82–85.

20. George White, "A Brief Account of the Life, Experience, Travels, and Gospel Labours of George White, an African" in Graham Russell Hodges, ed., *Black Itinerants of the Gospel: The Narratives of John Jea and George White*, 69 (Coker's influence in New York after having moved to Baltimore).

21. Accounts of Coker's childhood rely on Daniel Payne, *History of the African Methodist Episcopal Church*, 88–92 (Payne cited an 1852 conversation with "a half-brother of Brother Coker"—perhaps Abner Coker, another AME minister). See, for example, Phillips, *Freedom's Port*, 131; Leroy Graham, *Baltimore*, 63–64; George F. Bragg, *Men of Maryland*, 37–40; Wesley, *Richard Allen*, 130–31; and Campbell, *Songs of Zion*, 12.

22. Phillips, ibid., 133 (By 1810). "A Dialogue between a Virginian and an African Minister, Written by the Rev. Daniel Coker, a Descendant of Africa . . . Minister of the African Methodist Episcopal Church in Baltimore" in *Negro Protest Pamphlets: A Compendium*, ed. Dorothy Porter; Campbell, *Songs of Zion*, 23–24; Theophus H. Smith, *Conjuring Culture*, 184–90; Nash, *Forging Freedom*, 230; Dain, *A Hideous Monster of the Mind*, 70–72 discusses the *Dialogue*.

23. Coker, ibid., 4–5.

24. Ibid., 6–7.

25. Ibid., 9–11.

26. Jacob Oson, *A Search for Truth; or, An Inquiry for the Origin of the African Nation* (New York, 1817), 12 discusses Moses and David in an analogous argument. See Colin Kidd, *The Forging of Races*, 41–43 for Moses and miscegenation among European writers.

27. Coker, *Dialogue*, 28–29. See chap. 6 for Coker's move to Africa.

28. Martha Elizabeth Hodes, *White Women, Black Men* shows that sex between white women and black men was more common than once thought, and that localities in which it occurred openly were often less bothered by it than historians have assumed.

29. Coker, *Dialogue*, 39–43. A publication or speech provides evidence of talent. James Forten, for example, is credited for an appeal to Congress, not his success as an artisan and businessman. For his life and careers, see Julie Winch, *A Gentleman of Color*.

30. Nash, *Forging Freedom*, 230; and Campbell, *Songs of Zion*, 13 point this out. Smith, *Conjuring Culture*, 147 offers a different though not contradictory reading of the passage.

31. *New Century Bible: I Peter*, ed. Ernest Best; Paul J. Achtemeier, "I Peter," *The HarperCollins Bible Commentary*, rev. ed., 1168–77; H. A. A. Kennedy, "Peter, First Epistle of," *A New Standard Bible Dictionary*, ed. Melancthon W. Jacobus, Edward E. Nourse, Andrew C. Zenos, 699–700. Marrant preached on that text in Nova Scotia (John Saillant, "'Wipe Away All Tears from Their Eyes'").

32. Phillips, *Freedom's Port*, 132–33; 274n48.

33. Richard Allen to Daniel Coker, Feb. 16, 1816, in Tanner, *Outline of Our History*, 152–55.

34. Phillips, *Freedom's Port*, 133 notes the double meaning.

35. Jones made similar moves in the sermon, though more filiative claims to kinship predominated.

36. Of seven speeches commemorating the end of the slave trade collected in *Early Negro Writing, 1760–1837*, 34–35, 337–38, 345, 366, 375 (descendants); 391 (our parents), four authors are listed on the title page without a racial identifier (Absalom Jones, Joseph Sydney, George Lawrence, and Russell Parrott), and three are listed as "Descendant of Africa" (Peter Williams Jr., Henry Sipkins, and William Hamilton). They may, of course, have been introduced differently when they spoke; only the published versions survive.

37. Ibid., 35, 346, 366–67, 376–77. Wilson Jeremiah Moses, *Afrotopia*. Bruce Dain, *A Hideous Monster of the Mind*, 117 alludes to Edenic portrayals of Africa by black orators. Dain says Equiano portrays Africa similarly (50), but this conflates Eden with what Equiano calls the "Israel of the Patriarchs."

38. George Lawrence, "Oration on the Abolition of the Slave Trade, Delivered on the First Day of January, 1813, in the African Methodist Episcopal Church," *Early Negro Writing, 1760–1837*, 377.

39. Two partial exceptions strengthen the case, for they focus on what will no longer happen in Africa rather than on a progressive transformation: Henry Sipkins, "An Oration on the Abolition of the Slave Trade: Delivered in the African Church, in the City of New York, January 2, 1809," *Early Negro Writing, 1760–1837*, 372 ("No longer shall the shores of Africa be drenched with human gore. No longer shall its inhabitants be torn from their native soil; no longer shall they be brought on cruel shipboard, weighed down in chains. . . ."); Peter Williams Jr., "An Oration on the Abolition of the Slave Trade: Delivered in The African Church, in the City of New York, January 1, 1808," *Early Negro Writing, 1760–1837*, 349 ("Rejoice, Oh! Africans! No longer shall tyranny, war, and injustice, with irresistible sway, desolate your native country").

40. For most of these speaker/authors, one or two short published addresses constitute the only evidence of what they thought. Far too little survives to assert what

these men believed; I am instead reconstructing the patterns of discourse in which they participated. See below for Williams's alliance with Cuffe.

41. Williams Jr., "Oration," *Early Negro Writing, 1760–1837*, 353 closes with a plea suggesting a filiative sense of identity ("May the time speedily commence, when Ethiopia shall stretch forth her hands; when the sun of liberty shall beam resplendent on the whole African race; and its genial influences, promote the luxuriant growth of knowledge and virtue"). Also see William Miller, *A Sermon on the Abolition of the Slave Trade*.

42. Lamont D. Thomas, *Rise to Be a People*, 1–31; Amanda Lee Brooks, "Captain Paul Cuffe (1759–1817) and the Crown Colony of Sierra Leone," chaps. 2, 3 for a thorough account of Cuffe's early working life; Sally Loomis, "The Evolution of Paul Cuffe's Black Nationalism," in *Black Apostles at Home and Abroad*, 191–202; Rosalind Cobb Wiggins, "Introducing Captain Paul Cuffe, Friend," in *Captain Paul Cuffe's Logs and Letters, 1808–1817*, ed. Rosalind Cobb Wiggins, 45–69 (hereafter *Cuffe's Logs and Letters*); Sheldon H. Harris, *Paul Cuffe*; and H. N. Sherwood, "Paul Cuffe," 153–229 for biographical information. Cuffe's wife, like his mother, was Native American, and his network of friends and partners included white Quakers, Indians, and blacks.

43. William Dillwyn estimated that in 1809 Cuffe had "acquired about five thousand pounds sterling, in mercantile pursuits" (*Life of William Allen, with Selections from His Correspondence*, 1:85–86). See Thomas, ibid.; and Amanda Lee Brooks, "Captain Paul Cuffe" for biographical information.

44. Pemberton to Cuffe, Philadelphia, June 8, 1808; Cuffe to Pemberton, Westport, Mass., Sept. 14, 1808, in *Cuffe's Logs and Letters*, 77–78. Brooks, ibid., 111 reads this letter differently. For Quakers and antislavery views, see David Brion Davis, *The Problem of Slavery in the Age of Revolution*; Jean Soderlund, *Quakers and Slavery*; and Nash and Soderlund, *Freedom by Degrees*, esp. chaps. 2 and 3.

45. John Cuffe to Freelove Cuffe, Westport, Mass., Jan. 5, 1811, reel 1, Cuffe Microfilm, New Bedford Free Public Library (hereafter NBFPL).

46. Pemberton to Cuffe, Philadelphia, Sept. 27, 1808; Cuffe to John James and Alexander Wilson, Westport, Mass., Oct. 6, 1808, in *Cuffe's Logs and Letters*, 79–82.

47. Macaulay to Cuffe, Clapham, England, Aug. 29, 1809, in *Cuffe's Logs and Letters*, 84.

48. Log entry, Feb. 13, 1811, in *Cuffe's Logs and Letters*, 103.

49. Thomas Clarkson, *The History of the Rise, Progress, and Accomplishment of the Abolition of the African Slave-trade by the British Parliament*, 2:343–45 (quotes at 344 and 345). For Clarkson, see Ellen Gibson Wilson, *Thomas Clarkson: A Biography*; and Christopher Leslie Brown, *Moral Capital*, chap. 7.

50. Log entries, Mar. 1, 1811; Mar. 4, 1811; Mar. 6, 1811; Mar. 8, 1811; Mar. 9, 1811; Mar. 10, 1811; Mar. 11, 1811; Mar. 12, 1811, in *Cuffe's Logs and Letters*, 106–7.

51. Fyfe, *A History of Sierra Leone*, esp. chaps. 5–7 for recaptives; log entry, Dec. 8, 1811, in *Cuffe's Logs and Letters*, 172 (quotation).

52. Cuffe never recorded striking spiritual dreams, but his papers include a powerful dream that his niece Cyntha Cuff had in 1790, and that Ruth Cuffe recorded for Paul in 1807, indicating that the family believed in the spiritual significance of

dreams. See "A Remarkerble dream," June [7?], 1790, Cuffe microfilm, reel 1. See Mechal Sobel, *Teach Me Dreams*; and Ann Taves, *Fits, Trances and Visions: Experiencing Religion and Explaining Experience from Wesley to James*, part 1 for dreams and visions in early America.

53. Log entries, Mar. 13, 1811; Mar. 14, 1811; Mar. 18, 1811, in *Cuffe's Logs and Letters*, 108–9. *Letter from Elizabeth Webb to Anthony William Boehm. With His Answer*, 41–46 (quotes at 41, 45). Cuffe called this "a history of Elizabeth Webb a Quaker."

54. Stephen Crisp, *A Short History of a Long Travel from Babylon to Bethel*, 23. Cuffe called the text "a Short History of a Long travel from babel to Bethill" (*Cuffe's Logs and Letters*, 109).

55. Wiggins inserts an editorial comment to this effect at *Cuffe's Logs and Letters*, 115. William Allen, the British philanthropist and a leader of London's African Institution, commented on white settler hostility in Allen to Richard Reynolds, Jan. 1814, in Dillwyn, *Life of William Allen*, 1:137–39.

56. *Cuffe's Logs and Letters*, 115–17 (for both the petition to the governor and the "Epistle of the Society of Sierra Leone in Africa"). I have identified the Nova Scotians from my research files and from Graham Russell Hodges, ed., *The Black Loyalist Directory*.

57. "I fear their Children are indulged too much in idolness I have thought the morons [maroons] to be most industrious in Labour and the Novascotians most Constant in form of Religion etc" (from an unlabeled list of questions and answers, probably sent by Cuffe to the London African Institution, reel 1, Cuffe microfilm).

58. Cuffe to Allen, Sierraleone [*sic*], Apr. 22, 1811, in *Cuffe's Logs and Letters*, 118–20. The "servants" on whom the settlers relied were probably recaptives and other natives of Africa who were being pushed into apprenticeships that differed little from slavery. See Amanda Lee Brooks, "Captain Paul Cuffe," 158–66.

59. Log entry, Aug. 6, 1811, in *Cuffe's Logs and Letters*, 123.

60. Ibid., chap. 4 (quotes at 137, 148).

61. Log entry for July 28, 1811; and Cuffe to John Cuffe, Liverpool, Aug. 12, 1811, in ibid., 139, 144–45. Dillwyn, *Life of William Allen*, diary entry for July 30, 1811; and Apr. 12, 1812, 103, 107.

62. *Cuffe's Logs and Letters*, 158–67 reproduces Cuffe's ship log from the trip.

63. Log entries, Nov. 17, 1811; Nov. 24, 1811; Nov. 25, 1811; Dec. 1, 1811; Dec. 2, 1811; and Dec. 8, 1811, in *Cuffe's Logs and Letters*, 168, 170, 171, 172.

64. Log entry, Dec. 11, 1811, in *Cuffe's Logs and Letters*, 173. Fyfe, *A History*, 113 says that Cuffe "got one of the Methodist congregations to organize a co-operative trading society, the Friendly Society of Sierra Leone," but he also reports that John Kizell, a Baptist (62), was chosen first president.

65. Log entry, Dec. 18, 1811, in *Cuffe's Logs and Letters*, 174–75.

66. Log entries, Dec. 23, 1811; Dec. 28, 1811; Dec. 30, 1811, in *Cuffe's Logs and Letters*, 176, 178, 179.

67. Log entry, Jan. 2, 1812, *Cuffe's Logs and Letters*, 181.

68. Log entries, Dec. 21, 1811 (eight books); Jan. 23, 1812 (debating and we), in *Cuffe's Logs and Letters*, 176, 187.

69. See Amanda Lee Brooks, "Captain Paul Cuffe," 140 for a very different interpretation of Cuffe's careful record keeping.

CHAPTER 6

1. See Amanda Lee Brooks, "Captain Paul Cuffe (1759–1817) and the Crown Colony of Sierra Leone," chap. 12 for the fullest recounting of Cuffe's trip to Washington. Brooks is more cynical about Cuffe's motives than I am.

2. Log entries: Apr. 16, 1812; Apr. 25, 1812; May 2, 1812; May 4, 1812, in *Captain Paul Cuffe's Logs and Letters, 1808–1817*, ed. Rosalind Cobb Wiggins (hereafter, *Cuffe's Logs and Letters*), 208 (embargo), 210 (letters), 212–13 (Washington). His celebrity can be seen in the New York *Columbian* report on his trip: "Captain C. had been 18 months absent, and was unacquainted with the regulations of his native country. He went to Washington—and having stated his case to government, was very politely treated, and his vessel and cargo immediately restored" (May 14, 1812). For Jeffersonian attitudes that might have made them receptive to Cuffe's plan, see Peter S. Onuf, *Jefferson's Empire*, chap. 5; Peter S. Onuf, "Every Generation Is an 'Independent Nation': Colonization, Miscegenation, and the Fate of Jefferson's Children," 153–70; and James Sidbury, "Thomas Jefferson in Gabriel's Virginia," 199–219 (Jeffersonian fantasies of whitening).

3. Paul Cuffe, *A Brief Account of the Settlement and Present Situation of the Colony of Sierra Leone in Africa; as Communicated by Paul Cuffe (a Man of Colour) to His Friend in New York: Also an Explanation of the Object of His Visit, and Some Advice to the People of Colour in the United States.*

4. The entire "Address" and "Advice" are at *Brief Account*, 8–9. If my reading of "scattered" seems speculative, it is worth recalling that the book Cuffe gave the Temne king Thomas was an "Essa on Wars" (*Cuffe's Logs and Letters*, 108), and also worth noting that the paragraph preceding the "Address" in the *Brief Account* discusses indigenous involvement in the slave trade in Africa (7–8).

5. Log entry, May 6, 1812; May 12, 1812; May 14, 1812, in *Cuffe's Logs and Letters*, 214 (Baltimore; mode), 215 (Philadelphia), 216 (New York; colony). Cuffe to Allen, Westport, June 12, 1812, in *Cuffe's Logs and Letters*, 224–25.

6. Cuffe to Hannah Little, Westport, Feb. 18, 1813, in *Cuffe's Logs and Letters*, 237–38. See Catherine Allgor, *Parlor Politics*, esp. chap. 2 for Dolley Madison's political influence during her husband's administration; "The Memorial Petition to the Presedent Senate and House of Representatives," June 16, 1813, in *Cuffe's Logs and Letters*, 252–53.

7. Cuffe to the Friendly Society, Westport, Sept. 29, 1813; Cuffe to William Allen, Westport, Mar. 6, 1814; Cuffe to Richard Allen, Westport, Mar. 8, 1814; Cuffe to Benjamin Tucker, Westport, Aug. 6, 1814; Cuffe to Richard Allen, Westport, Aug. 6,

1814; Cuffe to Daniel Coker, Westport, Mar. 13, 1815; Cuffe to James Forten, Westport, Mar. 27, 1815, in *Cuffe's Logs and Letters*, 260–61, 274, 277, 292, 294–95, 322, 331. See Julie Winch, *A Gentleman of Color*, chap. 8 for these efforts in Philadelphia.

8. Cuffe to Laban Wheaton, Westport, Apr. 20, 1814; Prince Saunders to Cuffe, Boston, Mar. 21, 1815, in *Cuffe's Logs and Letters*, 281–82, 336–37. For McPherson, see Sidbury, *Ploughshares into Swords*, chap. 6; and Edmund Berkeley Jr., "Prophet without Honor: Christopher McPherson, Free Person of Color," 180–90; for Tyson, see Christopher Phillips, *Freedom's Port*, 49–50; and [John S. Tyson], *The Life of Elisha Tyson, the Philanthropist.*

9. Cuffe to James Forten, Westport, Jan. 27, 1815; Cuffe to William Allen, Westport, Mar. 13, 1815; Prince Saunders to Cuffe, Boston, Mar. 21, 1815, in *Cuffe's Logs and Letters*, 308–9, 326–27, 336–37.

10. Cuffe to Richard Dean, Westport, Oct. 29, 1815; Cuffe to James Forten, Westport, Oct. 28, 1815, in *Cuffe's Logs and Letters*, 384, 383.

11. Cuffe to J. Merecer, Westport, July 6, 1814; Cuffe to Samuel J. Mills, Westport, Mar. 15, 1814, in *Cuffe's Logs and Letters*, 289–90 (oppresed), 279–80 (African race). See also Cuffe to Samuel R. Fisher, Westport, Aug. 14, 1816, in *Cuffe's Logs and Letters*, 446 ("I . . . Noticed Thy arden Desire for the well being of the African race: It appers To me That Thare never [was] a time when it Calls Louder for Something To be Done for The African Nation").

12. Cuffe to Cato Sawyer, Westport, Feb. 17, 1814, in *Cuffe's Logs and Letters*, 271. Byrd, "Eboe, Country, Nation and Gustavus Vassa's *Interesting Narrative*," 123–49 discusses that author's complex use of *country* and *nation*.

13. Cuffe to James Wise, [Westport], Sept. 15, 1816, in *Cuffe's Logs and Letters*, 402.

14. Cuffe to Cato Sawyer, Westport, Feb. 17, 1814, in *Cuffe's Logs and Letters*, 271.

15. Cuffe to James Pemberton, Westport, Mass., Sept. 14, 1808, in *Cuffe's Logs and Letters*, 78.

16. Cuffe to Jedediah Morse, Westport, Aug. 10, 1816, in *Cuffe's Logs and Letters*, 436.

17. Cuffe to Samuel R. Fisher, Westport, Aug. 14, 1816; Cuffe to James Forten, Westport, Mar. 1, 1817, in *Cuffe's Logs and Letters*, 446, 509.

18. Cuffe to Peter Williams Jr., Westport, Aug. 30, 1816, in *Cuffe's Logs and Letters*, 450.

19. Cuffe to James Forten, Westport, Mar. 1, 1817, in *Cuffe's Logs and Letters*, 509.

20. *Poulson's American Daily Advertiser*, Jan. 20, 1817.

21. For discussions of Methodism's retreat, see Cynthia Lyn Lyerly, *Methodism and the Southern Mind, 1770–1810*, chap. 6; Donald G. Mathews, *Slavery and Methodism*; and David Hempton, *Methodism*, 82–85. Carol V. R. George, *Segregated Sabbaths*, chap. 3; and Gary B. Nash, *Forging Freedom*, 227–35 provide clear accounts of Philadelphia. See also Mary Corey, "Daniel Coker: Between an Oppressive Culture and a Liberating God," unpublished paper at the Maryland Episcopal Church Diocesan Archives, Baltimore, 20–25 for Baltimore. I am grateful to archivist Mary O. Klein for Corey's essay.

22. George, ibid., 84; David Smith, *Biography of Rev. David Smith of the A.M.E. Church*, 29 (Baltimore).

23. Nash, *Forging Freedom*, 227–33; George, ibid., chap. 2; Charles H. Wesley, *Richard Allen*, chap. 7.

24. Unfortunately, the only extant version of the sermon is a short excerpt in Herbert Aptheker, ed., *A Documentary History of the Negro People in the United States*, 68–69. His reference is *Sermon Delivered Extempore in the African Bethel Church in the City of Baltimore, on the 21st of January, 1816, to a numerous concourse of people, on account of the Coloured People gaining their Church (Bethel) in the Supreme Court of the State of Pennsylvania, by the Rev. D. Coker, Minister of said Church. To which is annexed a list of the African Preachers in Philadelphia, Baltimore, &c. who have withdrawn from under charge of the Methodist Bishops and Conference*, (BUT ARE STILL METHODISTS). (n.d., n.p.).

25. Allen to the Rev. Daniel Coker, minister of the African Bethel Church, Baltimore, Feb. 18, 1816, in Benjamin T. Tanner, *Outline of Our History and Government for African Methodist Churchmen, Ministerial and Lay*, 152–55. It seems unlikely that Coker would have sent the hymn without the sermon.

26. Ibid., 154. The Sharp Street loyalist was John Forty/Fortie. See "Class Records, 1799–1838," Lovely Lane United Methodist Church Museum, Baltimore, for John Fortie (Forty in Allen's letter). Forty/Fortie had, apparently, alleged some financial impropriety on Allen's part. Allen first asked Coker who he was, and then added: "N.B. Since writing the above, I have understood who this John Forty is, and I think him beneath my notice."

27. Phillips, *Freedom's Port*, 135.

28. P. J. Staudenraus, *The African Colonization Movement, 1816–1865* remains the standard institutional history of the ACS (see chap. 3 for the founding of the ACS), but also see Douglas R. Egerton, "'Its Origin Is Not a Little Curious': A New Look at the American Colonization Society," 462–80; and Eric Burin, *Slavery and the Peculiar Solution: A History of the American Colonization Society*. Some in the ACS discussed forming a colony in the American West or settling people in Haiti, but neither idea gained traction within the organization. Also see Floyd Miller, *The Search for a Black Nationality*, 45–53 for a discussion of Cuffe's relationship with the ACS; and Winch, *A Gentleman of Color*, 187–206 for Forten.

29. Staudenraus, ibid., chap. 3; Nash, *Forging Freedom*, 233–37; Douglas R. Egerton, *Charles Fenton Mercer and the Trial of National Conservatism*, chap. 7; Winch, ibid., 187–90.

30. Miller, *The Search for a Black Nationality*, chap. 2 (esp. 45–48); Winch, ibid., 187–88; Paul Cuffe to Robert Finley, Westport, Jan. 8, 1817; Paul Cuffe to James Forten, Westport, Jan. 8, 1817, in *Cuffe's Logs and Letters*, 492–94.

31. Aptheker, ed., *Documentary History*, 71–72 (Philadelphia resolutions); Nash, *Forging Freedom*, 237–39; Winch, ibid., 189–92; Miller, ibid., 48–50; Forten to Cuffe, Philadelphia, Jan. 25, 1817, in *Cuffe's Logs and Letters*, 501–3.

32. Richmond blacks sought territory on the Missouri River (Aptheker, ed., ibid., 70–71). The Georgetown group wanted "territory within the limits of our beloved union" (*Poulson's American Daily Advertiser*, Jan. 10, 1817).

33. *Poulson's American Daily Advertiser*, Jan. 10, 1817. Officers would include "the supreme head, the Right Reverend Father in God, Bishop—then thirty nine Vice Fathers and

Bishops—then thirty six managers or a majority of them, a recording secretary and his clerk, a corresponding secretary and his clerk, a treasurer and his clerk and a collector." For the early life of McPherson, clerk of the meeting and "corresponding secretary," see Berkeley Jr., "Prophet without Honor," 180–90; and Sidbury, *Ploughshares into Swords*, 214–16.

34. Forten to Cuffe, Philadelphia, Jan. 25, 1817, in *Cuffe's Logs and Letters*, 502 (Philadelphians' fears).

35. Staudenraus, *African Colonization*, chap. 4; Gardiner Spring, *Memoirs of the Rev. Samuel J. Mills, Late Missionary to the South Western Section of the United States and Agent of the American Colonization Society, Deputed to Explore the Coast of Africa*, chaps. 8, 9. Chapter 9 is the journal Mills kept while in Africa.

36. John Kizell to Paul Cuffe, Free Town, Feb. 19, 1817 (Kizell sought Cuffe's support for a settlement at Sherbro, in part by reporting that "the Governor seems dissatisfied with those that you brought out afore." Paul Cuffe Manuscripts, New Bedford Free Public Library (not microfilmed; hereafter NBFPL).

37. "Extracts from the Correspondence of Mr. John Kizell with Governor Columbine, respecting his Negotiations with the Chiefs on the River Sherbro, and giving an Account of that River," *Sixth Report of the Directors of the African Institution*, 113–53 (quote at 145). Kizell's letters have been edited—they lack the spelling and grammatical irregularities of the letters written in his own hand that are discussed below. Columbine sketched Kizell's biography on 144–45.

38. "Extract from the Correspondence," 145 (integrity); Spring, *Memoirs of Mills*, 182–83. Kizell sometimes spelled his name "Kezell," and it sometimes appeared "Kizzell," but his name is usually rendered Kizell in the secondary literature, and he sometimes used that spelling, so for the sake of consistency I have retained the most familiar usage. See John Kizell to Ebenezer Burgess, Freetown, Sierra Leone, Aug. 17, 182[3? 1?], Ebenezer Burgess Papers, Massachusetts Historical Society, Boston, for a letter in his hand signed "Kezell."

39. Most of these—getting governmental approval to found a colony and raising money to support it, for example—are peripheral to this chapter. See Staudenraus, *African Colonization* for such material.

40. Quote from unsigned introduction to Daniel Coker, *Journal of Daniel Coker, A Descendant of Africa*, v.

41. Phillips, *Freedom's Port*, 137–38; George, *Segregated Sabbaths*, 118–19; Corey, "Daniel Coker," 32–36. The main sources for Coker's life are Daniel Payne, *History of the African Methodist Episcopal Church*, 88–92 (who cites an 1852 conversation with "a half-brother of Brother Coker," probably Abner Coker); and Smith, *Biography of Rev. David Smith*, 34–37.

42. Payne, *History*, 15 (expulsion); Phillips, *Freedom's Port*, 137–38 (expulsion and bankruptcy). Richard Allen had founded and then been expelled from the Free African Society in Philadelphia. These incidents, and the rejection of colonization at the Philadelphia meeting of 1817, suggest that early free black organizations were unusually democratic. Payne decried the disappearance of democracy from black organizations over the nineteenth century (*History*, 15–16).

43. Smith, *Biography of the Rev. David Smith*, 36. Smith's memory was faulty—he recalled that Coker had become president of Liberia, though in fact Coker never lived in Liberia. Nonetheless, the Society might have promised Coker influence and those promises might have been alluring in the wake of his difficulties. See Bruce H. Mann, *Republic of Debtors*, chap. 4 for equation of imprisonment for debt and slavery.

44. He reported preaching "4 times to very large congregations" in New York City while waiting to embark for Africa (Daniel Coker to [Bishop James Kemp?], New York, Jan. 29, 1920); and he remained in regular contact with prominent Baltimore blacks after he settled in Sierra Leone (Coker to Rt. Rev. Bishop Kemp, Sierra Leone, Apr. 20, 1821, and Coker to Right Rev. Bishop Kemp, Hastings [Sierra Leone], n.d. [ca. 1825]), Maryland Episcopal Diocesan Archives, Baltimore.

45. Staudenraus, *African Colonization*, chap. 6; Thom W. Shick, *Behold the Promised Land*, chap. 2; Charles Henry Huberich, *The Political and Legislative History of Liberia*, 75–79; Antonio McDaniel, *Swing Low, Sweet Chariot*, chap. 3.

46. Archibald Alexander, *A History of Colonization on the West Coast of Africa*, 124 (secret influence); William Mervine to Edward Trenchard, USS *Cyane*, Nov. 1, 1820 (speculation); and John Dix to Edward Trenchard, USS *Cyane*, Nov. 22, 1820 (tyrant) in Huberich, *Liberia*, 121, 128. This portrayal found its way into "The Fourth Annual Report of the American Society for Colonizing the Free People of Colour of the United States. With an Appendix." Reprinted in *The Annual Reports of the American Society for Colonizing the Free People of Colour of the United States, Volumes 1–10, 1818–27.*

47. Spring, *Memoirs of Mills*, 182–83. This language echoes the battles the Nova Scotians had fought against the Sierra Leone Company during the 1790s, as well as the project of Paul Cuffe.

48. Mervine to Trenchard, USS *Cyane*, Nov. 1, 1820 (White Agents); and Kizell quoted in Dix to Trenchard, USS *Cyane*, Nov. 22, 1820 (colour—Dix interviewed Kizell), in Huberich, *Liberia*, 121, 130; American Colonization Society, *The Fourth Annual Report*, 56 (chief cause), which cites the letters of Mervine and Dix.

49. Huberich, ibid., 143 (present); Coker to Rt. Rev. Bishop Kemp, Sierra Leone, Apr. 20, 1821 (engraving), in Maryland Episcopal Church Diocesan Archives, Baltimore.

50. The pamphlet and a cover letter (Kizell to Ebenezer Burgess, Freetown, Sierra Leone, Aug. 17, 182[1]) are in the Ebenezer Burgess Papers, Massachusetts Historical Society, Boston. In the cover letter, Kizell wrote: "If you doe think proper to have it Pubblished you may." By 1821 the ACS had little to gain by rehashing the disasters of the previous summer, so Burgess might have left a brilliantly written account from Kizell to languish in his files.

51. Christian Wiltberger Diary, n.d., Christian Wiltberger Papers, Library of Congress, microfilm, frames 88–90 ("*Coker* . . . has done *more injury* to the cause *than any other man* living"); J. B. Winn to Smith Thompson, Fourah Bay, Sierra Leone, Aug. 6, 1821, in Huberich, *Liberia*, 174 ("had Mr. Coker . . . been as diligent and laborious in taking care of said property . . . as he was in writing home to America to building [*sic*] himself a name . . . there would have been less waste of property and the wreck and ruin not so great").

52. Coker, *Journal*, 25–26, 31, 36–38.

53. Ibid., 42–44.

54. Wiltberger Papers, microfilm, frames 149–50. This source is problematic. Wiltberger copied extracts from Johnson's diary into the diary that he sent back to the board of the ACS. It is impossible to know if or how he shaped the resulting text. Emphasis in original.

55. Sierra Leone Commissioners of Enquiry, 1827, vol. 2, appendix B and C, item 5, PRO 267/92, 22–27.

56. Matei Markwei, "The Rev. Daniel Coker of Sierra Leone," *Black Apostles at Home and Abroad: Afro-Americans and the Christian Mission from the Revolution to Reconstruction*, 203–10.

57. Coker to Right Rev. Bishop Kemp, Hastings, [Sierra Leone], [1823?], Maryland Episcopal Church Diocesan Archives, Baltimore.

58. Winch, *A Gentleman of Color*, 191–204. Allen would lay claim to the work "of Coker in Africa, this gathering 'of the little sons of Africa' into Sabbath School around him" as evidence that God had "'spread the work through our instrumentality, upon the barren shores of Africa'" (James A. Handy, *Scraps of African Methodist Episcopal History*, 39).

59. *Poulson's American Daily Advertiser*, Dec. 30, 1816 (quote); for further early coverage, see Jan. 2, 1816; Jan. 3, 1816; and Jan. 8, 1816. Forten to Cuffe, Philadelphia, Jan. 25, 1817, in *Cuffe's Logs and Letters*, 501–3. For Forten's response to the emigration/colonization controversies, see Winch, *A Gentleman of Color*, chap. 8 (176–87 for the period before the ACS was founded). Winch points to the anomaly of Forten using the third person to discuss black people's future in the United States ("until *they* come out") on 193.

CHAPTER 7

1. Sara Fanning, "The Roots of Early Black Nationalism: Northern African Americans' Invocations of Haiti in the Early Nineteenth Century," *Slavery and Abolition* (forthcoming); and Fanning, "'The Land of Promise': African America and Haiti from Revolutionary Solidarity to Emigration," (PhD dissertation, University of Texas, in progress).

2. P. J. Staudenraus, *The African Colonization Movement, 1816–1865*, chap. 6; Charles Henry Huberich, *The Political and Legislative History of Liberia*, chaps. 3, 4, 6–9; Archibald Alexander, *A History of Colonization on the Western Coast of Africa*, chaps. 8–16; Ralph Randolph Gurley, *Life of Jehudi Ashmun*, chaps. 5–12, 16, appendix.

3. John Saillant's introduction to Lott Cary, "Circular Addressed to the Colored Brethren and Friends in America: An Unpublished Essay by Lott Cary, Sent from Liberia to Virginia, 1827," 481–504; and Marie Tyler McGraw, "Richmond Free Blacks and African Colonization, 1816–1832," 207–24 (esp. 212–15); Miles Mark Fisher, "Lott Cary," 380–418; William A. Poe, "Lott Cary," 49–61. For the founding of Richmond's Baptist African Society see *The Third Annual Report of the Baptist Board of Foreign Missions*, 180; and Poe, "Lott Cary," 50–51.

4. *The Latter Day Luminary*, vol. 1, no. 8 (May 1819), 401.

5. Samuel Wilson to the Brethren Generally, Sierra Leone, May 18, 1818, in *The Latter Day Luminary*, vol. 1, no. 6 (Feb. 1819), 297. The other two letters, one written by Perry Locke and the other seemingly from the Friendly Society and signed first by John Kizell, were similar (298–300). Wilson had come with Cuffe (*Captain Paul Cuffe's Logs and Letters, 1808–1817*, ed. Rosaline Cobb Wiggins, [hereafter, *Logs and Letters of Cuffe*], 409). For discussions of dispensationalist interpretations of slavery, see John Saillant, *Black Puritan, Black Republican*; Joanna Brooks, *American Lazarus*; and chaps. 3 and 4 above.

6. John Kizell, William Martin, Geo. Pavis, Geo. Lewis, Robt. Robertson, Samuel Wilson, Peter Mitchell, Perry Locke, Thomas Williams, John Kizell Jr., Pompey Rutledge to Dear Friends and Brethren, Sierra Leone, May 21, 1818, in *The Latter Day Luminary*, vol. 1, no. 6 (Feb. 1819), 299–300.

7. Christian Wiltberger Diary, Mar. 30, 1821 (frames 25, 44), Christian Wiltberger Papers, 1820–21, Library of Congress microfilm (authority); Lott Carey to William Stoughton, Corresponding Secretary for the Baptist Board of Foreign Missions, Free Town, Mar. 13, 1821, in *Latter Day Missionary*, vol. 2, no. 18 (May 1821), 398–99 (missionary grounds).

8. Huberich, *Liberia*, 184–96; Claude A. Clegg III, *The Price of Liberty*, 36–38.

9. Clegg III, ibid., 77–81.

10. Huberich, *Liberia*, 1275 (sedition law); Christian Wiltberger Diary 1820–21, entries for Mar. 30, 1821; Dec, 19, 1821; Dec, 22, 1821 (American African Union Society).

11. Eli Ayres to E. B. Caldwell, Washington, Aug. 23, 1822, in Huberich, ibid., 199–213 (quote at 212).

12. Huberich, ibid., 214.

13. Ayres to the board of the American Colonization Society, Baltimore, Feb. 18, 1824, in Huberich, *Liberia*, 221.

14. E. B. Caldwell, by Order of the Board of the American Colonization Society, "Answer to the Petitioners," in Huberich, *Liberia*, 300–311 (quote at 310).

15. McGraw, "Richmond Free Blacks," 215–16.

16. Huberich, *Liberia*, 317–19 (Gurley and Ashmun), 1264–67 (plan of government); Ralph Randolph Gurley, *Life of Jehudi Ashmun, Late Colonial Agent in Liberia*, 211–16.

17. Quoted in Huberich, *Liberia*, 320. Huberich notes that the racism of the board of the American Colonization Society almost led them to overturn this success (329).

18. Lott Cary to William Crane, Monrovia, Apr. 23, 1826, in *Genius of Universal Emancipation and Baltimore Courier* 1 (June 10, 1826), 325.

19. For a remarkable analysis of this in the realm of material culture, see Max Belcher, Svend Holsoe, and Bernard Powers, *A Life and Land Remembered: Americo-Liberian Folk Architecture*.

20. Floyd J. Miller, *The Search for a Black Nationality*, chap. 3; and James Oliver Horton and Lois E. Horton, *In Hope of Liberty*, chap. 8 provide excellent accounts of this process throughout the North. For more detailed accounts of Philadelphia, see Gary B. Nash, *Forging Freedom*, chaps. 6, 7; Julie Winch, *A Gentleman of Color*, chaps.

8–10; Julie Winch, *Philadelphia's Black Elite*, chaps. 2–5. William Lloyd Garrison himself was the first to synthesize this narrative in *Thoughts on African Colonization* (1832; reprint, New York: Arno, 1969). Marie Tyler McGraw critiques this narrative in "Richmond Free Blacks" and shows that it does not hold in the South.

21. "Resolutions of the People of Color at a Meeting held on the 25th of January, 1831," in *Early Negro Writing, 1760–1837*, ed. Dorothy Porter, 282.

22. *Genius of Universal Emancipation*, vol. 2, no. 12 (1822), 155 ("After a religious service of praise, prayer and exhortation by the Rev. Mr. Allen, a colored preacher from Philadelphia"); "Letter from Bishop Allen," *Freedom's Journal*, Nov. 2, 1827.

23. William B. Davidson to R. R. Gurley, Philadelphia, Feb. 6, 1827, Letters Received, American Colonization Society Papers [hereafter ACSP], ser. 1, vol. 3, reel 1 (destruction); Man of Colour, "Communication," *Union United States Gazette and True American*, Dec. 11, 1819 (inhabited). I am indebted to Julie Winch for the "Man of Colour" letter and for its attribution to Forten.

24. [Charles C. Harper?] to R. R. Gurley, Baltimore, Dec. 13, 1826 (churches); Harper to Gurley, Baltimore, Dec. 28, 1826 (committee), ACSP, ser. 1, vol. 2, reel 1; Harper to Gurley, Baltimore, Sept. 23, 1828, ACSP, ser. 1, vol. 11, reel 4 (company); Harper to Gurley, Baltimore, Apr. 9, 1829, ACSP, ser. 1, vol. 14, reel 5 (intercourse). Grice eventually immigrated to Haiti. For a biographical sketch, see "The First Colored Convention," *The Anglo-African Magazine* 1 (Oct. 1859), 305–10. I am grateful to Randall Burkett for this reference.

25. John H. B. Latrobe to Gurley, Baltimore, July 13, 1829, ACSP, ser. 1, vol. 16, reel 6.

26. Clegg III, *Price of Liberty*, esp. chaps. 1–3 for North Carolina; Fanning, "The Land of Promise."

27. William Blackford to Gurley, Fredericksburg, June 2, 1828, ser. 1, vol. 10, reel 4; Jno. Kennedy to Gurley, Petersburg, Mar. 17, 1830; Jno. Kennedy to [Gurley, Petersburg, Mar. 1830], ACSP ser. 1, vol. 21, reel 7.

28. John C. Ehringhaus to Gurley, Elizabeth City, N.C., Jan. 16, 1827, ACSP, ser. 1, vol. 2, reel 1; John Ehringhaus to Gurley, Elizabeth City, N.C., June 23, 1827, ACSP, ser. 1, vol. 4, reel 2. Clegg III, *Price of Liberty*, chaps. 1–3; "A Coloured Baltimorean," probably William Watkins, underscored the sense among many blacks that the ACS ignored blacks' opinions and hopes—"have the members of that society ever come among us for the purpose of eliciting our true sentiments relative to colonization in Africa?"—in a letter published in the *Genius of Universal Emancipation* and republished in *Freedom's Journal*, July 11, 1828. Bettye J. Gardner, "Opposition to Emigration, a Selected Letter of William Watkins (the Colored Baltimorean)," 155–58 attributes the letter to Watkins.

29. John B. Hepburn to Gurley, Alexandria, Sept. 3, 1828; [L. P. Brewster?] to Gurley, Mt. Pleasant [Tennessee], Aug. 4, 1828 (Nashville); William Chamberlin to Gurley, Willstown, Cherokee Nation [Georgia], Sept. 27, 1828 (emphasis in original), ACSP, ser. 1, vol. 13, reel 4. Chamberlin was a white missionary in Willstown.

30. Antonio McDaniel, *Swing Low, Sweet Chariot*, 60–63.

31. The ACSP, ser. 1, Letters Received collection was filed by the date on each document. Thus the sheet on which these toasts were recorded (dated July 5, 1829) is at the beginning of vol. 16, reel 6. The sheet was sent with two letters from D. J. Burr, one of which is much later in vol. 16, and the other of which is at the beginning of vol. 17, reel 6: D. J. Burr to Gurley, Richmond, July 18, 1829; D. J. Burr to Gurley, Richmond, July 15, 1829. Inexplicably, the earlier letter is the one filed in vol. 17. Black Richmonders' interest in emigration is suggested by advertisements by Joseph Shippard, a free black teacher, for a school to prepare "for Liberia, callow chiefs and embryo statesmen" (*Freedom's Journal*, May 16, 1828 and other issues).

32. Similar celebrations occurred elsewhere. In 1827 the "Coloured Inhabitants of Fredercksburgh," Virginia, celebrated emancipation in New York and called for "Virginia and her sister slave states" to follow suit, and the "Friendship Society" of Baltimore—perhaps a descendant of the African Society that Cuffe and Coker had organized in 1813—cited the Declaration of Independence in calling on "every state in the Union" to follow New York's example (*Freedom's Journal*, July 13, 1827; and July 20, 1827). Neither set of toasts used the diasporic language used in Richmond.

33. *News from Africa. A Collection of Facts, Relating to the Colony in Liberia, for the Information of the Free People of Colour in Maryland.*

34. Thomas. C. Brown, *Examination of Mr. Thomas C. Brown, a Free Colored Citizen of S. Carolina, as to the Actual State of Things in Liberia in the Years 1833 and 1834*, 5, 14, 29–30.

35. "Memorial of the Free People of Colour," *Genius of Universal Emancipation and Baltimore Courier*, vol. 2, no. 12 (1826), 94–95.

36. Africanus essay, *Genius of Universal Emancipation and Baltimore Courier*, vol. 2, no. 18 (1827), 149; "A Colored Baltimorean" essay, ibid., 149–52.

37. Lott Cary, "Circular Addressed." Quotes at 500, 495, 502. In his insightful introductory essay, Saillant is more cynical about Cary's commitment to antislavery than I am, though given the subsequent history of relations between Americo-Liberians and the indigenous peoples of the region, the aspects of Cary's thought on which Saillant focuses sadly came to dominate life there. Cary sent the pamphlet to a white friend and commercial partner in Richmond.

38. Ibid., 496–97, 501, 499.

39. Amos J. Beyan, *African American Settlements in West Africa*, chap. 1; William M. Brewer, "John B. Russwurm," 413–22; Huberich, *Liberia*, 437–39.

40. John B. Russwurm, "The Condition and Prospects of Hayti," ed. Philip S. Foner, 393–97.

41. *Freedom's Journal*, Mar. 16, 1827.

42. Bella Gross, "Freedom's Journal and the Rights of All," 241–86 is the fullest treatment of the newspaper. Gross is harsh toward Russwurm. For recent discussions of *Freedom's Journal*, see Elizabeth McHenry, *Forgotten Readers*, chap. 2 (esp. 88–102); Horton and Horton, *In Hope of Liberty*, chaps. 7–8; Frederick Cooper, "Elevating the Race," 604–25 (esp. 605–9).

43. Listed agents changed from issue to issue. For this list see *Freedom's Journal*, Apr. 4, 1828.

44. Ibid., Feb. 14, 1829 (quote); Feb. 21, 1829; Feb. 28, 1829. Russwurm told the Colonization Society of his new opinion and began seeking a position in Liberia (Russwurm to Gurley, New York, Jan. 26, 1829, ACSP, ser. 1, vol. 13, reel 5).

45. *The Mind of the Negro as Reflected in Letters Written during the Crisis, 1800–1860*, ed. Carter G. Woodson, 160–63.

46. Russwurm, "The Condition and Prospects of Hayti," 397 (foundation), 395 (settle). Foner's introduction to the speech quotes his plan to emigrate from the *Eastern Argus*. When announcing his support for the ACS, Russwurm specified that he was not rejecting "Hayti or the able ruler at its head," but said that the negative reports of those who had returned from the island had created an "unwillingness of our people to emigrate" there (*Freedom's Journal*, Feb. 14, 1829).

47. *Freedom's Journal*, Feb. 14, 1829; Feb. 21, 1829.

48. C. C. Andrews to Gurley, June 25, [1829], ACSP, ser. 1, vol. 15, reel 5 (Williams); C. C. Andrews to Gurley, New York, July 1, 1829, ACSP, ser. 1, vol. 16, reel 6 (Cornish).

49. Peter Williams Jr. "To the Citizens of New York" (July 14, 1834; typescript). I am indebted to Randall Burkett for loaning me a copy of this typescript.

50. Russwurm to Gurley, New York, June 16, 1829, ACSP, ser. 1, vol. 15, reel 5.

51. Huberich, *Liberia*, 437–39; Penelope Campbell, *Maryland in Africa*, chaps. 3, 5–7; Beyan, *African American Settlements in West Africa*, chaps. 3–5.

52. The settlers' sense of their autonomy from Africa comes through in a memorial back to Maryland in which they praised the governor who preceded Russwurm for his success in making the "aberigences [*sic*] by which we are thickly surrounded and in many respects unavoidably associated, feel our superiority." Quoted in Samuel W. Laughon, "Administrative Problems in Maryland in Liberia, 1836–1851," 343. For settler-native relations reminiscent of early relations between English colonists and Indians, see Penelope Campbell, ibid., 127–29.

53. Laughon, ibid., 348–64; Penelope Campbell, ibid., esp. chap. 5.

54. W. Paul Quinn, "The Origin, Horrors, and Results of Slavery, Faithfully and Minutely Described," *Early Negro Writing, 1760–1837*, ed. Dorothy Porter, 614–36; Nathaniel Paul, "An Address, Delivered on the Celebration of the Abolition of Slavery, in the State of New-York, July 5, 1827," *Negro Protest Pamphlets: A Compendium*, ed. Dorothy Porter, 6–25.

55. Robert Alexander Young, "Ethiopian Manifesto," *Pamphlets of Protest*, 85–89; Robert Benjamin Lewis, *Light and Truth, from Ancient and Sacred History*. I am indebted to Randall Burkett for telling me of this title.

56. Joseph M. Corr, "Address Delivered Before the Humane Mechanics' Society on the 4th of July, 1834," *Early Negro Writing, 1760–1837*, 145–54; "Resolutions of the People of Color, at a Meeting held on the 25th of January, 1831. With an Address to the Citizens of New York, in Answer to Those of the New York Colonization Society," *Early Negro Writing, 1760–1837*, 281–85.

57. *The Colored American*, Mar. 4, 1837 (reproach); May 13, 1837 (brethren), box 3, Miscellaneous American Letters and Papers, Schomburg Center, New York Public Library.

58. David R. Roediger, *The Wages of Whiteness*, 13–14 and throughout. Alexander Saxton, *The Rise and Fall of the White Republic* incorporates American Indians and, to a lesser extent, Asian Americans.

EPILOGUE

1. Peter P. Hinks, ed., *David Walker's Appeal to the Coloured Citizens of the World*, 74–75 (sons), 22 (Hannibal), 44 (throat-cutting), 20 (Ham); Hinks, *"To Awaken My Afflicted Brethren."*

2. Leon Litwack, *North of Slavery*; James Oliver Horton and Lois E. Horton, *In Hope of Liberty*; C. Peter Ripley, ed., *Witness for Freedom*; Patrick J. Rael, *Black Identity and Black Protest in the Antebellum North*.

3. Leonard Richards, *"Gentlemen of Property and Standing"*; Paul Gilje, *Rioting in America*, chap. 4; David Grimsted, *American Mobbing, 1828–1861*, chap. 2 and throughout; Leon Litwack, *North of Slavery*; Donald Fehrenbacher, *The Slaveholding Republic*, compiled and edited by Ward M. McAfee; William W. Freehling, *The Road to Disunion: Secessionists at Bay: 1776–1854*.

4. Robert S. Levine, ed., *Martin Delany*, 200, 201.

5. The biographical information is drawn from Robert S. Levine, *Martin Delany, Frederick Douglass and the Politics of Representative Identity*; Toyin Falola, "Introduction" to *Martin Delany, the Condition, Elevation, Emigration, and Destiny of the Colored People of the United States and Official Report of the Niger Valley Exploring Party*; Tunde Adeleke, *Without Regard to Race*; Dorothy Sterling, *The Making of an Afro-American*. During the 1850s Delany won admission to Harvard Medical School and matriculated for a semester before being expelled because white students refused to attend classes with a black man (Levine, *Martin Delany, Frederick Douglass*, 61–62).

6. Levine, ed., *Martin R. Delany*, 144–48.

7. Ibid., 245–79. See Levine's insightful reading of the speech in his *Martin Delany, Frederick Douglass*, 194–97.

8. Levine, ed., *Martin R. Delany*, 246 (false impression), 247 (political economy), 248 (remedy). There is a perhaps-ironic resonance between his analysis of the problems of a permanent minority in a democracy and that which John Calhoun formulated at about the same time from a position of racial and economic privilege.

9. Levine, ed., ibid., 251 (Anglo-Saxon), 252 (colored races), 254 (countries), 315–76 (Africa).

10. Ibid., 251 (not identical), 252 (colored races).

11. See Levine, *Martin Delany, Frederick Douglass* for this split and its importance. Levine traces the efforts of each man to establish himself as the race's "representative figure."

Bibliography

MANUSCRIPT COLLECTIONS

Annapolis, Maryland
Maryland Hall of Records
    Records of the AME Bethel Church, Baltimore
Baltimore, Maryland
Lovely Lane United Methodist Church Museum
    Class Records, 1799–1838
    Plan of Appointments for Baltimore City Station
    City Station, Colored Classes, 1809–1822
    City Station 2, White and Colored Classes, 1804–1812
Maryland Historical Society
    African Masonic Friendship Lodge of Baltimore, Constitution and By–Laws
Diocesan Archives, Episcopal Church
    Daniel Coker Letters
Boston, Massachusetts
Boston Grand Masonic Lodge Library
    John Marrant Vertical File
    Primus Hall, 1758–1831, Military Service Record and Pension File (microfilm)
    Prince Hall Letterbooks (microfilm)
    Prince Hall Military Service Record and Pension File, microfilm
    Prince Hall Vertical File
Boston Public Library
    American Colonization Society, Records (microfilm); Series 1, Incoming Correspondence, Volumes 1–26

George W. Forbes Typescripts, Biographical Sketches and
Correspondence

Harvard University Libraries, Theatre Collection

Memoir and Theatrical Career of Ira Aldridge, The African Roscius

Ira Aldridge Clippings File

Massachusetts Historical Society

Ebenezer Burgess Papers

London, United Kingdom

British Library

Clarkson Papers, volumes 1–5

Papers Relating to Sierra Leone

Proceedings of the Committee for Abolition of the Slave Trade,
1787–1819

National Archives (Formerly the Public Record Office)

Colonial Office Records

Record group 217, volumes 58, 62, 70

Record group 218, volume 27

Record group 267, volumes 14, 35, 41, 91, 92

Record group 268, volume 5

Record group 270, volumes 2–7, 11, 14, 92

Record group 272, volume 72

Public Records Office Papers (Chatham Papers); 30/8/363

War Office Records; 1/352

New York City

Schomburg Center, New York Public Library

Mother Bethel AME Church Records, Philadelphia (microfilm)

The History of the New-York African Free Schools (microfilm)

Miscellaneous American Letters and Papers

African Free School Folder

African Colonization Folder

Aldridge, Ira Folder

Dann, Marty Folder

Washington, D.C.

Library of Congress

Houston H. Holloway Diary

Peter Force Collection; Diary of Daniel Coker
(microfilm)

Christian Wiltberger Papers, 1820–21
(microfilm)

Worcester, Massachusetts

American Antiquarian Society

Samuel Hodges Jr. Papers

NEWSPAPERS AND MAGAZINES

The Anglo-African Magazine
Evangelical Magazine
Freedom's Journal
Genius of Universal Emancipation (and Baltimore Courier)
The Latter Day Missionary
Poulson's American Daily Advertiser
The Royal Gazette and Sierra Leone Advertiser

PUBLISHED WORKS

Abzug, Robert H. *Cosmos Crumbling: American Reform and the Religious Imagination.* New York: Oxford University Press, 1994.

Achtemeier, Paul J. "I Peter." In *The Harpercollins Bible Commentary*, edited by James L. Mays et. al., 1168–77. San Francisco: HarperSanFrancisco, 2000.

Adeleke, Tunde. *Unafrican Americans: Nineteenth-Century Black Nationalists and the Civilizing Mission.* Lexington: University Press of Kentucky, 1998.

——. *Without Regard to Race: The Other Martin Delany.* Jackson: University Press of Mississippi, 2003.

Alexander, Archibald. *A History of Colonization on the Western Coast of Africa.* Reprint. Freeport, N.Y.: Books for Libraries Press, 1971.

Allen, Richard. *The Life Experience and Gospel Labors of the Rt. Rev. Richard Allen.* New York: Abindgon, 1960.

Allgor, Catherine. *Parlor Politics: In Which the Ladies of Washington Help Build a City and a Government.* Charlottesville: University Press of Virginia, 2000.

American Colonization Society. "The Fourth Annual Report of the American Society for Colonizing the Free People of Colour of the United States." In *The Annual Reports of the American Society for Colonizing the Free People of Colour of the United States, Volumes 1–10, 1818–27.* New York: Negro Universities Press, 1969.

Andrews, William L. *To Tell a Free Story: The First Century of Afro-American Autobiography.* Urbana: University of Illinois Press, 1986.

Anonymous. *News from Africa. A Collection of Facts, Relating to the Colony in Liberia, for the Information of the Free People of Colour in Maryland.* Baltimore: J. D. Toy, 1832.

——. "Resolutions of the People of Color at a Meetings Held on the 25th of January, 1831." In *Early Negro Writing, 1760–1837*, edited by Dorothy Porter, 282. Boston: Beacon, 1971.

Appiah, Kwame Anthony. *In My Father's House: Africa and the Philosophy of Culture.* New York: Oxford University Press, 1992.

Aptheker, Herbert, ed. *A Documentary History of the Negro People in the United States.* New York: Citadel, 1951.

Aravamudan, Srinivas. *Tropicopolitans: Colonialism and Agency.* Durham, N.C.: Duke University Press, 1999.

Armitage, David. *The Ideological Origins of the British Empire.* Cambridge: Cambridge University Press, 2000.

Aslakson, Kenneth. "Making Race: The Role of Free Blacks in the Development of New Orleans's Three Caste Society." Ph.D. diss, The University of Texas at Austin, 2007.

Axtell, James. *The Invasion Within: The Contest of Cultures in Colonial North America.* New York: Oxford University Press, 1985.

Baldwin, Lewis V. *"Invisible" Strands in African Methodism: A History of the African Union Methodist Protestant and Union American Methodist Episcopal Churches, 1805–1890.* Metuchen, N.J.: Scarecrow, 1983.

Bangs, Nathan. *The Life of the Rev. Freeborn Garrettson: Compiled from His Printed and Manuscript Journals, and Other Authentic Documents.* New York: G. Lane and C. B. Tippett, 1845.

Baptist Board of Foreign Missions. *Third Annual Report of the Baptist Board of Foreign Missions.* Philadelphia, 1817.

Barker, Anthony J. *The African Link: British Attitudes to the Negro in the Era of the Atlantic Slave Trade, 1550–1807.* London: Frank Cass, 1978.

Bartels, Emily C. "Othello and Africa: Postcolonialism Reconsidered." *William and Mary Quarterly*, 3rd ser., 54 (1997): 45–64.

Bassard, Katherine Clay. *Spiritual Interrogations: Culture, Gender, and Community in Early African American Women's Writing.* Princeton, N.J.: Princeton University Press, 1999.

Belcher, Max, Svend Holsoe, and Bernard Powers. *A Life and Land Remembered: Americo-Liberian Folk Architecture.* Athens: University of Georgia Press, 1988.

Bender, Thomas, ed. *The Antislavery Debate: Capitalism and Abolitionism as a Problem in Historical Interpretation.* Berkeley and Los Angeles: University of California Press, 1992.

Bercovitch, Sacvan. "The Typology of America's Mission." *American Quarterly* 30 (1978): 135–55.

Berkeley, Edmund Jr. "Prophet without Honor: Christopher McPherson, Free Person of Color." *The Virginia Magazine of History and Biography* 77, no. 1969 (1969): 180–90.

Berlin, Ira. *Generations of Captivity: A History of African-American Slaves.* Cambridge, Mass.: Harvard University Press, 2003.

——. *Many Thousands Gone: The First Two Centuries of Slavery in North America.* Cambridge, Mass.: Harvard University Press, 1998.

Bernal, Martin. *Black Athena: The Afroasiatic Roots of Classical Civilization.* New Brunswick, N.J.: Rutgers University Press, 1987.

Best, Ernest, ed. *New Century Bible: I Peter.* London: Oliphants, 1971.

Bethel, Elizabeth Rauh. *The Roots of African-American Identity: Memory and History in Antebellum Free Communities.* New York: St. Martin's, 1997.

Beyan, Amos J. *African American Settlements in West Africa: John Brown Russwurm and the American Civilizing Efforts*. New York: Palgrave Macmillan, 2005.

Blackburn, Robin. *The Overthrow of Colonial Slavery, 1776–1848*. London: Verso, 1988.

Bloch, Marc. *The Historian's Craft*. Translated by Joseph A. Strayer. New York: Vintage, 1953.

Bolster, Jeffrey W. *Black Jacks: African American Seamen in the Age of Sail*. Cambridge, Mass.: Harvard University Press, 1997.

Boulukos, George Eleftherios. "The Grateful Slave: Representations of Slave Plantation Reform in the British Novel, 1720–1805." Ph.D. diss., University of Texas, Austin, 1998.

Bragg, George F. *Heroes of the Eastern Shore*. Baltimore, 1939.

——. *Men of Maryland*. Baltimore: Church Advocate, 1914.

Braidwood, Stephen J. *Black Poor and White Philanthropists: London's Blacks and the Foundation of the Sierra Leone Settlement, 1786–1791*. Liverpool: Liverpool University Press, 1994.

Braude, Benjamin. "The Sons of Noah and the Construction of Ethnic and Geographical Identities in the Medieval and Early Modern Periods." *William and Mary Quarterly*, 3rd ser., 54 (1997): 103–42.

Breen, T. H. "Creative Adaptations: Peoples and Cultures." In *Colonial British America: Essays in the New History of the Early Modern Era*, edited by Jack P. Greene and J. R. Pole, 195–232. Baltimore: Johns Hopkins University Press, 1984.

Brekus, Catherine A. *Strangers and Pilgrims: Female Preaching in America*. Chapel Hill: University of North Carolina Press, 1998.

Brewer, William M. "John B. Russwurm." *Journal of Negro History* 13 (1928): 413–22.

Brooke, John L. *The Refiner's Fire: The Making of Mormon Cosmology, 1644–1844*. Cambridge: Cambridge University Press, 1996.

Brooks, Amanda Lee. "Captain Paul Cuffe (1759–1817) and the Crown Colony of Sierra Leone: The Liminality of the Free Black." Ph.D. diss., University of Chicago, 1988.

Brooks, Joanna. *American Lazarus: Religion and the Rise of African-American and Native American Literatures*. New York: Oxford University Press, 2003.

Brooks, Joanna, and John Saillant, ed. *"Face Zion Forward": First Writers of the Black Atlantic, 1785–1798*. Boston: Northeastern University Press, 2002.

Brown, Christopher Leslie. "The Empire without Slaves: British Concepts of Emancipation in the Age of the American Revolution." *William and Mary Quarterly*, 3rd ser., 55 (1999): 273–306.

——. *Moral Capital: Foundations of British Abolitionism*. Chapel Hill: University of North Carolina Press for the Omohundru Institute of Early American History and Culture, 2006.

Brown, Kathleen M. *Good Wives, Nasty Wenches and Anxious Patriarchs: Gender, Race, and Power in Colonial Virginia*. Chapel Hill: University of North Carolina Press for the Institute of Early American History and Culture, 1996.

Brown, Thomas C. *Examination of Mr. Thomas C. Brown, a Free Colored Citizen of S. Carolina, as to the Actual State of Things in Liberia in the Years 1833 and 1834*. New York: S. W. Benedict and Co., 1834.

Bruce, Dickson D. Jr. *The Origins of African American Literature, 1680–1865*. Charlottesville: University Press of Virginia, 2001.

Bullock, Stephen C. *Revolutionary Brotherhood: Freemasonry and the Transformation of the American Social Order, 1730–1840*. Chapel Hill: University of North Carolina Press for the Institute of Early American History and Culture, 1996.

Burin, Eric. *Slavery and the Peculiar Solution: A History of the American Colonization Society*. Gainesville: University Press of Florida, 2005.

Bushman, Richard. *From Puritan to Yankee: Character and the Social Order in Connecticut, 1690–1765*. Cambridge, Mass.: Harvard University Press, 1967.

Byrd, Alexander X. "Eboe, Country, Nation and Gustavus Vassa's *Interesting Narrative*." *William and Mary Quarterly*, 3rd ser., 63 (2006): 123–49.

Campbell, James T. *Middle Passage: African American Journeys to Africa, 1787–2005*. New York: Penguin, 2006.

——. *Songs of Zion: The African Methodist Episcopal Church in the United States and South Africa*. New York: Oxford University Press, 1995.

Campbell, Mavis Christine, ed. *Back to Africa: George Ross and the Maroons: From Nova Scotia to Sierra Leone*. Trenton, N.J.: Africa World Press, 1993.

——. *The Maroons of Jamaica, 1655–1796: A History of Resistance, Collaboration and Betrayal*. Granby, Mass.: Bergin & Garvey, 1988.

Campbell, Penelope. *Maryland in Africa: The Maryland Colonization Society, 1831–1857*. Urbana: University of Illinois Press, 1971.

Carey, Brycchan. "The Extraordinary Negro': Ignatius Sancho, Joseph Jekyll, and the Problem of Biography." *British Journal for Eighteenth-Century Studies* 26 (2003): 1–14.

Carretta, Vincent. *Equiano, the African: Biography of a Self-Made Man*. Athens: University of Georgia Press, 2005.

——. "Introduction." In *Letters of the Late Ignatius Sancho, an African*. Edited with an introduction and notes by Vincent Carretta, ix–xxxii. New York: Penguin, 1998.

——. "Introduction." In *Quobna Ottobah Cugoano, Thoughts and Sentiments on the Evil of Slavery*. Edited with an introduction and notes by Vincent Carretta, ix–xxviii. New York: Penguin, 1999.

——. "Introduction." In *Phillis Wheatley, Complete Writings*. Edited with an introduction and notes by Vincent Carretta, xiii–xxxviii. New York: Penguin, 2001.

——. "Olaudah Equiano or Gustavus Vassa? New Light on an Eighteenth-Century Question of Identity." *Slavery and Abolition* 20 (1999): 96–105.

——. "'Property of the Author': Olaudah Equiano's Place in the History of the Book." In *Genius in Bondage: Literature of the Early Black Atlantic*, 130–50. Lexington: University Press of Kentucky, 2001.

——. "Review of 'Face Zion Forward': First Writers of the Black Atlantic." *Early American Literature* 39 (2004): 175–77.

——. "Soubise, Julius (C. 1754–1798)." New York: Oxford University Press, http://www.oxforddnb.com.content.lib.utexas.edu:2048/view/article/6084.

——. "Three West Indian Writers of the 1780s Revisited and Revised." *Research in African Literatures* 18 (Winter 1998): 73–87.

——. ed. *Unchained Voices: An Anthology of Black Authors in the English-Speaking World of the 18th Century*. Lexington: University Press of Kentucky, 1996.

——. "Who Was Francis Williams?" *Early American Literature* 38 (2003): 213–37.

Carretta, Vincent, and Philip Gould. "Introduction." In *Genius in Bondage: Literature of the Early Black Atlantic*, edited by Vincent Carretta and Philip Gould. Lexington: University Press of Kentucky, 2001.

Cary, Lott. "Circular Addressed to the Colored Brethren and Friends in America: An Unpublished Essay by Lott Cary, Sent from Liberia to Virginia, 1827." Edited with an introduction and notes by John Saillant. *Virginia Magazine of History and Biography* 104 (1996): 481–504.

Chambers, Douglas B. *Murder at Montpelier: Igbo Africans in Virginia*. Jackson: University Press of Mississippi, 2005.

Chaplin, Joyce E. "Race." In *The British Atlantic World, 1500–1800*, edited by David Armitage and Michael J. Braddick. New York: Palgrave Macmillan, 2002.

Clarkson, John. "Diary of Lieutenant Clarkson, R.N." *Sierra Leone Studies* 8 (1927): 1–114.

——. "Governor Clarkson's Diary." In *Sierra Leone after a Hundred Years*, edited by E. G. Ingham. London: Frank Cass, 1968.

Clarkson, Thomas. *The History of the Rise, Progress, and Accomplishment of the Abolition of the African Slave-Trade by the British Parliament*. 2 vols. London: Longman, Hurst, Rees, and Orme, 1808.

Clegg, Claude A. III. *The Price of Liberty: African Americans and the Making of Liberia*. Chapel Hill: University of North Carolina Press, 2004.

Coker, Daniel. "A Dialogue between a Virginian and an African Minister, Written by the Rev. Daniel Coker, a Descendant of Africa . . . Minister of the African Methodist Episcopal Church in Baltimore." In *Negro Protest Pamphlets: A Compendium*, edited by Dorothy Porter. New York: Arno, 1969.

——. *Journal of Daniel Coker, a Descendant of Africa*. Baltimore: Edward J. Coale, 1820.

Coleman, Deirdre. *Romantic Colonization and British Anti-Slavery*. Cambridge: Cambridge University Press, 2005.

Colley, Linda. *Britons: Forging the Nation, 1707–1837*. New Haven, Conn.: Yale University Press, 1992.

Constanzo, Angelo. *Surprising Narrative: Olaudah Equiano and the Beginning of Black Autobiography*. Westport, Conn.: Greenwood, 1987.

Cooper, Frederick. "Elevating the Race: The Social Thought of Black Leaders, 1827–1850." *American Quarterly* 24 (1972): 604–25.

Corey, Mary. "Daniel Coker: Between an Oppressive Culture and a Liberating God," 20–25. Baltimore: Maryland Episcopal Church Diocesan Archives.

Corr, Joseph M. "Address Delivered before the Human Mechanics' Society on the 4th of July, 1834." In *Early Negro Writing, 1760–1837*, edited by Dorothy Porter, 145–54. Boston: Beacon, 1971.

——. "Resolutions of the People of Color, at a Meeting Held on the 25th of January, 1831. With an Address to the Citizens of New York, in Answer to Those of the New

York Colonization Society." In *Early Negro Writing, 1760–1837*, edited by Dorothy Porter, 281–85. Boston: Beacon, 1971.

Crane, Elaine Forman. *A Dependent People: Newport Rhode Island in the Revolutionary Era*. New York: Fordham University Press, 1992.

Craton, Michael. *Testing the Chains: Resistance to Slavery in the British West Indies*. Ithaca, N.Y.: Cornell University Press, 1982.

Crisp, Stephen. *A Short History of a Long Travel from Babylon to Bethel*. New Haven, Conn., 1797.

Cuffe, Paul. *A Brief Account of the Settlement and Present Situation of the Colony of Sierra Leone in Africa; as Communicated by Paul Cuffe (a Man of Colour) to His Friend in New York: Also an Explanation of the Object of His Visit, and Some Advice to the People of Colour in the United States*. New York: Samuel Wood, 1812.

Cugoano, Quobna Ottobah. *Thoughts and Sentiments on the Evil of Slavery*. Edited with an introduction and notes by Vincent Carretta. New York: Penguin, 1999.

Curtin, Philip D. *The Image of Africa: British Ideas and Actions, 1780–1850*. Madison: University of Wisconsin Press, 1964.

Dain, Bruce. *A Hideous Monster of the Mind: American Race Theory in the Early Republic*. Cambridge, Mass.: Harvard University Press, 2002.

Davis, Charles T., and Henry Louis Gates Jr., ed. *The Slave's Narrative*. New York: Oxford University Press, 1985.

Davis, David Brion. "Constructing Race: A Reflection." *William and Mary Quarterly*, 3rd ser., 54, no. 1 (1997): 7–18.

——. *Inhuman Bondage: The Rise and Fall of Slavery in the New World*. New York: Oxford University Press, 2006.

——. *The Problem of Slavery in the Age of Revolution, 1770–1823*. Ithaca, N.Y.: Cornell University Press, 1975.

——. *Slavery and Human Progress*. New York: Oxford University Press, 1984.

Davis, Harry E. "Documents Relating to Negro Masonry in America." *Journal of Negro History* 21 (1936): 411–32.

Desrochers, Robert Jr. "'Surprizing Deliverance'?: Slavery and Freedom, Language and Identity in the *Narrative* of Briton Hammon." In *Genius in Bondage: Literature of the Early Black Atlantic*, edited by Vincent Carretta and Philip Gould, 153–74. Lexington: University Press of Kentucky, 2001.

Dillwyn, William. *Life of William Allen, with Selections from His Correspondence*. 2 vols. Philadelphia: Henry Lonstreth, 1847.

Diouf, Sylviane A. *Servants of Allah: African Muslims Enslaved in the Americas*. New York: New York University Press, 1998.

Douglass, William. *Annals of the First African Church, in the United States of America, Now Styled the African Episcopal Church of St. Thomas, Philadelphia: On Account of the Abolition of the African Slave Trade*. Philadelphia: King & Baird, 1862.

Dow, Lorenzo. *Quintessence of Lorenzo's Works*. Philadelphia: Joseph Rakestraw, 1816.

Drescher, Seymour. *Capitalism and Antislavery: British Mobilization in Comparative Perspective.* New York: Oxford University Press, 1986.

Dubois, Laurent. *Avengers of the New World: The Story of the Haitian Revolution.* Cambridge, Mass.: Harvard University Press, 2004.

DuBois, W. E. Burghardt. *The Philadephia Negro: A Social Study.* New York: Benjamin Blom, 1967.

Edwards, Paul. "Three West African Writers of the 1780s." In *The Slave's Narrative*, edited by Charles D. Davis and Henry Louis Gates Jr. New York: Oxford University Press, 1985.

Egerton, Douglas R. *Charles Fenton Mercer and the Trial of National Conservatism.* Jackson: University Press of Mississippi, 1989.

Egerton, Douglas R. "'Its Origin Is Not a Little Curious': A New Look at the American Colonization Society." *Journal of the Early Republic* 5 (1985): 462–80.

Ellis, Markman. "Ignatius Sancho's Letters: Sentimental Libertinism and the Politics of Form." In *Genius in Bondage: Literature of the Early Black Atlantic*, edited by Vincent Carretta and Philip Gould, 199–217. Lexington: University Press of Kentucky, 2001.

Ellison, Julie. *Cato's Tears and the Making of Anglo-American Emotion.* Chicago: University of Chicago Press, 1999.

Eltis, David. *The Rise of African Slavery in the Americas.* Cambridge: Cambridge University Press, 2000.

Eltis, David, Stephen D. Behrendt, David Richardson, and Herbert S. Klein. *The Trans-Atlantic Slave Trade: A Database on CD-ROM.* Cambridge: Cambridge University Press, 1999.

Ely, Melvin Patrick. *Israel on the Appomattox: A Southern Experiment in Black Freedom from the 1790s through the Civil War.* New York: Vintage, 2004.

Equiano, Olaudah. *The Interesting Narrative and Other Writings.* Edited with an introduction and notes by Vincent Carretta. New York: Penguin, 1995.

Erkkila, Betsy. *Mixed Bloods and Other Crosses: Rethinking American Literature from the Revolution to the Culture Wars.* Philadelphia: University of Pennsylvania Press, 2005.

———. "Phillis Wheatley and the Black American Revolution." In *A Mixed Race: Ethnicity in Early America*, edited by Frank Shuffleton. New York: Oxford University Press, 1993.

Eze, Emmanuel Chukwudy, ed. *Race and the Enlightenment: A Reader.* Cambridge, Mass.: Blackwell, 1997.

Falconbridge, Anna Maria. *Narrative of Two Voyages to the River Sierra Leone during the Years 1791-1792-1793.* Edited by Christopher Fyfe. Liverpool: Liverpool University Press, 2000.

Falola, Toyin. "Introduction." In Martin Delany, *The Condition, Elevation, Emigration, and Destiny of the Colored People of the United States and Official Report of the Niger Valley Exploring Party.* Amherst, N.Y.: Humanity, 2004.

Falola, Toyin, and Matt Childs, ed. *The Yoruba Diaspora in the Atlantic World.* Bloomington: Indiana University Press, 2004.

Fanning, Sara. "'The Land of Promise': African Americans and Haiti from Revolutionary Solidarity to Emigration." Ph.D. dissertation, University of Texas, Austin, forthcoming.

——. "The Roots of Early Black Nationalism: Northern African Americans' Invocations of Haiti in the Early Nineteenth Century." In *Slavery and Abolition*, forthcoming.

Fehrenbacher, Donald. *The Slaveholding Republic: An Account of the United States Government's Relations to Slavery*, compiled and edited by Ward M. McAfee. New York: Oxford University Press, 2001.

Fenn, Elizabeth A. *Pox Americana: The Great Smallpox Epidemic of 1775–1782*. New York: Hill and Wang, 2001.

Fergusson, Charles Bruce, ed. *Clarkson's Mission to America 1791–1792*. Halifax: Public Archives of Nova Scotia, 1971.

Fisher, Miles Mark. "Lott Cary: The Colonizing Missionary." *Journal of Negro History* 7 (1922): 380–418.

Frazier, E. Franklin. *The Free Negro Family: A Study of Family Origins before the Civil War*. Nashville: Fisk University Press, 1932.

Frederickson, George M. "Redcoat Liberation." *The New York Review of Books* 53 (August 10, 2006): 51–53.

Freehling, William W. *The Reintegration of American History: Slavery and the Civil War*. New York: Oxford University Press, 1994.

——. *The Road to Disunion: Secessionists at Bay, 1776–1854*. Vol. 1. New York: Oxford University Press, 1990.

Frey, Sylvia. *Water from the Rock: Black Resistance in a Revolutionary Age*. Princeton, N.J.: Princeton University Press, 1991.

Frey, Sylvia, and Betty Wood. *Come Shouting to Zion: African American Protestantism in the American South and the British Caribbean*. Chapel Hill: University of North Carolina Press, 1998.

Fyfe, Christopher. *A History of Sierra Leone*. London: Oxford University Press, 1962.

——, ed. *Sierra Leone Inheritance*. London: Oxford University Press, 1964.

Fyfe, Christopher with a contribution by Charles Jones ed. *"Our Children Free and Happy": Letters from Black Settlers in Africa in the 1790s*. Edinburgh: Edinburgh University Press, 1991.

Gallay, Allan. "Planters and Slaves in the Great Awakening." In *Masters and Slaves in the House of the Lord*, edited by John B. Boles, 19–36. Lexington: University Press of Kentucky, 1988.

Gardner, Bettye J. "Opposition to Emigration, a Selected Letter of William Watkins (the Colored Baltimorean)." *Journal of Negro History* 67 (1982): 155–58.

Garrison, William Lloyd. *Thoughts on African Colonization*. New York: Arno, 1969. Originally published in 1832.

Gates, Henry Louis Jr. "Editor's Introduction: Writing, 'Race' and the Difference It Makes." In *"Race," Writing, and Difference*, edited by Henry Louis Gates Jr., 1–20. Chicago: University of Chicago Press, 1986.

——. *Figures in Black: Words, Signs, and the "Racial" Self*. New York: Oxford University Press, 1987.

——. *The Signifying Monkey: A Theory of African-American Literary Criticism.* New York: Oxford University Press, 1988.

Geggus, David Patrick. *Haitian Revolutionary Studies.* Bloomington: Indiana University Press, 2002.

——. *Slavery, War, and Revolution: The British Occupation of Saint Domingue, 1793–1798.* Oxford: Oxford University Press, 1982.

George, Carol V. R. *Segregated Sabbaths: Richard Allen and the Emergence of Independent Black Churches, 1760–1840.* New York: Oxford University Press, 1973.

Gerzina, Gretchen. *Black London: Life before Emancipation.* New Brunswick, N.J.: Rutgers University Press, 1995.

Gilje, Paul. *Rioting in America.* Bloomington: Indiana University Press, 1996.

Gilroy, Paul. *The Black Atlantic: Modernity and Double Consciousness.* Cambridge, Mass.: Harvard University Press, 1993.

Glaude, Eddie S. *Exodus!: Religion, Race, and Nation in Early Nineteenth-Century Black America.* Chicago: University of Chicago Press, 2000.

Gomez, Michael A. *Exchanging Our Country Marks: The Transformation of African Identities in the Colonial and Antebellum South.* Chapel Hill: University of North Carolina Press, 1998.

Gould, Elijah H. *The Persistence of Empire: British Political Culture in the Age of the American Revolution.* Chapel Hill: University of North Carolina Press for the Omohundru Institute of Early American History and Culture, 2000.

Gould, Philip. *Barbaric Traffic: Commerce and Antislavery in the Eighteenth-Century Atlantic World.* Cambridge, Mass.: Harvard University Press, 2003.

Graham, Leroy. *Baltimore: The Nineteenth-Century Black Capital.* Washington, D.C.: University Press of America, 1982.

Green, James. "The Publishing History of Olaudah Equiano's Interesting Narrative." *Slavery and Abolition* 16 (1995): 362–75.

Greene, Jack P. "Empire and Identity from the Glorious Revolution to the American Revolution." In *The Oxford History of the British Empire,* edited by P. J. Marshall. Oxford: Oxford University Press, 1998.

Grimsted, David. *American Mobbing, 1828–1861.* New York: Oxford University Press, 1998.

——. "Anglo-American Racism and Phillis Wheatley's 'Sable Veil,' 'Length'ned Chain,' and 'Knitted Hearth'." In *Women in the Age of the American Revolution,* edited by Ronald Hoffman and Peter J. Albert, 338–444. Charlottesville: University Press of Virginia, 1989.

Gross, Bella. "Freedom's Journal and the Rights of All." *Journal of Negro History* 17 (1932): 241–86.

Gurley, Ralph Randolph. *Life of Jehudi Ashmun: Late Colonial Agent in Liberia.* Freeport, N.Y.: Books for Libraries Press, 1971.

Hahn, Steven. *A Nation under Our Feet: Black Political Struggles in the Rural South from Slavery to the Great Migration.* Cambridge, Mass.: Harvard University Press, 2003.

Hall, Gwendolyn Midlo. *Slavery and African Ethnicities in the Americas: Restoring the Links.* Chapel Hill: University of North Carolina Press, 2005.

Hall, Prince. "Letters and Sermons by Prince Hall, 1787–1802." In *Prince Hall Records by H. V. B. Voorhis*. Boston: Boston Grand Masonic Lodge Library.

Hancock, David. *Citizens of the World: London Merchants and the Integration of the British Atlantic Community, 1735–1785*. Cambridge: Cambridge University Press, 1995.

Handy, James A. *Scraps of African Methodist Episcopal History*. Philadelphia: A.M.E. Book Concern, n.d. [1902].

Hanger, Kimberly. *Bounded Lives, Bounded Places: Free Black Society in Colonial New Orleans, 1769–1803*. Durham, N.C.: Duke University Press, 1997.

Hannaford, Ivan. *Race: The History of an Idea in the West*. Washington, D.C.: Woodrow Wilson Center Press, 1996.

Harris, Sheldon H. *Paul Cuffe: Black America and the African Return*. New York: Simon and Shuster, 1972.

Hempton, David. *Methodism: Empire of the Spirit*. New Haven, Conn.: Yale University Press, 2005.

Herskovits, Melville J. *Life in a Haitian Valley*. New York: Knopf, 1937.

Hinks, Peter P., ed. *David Walker's Appeal to the Coloured Citizens of the World*. University Park: Pennsylvania State University Press, 2000.

——. *"To Awaken My Afflicted Brethren": David Walker and the Problem of Antebellum Slave Resistance*. University Park: The Pennsylvania State University Press, 1997.

Hodes, Martha Elizabeth. *White Women, Black Men: Illicit Sex in the Nineteenth–Century South*. New Haven, Conn.: Yale University Press, 1997.

Hodges, Graham Russell, ed. *The Black Loyalist Directory: African Americans in Exile after the American Revolution*. New York: Garland, 1996.

Hodges, Graham Russell. *Root and Branch: African Americans in New York and East Jersey, 1613–1863*. Chapel Hill: University of North Carolina Press, 1999.

Holt, Thomas C. *The Problem of Freedom: Race, Labor and Politics in Jamaica and Britain, 1832–1938*. Baltimore: Johns Hopkins University Press, 1992.

Horton, James Oliver. *Free People of Color: Inside the African American Community*. Washington, D.C.: Smithsonian Institution Press, 1993.

Horton, James Oliver, and Lois E. Horton. *In Hope of Liberty: Culture, Community and Protest among Northern Free Blacks, 1700–1860*. New York: Oxford University Press, 1997.

Huberich, Charles Henry. *The Political and Legislative History of Liberia*. New York: Central Book Company, 1947.

Ingersoll, Thomas N. "Free Blacks in a Slave Society: New Orleans, 1718–1812." *William and Mary Quarterly*, 3rd ser., 48 (1991): 173–200.

Ingham, E. G., ed. *Sierra Leone after a Hundred Years*. Reprint, London: Frank Cass & Co., 1968.

Innes, Stephen. *Creating the Commonwealth: The Economic Culture of Puritan New England*. New York: Norton, 1995.

Isaac, Rhys. *Landon Carter's Uneasy Kingdom: Revolution and Rebellion on a Virginia Plantation*. New York: Oxford University Press, 2004.

Jacob, Margaret C. *Living the Enlightenment: Freemasonry and Politics in Eighteenth-Century Europe*. New York: Oxford University Press, 1991.

Jones, Absalom. "A Thanksgiving Sermon, Preached January 1, 1808, in St. Thomas's, or the African Episcopal, Church, Philadelphia: On Account of the Abolition of the African Slave Trade." In Dorothy Porter, ed. *Early Negro Writing, 1760–1837*. Boston: Beacon, 1971

Jordan, Winthrop D. *White over Black: American Attitudes toward the Negro, 1550–1812*. Chapel Hill: University of North Carolina Press for the Institute of Early American History and Culture, 1968.

Judy, Ronald A. *(Dis)Forming the American Canon: African-Arabic Slave Narratives and the Vernacular*. Minneapolis: University of Minnesota Press, 1993.

Juster, Susan. *Doomsayers: Anglo-American Prophecy in the Age of Revolution*. Philadelphia: University of Pennsylvania Press, 2003.

Kaplan, Sidney, and Emma Nogrady Kaplan. *The Black Presence in the Era of the American Revolution*. Rev. ed. Amherst: University Press of Massachusetts, 1989.

Kennedy, H. A. A. "Peter, First Epistle Of." In *A New Standard Bible Dictionary*, edited by Edward E. Nourse, Melancthon W. Jacobus, and Andrew C. Zenos. New York: Funk and Wagnalls, 1926.

Kidd, Colin. *The Forging of Races: Race and Scripture in the Protestant Atlantic World, 1600–2000*. Cambridge: Cambridge University Press, 2006.

Kizell, John. "Extracts from the Correspondence of Mr. John Kizell with Governor Columbine, Respecting His Negotiations with the Chiefs on the River Sherbro, and Giving an Account of That River." In *Sixth Report of the Directors of the African Institution*, 113–53. London: Ellerton and Henderson, 1812.

Knutsford, Viscountess. *Life and Letters of Zachary Macaulay*. London: Edward Arnold, 1900.

Krise, Thomas W., ed. *Caribbeana: An Anthology of English Literature in the West Indies, 1657–1777*. Chicago: University of Chicago Press, 1999.

Laughon, Samuel W. "Administrative Problems in Maryland in Liberia." *Journal of Negro History* 26 (1941): 325–64.

Lawrence, George. "Oration on the Abolition of the Slave Trade, Delivered on the First Day of January, 1813, in the African Methodist Episcopal Church." In *Early Negro Writing, 1760–1837*, edited by Dorothy Porter. Boston: Beacon, 1971.

Levine, Robert S., ed. *Martin Delany: A Documentary Reader*. Chapel Hill: University of North Carolina Press, 2003.

——. *Martin Delany, Frederick Douglass and the Politics of Representative Identity*. Chapel Hill: University of North Carolina Press, 1997.

Lewis, Robert Benjamin. *Light and Truth, from Ancient and Sacred History*. Portland, Me.: D. C. Colesworthy, 1836.

Lin, Rachel Chernos. "The Rhode Island Slave-Traders: Butchers, Bakers and Candlestick Makers." *Slavery and Abolition* 23 (2002): 21–38.

Linebaugh, Peter, and Marcus Rediker. *The Many-Headed Hydra: Sailors, Slaves, Commoners, and the Hidden History of the Revolutionary Atlantic*. Boston: Beacon, 2000.

Little, Thomas J. "George Liele and the Rise of Independent Black Baptist Churches in the Lower South and Jamaica." *Slavery and Abolition* 16 (1995): 188–204.

Litwack, Leon. *North of Slavery: The Negro in the Free States, 1790–1860*. Chicago: University of Chicago Press, 1961.

Loomis, Sally. "The Evolution of Paul Cuffe's Black Nationalism." In *Black Apostles at Home and Abroad: Afro-Americans and the Christian Mission from the Revolution to Reconstruction*, edited by David W. Wills and Richard Newman, 191–202. Boston: G. K. Hall, 1982.

Love, Emanuel King. *History of the First African Baptist Church, from Its Organization January 20th, 1788, to July 1st, 1888. Including the Centennial Celebration, Addresses, Sermons, Etc.* Savannah: The Morning News Print, 1888.

Lovejoy, Paul. "Autobiography and Memory: Gustavus Vassa, Alias Olaudah Equiano, the African." http://72.14.221.104/search?q=cache:3vwGUiyOCnEJ:www.yorku.ca/nhp/seminars/2005_06/Vassa_and_Abolition_Slavery_and_Abolition.pdf+joanna+vassa&hl=en&gl=uk&ct=clnk&cd=2.

Lyerly, Cynthia Lyn. *Methodism and the Southern Mind, 1770–1810*. New York: Oxford University Press, 1998.

Mann, Bruce H. *Republic of Debtors: Bankruptcy in the Age of American Independence*. Cambridge, Mass.: Harvard University Press, 2002.

Manning, Patrick. *Slavery and African Life: Occidental, Oriental, and African Slave Trades*. Cambridge: Cambridge University Press, 1990.

Manuel, Frank E. *The Broken Staff: Judaism through Christian Eyes*. Cambridge, Mass.: Harvard University Press, 1992.

———. *The Changing of the Gods*. Hanover, N.H.: University Press of New England, 1983.

Markwei, Matei. "The Rev. Daniel Coker of Sierra Leone." In *Black Apostles at Home and Abroad: Afro-Americans and the Christian Mission from the Revolution to Reconstruction*, edited by David W. Wills and Richard Newman, 203–10. Boston: G. K. Hall, 1982.

Marshall, Herbert, and Mildred Stock. *Ira Aldridge: The Negro Tragedian*. London: Rockliff, 1958.

Matthews, Donald G. *Slavery and Methodism: A Chapter in American Morality, 1780–1845*. Princeton, N.J.: Princeton University Press, 1965.

Matthews, John. *A Voyage to the River Sierra Leone on the Coast of Africa*. London: White and Son, 1788.

McDaniel, Antonio. *Swing Low, Sweet Chariot: The Mortality Cost of Colonizing Liberia in the Nineteenth Century*. Chicago: University of Chicago Press, 1995.

McGraw, Marie Tyler. "Richmond Free Blacks and African Colonization, 1816–1832." *Journal of American Studies* 21 (1987): 207–24.

McHenry, Elizabeth. *Forgotten Readers: Recovering the Lost History of African American Literary Societies*. Durham, N.C.: Duke University Press, 2002.

Meacham, Standish. *Henry Thornton of Clapham, 1760–1815*. Cambridge, Mass.: Harvard University Press, 1964.

Meek, Ronald L. *Social Science and the Ignoble Savage*. Cambridge: Cambridge University Press, 1976.

Melish, Joanne Pope. *Disowning Slavery: Gradual Emancipation and "Race" in New England, 1780–1860.* Ithaca, N.Y.: Cornell University Press, 1998.

Miller, Floyd J. *The Search for a Black Nationality: Black Emigration and Colonization, 1787–1863.* Urbana: University of Illinois Press, 1975.

Miller, William. *A Sermon on the Abolition of the Slave Trade: Delivered in the African Church, New York.* New York: John C. Totten, 1810.

Mintz, Sidney W. *Caribbean Transformations.* Baltimore: Johns Hopkins University Press, 1984.

Mintz, Sidney W., and Richard Price. *The Birth of African-American Culture: An Anthropological Perspective.* Boston: Beacon, 1992.

Molineux, Catherine. "Hogarth's Fashionable Slaves: Moral Corruption in Eighteenth–Century London." *English Literary History* 72 (2005): 495–520.

———. "The Peripheries Within: Race, Slavery, and Empire in Early Modern England." Ph.D. diss., Johns Hopkins University, 2005.

Morgan, Edmund S. *The Gentle Puritan: A Life of Ezra Stiles, 1727–1795.* New York: Norton, 1983.

Morgan, Philip D. "British Encounters with Africans and African–Americans, Circa 1600–1780." In *Strangers within the Realm: Cultural Margins of the First British Empire,* edited by Bernard Bailyn and Philip D. Morgan, 157–219. Chapel Hill: University of North Carolina Press for the Institute of Early American History and Culture, 1991.

———. "The Cultural Implications of the Atlantic Slave Trade: African Regional Origins, American Destinations and New World Developments." In *Routes to Slavery: Direction, Ethnicity and Mortality in the Transatlantic Slave Trade,* edited by David Eltis and David Richardson. London: Frank Cass, 1997.

Moses, Wilson Jeremiah. *Afrotopia: The Roots of African American Popular History.* Cambridge: Cambridge University Press, 1998.

———. *The Golden Age of Black Nationalism, 1850–1925.* New York: Oxford University Press, 1978.

Murphy, Geraldine. "Olaudah Equiano, Accidental Tourist." *Eighteenth–Century Studies* 27 (1994): 551–68.

Nash, Gary B. *Forging Freedom: The Formation of Philadelphia's Black Community, 1720–1840.* Cambridge, Mass.: Harvard University Press, 1988.

———. *The Forgotten Fifth: African Americans in the Age of Revolution.* Cambridge, Mass.: Harvard University Press, 2006.

———. *Race, Class, and Politics: Essays on American Colonial and Revolutionary Society.* Urbana: University of Illinois Press, 1986.

Nash, Gary B. "Thomas Peters: Millwright and Deliverer." *Struggle and Survival in Colonial America* edited by Gary B. Nash and David J. Sweet, 69–85. Berkeley and Los Angeles: University of California Press, 1981.

Nash, Gary B., and Jean R. Soderlund. *Freedom by Degrees: Emancipation in Pennsylvania and Its Aftermath.* New York: Oxford University Press, 1991.

Nichols, Charles H. "The Slave Narrators and the Picaresque Mode: Archetypes for Modern Black Personae." In *The Slave's Narrative*, edited by Charles T. Davis and Henry Louis Gates Jr., 283–98. New York: Oxford University Press, 1985.

Niven, Laird, and Stephen A. Davis. "Birchtown: The History and Material Culture of an Expatriate African American Community." In *Moving On: Black Loyalists in the Afro-Atlantic World*, edited by John W. Pulis, 59–84. New York: Garland, 1999.

Norton, Mary Beth. "The Fate of Some Black Loyalists of the American Revolution." *Journal of Negro History* 58 (1973): 402–26.

Odell, Margaretta Matilda. *Memoir and Poems of Phillis Wheatley, a Native African and a Slave*. Boston: George W. Light, 1834.

O'Neale, Sondra. "A Slave's Subtle War: Phillis Wheatley's Use of Biblical Myth and Symbol." *Early American Literature* 21 (1986): 144–65.

Onuf, Peter S. "Every Generation Is an 'Independent Nation': Colonization, Miscegenation, and the Fate of Jefferson's Children." *William and Mary Quarterly*, 3rd ser., 57 (2000): 153–70.

——. *Jefferson's Empire: The Language of Nationhood*. Charlottesville: University Press of Virginia, 2000.

Oson, Jacob. *A Search for Truth; or, an Inquiry for the Origin of the African Nation*. New York, 1817.

Paul, Nathaniel. "An Address, Delivered on the Celebration of the Abolition of Slavery, in the State of New-York, July 5, 1827." In *Negro Protest Pamphlets: A Compendium*, edited by Dorothy Porter, 6–25. New York: Arno, 1969.

Payne, Daniel. *History of the African Methodist Episcopal Church*. Nashville: A.M.E. Sunday-School Union, 1891.

Peterson, John. *A Province of Freedom: A History of Sierra Leone 1787–1870*. Evanston, Ill.: Northwestern University Press, 1969.

Phillips, Christopher. *Freedom's Port: The African American Community of Baltimore, 1790–1860*. Urbana: University of Illinois Press, 1997.

Piersen, William D. *Black Yankees: The Development of an Afro-American Subculture in Eighteenth-Century New England*. Amherst: University of Massachusetts Press, 1988.

Pocock, J. G. A. *Barbarism and Religion: Barbarians, Savages and Empires*. Vol. 4. Cambridge: Cambridge University Press, 2005.

Poe, William A. "Lott Cary: Man of Purchased Freedom." *Church History* 39 (1970): 49–61.

Pole, J. R. *Political Representation in England and the Origins of the American Republic*. New York: St. Martin's, 1966.

Porter, Dorothy, ed. *Early Negro Writing, 1760–1837*. Boston: Beacon, 1971.

Potkay, Adam. "Introduction." In *Black Atlantic Writers of the Eighteenth Century: Living the New Exodus in England and the Americas*, edited by Adam Potkay and Sandra Burr, 1–22. New York: St. Martin's, 1995.

——. "Olaudah Equiano and the Art of Spiritual Autobiography." *Eighteenth-Century Studies* 27 (1994): 677–92.

Potkay, Adam, and Sandra Burr, ed. *Black Atlantic Writers of the Eighteenth Century: Living the New Exodus in England and the Americas*. New York: St. Martin's, 1995.

Pybus, Cassandra. *Epic Journeys of Freedom: Runaway Slaves of the American Revolution and Their Global Quest for Liberty*. Boston: Beacon, 2006.

——. "Jefferson's Faulty Math: The Question of Slave Defections in the American Revolution." *William and Mary Quarterly*, 3rd ser., 62 (2005): 243–64.

Quarles, Benjamin. *The Negro in the American Revolution*. New York: Norton, 1973.

Quinn, W. Paul. "The Origin, Horrors, and Results of Slavery, Faithfully and Minutely Described." In *Early Negro Writing, 1760–1837*, edited by Dorothy Porter, 614–36. Boston: Beacon, 1971.

Raboteau, Albert J. *A Fire in the Bones: Reflections on African-American Religious History*. Boston: Beacon, 1995.

Rael, Patrick J. *Black Identity and Black Protest in the Antebellum North*. Chapel Hill: University of North Carolina Press, 2002.

Richards, Leonard. *"Gentlemen of Property and Standing": Anti-abolition Mobs in Jacksonian America*. New York: Oxford University Press, 1970.

Richards, Phillip. "The 'Joseph Story' as Slave Narrative: On Genesis and Exodus as Prototypes for Early Black Anglophone Writing." In *African Americans and the Bible: Sacred Texts and Social Textures*, edited by Vincent L. Wimbush, 221–35. New York: Continuum, 2000.

Ripley, C. Peter, ed. *Witness for Freedom: African American Voices on Race, Slavery, and Emancipation*. Chapel Hill: University of North Carolina Press, 1993.

Ripley, Dorothy. *The Extraordinary Conversion and Religious Experience*. New York: Waites, 1810.

Roberts, William. *Memoirs of the Life and Correspondence of Mrs. Hannah More*. 2 vols. New York: Harper, 1834.

Robinson, William H. *Black New England Letters: The Uses of Writings in Black New England*. Boston: Trustees of the Public Library of the City of Boston, 1977.

——. *Phillis Wheatley and Her Writings*. New York: Garland, 1984.

——, ed. *The Proceedings of the Free African Union Society and African Benevolent Society, Newport, Rhode Island, 1780–1824*. Providence, R.I.: The Urban League of Rhode Island, 1976.

Roediger, David R. *The Wages of Whiteness: Race and the Making of the American Working Class*. London: Verso, 1991.

Russell, Dick. *Black Genius and the American Experience*. New York: Carroll & Graf, 1998.

Russwurm, John B. "The Condition and Prospects of Hayti," edited by Philip S. Foner. *Journal of Negro History* 54 (1969): 393–97.

Said, Edward W. *Beginnings: Intention and Method*. New York: Columbia University Press, 1985.

Saillant, John. *Black Puritan, Black Republican: The Life and Thought of Lemuel Haynes, 1753–1833*. New York: Oxford University Press, 2003.

Saillant, John. "'Wipe Away All Tears from Their Eyes': John Marrant's Theology in the Black Atlantic, 1785–1808." *Journal of Millenial Studies* (1999), www.mille.org/journal.html.

Sancho, Ignatius. *Letters of the Late Ignatius Sancho, an African.* Edited with an introduction and notes by Vincent Carretta. New York: Penguin, 1998.

Sandhu, S. S. "Ignatius Sancho and Laurence Sterne." *Research in African Literatures* 29 (1998): 88–106.

Sanneh, Lamin. *Abolitionists Abroad: American Blacks and the Making of Modern West Africa.* Cambridge, Mass.: Harvard University Press, 1999.

Saxton, Alexander. *The Rise and Fall of the White Republic: Class Politics in Nineteenth-Century America.* London: Verso, 1990.

Schama, Simon. *Rough Crossings: Britain, the Slaves and the American Revolution.* London: BBC, 2005.

Scott, Julius Sherrard III. "A Common Wind: Currents of Afro-American Communications in the Age of the Haitian Revolution." Ph.D. diss., Duke University, 1986.

Sernett, Milton C. *Black Religion and American Evangelicalism: White Protestants, Plantation Missions, and the Flowering of Negro Christianity, 1787–1865.* Metuchen, N.J.: Scarecrow, 1975.

Sherwood, H. N. "Paul Cuffe." *Journal of Negro History* 8 (1923): 153–229.

Shick, Thom W. *Behold the Promised Land: A History of Afro–American Settler Society in Nineteenth-Century Liberia.* Baltimore: Johns Hopkins University Press, 1980.

Shields, John C. "Phillis Wheatley's Struggle for Freedom in Her Poetry and Prose." In *Collected Works of Wheatley,* edited by John C. Shields, 229–70. New York: Oxford University Press, 1989.

Shuffleton, Frank. "On Her Own Footing: Phillis Wheatley in Freedom." In *Genius in Bondage: Literature of the Early Black Atlantic,* edited by Vincent Carretta and Philip Gould, 175–89. Lexington: University Press of Kentucky, 2001.

Shyllon, Folarin. *Black People in Britain, 1555–1833.* London: Oxford University Press, 1977.

Sidbury, James. "Early Slave Narratives and the Culture of the Atlantic Market." In *Empire and Nation,* edited by Eligah H. Gould and Peter S. Onuf, 260–74. Baltimore: Johns Hopkins University Press, 2005.

——. *Ploughshares into Swords: Race, Rebellion, and Identity in Gabriel's Virginia, 1730–1810.* Cambridge: Cambridge University Press, 1997.

——. "Thomas Jefferson in Gabriel's Virginia." In *The Revolution of 1800: Democracy, Race, and the New Republic,* edited by Jan Ellen Lewis, James Horn, and Peter S. Onuf, 199–219. Charlottesville: University of Virginia Press, 2002.

Sierra Leone Company. *Substance of the Report of the court of directors of the Sierra Leone Company, Delivered to the General Court of Proprietors, on Thursday, the 26th Day of February, 1795.* Philadelphia: Thomas Dobson, 1795.

Sipkins, Henry. "An Oration on the Abolition of the Slave Trade: Delivered in the African Church, in the City of New York, January 2, 1809." In *Early Negro Writing, 1760–1837,* edited by Dorothy Porter. Boston: Beacon, 1971.

Smith, David. *Biography Of Rev. David Smith Of The A.M.E. Church; Being A Complete History, Embracing Over Sixty Years' Labor In The Advancement Of The Redeemer's Kingdom On Earth*. Xenia, Ohio: Xenia Gazette Office, 1881.

Smith, Theophus H. *Conjuring Culture: Biblical Formations of Black America*. New York: Oxford University Press, 1994.

Sobel, Mechal. *Teach Me Dreams: The Search for the Self in the Revolutionary Era*. Princeton, N.J.: Princeton University Press, 2000.

——. *Trabelin' On: The Slave Journey to an Afro-Baptist Faith*. Princeton, N.J.: Princeton University Press, 1988.

——. *The World They Made Together: Black and White Values in Eighteenth-Century Virginia*. Princeton, N.J.: Princeton University Press, 1987.

Soderlund, Jean R. *Quakers and Slavery: A Divided Spirit*. Princeton, N.J.: Princeton University Press, 1985.

Sollors, Werner. *Beyond Ethnicity: Consent and Descent in American Culture*. New York: Oxford University Press, 1986.

Sparks, Randy. *The Two Princes of Calabar: An Eighteenth-Century Atlantic Odyssey*. Cambridge, Mass.: Harvard University Press, 2004.

Spilsbury, F. B. *Account of a Voyage to the Western Coast of Africa*. London: Printed for Richard Phillips, 1807.

Spring, Gardiner. *Memoirs of the Rev. Samuel J. Mills, Late Missionary to the South Western Section of the United States and Agent of the American Colonization Society, Deputed to Explore the Coast of Africa*. New York: New York Evangelical Missionary Society, 1820.

Staudenraus, P. J. *The African Colonization Movement, 1816–1865*. New York: Columbia University Press, 1961.

Sterling, Dorothy. *The Making of an Afro-American: Martin Robinson Delany, 1812–1885*. Garden City, N.Y.: Doubleday, 1971.

Stuckey, Sterling. *Slave Culture: Nationalist Theory and the Foundations of Black America*. New York: Oxford University Press, 1987.

Sweet, John Wood. *Bodies Politic: Negotiating Race in the American North, 1730–1830*. Baltimore: Johns Hopkins University Press, 2003.

Tanner, Benjamin T. *Outline of Our History and Government for African Methodist Churchmen, Ministerial and Lay*. Philadelphia, 1884.

Taves, Ann. *Fits, Trances and Visions: Experiencing Religion and Explaining Experience from Wesley to James*. Princeton, N.J.: Princeton University Press, 1999.

Taylor, Alan. "The Early Republic's Supernatural Economy: Treasure Seeking in the American Northeast, 1780–1830." *American Quarterly* 38 (1986): 6–34.

Thomas, Karin Michele. "Traveling Eyes: African American Travelers Create a World, 1789–1930." Ph.D. diss., Yale University, 2001.

Thomas, Lamont D. *Rise to Be a People: A Biography of Paul Cuffe*. Urbana: University of Illinois Press, 1986.

Thompson, E. P. *Witness against the Beast: William Black and the Moral Law*. Cambridge: Cambridge University Press, 1993.

Thompson, George A. Jr., ed. *A Documentary History of the African Theatre*. Evanston, Ill.: Northwestern University Press, 1998.

Thompson, Robert Farris. *Flash of the Spirit: African and Afro-American Art and Philosophy*. New York: Vintage, 1983.

Thornton, John. *Africa and Africans in the Making of the Atlantic World: 1400–1680*. Cambridge: Cambridge University Press, 1992.

Tuveson, Ernest Lee. *Millennium and Utopia: A Study in the Background of the Idea of Progress*. Berkeley and Los Angeles: University of California Press, 1949.

Tyson, John S. *The Life of Elisha Tyson, the Philanthropist*. Baltimore: B. Lundy, 1825.

Vaughan, Alden T., and Virginia Mason Vaughan. "Before Othello: Elizabethan Representations of Sub–Saharan Africans." *William and Mary Quarterly*, 3rd ser., 54 (1997): 19–44.

Vaughan, Virginia Mason. *Performing Blackness on English Stages, 1500–1800*. Cambridge: Cambridge University Press, 2005.

Volney, C. F. *The Ruins, or, Meditation on the Revolutions of Empires: And the Law of Nature*. Baltimore: Black Classics, 1991.

Walker, James W. St. G. *The Black Loyalists: The Search for a Promised Land in Nova Scotia and Sierra Leone, 1783–1870*. New York: Africana, 1976.

Walters, Ronald G. *American Reformers, 1815–1860*. New York: Hill and Wang, 1978.

Walvin, James. *England, Slaves and Freedom, 1776–1838*. Jackson: University Press of Mississippi, 1986.

Webb, Elizabeth, *Letter from Elizabeth Webb to Anthony William Boehm. With His Answer*. Philadelphia: Henry Tuckniss, 1798.

Wesley, Charles H. *Prince Hall: Life and Legacy*. 2nd ed. Washington, D.C.: United Supreme Council, Southern Jurisdiction, Prince Hall Affiliation, 1983.

——. *Richard Allen: Apostle of Freedom*. Washington, D.C.: Associated Publishers, 1935.

West, Richard. *Back to Africa: A History of Sierra Leone and Liberia*. London: Jonathan Cape, 1970.

Wheatley, Phillis. *Complete Writings*. Edited with an introduction and notes by Vincent Carretta. New York: Penguin, 2001.

Wheeler, Roxann. *The Complexion of Race: Categories of Difference in Eighteenth-Century British Culture*. Philadelphia: University of Pennsylvania Press, 2000.

White, George. "A Brief Account of the Life, Experience, Travels, and Gospel Labours of George White, an African." In *Black Itinerants of the Gospel: The Narratives of John Jea and George White*, edited by Graham Russell Hodges. Madison, Wisc.: Madison House, 1993.

White, Shane. "'It Was a Proud Day': African Americans, Festivals, and Parades in the North, 1741–1834." *Journal of American History* 81 (1994): 13–50.

——. *Somewhat More Independent: The End of Slavery in New York City, 1770–1810*. Athens: University of Georgia Press, 1991.

——. *Stories of Freedom in Black New York*. Cambridge, Mass.: Harvard University Press, 2002.

Wiggins, Rosalind Cobb. "Introducing Captain Paul Cuffe, Friend." In *Captain Paul Cuffe's Logs and Letters, 1808–1817*, edited by Rosalind Cobb Wiggins. Washington, D.C.: Howard University Press, 1996.

Wilentz, Sean. *The Rise of American Democracy: Jefferson to Lincoln*. New York: Norton, 2005.

Williams, Peter Jr. "An Oration on the Abolition of the Slave Trade: Delivered in the African Church, in the City of New York, January 1, 1808." In *Early Negro Writing, 1760–1837*, edited by Dorothy Porter. Boston: Beacon, 1971.

———. "To the Citizens of New York (July 14, 1834)." 1834 (typescript in possession of author).

Wilson, Ellen Gibson. *John Clarkson and the African Adventure*. London: Macmillan, 1980.

———. *The Loyal Blacks*. New York: Capricorn, 1976.

———. *Thomas Clarkson: A Biography*. London: Macmillan, 1989.

Wilson, Kathleen. *The Sense of the People: Politics, Culture, and Empire in England, 1715–1785*. Cambridge: Cambridge University Press, 1995.

Winch, Julie. *A Gentleman of Color: The Life of James Forten*. New York: Oxford University Press, 2002.

———. *Philadelphia's Black Elite: Activism, Accommodation, and the Struggle for Autonomy, 1787–1848*. Philadelphia: Temple University Press, 1988.

Winterbottom, Thomas. *An Account of the Native Africans in the Neighborhood of Sierra Leone*. 2 vols. London: Frank Cass, 1969.

Wood, Peter H. "'Liberty Is Sweet': African-American Freedom Struggles in the Years before White Independence." In *Beyond the American Revolution: Explorations in the History of American Radicalism*, edited by Alfred F. Young, 149–84. DeKalb: Northern Illinois University Press, 1993.

Woodard, Helena. *African-British Writings in the Eighteenth Century: The Politics of Race and Reason*. Westport, Conn.: Greenwood, 1999.

Woodson, Carter G. *The History of the Negro Church*. 2nd ed. Washington, D.C.: Associated Publishers, 1921.

———, ed. *The Mind of the Negro as Reflected in Letters Written during the Crisis, 1800–1860*. Washington, D.C.: Association for the Study of Negro Life and History, 1926.

Wright, Josephine R. B. "Introduction." In *Ignatius Sancho (1720–1780): An Early African Composer in England: The Collected Editions of His Music in Facsimile*. Edited by Josephine R. B. Wright. New York: Garland, 1981.

Young, Robert Alexander. "Ethiopian Manifesto." In *Pamphlets of Protest: An Anthology of Early African-American Protest Literature, 1790–1860*, edited by Richard Newman, Patrick Rael, and Philip Lapsansky, 85–89. New York: Routledge, 2001.

Zafar, Rafia. *We Wear the Mask: African Americans Write American Literature, 1760–1870*. New York: Columbia University Press, 1997.

Zilversmit, Arthur. *The First Emancipation: The Abolition of Slavery in the North*. Chicago: University of Chicago Press, 1967.

Index

Brown, Thomas C., 194–95
Bryan, Andrew, 70–72, 77
Burgess, Ebenezer, 171–72
Burr, D.J., 252n31
Bushman, Richard, 59

Calhoun, John, 254n8
California, 204–5
Cape Mesurado, 173, *186*
  acquisition of, 185–87
Carleton, Guy, 81, 83
Carretta, Vincent, 45, 220n25
  on African authors, 218n4
  on Equiano, 218n2
Cary, Lott, 183–87, 189, 194, 195, 196
  commitment to antislavery of, 252n37
  death of, 198
Catholicism, 100
Channel, Scipio, 108
Christianity, 3, 50. *See also* evangelical
    Christianity
  Africa and, 30–33, 57, 79, 147, 177
  brotherhood/equality relating to,
    138–39
  commerce and, 76
  conversion to, 8, 53
  Dark Continent to be redeemed
    through, 128–29, 147, 179
  enlightenment through, 65
  Equiano's rebirth into, 49–50
  Macaulay's vision of society based on,
    117
  missions for, 128–29
  in plantation colonies, 95
  racial uplift and, 159
  of Sancho/Wheatley, P., 21–22
  spreading, 58–59
  universalist, 122–23
church(es), 9–11
  African, 12, 67–68, 165–67
  African identity relating to, 143–44
  segregation of, 72–73

separate movements of, 131–42
  universalist, 71
Church of England, 69
Clarkson, John, 86, 91, 231n8
  on abolition of slave trade, 148–49
  correspondence with Nova Scotians,
    114
  emigrants recruited by, 230n3
  Freetown led by, 101–6
  as governor, 98–99
  leading Sierra Leone settlers, 92–96,
    233n42
  memo book of, 229n52
  Nova Scotians and, 128
  Peters challenging, 102–03, 232n29,
    233n32
  settlers complaints to, 111
Coker, Daniel, 11–12, 14, *140*, 168, 195,
    209–10
  childhood of, 240n21
  excommunication of, 172
  as first black teacher in African school,
    138–39
  as follower of Cuffe, 202
  on God, 141–42
  Kizell and, 174–75
  Liberia and, 248n43
  life of, 139–40
  new denomination formed by, 165
  publications of, 167
  records kept by, 155
  as religious leader, 173–74
  sermon of, 246n24–25
  in Sierra Leone, 248n44
  on slave trade, 143
colonization, 13–14. *See also* American
    Colonization Society
  in Africa, 251n28
  arguments in favor of, 199
  opposition to, 181–82
  repudiation of, 169–70
  supporters of, 172